ROYAL FLYING CORPS COMMUNIQUÉS

1917-1918

EDITED BY
CHAZ BOWYER

GRUB STREET • LONDON

Published by Grub Street
The Basement
10 Chivalry Road
London
SW11 1 HT

Edited by Chaz Bowyer

A catalogue record for this book is available from the British Library

ISBN 1 898697 79 5

Printed and bound in Great Britain by
Biddles Ltd, Guildford and King's Lynn

Contents

INTRODUCTION

In this volume the weekly communiqués issued by the Royal Flying Corps Headquarters in France – known irreverently to all RFC air crews as "Comic Cuts" after a popular children's magazine of that time – cover the period January 1917 to March 1918 inclusive. These concerned only RFC operations over the Western Front in France, plus certain squadrons of the Royal Naval Air Service temporarily attached to the RFC. As with previously published companion volumes of the 1915-16 and 1918 communiqués, operations routinely carried out by the bomber and army co-operation squadrons have been omitted with only certain individual actions being high-lighted – however, the emphasis on reporting details of aerial combats tends to offer an unbalanced view of the overall efforts of the Corps, and it should be well remembered that the *raison d'etre* of the RFC was primarily support for the P.B.I. ("Poor Bloody Infantry") and the role of the scout (fighter) squadrons was to gain freedom of the skies for the army co-operation units and their protection in order that they could carry out their vital duties unimpeded by enemy aircraft. The 15 months of operations covered in this volume saw the RFC's fortunes vary widely. At the beginning of 1917 the Corps was still equipped with a high proportion of out-dated types of aircraft, and was opposed by enemy aircraft, in the main, superior in design, performance and armament. This situation had been bluntly emphasised to higher authority by Hugh Trenchard, commander of the RFC in France, for several months in late 1916, but promised better aircraft designs, such as the SE5, Bristol Fighter and Sopwith Camel, only reached France in small numbers in the spring and early summer of 1917. Thus, initially, the German air services enjoyed a period of aerial superiority. By mid-summer, 1917, the arrival of fresh squadrons and new aircraft had given the RFC a numerical advantage of four to one, and aerial dominance was slowly being established. In the autumn and early winter of the year the RFC scout squadrons in particular were given a fresh tactical role, that of harassing – "ground strafing" – enemy troops and emplacements from low levels in direct support of the British front-line infantry; operations which resulted in high casualty rates in men and machines as high as 30 per cent in a single day, apart from the attrition of aerial combats. The early weeks of 1918 were a period of preparation by the German air services for the long-planned "Great Battle of France"; a massive land offensive due to commence in late March intended to secure victory before American reinforcements and resources could have any effect on the struggle. The nullification of that ambition owed no small part to the intensive operations by the RFC and RNAS air crews opposing the German advance. By 1st April 1918, on which date the two British air services ceased to exist with the birth of the single service, the Royal Air Force, the German offensive had been halted. With regard to the communiqués themselves, it should be borne in mind that each day reported is concerned with events between the hours of 6am and 6pm; thus operations after 6pm are often included in a following day's summary. On the matter of combat claims, the bulk of these were termed "Out of Control", whereby the actual fate of any enemy aircraft so claimed was not actually witnessed though such 'victories' have often been included by latter-day historians in individual pilots' so-termed 'scores'. Compiled by staff officers on a selective basis, with no pretensions to literary quality, nevertheless, these communiqués reflect the outstanding courage and dedication of a generation of young airmen whose deeds provided a concrete foundation of a tradition for the future Royal Air Force.

Chaz Bowyer, Norwich, 1998

COMMUNIQUÉ No.69

1 - 6 JANUARY 1917

Throughout this week emphasis was given to artillery co-operation operations and reconnaissance. On 1 January No.53 Squadron (BE2e) arrived in France.

JANUARY 1
Low clouds and strong wind all day made service flying impossible.
Casualties – Killed – Lt T K Robertson & Lt E F Clark, No. 52 Squadron (accident).

JANUARY 2
Artillery Co-operation – Nine targets were dealt with by artillery of the First Army, co-operating with aeroplanes of the 1st Brigade. One hostile battery was silenced under zone call. Artillery of the Second Army with observation by aeroplanes of the 2nd Brigade obtained 11 direct hits on battery positions.
Bombing – bombs were dropped on trenches and places of military importance by aeroplanes of the 1st Brigade.

JANUARY 3
Nothing to report.

JANUARY 4
Artillery Co-operation – Twenty-seven targets were successfully engaged with aeroplane observation. Siege artillery of the First Army co-operating with aeroplanes of the 1st Brigade obtained three direct hits on gun pits and caused an explosion of ammunition. Artillery of the Second Army, with observation by aeroplanes of the 2nd Brigade obtained four direct hits on hostile batteries.
Hostile Aircraft – A patrol of No.8 RNAS Squadron had several combats. Flight Sub-Lt E R Grange engaged and drove down a German aeroplane in badly damaged condition north of Bapaume. When south of Bapaume this pilot engaged two more hostile machines, one of which was driven down. Later he had an engagement with a German aeroplane near Ypres and again drove his opponent down in damaged condition. Flight Sub-Lt R A Little of the same patrol saw one of the damaged German aeroplanes on its back in a field, surrounded by people.
Bombing – Aeroplanes of the 1st Brigade dropped 70 20lb bombs
behind the German lines.
Casualties – Killed – No.15592 1/AM A A Stooke, 4th Balloon Wing. Missing – Flight Sub-Lt A S Todd, No.8 Squadron RNAS & Flight Sub-Lt J C Croft, No.8 Squadron RNAS.

JANUARY 5
Artillery Co-operation – Seventy-seven targets were engaged by aeroplane observation. Three direct hits were obtained by artillery co-operating with aeroplanes of the 1st Brigade. Artillery of the Second Army, with observation by aeroplanes of the 2nd Brigade, successfully engaged eight hostile batteries. Three gun pits were hit and an explosion of ammunition caused. Artillery of the Fourth Army, with observation by

aeroplanes of the 4th Brigade, engaged 18 hostile batteries. Nine direct hits were obtained and seven batteries were silenced. Five direct hits were obtained on trenches. With observation by aeroplanes of the 5th Brigade, artillery successfully engaged 12 hostile batteries. Seven direct hits were obtained on gun positions. Four gun pits were damaged and an explosion of ammunition caused. The 76th Siege Battery, with observation by 2nd Lt Hewitt, No.4 Squadron, obtained three direct hits on a bridge over the Ancre. The bridge was totally destroyed and the approaches damaged.

Night Bombing – on the night of the 4th/5th,aeroplanes of the 1st Brigade dropped 6-112lb bombs on Hantay, all of which were seen to burst on houses in the village. Aeroplanes of the 5th Brigade dropped bombs on St Leger and Achiet-le-Grand. All the bombs were seen to hit their objectives and one burst on the station at St Leger. The bombing machines attacked anti-aircraft guns and rocket batteries with machine gun fire.

Bombing – During the day of the 5th,several places of military importance behind the German lines were attacked with bombs by machines of the 1st & 5th Brigades. A factory on which bombs were dropped by aeroplanes of the 1st Brigade was considerably damaged and set on fire.

Photography – 261 photographs were taken during the day.

Casualties – Killed – 2nd Lt H Jameson & Lt W D Thomson, both of No.6 Squadron. Wounded – Lt D Faure, No.32 Squadron, and Lt W F T James, No.24 Squadron.

JANUARY 6

Artillery Co-operation – Field Artillery of the First Army with observation by aeroplanes of the 1st Brigade obtained four direct hits on trench targets. In co-operation with aeroplanes of the 3rd Brigade, artillery silenced four hostile batteries. Three direct hits were obtained on a trench by artillery of the Fourth Army, with observation by aeroplanes of the 4th Brigade. Co-operating with aeroplanes of the 5th Brigade, artillery successfully engaged one hostile battery and caused an explosion of ammunition.

Bombing – Places of military importance behind the German lines were attacked by aeroplanes of the 1st and 5th Brigades.

Casualties – Killed – 2nd Lt D W L Young,53 Squadron. 2nd Lt L C F Lukis,27 Squadron.

COMMUNIQUÉ No.70

7 – 13 January 1917

Despite unfavourable weather conditions, this week included two particularly notable actions. The successful 'decoy' operation by two officers of No.2 Squadron on January 10th, and the selfless courage of Sergeant Thomas Mottershead, DCM on January 7th. He was awarded a posthumous Victoria Cross. Flight Lt Robert Little, an Australian by birth, was to be credited with a total of 47 combat victories before being killed in action on 27th May 1918.

JANUARY 7
Artillery Co-operation – Seventy-six targets were successfully engaged with aeroplane observation.

Hostile Aircraft – Flight Lt R A Little, RNAS, observed a hostile machine engaging a BE over Grevillers. He dived at the hostile machine and fired about 60 rounds, The German fell out of control and was last seen turned on its back. Owing to the presence of other hostile machines its ultimate fate was not ascertained. An Offensive Patrol of No.32 Squadron engaged and dispersed a hostile formation north of the Bois des Vaux. One of the hostile machines was obviously hit. It side-slipped and nose-dived, but flattened out again when it had gone down 3000 feet.

Bombing – During the day 80-20lb bombs were dropped by the 1st Brigade on various objectives with satisfactory results. Twenty-one 20lb bombs were dropped on Miraumont by the 5th Brigade.

Casualties – Killed – 2nd Lt E G W Bisset,No.6 Squadron. Wounded – No.1396 Sergt T Mottershead & Lt W E Gower, 20 Squadron; 2nd Lt J W Eckles, No.22 Squadron; Flight Sub-Lt A H S Lawson, No.8 Squadron RNAS, & Flight Lt E R Grange,No.8 Squadron RNAS. Missing – 2nd Lt E G S Wagner,No.32 Squadron; Major L Parker & 2nd Lt F A Mann,No.52 Squadron.

JANUARY 8
Weather was unfavourable and very little work was accomplished. During an artillery patrol 2nd Lt Johnson & Lt Bird, No.4 Squadron, engaged 3 hostile machines, one of which was apparently damaged. January 9: Nothing to report.

JANUARY 10
Weather continued unfavourable and little work was accomplished.

Hostile Aircraft – No.2 Section's balloon was attacked and brought down in flames. Lt S Gavin and 2nd Lt Whitlock made successful parachute descents and landed unhurt. No.10 Section's balloon was also attacked but was hauled down safely.

Bombing – On the night 9th/10th inst. bombs were dropped by No. 18 Squadron on hostile aerodromes. Six were dropped on Velu (or Lebucquiere), all of which were seen to burst and a large explosion caused. Six more were dropped on Villers les Cagnicourt. One fell among the hangars and the remainder on or about the aerodrome. Six bombs were also dropped on Buissy from a height of 500 feet, all of which fell on the north-east edge of the aerodrome.

Contact Patrols – 2nd Lt J H Sayer and 2nd Lt H J Davis, No.15 Squadron, carried out a successful contact patrol at low altitudes gaining valuable information as to the position of our troops and the condition of the enemy's positions. On a pre-arranged plan, Captain G C Bailey & 2nd Lt L S White, No. 2 Squadron, flew over the enemy's trenches just north of the double Crassier at a low altitude and opened machine gun fire. They fired Very Lights and generally attracted the enemy in the trenches, who thus had their backs turned to the front line and were firing at the aeroplane with rifle and machine gun fire. The Germans were so occupied with this work that our troops were enabled to leave their trenches and cross "No Man's Land" without being perceived, and without any previous artillery preparation. Two parties entered the German trenches, took eight prisoners, and bombed dugouts which were full of Germans. Captain Bailey's machine was hit in a few places by AA fire but was untouched by rifle or machine gun fire. During the flight he and his Observer located 13 active hostile batteries.

JANUARY 11
Very little work was possible on account of clouds and snow.

Contact Patrol – In connection with the operations of the Fifth Army a very successful contact patrol was accomplished by 2nd Lt J H Sayer & 2nd Lt H J Davis, No.15 Squadron, from a height of 300 feet. Flares were located in the captured objective, and our men were seen waving their hands.

Bombing – On the night 10th/11th instant, two hostile aeroplanes dropped bombs on No.16 Squadron's aerodrome at Bruay. One bomb hit a hangar, destroying five aeroplanes which were in it, and wounding one NCO and two men. In retaliation, aeroplanes of No. 2 Squadron left to attack the aerodrome at Provin. Owing to mist they were unable to find the objective and dropped bombs with good results on Pont-a-Vendin, Carvin and Salome. *Casualties* – Killed – 2nd Lt R Hopper, No.60 Squadron. Wounded – No.24977 Sergt J Drew; No.10726 1/AM A Best, & No. 16398 2/AM W J Callaghan, all of No.16 Squadron.

On January 7th, Sergeant T Mottershead, DCM and his Observer, Lt W E Gower, No. 20 Squadron, were attacked by a German aeroplane when about 9000 feet over Ploegsteert Wood. The petrol tank of the FE2d was pierced almost immediately and the machine burst into flames, compelling the pilot to break off the fight and make towards our lines. Two officers of the A/153rd Brigade, RFA, witnessed the descent, and could see the pilot enveloped in flames being sprayed with a fire extinguisher by Lt Gower. Sergeant Mottershead selected a suitable landing ground in a difficult country, and made a successful landing in spite of the condition of his machine and the seriousness of his wounds. On touching the ground the machine collapsed, throwing the Observer clear, but pinning Sergeant Mottershead under the burning wreckage. Again Lt Gower checked the flames as much as possible by the use of his extinguisher. Sergeant Mottershead has since died of his wounds.

(Editor's note: The FE2d, A39, was shot down by Vizefeldwebel Göttsch of Jagdstaffel 8 who was to be killed in action on 10 April 1918 after gaining his 20th combat victory. Lt Gower received a Military Cross for his actions.)

JANUARY 12: Unfavourable weather. Nothing to report.

JANUARY 13
Practically no flying. Low clouds, snow and rain all day.

Casualties – Missing – 2nd Lt G W Bentley & 2nd Lt D R Hinkley, 12th Yorks & Lancs Regiment (attached No.5 Squadron for signalling purposes).

COMMUNIQUÉ No.71

14 – 20 January 1917

JANUARY 14TH TO 20TH INCLUSIVE – During this period there has been practically no flying owing to adverse weather conditions.

Casualties – With reference to January 13th Casualty Report of 2nd Lt Bentley & 2nd Lt Hinckley (Missing). An officer of No.5 Squadron visited today the part of the Line in the Third Army where a British machine was reported to have made a landing in No Man's Land yesterday. Infantry at this point report that the machine made a perfect landing. The enemy immediately opened a very heavy rifle and machine gun fire, and came out into the open and proceeded to take away heavy objects from the machine. These "objects" were supposed to be the bodies of the two officers. British infantry did not open fire on the German party for fear of hitting the pilot and Observer, who might only have been wounded. A party went out to the spot during the night but no sign of the aeroplane could be seen and nothing was to be seen this morning of it. Killed – 2nd Lt G A Exley, No.29 Squadron. Wounded – Captain J McArthur, 12 Squadron; Lt Ball, 6th Corps Intelligence officer, attached to No.12 Squadron.

COMMUNIQUÉ No.72

21 – 26 January 1917

In a week of continuing close co-operation with the ground forces, RFC strength was increased by the arrival on January 26 of No.35 Squadron, equipped with Armstrong Whitworth FK8 two-seaters. 2nd Lt Stanley Vincent of 60 Squadron later rose to Air Vice-Marshal, RAF and flew operationally in the 1940 Battle of Britain.

JANUARY 21

Hostile Aircraft – A German Rumpler two-seater biplane, which lost its way in the thick mist, landed at Tinques. The Observer got out to ascertain his position and was captured. The pilot then flew off, but seeing three Nieuports of No.60 Squadron leaving the ground he landed and surrendered. Before surrendering, however, he blew up his machine.

Contact Patrol – Some successful contact patrol work was accomplished by pilots of No.42 Squadron, who flew at a height of 150 to 200 feet in order to ascertain the condition of the enemy's barbed wire previous to an attack by our troops.

Casualties – Killed – 2nd Lt A H Hodgson No.52 Squadron; 2nd Lt F R White, 2nd Lt S W Woodley & 2nd Lt W Kellett, No. 10 Squadron. Wounded – Capt C E W Foster, No.10 Squadron.

JANUARY 23

Hostile Aircraft – 2nd Lt B Mews & 2nd Lt A V Blenkiron, No.25 Squadron, engaged and destroyed a German aeroplane near Lens. 2nd Lt J Hay, No.40

Squadron, engaged a hostile machine over La Bassée. The wings were seen to break away from the German machine before it crashed. 2nd Lt Hay then attacked and destroyed the leading machine of a formation of eight. He was then brought down himself and killed. A hostile machine, engaged by 2nd Lt S W Taylor, No.41 Squadron, was driven down in a damaged condition. While on Offensive Patrol, Capt W G B Williams, No.45 Squadron, engaged several German aeroplanes, one of which he drove down out of control and a second was badly damaged by him. Lt E V C Hamilton and Gunner Lambert, No.45 Squadron, engaged several German aeroplanes over Menin and drove one down in a badly damaged condition. A hostile machine was brought down in flames and destroyed by 2nd Lt J G Kidd & 2nd Lt T C Lowe, No.9 Squadron, who were on artillery observation work at the time. This machine fell on our side of the lines. Lt E C Pashley, No.24 Squadron, destroyed a Halberstadt scout which was attacking a BE2e. The German machine fell in our lines. A German aeroplane which attacked Capt J C McMillan & 2nd Lt Hopkins, No.4 Squadron, was hit in the petrol tank and fell in flames. Flight Lt C D Booker, Naval Squadron No.8, drove down a German aeroplane out of control near Bapaume. Some object, believed to be the pilot, was seen to fall from the machine as it fell. Flight Commander P Huskisson, Naval Squadron No.8, encountered several hostile machines and succeeded in hitting the Observer of one machine.

Photography – 992 photographs were taken during the day.

Casualties – Killed – 2nd Lt J Hay, No.40 Squadron. Wounded – Capt E A Beaulah, No.6 Squadron; 2nd Lt T F Northcote, No.45 Squadron. Missing – 2nd Lt S F Cody, No.41 Squadron; 2nd Lt J V Lyle & Bombardier A Harrison, No.45 Squadron.

JANUARY 24

Hostile Aircraft – 2nd Lt J L Leith & 2nd Lt W D Matheson,No.25 Squadron, engaged and drove down out of control a hostile machine which had forced one of our aeroplanes to land in German territory. Sergeant C S Tooms, No.41 Squadron, who was brought down and killed by a German aeroplane had previously destroyed two hostile machines. 2nd Lt S F Vincent, No.60 Squadron, engaged and drove down a two-seater German machine out of control near Monchy. Capt H A Wood and Lt A E McKay, both of No.24 Squadron, attacked a two-seater German machine over Fins. The German machine turned towards our lines and landed, It was seen to be on fire. The crew were taken prisoner.

Photography – 882 photographs were taken during the day.

Casualties – Killed – 2nd Lt E G Waters, No.6 Squadron; No.1678 Sergt C S Tooms, No.41 Squadron; No.60717 Sergt L Booth, No.23 Squadron. Wounded – Capt R H Rusby, No.22 Squadron; 2nd Lt A Dennison, No.41 Squadron. Missing – Capt O Grieg & 2nd Lt J E MacLennan, No.25 Squadron; Flight Lt C R Mackenzie, Naval Squadron No.8; Lt T F Preston & Lt C M Buck,No.53 Squadron.

JANUARY 25

Hostile Aircraft – 2nd Lt H S Pell, No.40 Squadron, engaged and drove down a German aeroplane out of control south of Lens. Three Halberstadt scouts were encountered by Lt F T Woods & Lt G W W Swann, No.70 Squadron, who drove down one of their opponents out of control. Lt T C H Lucas & 2nd Lt W T Gilson, No.20 Squadron, engaged five hostile machines, one of which they destroyed. Capt J B Quested & 2nd Lt H J H Dicksee, No.11 Squadron, drove down two German aeroplanes – one fell out of control, and the other went down in a badly damaged condition. When at 16,000 feet, Capt A Lees, No.54 Squadron, observed a hostile aeroplane below him. He dived at this machine and destroyed it. A two-seater LVG was engaged by Capt S H Long, No.24 Squadron. This machine burst into flames, and the pilot and Observer were both seen to jump out of the aeroplane. The machine fell in our lines. Lt D H M Carbery & 2nd Lt H A D Mackay, No.52 Squadron, engaged a hostile machine near Maricourt. This machine was brought down and fell in our lines. Lt A E McFay, No.24 Squadron, destroyed a single-seater Albatros, which also fell in our lines. Capt A Lees, No.54 Squadron, engaged and drove down a German two-seater out of control. A German aeroplane was brought down in our lines by machine gun fire.

Photography – 852 photographs were taken during the day.

Miscellaneous – Between 10.20am and 12-noon, the aerodrome of No. 18 Squadron was shelled. Twenty-eight shells of about 7.5" calibre fell in the vicinity of the aerodrome. No damage was done to personnel but slight damage was done to four machines.

Casualties – Killed – No.33728 2/AM B Hartley, HQ 14th Wing . Wounded – 2nd Lt J R Houghton, No.53 Squadron; No.34070 2/AM A T Gingell, HQ 14th Wing. Missing – Lt S Alder & Lt R W White, both of No.20 Squadron.

JANUARY 26

Hostile Aircraft – A reconnaissance of No.20 Squadron encountered five hostile aeroplanes. Lt J K Stead & 2nd Lt W T Gilson brought one down, which crashed near Westroosebeke. Another hostile machine was destroyed by 2nd Lt R B Wainwright & Lt H M Golding.

Casualties – Wounded – 2nd Lt P C Hollingsworth, No.6 Squadron; No.290 Flight Sergt C J Cox, No.20 Squadron. Missing – No.191 Flight Sergt W G Webb & 14454 Corpl R D Fleming, No.45 Squadron.

COMMUNIQUÉ No.73

27 January – 3 February

On February 1st, No.8 Squadron RNAS ceased to be attached to the RFC, but No.3 Squadron RNAS (Sopwith Pups) replaced it the same day. Of the various airmen mentioned in this communiqué, 2nd Lt Hugh G White, No.20 Squadron, later rose to Air Rank in the RAF, while 2nd Lt J T B McCudden, No.29 Squadron, claimed his third of an eventual 57 accredited combat victories. As Major McCudden, VC, DSO, MC, MM, he was killed in a flying accident on 9 July 1918.

JANUARY 27
Artillery Co-operation – Forty-six targets were engaged with aeroplane observation.
Hostile Aircraft – Capt S H Long, No.24 Squadron, destroyed a German aeroplane, which fell in our lines, near Morval. A hostile machine, engaged by Lt F N Hudson, 54 Squadron, fell in "No Man's Land" near Courcelette. A third German aeroplane, attacked by Lt Woodhouse & Lt Nickalls, No.52 Squadron, fell on our side of the lines at Maurepas. An Offensive Patrol of No.32 Squadron met two hostile aeroplanes near Ervillers. The patrol dived on to one of the machines, which fell in flames and was seen to crash near St Leger. Lt Taylor of the same squadron engaged and drove down a second German aeroplane out of control. Lt A Dennison, No.41 Squadron, while on patrol on the 24th inst., engaged two hostile aeroplanes. He was severely wounded in the arm, but continued the engagement and drove down one hostile machine. Infantry report that this machine fell out of control. Lt Dennison continued fighting the second enemy aeroplane until his engine was hit, when he glided over the lines and landed safely.
Casualties – Wounded – 2nd Lt L G Fauvel, 20 Squadron; 2nd Lt H Butler, 70 Squadron.

JANUARY 28
Artillery Co-operation – Fifty-six targets were engaged with aeroplane observation.
Hostile Aircraft – 2nd Lt J V Aspinall & 2nd Lt J M R Miller, 22 Squadron, engaged a hostile aeroplane over Villers-au-Flos. The hostile machine was driven down and crashed between Barastre and Bus.
Casualties – Killed – Lt F G Russell, 21 Squadron. Wounded – 2nd Lt A F Barker, 41 Squadron; 2nd Lt E G Herbert, 60 Squadron; Lt B S Cole, 1 Squadron. Missing – 2nd Lt P C E Johnson & Lt C B Bird, MC, 4 Squadron.

JANUARY 29
Artillery Co-operation – Sixty-five targets were engaged with aeroplane observation.
Hostile Aircraft – Five FE2bs, No.25 Squadron, accompanied by three FE8s, No.40 Squadron, encountered a formation of 12 hostile scouts, all Halberstadts, while on photographic reconnaissance. 2nd Lt A V Blenkiron, 25 Squadron, was hit in the thigh at the beginning of the encounter, but managed to stand up and fire at a hostile aeroplane at point-blank range. This machine went down out of control with columns of smoke and then flames coming out of it. This was confirmed by two other pilots. 2nd Lt J L Leith in another FE dived to the help of 2nd Lt Blenkiron and fired a drum at 15 yards range into another hostile aeroplane. This German machine

stalled and side-slipped and was seen to fall out of control. Two more Halberstadts were forced to land and the formation was entirely broken up. Capt H Meintjes, 60 Squadron, engaged a German aeroplane at a range of 35 yards. The hostile machine was seen to fall out of control and crash. Lt A N Benge, 29 Squadron, also engaged and destroyed a German aeroplane. 2nd Lt K L Caldwell, on a Nieuport Scout, attacked and drove down a machine. It was not seen to crash. He was forced to leave the formation owing to his petrol and oil tank being shot through, but landed safely.

Capt B L Dowling & Lt C F Lodge, 11 Squadron (FE2bs), whilst leading an Offensive Patrol on the afternoon of the 29th, had an anti-aircraft high explosive shell burst just behind the right lower wing. The machine was completely riddled. Three tail booms were cut, one blade of the propeller was blown away, and all the controls except the elevator were put out of action. The lower right-hand tail boom was completely severed by the destroyed propeller blade, and the aeroplane became uncontrollable. Realising this, Lt Lodge climbed out three-quarters of the way to the right wing tip, in order to balance the machine. When about 900 feet from the ground, owing to a slight movement on the part of the Observer, the machine again began to spin, but the pilot was able to stall the aeroplane from a height of about ten feet and both pilot and Observer escaped unhurt. This machine was hit just over the lines, but owing to a strong east wind was blown about 2000 yards over our front line.

Casualties – Wounded – Lt S E Goodwin, 53 Squadron; 2nd Lt A W Clarke, 5 Squadron; Lt H W Golding, 20 Squadron; 2nd Lt A V Blenkiron, 25 Squadron; 2nd Lt H A Whistler, 3 Squadron; Corpl E J Hare, 3 Squadron.

JANUARY 30
Casualty – 2nd Lt H G White, No.20 Squadron.

FEBRUARY 1
Artillery Co-operation – Fifty-two targets were dealt with by aeroplane Observers.
Casualties – Wounded – Lt J K Stead, 20 Squadron; Lt K B Brigham, 2 Squadron; Capt G M Moore, 15 Squadron. Missing – 2nd Lt W A Reeves & 2nd Lt F H Bronskill, 20 Squadron; 2nd Lt E D Spicer & Capt C M Carbert, MC, 20 Squadron; Lt P W Murray & Lt D J McRae, 16 Squadron, Capt A P V Daly, 29 Squadron.

FEBRUARY 2
Artillery Co-operation – Fifty-eight targets were dealt with by aeroplane observation.
Hostile Aircraft – Capt H E Hartney & 2nd Lt H R Wilkinson,20 Squadron, engaged and destroyed a Halberstadt near Lille. A German aeroplane was driven down out of control by Major A W Grattan Bellew & 2nd Lt J T B McCudden, both of 29 Squadron. In a general engagement between No.32 Squadron and nine hostile aircraft, one enemy machine was driven down out of control and another forced to land.
Casualties – Wounded – 2nd Lt J M R Miller, 22 Squadron. Missing – 2nd Lt H Blythe,32 Squadron; Flight Sub-Lt W E Traynor, 3 RNAS Squadron; 2nd Lt R F Whitney & Lt T G Holley, 23 Squadron.

FEBRUARY 3
Hostile Aircraft – 2nd Lt C Gordon-Davis & Capt R M Knowles,20 Squadron, engaged seven hostile aircraft during a patrol near Wervicq, and one German machine was driven down out of control.
Casualty – Wounded – Capt J C McMillan, 4 Squadron.

COMMUNIQUÉ No.74

4 – 10 February 1917

FEBRUARY 4

Artillery Co-operation – Forty-five targets were dealt with by aeroplane observation. On the night of the 3rd/4th inst., Major G L P Henderson & 2nd Lt A N Nesbitt, 5 Squadron, located and reported by zone call 19 active hostile batteries. During this patrol a searchlight was attacked and extinguished by machine gun fire from the aeroplane.

Hostile Aircraft – As a result of an encounter with a German aeroplane, 2nd Lt H M Massey & 2nd Lt N M H Vernham, 16 Squadron, had their machine brought down on fire. 2nd Lt Massey was wounded and 2nd Lt Vernham killed. Artillery officers state that the German machine was also shot down in this combat. Lt J W Boyd & 2nd Lt A H Steele, 16 Squadron, drove down a German machine, which went down under control but crashed on landing. Capt H R Hawkins & Sergt Johnson, 22 Squadron, engaged three hostile aeroplanes near Haplincourt, one of which they destroyed. Capt C M Clement & Lt M K Parlee, 22 Squadron, while on Offensive Patrol, were attacked by three hostile machines, one of which was hit and the propeller was seen to stop, but it glided away under control. Later, assisted by a De Havilland 2, this pilot and Observer destroyed a German aeroplane near Rocquigny. Two German aeroplanes were attacked by Capt H W von L Poellnitz, 24 Squadron, near St Pierre Vaast Wood. The hostile machines were driven down and one fell apparently out of control. Lt E C Pashley and Lt R H M S Saundby, both of 24 Squadron, observed eight German aeroplanes attacking five FEs. They dived at the hostile machines and succeeded in destroying one of them. A second German aeroplane was driven down out of control by an Offensive Patrol of 24 Squadron. An Offensive Patrol of 32 Squadron encountered a hostile formation near Achiet. A general encounter ensued in which Capt W G S Curphey drove down one of the hostile machines and succeeded in spite of several of our machines being badly hit. The patrol returned to their aerodrome, where Capt Curphey and 2nd Lt A C Randall changed their machines and went in search of the hostile aeroplanes. They had several combats, in one of which Capt Curphey, assisted by the other pilot, brought down a hostile machine although he had been wounded in the head. 2nd Lt R W Farquhar & 2nd Lt G N Blennerhasset, 18 Squadron, while on line patrol, were attacked by four German aeroplanes. One of these was driven down out of control.

Casualties – Killed – Lt J W Boyd, 2nd Lt A H Steele, 2nd Lt N M H Vernham, all of 16 Squadron; 2nd Lt H L Villiers, 11 Squadron. Wounded – 2nd Lt H M Massey, 16 Squadron; 2nd Lt A B Coupal, 11 Squadron; Capt W G S Curphey, 32 Squadron. Missing – No.917 Sergt J F Shaw, 15 Squadron; 2nd Lt G W B Bradford, 15 Squadron.

FEBRUARY 5

Hostile Aircraft – Captain G M Boumphrey & Captain L Findlay, 46 Squadron, while on artillery observation, were attacked from behind by a Roland two-seater. An armour-piercing bullet struck a drum, with the result that six rounds exploded and Captain Findlay was wounded, but he continued fighting. Anti-aircraft gunners report that the German aeroplane fell out of control. An Offensive Patrol of 32

Squadron met nine hostile aircraft near Grevillers. In the general combat which ensued, Captain H W G Jones drove down a hostile machine which fell completely out of control.

Bombing – Douai aerodrome was attacked by aeroplanes of the 1st Brigade. The majority of the bombs, both 112lb and 20lb, were seen to burst on and around the aerodrome.

Casualties – Wounded – Captain G M Boumphrey & Captain L Findlay, 46 Squadron.

FEBRUARY 6

Artillery Co-operation – Thirty-five targets were dealt with by aeroplane observation.

Hostile Aircraft – Capt R J Mounsey & Lt L M Elworthy, 2 Squadron, while on artillery observation registration, were attacked by two hostile aeroplanes. The Observer of one of the German machines was hit and seen to fall into the machine. 2nd Lt E B W Bartlett, 41 Squadron, engaged a hostile machine which he drove down in a vertical nose-dive, apparently out of control. A second hostile machine was driven down by a reconnaissance patrol of 20 Squadron, and was last seen in a vertical nose-dive. 2nd Lt J T B McCudden, 29 Squadron, and Lt S Cockerell, 24 Squadron, each engaged and drove down a hostile aeroplane out of control.

Bombing – On the night of the 6th/7th bombs were dropped on Provin aerodrome by aeroplanes of the 1st Brigade. The bombs were seen to explode near the hangars. Bombs dropped on a dump at Provin Station were seen to burst on the objective. Bombs were also dropped on a train and on billets at Berclau.

Casualties – Killed – 2nd Lt H L Pateman & 2nd Lt H J Davis, both of 15 Squadron. Wounded – 2nd Lt F W A Vickery, 23 Squadron; Lt W B McDonald, 22 Squadron. Missing – Lt E B Maule & Lt T C H Lucas, both of 20 Squadron; 2nd Lt M E Woods & 2nd Lt J T Gibbon, both of 20 Squadron.

FEBRUARY 7

Artillery Co-operation – Sixty-nine targets were dealt with by aeroplane observation.

Hostile Aircraft – A patrol of 40 Squadron engaged a German aeroplane which was driven down under control but in a badly damaged condition. Sergt J A Cunniffe & 2/AM Walker, 23 Squadron, whilst on line patrol, were attacked by five hostile aeroplanes near Combles. One of the German machines was driven down out of control and seen to crash. A line patrol of 32 Squadron was attacked by nine hostile machines. One of the German machines, engaged by Capt W G S Curphey, went down in a spinning nose-dive with its engine full on. The fate of this machine could not be ascertained owing to the presence of other hostile aircraft. A second German aeroplane fell completely out of control after being engaged by 2nd Lt H D Davies.

Photography – 410 photographs were taken during the day.

Casualties – Missing – 2nd Lt E E Erlebach & 2/AM F Ridgway, 25 Squadron.

FEBRUARY 8

Artillery Co-operation – 71 targets were dealt with by aeroplane observation.

Hostile Aircraft – 2nd Lt G F Haseler, 40 Squadron, drove down an Albatros two-seater. This machine landed in a field and turned on its back after landing.

Casualty – Wounded – Lt W H Copeland, 4 Squadron.

FEBRUARY 9

Artillery Co-operation – Sixty-eight targets were dealt with by aeroplane observation.

Hostile Aircraft – A German aeroplane which was engaged by Lt Dunlop & 2nd Lt J B Weir, 25 Squadron, was driven down and fell in flames. Sergt Munro & Sergt King, 25 Squadron, also drove down a hostile aeroplane in a damaged condition. An Offensive Patrol of 32 Squadron engaged and drove down a hostile machine which is believed to be badly damaged.

Photography – 453 photographs were taken during the day.

Bombing – Provin aerodrome was attacked by aeroplanes of the 1st Brigade. A number of bombs fell on the aerodrome and one hangar was destroyed.

Casualties – Wounded – 2nd Lt H V Puckeridge & Lt A N Nesbitt, 5 Squadron.

FEBRUARY 10

Artillery Co-operation – Sixty-eight targets were dealt with by aeroplane observation.

Hostile Aircraft – Capt L P Aizlewood, 32 Squadron, while on an Offensive Patrol, engaged and drove down a German aeroplane which was reported to have fallen out of control.

Casualties – Killed – Lt R J Docking, 43 Squadron; Lt W A Porkess & 2nd Lt E Roberts, 10 Squadron. Wounded – Lt A G Stewart, 20 Squadron; Capt L P Aizlewood, 32 Squadron; 2nd Lt T S Edelston, 43 Squadron; Lt J M J C I Rock & 2nd Lt A E P Smith, 43 Squadron.

Photography – From the 4th to the 10th inclusive 2643 photographs were taken.

COMMUNIQUÉ No.75

11 – 17 February 1917

While maintaining their daily close co-operation with the armies the RFC's reconnaissance squadrons received extra support with the arrival in France of No.59 Squadron, equipped with RE8 two-seaters, on February 13. Further strength was added to the scout (ie fighter) units when No.1 Squadron RNAS, flying Sopwith Triplanes, was officially attached to the RFC with effect from February 15; this attachment lasting until 2 November 1917.

FEBRUARY 11
Hostile Aircraft – Four machines of 40 Squadron encountered four Halberstadts and one Albatros. One of the hostile machines was brought down in flames behind the German lines.
Photography – 366 plates were exposed.
Miscellaneous – Several trench and flash reconnaissances were carried out. 2nd Lt J H Sayer & 2nd Lt V C Morris, 15 Squadron, carried out a successful contact patrol. Several posts were located and communication obtained with Battalion HQ.
Casualties – Wounded – No.3232 Corpl H Cottingham, 13 Squadron; 2nd Lt L L Brown, 15 Squadron; 2nd Lt F J Fleming, 34 Squadron. Missing – Capt J Thorburn & 2nd Lt J K Howard, 13 Squadron.

FEBRUARY 12
Contact Patrol – 2nd Lt J H Sayer & 2nd Lt V C Morris,15 Squadron, carried out a successful contact patrol. No other work was possible owing to bad weather.

FEBRUARY 13
Artillery Co-operation – Eight targets were dealt with by aeroplane observation.
Hostile Aircraft – 2nd Lt F N Hudson, 54 Squadron, engaged a hostile aeroplane near Le Transloy. The German machine was hit and went down in a vertical dive. Lt Burcher & 2nd Lt Stroud, 9 Squadron, engaged two Albatros scouts near Sailly-Saillisel. One Albatros was brought down in our lines.
Photography – 197 photographs were taken during the day.
Casualties – Killed – Lt T S Green & 2nd Lt W K Carse, 3 Squadron.

FEBRUARY 14
Artillery Co-operation – Sixty-nine targets were dealt with by aeroplane observation.
Hostile Aircraft – Two German aeroplanes were driven down out of control during the day – one by a patrol of 60 Squadron near Monchy, and one by Flight Lt R G Mack, No 3 Squadron RNAS, near Warlencourt. Lt D H M Carbery & Lt Vaile, 52 Squadron, destroyed a German aeroplane near Bouchavesnes.
Photography – 754 photographs were taken during the day.
Casualties – Killed – 2nd Lt F C Young & 2nd Lt A G S de Ross, 3 Squadron; 2nd Lt F W Nisbet & No.45071 2/AM P E Knightly, 46 Squadron; 2nd Lt F M Myers, 20 Squadron. Wounded – Capt H E Hartney & 2nd Lt W T Jourdan, 20 Squadron; 2nd Lt F J Taylor, 20 Squadron; 2nd Lt C F Uwins, No.1 A.D.; Capt G C Bailey, DSO, 2

Squadron; 2nd Lt W J Pearson, 8 Squadron. Missing – 2nd Lt C D Bennett & 2nd Lt H A Croft, 2 Squadron; 2nd Lt J V Fairbairn, 54 Squadron.

FEBRUARY 15

Artillery Co-operation – 100 targets were dealt with by aeroplane observation.

Hostile Aircraft – Hostile aircraft were driven down out of control by the following; One by a patrol of 25 Squadron near Avion. One by a patrol of No.1 Squadron near Hollebeke. One by Flight Sub-Lt R Collishaw, No.3 Squadron RNAS, near Bapaume. Capt H W G Jones, 32 Squadron, drove down a German aeroplane out of control near Grevillers. Although twice wounded, and with his machine badly shot about, he carried on with the patrol until the hostile formation was driven off. 2nd Lt S H Pratt & 2nd Lt Bryers, 46 Squadron, brought down a German Albatros scout which fell in our lines near Vlamertinghe. 2nd Lt J T B McCudden, 29 Squadron, engaged two hostile aircraft over Adinfer Wood. One of the hostile machines was destroyed and crashed east of Monchy. While on patrol, 2nd Lt V H Collins, No.1 Squadron, engaged and destroyed a German aeroplane. A fourth hostile machine was destroyed west of Bapaume by 2nd Lt V H Huston & 2nd Lt Taylor, 18 Squadron. Lt E L Benbow, 40 Squadron,drove down a hostile aeroplane which crashed near Douai.

Photography – 441 photographs were taken during the day.

Casualties – Killed – Lt H E Mulock & No.O/79593 Pte T A Booth, 52 Squadron; 2nd Lt A E Townsend & No.21732 2/AM H J Honour, 34 Squadron. Wounded – 2nd Lt H E Rathkins & Lt W A Landry, 42 Squadron; Capt H W G Jones, 32 Squadron; Lt R B Wainwright, 20 Squadron. Missing – 2nd Lt E Hamilton & Cap C L M Scott, 54 Squadron; Lt C H March, 32 Squadron; Capt J M E Shepherd, 1 Squadron.

FEBRUARY 16

Artillery Co-operation – Twenty-eight targets were dealt with by aeroplane observation.

Hostile Aircraft – A German aeroplane which was attacked by 2nd Lt D Mc C Kerr & 2nd Lt F C Elstob, 53 Squadron, fell out of control near Wytschaete. Sergt H G Smith & Lt J Aldred, 5 Squadron, brought down an Albatros scout which crashed near Hebuterne. A patrol of 32 Squadron encountered four hostile machines near Bapaume. The Observer in one of the machines was hit and seen to fall forward.

Photography – Eighty-six photographs were taken during the day.

Casualties – Killed – Capt F W H Simpson & No.766 Sergt C J Trumpeter, 53 Squadron (accident). Wounded – No.23921 Sergt H G Smith, 5 Squadron.

Missing – 2nd Lt E W Lindley & 2nd Lt L V Munn, 16 Squadron.

FEBRUARY 17

Owing to adverse weather conditions, only one successful flight was carried out. This was a patrol by 2nd Lt T Ure & 2nd Lt V C Manuel, 10 Squadron, during a raid by XI Corps. Flares lit by our men in the enemy's trenches were observed and SOS signals made by the enemy were also noted.

COMMUNIQUÉ No.76

From February 18th to 24th inclusive, no service flying was possible owing to unfavourable weather.

COMMUNIQUÉ No.77

25 February – 3 March 1917

In a week of unsettled weather very little flying was possible. Further reinforcement for the front-line RFC units in France was the arrival of 66 Squadron, equipped with Sopwith Pups, on March 3.

FEBRUARY 25

Hostile Aircraft – A Halberstadt scout, which was attacked by Lt H Fowler & Lt F E Brown,2 Squadron, burst into flames and fell to earth near Lens. Lt Probyn & Lt Wood,34 Squadron drove down a German aeroplane near Marrieres Wood. This machine is believed to have been destroyed.

Casualties – Killed – Lt J G B Baines, 23 Squadron (accident). Wounded – Lt R J S Lund, 29 Squadron (combat).

FEBRUARY 26

Photography – 186 photographs were taken during the day.

Artillery Co-operation – Eleven targets were dealt with by aeroplane observation.

Hostile Aircraft – Lt C E M Pickthorn, 32 Squadron, dived at a hostile machine which was attacking a BE2e, and fired half a drum of ammunition at close range. The enemy went down in a vertical nose-dive, but was lost in the clouds.

Casualties – Killed – Lt G Vaughan Jones, 18 Squadron. Wounded – Lt J F Ferguson, 18 Squadron; 2nd Lt L L Carter, 29 Squadron; Lt H E Bagot, 16 Squadron; 2nd Lt R L M Jack, 16 Squadron (since died); Lt H Q Nickalls, 52 Squadron; Capt E Fletcher & 2nd Lt A M Morgan, 5 Squadron; No.P43412 2/AM E Campbell, 22 Squadron.

FEBRUARY 27

Artillery Co-operation – 28 targets were dealt with by aeroplane observation.

Hostile Aircraft – Three of our machines were brought down by hostile aircraft during the day. 2nd Lt H F Mackain, pilot, and 2nd Lt J A E R Daly, Observer, of 13 Squadron, whilst on artillery patrol at Arras, were surrounded by six hostile aircraft. One hostile aircraft dived on them from above. The Observer opened fire and the hostile machine dived straight towards its own lines. Noticing that his pilot had no control over his machine, Lt Daly concluded that he was either dead or wounded. He thereupon climbed from the Observer's seat across the wing into the pilot's seat and, sitting on the pilot's lap with his left foot on the wing, rectified the machine and landed in the biggest field he could find.

Casualties – Killed – Capt J McArthur, 12 Squadron; 2nd Lt E A Pope & 2nd Lt H A Johnson, 8 Squadron; 2nd Lt H F Mackain, 13 Squadron; No.15814 Pte J Whiteford, 12 Squadron.

FEBRUARY 28

No work was possible.

MARCH 1
Artillery Co-operation – 82 targets were dealt with by aeroplane observation.
Hostile Aircraft – A patrol of 25 Squadron was attacked by eleven Halberstadts near Mericourt. 2nd Lt J L Leith drove down one Halberstadt which fell in a spinning nose-dive. Capt A G Saxty & 2/AM McMillan, 70 Squadron, engaged and drove down an Albatros scout near Vimy.
Photography – 324 photographs were taken during the day.
Casualties – Wounded – 2nd Lt G R F Waner, 25 Squadron; Lt G K Simpson, No.14 KBS; 1/AM W Bond (No.7653), 6 Squadron; 2nd Lt D R C Gabell, 5 Squadron.

MARCH 2
Casualties – Wounded – 2nd Lt H J Q Campbell, 8 Squadron; 2nd Lt A R M Scrase Dickens, 23 Squadron (accident). Missing – 2nd Lt C S Cravos & No.1054 F/Sgt A G Shepherd, 5 Squadron.

MARCH 3
Nothing to report.

COMMUNIQUÉ No.78

4 – 10 March 1917

This week saw increased activity from German aircraft. The combat on March 9, in particular, evidenced the obsolescence of the FE8 as a fighter aircraft when matched against German Albatros scouts; in this instance led by Rittmeister Manfred von Richthofen of Jagdstaffel 11. Of the many Allied pilots named here, C J Q Brand, R H M S Saundby, R Collishaw and H H Balfour were later to achieve high ranks in the postwar RAF; Harold Balfour becoming Under-Secretary of State for Air in World War Two. Two more fresh squadrons arrived in France this week; 55 Squadron, equipped with De Havilland 4 two-seat bombers, on March 5, and 48 Squadron, flying Bristol F2a two- seat fighter-reconnaissance aircraft. In each case, these units were introducing new aircraft types to operations. This communiqué was the last to include individual lists of casualties.

MARCH 4
Artillery Co-operation – Fifty-two targets were dealt with by aeroplane observation.
Hostile Aircraft – Hostile aircraft were destroyed by the following during the day: One by 2nd Lt C P Thornton & Sergt R Dunn, 43 Squadron; one by 2nd Lt C J Q Brand & Lt V G A Bush, 1 Squadron; one by 2nd Lt E S T Cole, 1 Squadron; one by 2nd Lt G P Kay & 2nd Lt W W Steuart, 46 Squadron; one by 2nd Lt A Fraser and Lt R H M S Saundby, 41 Squadron. A German machine was also shot down in our lines near Verbranten Molen. This machine was heavily shelled by the Germans. An Albatros scout which was attacked by Lt A J Pearson, 29 Squadron and Lts Graham & Boddy, 11 Squadron, landed near Tilloy. The pilot (Ltn Max Bohme, Jagdstaffel 5) was taken prisoner. Hostile aircraft were driven down damaged by 2nd Lt W B Hills, 40 Squadron, 2nd Lt R E Neve, 40 Squadron, Lt T F Hazell, 1 Squadron, one by two FE2bs of 11 Squadron, and one each by the following pilots of No.3 Squadron RNAS; Flight Sub-Lt L Rochford, Flight Sub-Lt R Collishaw, Flight Cdr T C Vernon, Flight Lt J Malone, and Flight Sub-Lt H Wigglesworth.
Photography – 1187 photographs were taken during the day.
Casualties – Killed – 2nd Lt V M Bowling, 29 Squadron; No.626 F/Sgt R J Moody & 2nd Lt E E Horn, 8 Squadron; 2nd Lt B W Hill & 2nd Lt W Harms, 59 Squadron. Wounded – Lt R W Scoles & 2nd Lt B A Morgan (since died), 53 Squadron; 2nd Lt W A Golding, 23 Squadron; No.2008 F/Sgt J E Prance, 2 Squadron; Lt H Lambourne, 18 Squadron; No.578 Pte J Collinson, 18 Squadron; Flight Sub-Lt L A Powell (since died), 3 Squadron RNAS; 2nd Lt W W Steuart (since died), 46 Squadron; 2nd Lt F H E Reeve, 15 Squadron. Missing – 2nd Lt P L Woods & 2nd Lt A H Fenton, 43 Squadron; Capt A Lees, 54 Squadron; Flight Lt H R Wambolt & Flight Sub-Lt J P White, 3 Squadron RNAS; 2nd Lt A W Reid, 43 Squadron.

MARCH 5
Weather was unsatisfactory for flying.

MARCH 6
Artillery Co-operation – Sixty-five targets were dealt with by aeroplane observation.

Hostile Aircraft – Hostile aircraft were exceptionally active during the day and a great number of combats took place. About 70 hostile aeroplanes were observed opposite the First Army front; 23 of these crossed the lines. 2nd Lt C P Thornton & Lt H D Blackburn, 43 Squadron, brought down a Halberstadt Scout in flames south of Lens. Lt E L Benbow, 40 Squadron, drove down a hostile machine which also fell in flames near Givenchy. Capt H H Balfour & 2nd Lt Roberts, 43 Squadron, drove down a hostile machine out of control near Givenchy. Confirmation has been received that this machine crashed. Capt S H Long & Lt E C Pashley, 24 Squadron, drove down a German aeroplane in which the Observer was hit. Confirmation has been received that this machine was destroyed. The 34th Heavy Artillery Group report that a hostile machine was brought down east of Bapaume. This is believed to have been engaged by two De Havilland 2s of 32 Squadron, both of which failed to return. A Halberstadt scout engaged by Capt Bryant & 2nd Lt Elliott, 23 Squadron, was driven down out of control.

Casualties – Killed – 2nd Lt D E Greenhow, 45 Squadron; Lt W F W Hills & 2nd Lt W S Gardner, 57 Squadron; Major E P Graves, 60 Squadron; 2nd Lt V A Berridge & No.3131 1/AM S Lamplugh, 34 Squadron; 2nd Lt C M G Bibby & Lt G J O Brichton, 16 Squadron; Lt C W Short, 3 Squadron. Wounded – 2nd Lt S M Frazer, 3 Squadron; Lt C E M Pickthorn, 32 Squadron; Lt J W Lockhart, 52 Squadron; 2nd Lt G H Harrison & 2nd Lt O G S Crawford, 23 Squadron; 2/AM P Brown (No.P/17888), 23 Squadron; 2nd Lt O R Knight, 16 Squadron. Missing – Capt R S R Bloomfield & 2nd Lt V O Lonsdale, 57 Squadron; 2nd Lt F E Hills & 2nd Lt A G Ryale, 57 Squadron; Lt S J Pepler & Capt J D Stuart, 43 Squadron; 2nd Lt P S Joyce, 60 Squadron; 2nd Lt Underwood & 2nd Lt A E Watts, 16 Squadron; 2nd Lt M J J G Mare-Montembault & Lt H G Southon, 32 Squadron.

MARCH 7, MARCH 8
Very little work possible owing to unsatisfactory weather.

MARCH 9
Artillery Co-operation – Twenty-one targets were dealt with by aeroplane observation.

Hostile Aircraft – Nine FE8s of 40 Squadron, whilst patrolling over Oppy in the morning, were unusually heavily fired at by anti-aircraft guns for about five minutes. Two hostile aircraft appeared well to the east of the patrol. The anti-aircraft fire suddenly ceased and eight or more hostile machines dived from above the clouds onto the FE patrol. Apparently the two machines, the anti-aircraft and the formation of hostile aircraft were working in accordance with a pre-arranged plan. In the combat that ensued at least one hostile machine was destroyed. Three of our machines failed to return and the remainder were badly shot about. One FE just succeeded in reaching our lines when it burst into flames. The pilot, who had been twice wounded, jumped from the machine. The fight lasted for about half an hour.

Casualties – Missing – 2nd Lt W B Hills, 2nd Lt G F Haseler, 2nd Lt T Shepard, all of 40 Squadron; 2nd Lt A J Pearson, 29 Squadron. Wounded – 2nd Lt R E Neve, 40 Squadron.

MARCH 10
No work possible owing to unsatisfactory weather.

COMMUNIQUÉ No.79

11 – 17 March 1917

The bulk of activity by the Allied squadrons continued to be close co-operation with their armies, a daily task undertaken by crews flying aircraft which were – in the main – no real match to the Albatros and Halberstadt Jagdstaffeln opposing them, though such crews fought valiantly, with no few successes. On March 15, No.6 Squadron RNAS, flying Nieuport Scouts, was officially attached to the RFC in France and remained so until the unit's disbandment in August 1917. 2nd Lt W G Barker, a pilot with 15 Squadron, mentioned in the report for March 14, later became Major, VC, DSO, MC in 1918.

MARCH 11
Artillery Co-operation – 102 targets were dealt with by aeroplane observation.
Hostile Aircraft – Hostile aircraft were extremely active, about 81 machines being observed on the First Army front. 2nd Lt V W B Castle, 1 Squadron, engaged an Albatros two-seater near Poezelboek which was reported as falling in flames. A line patrol of six machines of 32 Squadron engaged nine hostile aircraft east of Bapaume. One hostile aeroplane was destroyed by Lt C E M Pickthorn. Lt Howe fired a double drum at another machine at a range of from ten to 20 yards. The German pilot was seen to throw up his hands and fall forward in his machine which fell completely out of control. A general engagement took place between hostile machines and aeroplanes of 18 Squadron. Lt Boustead & 2nd Lt Smith destroyed one hostile machine and drove down a second out of control. At least three other hostile aircraft are believed to have been driven down during this fight. Capt R Oxspring, 54 Squadron, engaged and destroyed a hostile machine near Achiet-le-Grand. A German machine was driven down out of control by two FE2bs of 11 Squadron near Monchy-le-Preux. Hostile machines were driven down out of control by Lt Davies & 2/AM Taylor, 25 Squadron; Lt A C Randall, 32 Squadron, and by Flight Cdr C D Bell and Flight Lt H G Travers, both of 3 Squadron RNAS.

MARCH 12
Artillery Co-operation – Sixteen targets were dealt with by aeroplane observation.

MARCH 14
Very little work was possible owing to low clouds, mist and rain. Two machines of 4 Squadron carried out successful trench reconnaissances, and a successful contact patrol was flown by 2nd Lt W G Barker & Lt G S Goodfellow of 15 Squadron.

MARCH 15
Artillery Co-operation – Thirty-three targets were dealt with by aeroplane observation.
Hostile Aircraft – Capt G J Q Brand, 1 Squadron, destroyed an LVG east of Zillebeke. 2nd Lt C C Clark, 1 Squadron, destroyed an Albatros scout. A patrol of No.1 Squadron engaged three Albatros scouts. One of these fell out of control and the other two driven down. A patrol of 11 Squadron destroyed a hostile machine

near Hoppy, and drove down a second machine out of control. A hostile machine was destroyed by machines of No.22 Squadron.

MARCH 16
Hostile Aircraft – An Offensive Patrol of six FE2bs of 25 Squadron and two Sopwith 1½ Strutters of 43 Squadron met eight hostile machines near Lens, which were immediately reinforced by eight more enemy scouts. A combat lasting 20 minutes ensued in which one hostile machine was brought down by Sergt Mackie & Sergt J H Brown, 25 Squadron. Lt Munro, 43 Squadron, and Lt Whitaker, 25 Squadron each drove one down out of control. All our machines returned.

MARCH 17
Artillery Co-operation – 83 targets were dealt with by aeroplane observation, and 12 with Kite Balloon observation.
Hostile Aircraft – Eighteen aeroplanes of the 1st Brigade taking photographs in the rear of the enemy's lines encountered 19 hostile machines. As the result of the fight, three hostile machines were destroyed, three driven down damaged, and one down out of control. The hostile formation was broken up and the photographic machines completed their work. Ten other hostile machines were brought down completely out of control by pilots of Nos 1 and 6 Squadrons, and pilots of the 2nd, 4th, 5th Brigades and the 9th Wing.

COMMUNIQUÉ No.80

18 – 24 March 1917

Further reinforcement for the RFC in France this week was the arrival on March 21 of No.100 Squadron, equipped with FE2bs and BE2cs. Lt Pickthorn's victim that same day was Prince Friedrich Karl of Prussia, who force-landed his Albatros scout in front of some Allied trenches. Attempting to reach the German lines, he was shot by Australian infantry and died of his wounds on 11 April 1917.

MARCH 18
Artillery Co-operation – Thirty targets were dealt with by aeroplane observation and six with balloon observation.
Hostile Aircraft – A hostile machine was shot down by Lt J D Belgrave & 2nd Lt Truscott, 45 Squadron, and one driven down by Flight Sub Lt F D Casey, 3 Squadron RNAS.

MARCH 19
Bombing – Machines of the 9th Wing dropped 48 bombs on the ammunition depot at Aulnoye from a height of 6000 feet. Two direct hits were observed.
Hostile Aircraft – Hostile aircraft were active well behind the enemy lines. Lt E J Y Grevelink, 54 Squadron, drove down a hostile machine in flames. 2nd Lt E R Pennell, 27 Squadron, drove down a Halberstadt completely out of control. A hostile machine was driven down out of control by Flight Sub-Lt J J Malone, 3 Squadron RNAS.

MARCH 20
No flying possible owing to weather.

MARCH 21
Hostile Aircraft – Lt C E M Pickthorn, 32 Squadron, got on the tail of an Albatros scout which he forced to land within our lines near Vaulx-Vraucourt.

MARCH 22
Hostile Aircraft – Little activity, there were two indecisive combats.

MARCH 23
Artillery Co-operation – Four targets were engaged with aeroplane and ten with kite balloon observation.
Photography – 112 plates were exposed.
Hostile Aircraft – Activity below normal.

MARCH 24
Artillery Co-operation – Thirty-five targets were engaged with aeroplane and two with kite balloon observation.
Photography – A total of 1019 plates were exposed during the day.
Bombing – Eighteen 112lb bombs were dropped by machines of 20 Squadron on

Cambrai Goods Station. Machines of 27 Squadron dropped twelve 112lb bombs on Busigny Station and sidings.

Hostile Aircraft – F/Sgt C Ryder & Lt J E S Alexander, 2 Squadron, drove down a Halberstadt out of control. During a reconnaissance by machines of 11 Squadron, two hostile machines were driven down completely out of control; one by Lt E T Curling & Lt H E Guy, the other by 2nd Lt R Savery & 2/AM Totterfield. Flight Cdr C D Bell, 3 Squadron RNAS, and 2nd Lt E L Zink & 2/AM Walker, 18 Squadron, both drove down hostile machines out of control. A reconnaissance of 70 Squadron, consisting of six machines, were attacked by a hostile formation of 12 machines, two of which were driven down out of control. After 15 minutes fighting only four hostile machines were seen and these made no attempt to continue the combat. 2nd Lt Harker & 2nd Lt Fernald, 57 Squadron, drove down a hostile machine out of control. Most of the above machines were almost certainly destroyed, and in addition several others were driven down.

COMMUNIQUÉ No.81

25 – 31 March 1917

On March 27, No.8 Squadron RNAS (Sopwith Pups) was re-attached to the RFC in France. The Canadian W A "Billy" Bishop's victory on March 31 was his second of an eventual accredited 72 combat victories. As Air Marshal, VC, CB, DSO, MC, DFC, he died in his sleep on 11 September 1956. The invaluable work of Kite Balloon observers should be noted in co-operation with the artillery.

MARCH 25
Artillery Co-operation – Fifty-five targets were dealt with by aeroplane and 12 with kite balloon observation. Eleven direct hits were obtained by artillery of the Third Army on hostile batteries, nine of which were obtained with observation by 2nd Lt Morris & 2nd Lt de Street, 8 Squadron with the 213th Siege Battery. Four direct hits were obtained on trenches.

Hostile Aircraft – Two hostile machines were brought down near Mercatel on our side of the lines by Lts A Binnie and F Bower, 60 Squadron. A reconnaissance of 11 Squadron encountered seven hostile aircraft in the Scarpe Valley. 2nd Lt Mackrell & 2nd Lt Boddy, and 2nd Lt Calvey & AM Hadlow drove down one machine which is believed to have crashed. A second machine was driven down in a vertical nose-dive. A hostile aeroplane attacked by a patrol of 54 Squadron was driven down and is believed to have crashed. On the 24th inst., Sergt J F Ridgway & 2nd Lt E J Hare, 15 Squadron, whilst on a photographic flight, were attacked by hostile aircraft near Heninel. The hostile aircraft were driven off. The photographic machine was then hit by an anti-aircraft shell which killed the Observer, wounded the pilot, and considerably damaged the machine. Two hostile aircraft then attacked the machine and the pilot was shot in the leg. He, however, succeeded in recrossing the line and landing his machine. The photographs of the Hindenburg Line were of much value.

Photography – 202 photographs were taken.

Hostile Kite Balloons – A hostile kite balloon was attacked by Capt E D Atkinson, 1 Squadron, and brought down in flames near Wervicq.

MARCH 26
Artillery Co-operation – Four targets were dealt with by aeroplane and 16 with Kite Balloon observation.

MARCH 27
Practically no work was possible owing to unfavourable weather.

MARCH 28
Artillery Co-operation – Thirty-seven targets were dealt with artillery with aeroplane observation.

Hostile Aircraft – 2nd Lt E S T Cole, 1 Squadron, drove down an Albatros scout out of control near Ronchin. 2nd Lt C C Clark, 1 Squadron, engaged a hostile machine near Lesquin which he drove down completely out of control.

Photography – 204 photographs were taken during the day.

MARCH 29
Weather was unfavourable for air work.
Artillery Co-operation – Eleven targets were dealt with by aeroplane and 12 with observation by kite balloon.

MARCH 30
Artillery Co-operation – Fourteen targets were dealt with by aeroplane observation.
Hostile Aircraft – Capt R W Gregory, 40 Squadron, dived at two hostile machines near Bailleul, one of which he drove down apparently badly damaged.

MARCH 31
Artillery Co-operation – Twenty-eight targets were dealt with by aeroplane observation.
Hostile Aircraft – Major A J L Scott, Squadron Commander 60 Squadron, destroyed a hostile machine south-east of Arras. Capt C T Black, 60 Squadron, assisted Major Scott. A second hostile aeroplane was destroyed north-east of Arras by Lt W A Bishop, 60 Squadron. A patrol of three Nieuports, 29 Squadron, drove down a hostile machine out of control in the vicinity of Gavrelle. Two other German machines were forced to land after having been engaged by Lts A Binnie and W E Molesworth, both of 60 Squadron.

COMMUNIQUÉ No. 82

1 – 7 April 1917

The month of April 1917 – later to be dubbed 'Bloody April' – saw the RFC in France suffer its highest casualty figures for one month in the entire air war of 1914-18 (See Appendix 4). The recently formed Jagdstaffeln (fighter units) of the German air service had become increasingly more aggressive, having discarded the former policy of mainly defensive tactics behind the German lines and now adopting the offensive, seeking Allied aircraft over their own territory. The RFC's constant policy of the offensive, as proscribed by the RFC's commander, Hugh Trenchard, was maintained, but with most squadrons still flying obsolescent types of aircraft, eg BE2cs, these were relatively easy targets for the superior Albatros scouts now in service in increasing numbers. Fresh aircraft designs for the RFC frontline units were still to make their impact. The Bristol F2as of 48 Squadron flew their first war patrols on April 5, with disastrous results, while the first unit to be equipped with the new SE5 fighter, No.56 Squadron, only arrived on April 7 and did not commence operations until April 22. On April 6 the United States of America officially declared war on Germany and her allies.

APRIL 1
Artillery Co-operation – Twenty-five targets were dealt with by aeroplane observation.
Hostile Aircraft – 2nd Lt D Gordon & 2nd Lt H E Baker, 12 Squadron, engaged a hostile aeroplane near Arras, which was seen to break in the air and to crash.

APRIL 2
Artillery Co-operation – Thirty-two targets were dealt with by aeroplane observation and five by kite balloon observation.
Hostile Aircraft – On March 30 a patrol of 60 Squadron pursued six hostile aircraft to east of Douai in a very strong westerly wind. 2nd Lt F Bower was shot through the stomach but flew west and landed his machine completely undamaged except for enemy bullets, four miles south of Chipilly. 2nd Lt Bower died from his wound the next day. 2nd Lt C E Berigny & 2/AM E Bowen, 43 Squadron, engaged and drove down an Albatros scout which fell in flames east of Vimy. Lt O M Sutton, 54 Squadron, drove down a German aeroplane out of control east of Peronne. A patrol of 24 Squadron engaged a number of hostile scouts near Bois D'Havrincourt and destroyed two of them; one by Lt K Crawford and the other by Lt S Cockerell. A line patrol of 57 Squadron engaged six single-seater Albatros south-east of Arras. One hostile machine fell in flames and a second went down apparently out of control. A two-seater Albatros crossed the lines on the Fifth Army front and was brought down by anti-aircraft fire. The machine was little damaged and the passengers were taken prisoners.

APRIL 3
Artillery Co-operation – Twenty-seven targets were dealt with by aeroplane observation.

Hostile Aircraft – Capt H H Balfour & 2nd Lt A Roberts, 43 Squadron, while on photographic reconnaissance were attacked by four hostile scouts which they drove off. They were then attacked by two more, one of which they drove down in flames.

Photography – 630 photographs were taken.

Kite Balloons – The balloons of Nos.13 and 18 KBS were brought down by hostile aircraft. The passengers in each made successful parachute descents.

APRIL 4

Artillery Co-operation – Fifty-four targets were dealt with by aeroplane and 14 with observation by kite balloons.

APRIL 5

Artillery Co-operation – 119 targets were dealt with by aeroplane observation and nine by kite balloon observation.

Hostile Aircraft – Our Offensive Patrols were successful in keeping hostile aircraft well over the lines and our artillery machines were able to carry out their work without interference. There was much hard fighting during the day and although the combats took place mostly far over the enemy's lines, he suffered far more heavily than we. Lt C R O'Brien & Lt J L Dickson, 43 Squadron, engaged three hostile machines east of La Bassée. One of these was driven down out of control and the other two broke off the combat. Flight Lt R J O Compston, 8 Squadron RNAS, on a Sopwith Triplane, pursued three hostile aeroplanes and attacked the rear one which went down out of control. An Albatros scout which had been engaged by Sergt J Dempsey & Sergt C H Nunn, 25 Squadron, fell out of control. 2nd Lt H G White & Pte T Allum, 20 Squadron, were attacked by two Albatros scouts near St Eloi. Two-thirds of a drum was fired at one hostile aircraft which was forced to land near Neuve Eglise, and the pilot, who was wounded, was taken prisoner. Two Halberstadts were driven down out of control by a patrol of 20 Squadron. Capt G J Mahoney-Jones and Capt R M Knowles who, with others, engaged these machines, believed that both were destroyed. A patrol of 48 Squadron, led by Capt W L Robinson, VC, engaged 12 hostile aircraft near Douai. Capt Robinson engaged one hostile machine which he drove down out of control. Another hostile machine engaged by Lt Pike & Lt H B Griffith was brought down apparently out of control. These two officers lost the formation and on returning home fought two rearguard actions, in one of which they drove down one hostile aeroplane. A second patrol of 48 Squadron, led by Capt A M Wilkinson, saw three HA near Douai and engaged and drove down two of them – one out of control. Later, they engaged another and drove it down. Another patrol of 48 Squadron, led by Capt D M Tidmarsh, engaged a two-seater HA east of Douai – the HA disappeared in the clouds. Lt O W Berry engaged another HA south-east of Douai and drove it down in a steep spiral. Lt G N Brockhurst then dived on a red single-seater which was also driven down.

(NB: See Editor's note on 48 Squadron at end of this communiqué).

Flight Cdr E W Norton, 6 Squadron RNAS, drove down one hostile aeroplane in flames and one out of control west of Douai. Flight Sub-Lt Thorne, 6 Squadron RNAS, also drove down a hostile machine out of control. An Offensive Patrol of five Nieuports of 29 Squadron fought six HA near Arras and one HA was driven

down out of control. Lt T Langwill, with a patrol of 60 Squadron, engaged four HA. One HA dropped vertical and appeared to crash. During the patrol two other HA were driven down out of control – one by Lt C S Hall and one by Lt J McC Elliott. An Albatros scout was driven down out of control by Lt C V de B Rogers,29 Squadron, near Vitry-en-Artois. A patrol of 24 Squadron engaged three HA near Honnecourt. Lt H W Woollett drove down one HA which was seen to crash east of Honnecourt. Flight Cdr R S Dallas, 1 Squadron RNAS, drove down an Albatros scout out of control south-east of St Quentin. A patrol of 22 Squadron drove down a German aeroplane out of control near Honnecourt. Lt V H Huston & 2nd Lt G N Blennerhassett, 18 Squadron, who were part of a photographic patrol, drove down two HA out of control and drove off several others. Capt Platt & 2nd Lt Margerison, 57 Squadron, drove down a single-seater biplane which landed in a ploughed field.
Photography – 1000 photographs were taken.

APRIL 6

Artillery Co-operation – 123 targets were dealt with by aeroplane observation.
Hostile Aircraft – 2nd Lt H S Pell, 40 Squadron, drove down an HA south of Bailleul. This machine was observed by anti-aircraft to crash. 2nd Lt A Roulstone & 2nd Lt E G Green, 25 Squadron, saw a hostile scout attacking one of our artillery machines and immediately dived at it. The HA was sent down in flames and crashed. 2nd Lt B King & Corpl L Emsden, 25 Squadron, attacked a Halberstadt scout which was harassing a BE engaged on artillery work. The Halberstadt was destroyed. 2nd Lt E O Perry & Pte T Allum, 20 Squadron, destroyed a Halberstadt scout near Ledeghem. 2nd Lt R Smart & 2nd Lt H N Hampson, 20 Squadron, while on a bombing raid, attacked three HA. The pilot of one HA was shot and the machine broke in the air and fell. The second machine was driven down in a spinning nose-dive, while the third after having been attacked dived vertically. 2nd Lt G H Cock & 2nd Lt J T M Murison, 45 Squadron, destroyed an HA near Lille, and a second was driven down out of control near Templeuve. While on photographic work, Lt J P V Lavarack & 2nd Lt Baker-Jones, 12 Squadron, were attacked by an HA. The HA finally burst into flames and fell. Lt G O Smart, 60 Squadron, while on Offensive Patrol, engaged three HA near Arras. One HA was driven down in a spin, and the other two driven off. Later this patrol of 60 Squadron engaged six HA and two HA were driven down and a third appeared to be hit. 2nd Lt J H Muir,29 Squadron, engaged a two-seater biplane north- east of Arras. The Observer in the HA was shot whereupon the enemy pilot broke off the combat. Lt F P Holliday & Capt A H Wall, 48 Squadron, drove down an HA out of control in the same locality with its pilot apparently shot. 2nd Lt W T Price & 2nd Lt M A Benjamin of the same patrol drove down an HA out of control near Douai. A formation of 54 Squadron, while acting as escort, was attacked by a fast HA scout. The enemy pilot appeared to be very good and manoeuvred with great skill. Finally, however, he was enticed to attack one of our machines from behind, whereupon Lt O Stewart dived at the HA and destroyed it. A patrol of 22 Squadron succeeded in destroying one HA and driving down a second near Fontaine Uterte. Capt F N Hudson, 54 Squadron, and Lt T C Arnot, 24 Squadron, each drove down an HA out of control. Flight Cdr B C Clayton, 1 Squadron RNAS, engaged an HA which was painted partially red and drove it down out of control. Flight Sub-Lt T G Culling, also 1 Squadron RNAS, engaged a two-seater biplane north-east of St Quentin, which was driven down

completely out of control. Capt K C McCallum, 23 Squadron, engaged four HA. He drove down one apparently out of control. Flight Lt L S Breadner, 3 Squadron RNAS, while escorting BEs on a bombing raid, engaged four HA who were endeavouring to intercept the BEs. He drove one down and followed, firing at it, until it crashed near Bois de Bourlon. A second HA was destroyed in the same locality by Flight Sub-Lt J S T Fall from the same escort. 2nd Lt Reid & 2nd Lt G N Blennerhassett, 18 Squadron, drove down an HA which was interfering with a photographic reconnaissance. This machine fell completely out of control and anti-aircraft report that it crashed. 2nd Lt Parkinson & 2nd Lt Power of the same squadron also fired on this HA. Flight Sub-Lt A W Carter, 3 Squadron RNAS, while acting as escort, drove down an HA out of control. 2nd Lt A H Vinson & 2nd Lt E C L Gwilt, 15 Squadron, were taking photographs over Bullecourt when they were attacked by six Albatros scouts. Unfortunately, both machine guns fell out of their BE and it was forced to land near Lagnicourt as one HA pursued and kept firing at it. The pilot and Observer jumped out and got into shell holes. The enemy artillery opened fire on our machine, but just before it was hit by an eight-inch shell, 2nd Lt Vinson managed to obtain the exposed plates, which produced good photographs of the Hindenburg Line and Bullecourt. 2nd Lt D P Collis, 23 Squadron, drove down an HA near St Quentin. An Offensive Patrol of Sopwith Scouts of 66 Squadron shot the Observer in an HA and he was seen to fall from the aeroplane. They drove off three HA which were interfering with our artillery machines.

Photography – 700 photographs were taken.

Bombing – On the night of the 5th/6th, eight 112lb bombs and 20lb bombs were dropped on Provin aerodrome. All bombs dropped on the sheds and on the aerodrome. On the same night Douai aerodrome was attacked twice by machines of 100 Squadron. Four hangars were completely destroyed and other damage done. Six De Havilland 4s of 55 Squadron attacked an ammunition dump at Valenciennes. Bombs were dropped from a height of 11,500 feet. Two bombs were seen to fall in the station, two near the engine depot, and the remainder on or about the objective. On the return flight the De Havillands were pursued by hostile scouts but owing to the superior speed of our machines the HA were soon outdistanced.

Hostile Kite Balloons – Five Nieuports of 40 Squadron proceeded to attack hostile kite balloons. The balloons were rapidly hauled down but 2nd Lt A S Todd succeeded in destroying one by firing three rockets into it at a range of about ten yards. The balloon was then 500 feet from the ground.

APRIL 7

Reconnaissances – 2nd Lt J S Black & 2nd Lt S Cooper, 16 Squadron, carried out a special reconnaissance at a height of 500 feet and made some useful observations.

Artillery Co-operation – Fifty-seven targets were dealt with by aeroplane observation.

Hostile Aircraft – A German aeroplane, said to resemble a Nieuport, attacked and destroyed one of our kite balloons. This HA had been observed by one of our artillery machines, but until the attack the BE pilot had failed to realise that the machine was hostile. Lt W A Bishop, 60 Squadron, drove down an HA, after which he attacked a hostile balloon on the ground and set it on fire. Lt A Binnie, 60 Squadron, also attacked a hostile balloon on the ground but, although hit, it did not burn.

Bombing – Provin aerodrome was attacked twice during the day. One bomb dropped by 2nd Lt D Gordon, 10 Squadron, fell on the engine of a train going south-east of Provin-Carvin railway. The boiler exploded and the engine and trucks left the line.

Photography – 221 photographs were taken during the day.

Editor's footnote: The first operations by 48 Squadron's Bristol F2As on April 5 were initially attacked by Albatros scouts from Jagdstaffel 11, led by Rittmeister Manfred von Richthofen who personally claimed two F2As as his victims. Two other F2As were shot down from Capt W L Robinson's Flight, including himself. Claims by all F2A crews that day for three HA out of control and five others 'Driven down' were optimistic – no German aircraft was lost in these encounters. Capt Robinson, VC, a victim of Vizefeldwebel Sebastian Festner, Jagdstaffel 11, became a prisoner of war, and died on 31 December 1918 after repatriation.

COMMUNIQUÉ No.83

8 – 14 April 1917

With an Allied ground offensive due to commence on April 9 – the Battle of Arras – aerial activity intensified in the opposing air services. One of 48 Squadron's victims on April 8 was the 19-victory German ace, Wilhelm Frankl of Jagdstaffel 4.

APRIL 8

Artillery Co-operation – 96 targets were dealt with by aeroplane and 34 by kite balloon observation.

Hostile Aircraft – Flight Sub-Lt R A Little, 8 Squadron RNAS, destroyed an HA near Lens. Lt F M Kitto & 2/AM A Cant, 43 Squadron, while on line patrol, were attacked by five hostile aircraft. One HA was driven down completely out of control. Flight Cdr A R Arnold, 8 Squadron RNAS, drove down a hostile scout out of control near Beaumont. Lt R L Robertson & 2nd Lt L G Fauvel, 20 Squadron, drove down a single-seater Albatros out of control near Tourcoing. Lt W A Bishop, 60 Squadron, drove down two HA out of control and forced three others to go down apparently damaged. Major A J L Scott, 60 Squadron, also drove down an HA out of control. A patrol of 48 Squadron drove down six hostile aircraft; two of them fell out of control. No.54 Squadron destroyed an HA, and 1 Squadron, RNAS, drove one down which is believed to have been destroyed. Two HA were driven down out of control – one by Flight Sub-Lt F D Casey, and one by Flight Lt H G Travers, both of 8 Squadron RNAS. Capt K C McCallum, 23 Squadron, drove down an HA and forced it to land in a field near the Canal du Nord. An Offensive Patrol of 66 Squadron encountered six Halberstadt scouts, and three of them were driven down out of control by Capt G W Roberts and Lts C C S Montgomery and A J Lucas. Lt J T Collier on the same patrol drove down a fourth machine in damaged condition. An Offensive Patrol of 57 Squadron engaged six HA east of Arras, although none of the HA were seen to fall, when the combat ceased only three of them were seen. On the evening of the 6th a patrol of 57 Squadron engaged ten HA south of Douai. The fighting was very severe and several HA are believed to have been badly hit.

Hostile Kite Balloons – Two hostile kite balloons were attacked and brought down in flames near Moorslede and Quesnoy respectively by machines of 1 Squadron.

Bombing – On the night of 7th/8th, five 112lb bombs and 22 – 20lb bombs were dropped on Provin aerodrome. Douai aerodrome was attacked twice during the night of the 7th/8th by machines of 100 Squadron. Aulnoye engine sheds were attacked by 27 Squadron, while an ammunition dump at Valenciennes was attacked by 55 Squadron.

APRIL 9

Artillery Co-operation – Sixty-one targets were dealt with by aeroplane and 55 with kite balloon observation.

Hostile Aircraft – Flight Sub-Lt R A Little, 8 Squadron RNAS, drove down a hostile scout out of control. Capt A M Wilkinson & Lt H B Griffiths, 48 Squadron, destroyed a hostile two-seater near Lens, and drove down an Albatros two-seater out of control. 2nd Lt W T Price & 2nd Lt M A Benjamin, 48 Squadron, destroyed a hostile machine east of Arras. Capt A M Wilkinson & Lt L W Allen, Lts J H Letts & H G Collins, in two machines of 48 Squadron, attacked five hostile aircraft near Arras. They destroyed one and drove down another out of control. Flight Cdr E W Norton, 6 Squadron RNAS, drove down two hostile aircraft out of control near Cambrai. No.22 Squadron destroyed an HA near Regny and drove down two in damaged condition – one at Mont d'Origny and the other near Marcy.

APRIL 10
Artillery Co-operation – Eleven targets were dealt with by aeroplane observation and 12 with kite balloon observation.
Hostile Aircraft – Lt T N Southorn & 2nd Lt H E Freeman-Smith, 25 Squadron, were attacked by a formation of hostile scouts and they drove one of them down out of control.

APRIL 11
Artillery Co-operation – Twenty-five targets were dealt with by aeroplane observation.
Hostile Aircraft – Anti-aircraft report that they watched a fight between four Bristol Fighters (48 Squadron) and four hostile aircraft. They saw two of the latter brought down and the other two break off the combat and fly east. Two Bristol Fighters were observed by No.12 Squadron to land under control in hostile territory. 2nd Lts A G Riley & L G Hall, 48 Squadron, drove down a hostile machine out of control. No.3 Squadron RNAS, when acting as escort to a bombing raid on Cambrai, was attacked by HA. Flight Lt L S Breadner engaged one machine which fell completely out of control and in flames. Later, a formation of HA attempted to attack the bombing machines. Flight Lt Breadner drove down an Albatros scout and then attacked a second which went down in a spinning nose-dive and one wing was observed to break off. Flight Sub-Lt J S T Fall also drove down one of the attacking machines in flames. In the fighting he became detached from the rest of the formation and was attacked by three HA. He drove down one hostile scout out of control but the remaining two continued to attack. After considerable fighting one of the HA broke off the combat. Flight Sub-Lt Fall, by skilful manoeuvring, obtained a favourable position from which to attack the remaining machine. He opened fire and the HA crashed. During certain periods the fighting took place at a height of only 50 feet from the ground. Flight Sub-Lt Fall landed at one of our aerodromes unhurt but with his machine riddled with bullets from hostile gunfire from aircraft, infantry and cavalry. Flight Sub-Lt P G MacNeill of the same escort also drove down an enemy machine completely out of control.

APRIL 12
Hostile Aircraft – Capt A M Wilkinson & Lt L W Allen, 2nd Lt W O D Winkler & 2nd Lt E S Moore, 48 Squadron, drove down out of control one of seven hostile machines which they engaged. 2nd Lt E W P Hunt & 2nd Lt K Fearnside-Speed, 18 Squadron, and Flight Sub-Lt F C Armstrong, 8 Squadron RNAS, drove down a black single-seat HA out of control. Flight Sub-Lt A T Whealey of the same squadron also drove down an HA out of control. During the combat a German aeroplane was seen to fall with its wings completely broken. It is believed to have been brought down by Flight Cdr R G Mack, who is missing.

APRIL 13

Artillery Co-operation – Twenty-six targets were dealt with by aeroplane observation.

Hostile Aircraft – Lt H E O Ellis, 40 Squadron, engaged and destroyed an Albatros two-seater near Courrieres. Capt K Oxspring, 66 Squadron, drove down a two-seat biplane near Douai. Lt G S Buck, 19 Squadron, assisted by another pilot, drove down an Albatros scout out of control.

Bombing – On the night 12th/13th, bombs were dropped on Henin Lietard, Billy Montigny, Dourges, Sallaumines, Mericourt, La Bassée, Lambersart, Tournai, Wervicq, and Mouveaux aerodrome. By day on the 13th, bombs were dropped on Essigny-le-Petit, Busigny Station, Henin Lietard Station.

APRIL 14

Artillery Co-operation – Thirty-five targets were dealt with by aeroplane observation and 32 by kite balloon observation.

Hostile Aircraft – FEs of 25 Squadron engaged five hostile scouts and one was destroyed by Sergt W J Burtenshaw & Sergt J H Brown. A second was destroyed by 2nd Lt R G Malcolm & Cpl W J Emsden. 2nd Lt Buckton & 2nd Lt Barritt, 5 Squadron, were attacked by two Halberstadts. The BE was considerably shot about and as the pilot was unable to flatten out it flew into the ground and was completely wrecked. The occupants were uninjured. They took the guns from the wrecked machine and sought shelter in a sunken road. A patrol of eight Germans approached and our men opened fire on them. The Germans retreated and 2nd Lts Buckton and Barritt shortly after fell into the hands of a Canadian advance patrol. They found an RE8 of 59 Squadron which had been brought down a few days previously. The pilot and Observer, 2nd Lt R W M Davies and 2nd Lt J C D Wordsworth were both killed. Flight Lt C D Booker and Flight Sub-Lt E D Crundall, 8 Squadron RNAS, each drove down an Albatros out of control. Flight Sub-Lt R R Soar drove off three Albatros scouts. On the evening of the 13th a patrol of 48 Squadron engaged about 20 hostile aircraft near Vitry-en-Artois. One HA was destroyed by Capt A M Wilkinson & Lt L W Allen, and a second was driven down completely out of control by Lt Warren & 2nd Lt H B Griffith. One HA was driven down by each of the following; 2nd Lt A G Jones-Williams, 29 Squadron; 2nd Lt R Savery & Cpl Tollerfield, 11 Squadron; 2nd Lt G A Exley & Capt J A le Royer, 11 Squadron; and Flight Cdr T F N Gerrard, 1 Squadron RNAS. 2nd Lt Aspinall & Lt M K Parlee, 22 Squadron, destroyed an Albatros scout, and Capt W V Strugnell, 54 Squadron, and 2nd Lt M B Cole, also 54 Squadron, each drove down an HA out of control. Five HA were driven down by 23 Squadron. One HA was driven down out of control by Lt W E Reid, 19 Squadron.

Photography – Nearly 500 photographs were taken during the day.

COMMUNIQUÉ No.84

15 – 21 April 1917

Of the individuals mentioned in this communiqué, Lt Pidcock of 60 Squadron later became Air Vice-Marshal, RAF, while Lt F F Wessel, 15 Squadron, was unique as the only Danish operational pilot to serve in the RFC.

APRIL 15

Artillery Co-operation – Fourteen targets were dealt with by aeroplane and three by kite balloon observation. 2nd Lt W Buckingham & 2nd Lt W R Cox, 15 Squadron, did an artillery patrol at a height of 500 feet. The zone call was sent down and five parties of infantry, varying from 100 to 300 strong, were engaged by our artillery. On the evening of the 14th, Capt L C Coates & 2nd Lt J C Cotton, 5 Squadron, while on artillery work, were attacked by five HA. At the commencement of the fight 2nd Lt Cotton was wounded in seven places and Captain Coates was also wounded, but they succeeded in destroying one HA and landed safely in spite of the fact that their machine was considerably damaged by machine gun fire. 2nd Lt B King & Cpl Taylor, 25 Squadron, attacked two HA that were interfering with artillery patrols and drove one HA down in badly damaged condition. Lt D de Burgh and Lt I P R Napier, 40 Squadron, dived on three hostile scouts, one of which landed in a field and was seen to burst into flames. Flight Sub-Lt E D Crundall, 8 Squadron RNAS, drove down an Albatros two-seater out of control, in addition to one already reported on the 14th inst. On the evening of the 15th, Lt L P Beynon & 2nd Lt Lutyens, 3 Squadron, engaged two HA near Queant. The Observer had his collar bone broken but continued fighting, and one HA was forced to land in a field.

APRIL 16

Hostile Aircraft – Lt G H Pidcock, 60 Squadron, drove down two hostile aircraft. A photographic patrol by 18 Squadron engaged six HA scouts over Cagnicourt. 2nd Lt S J Young & 2nd Lt E N Blennerhassett attacked one HA which was engaging one of our machines and fired a whole drum into it. The HA fell completely out of control. They then attacked and downed a second HA. A third HA was driven down and fell out of control by 2nd Lt E W A Hunt & 2nd Lt O J Partington.
Photography – 426 photographs were taken during the day.

APRIL 17

Artillery Co-operation – Lt F F Wessel, 15 Squadron, successfully ranged the 152nd Siege Battery on to wire, and five direct hits were observed. This work was carried out under most unfavourable conditions and at a height of only 500 feet.

APRIL 20

Hostile Aircraft – Lt W A Bishop, 60 Squadron, drove down in flames a German two-seat machine. *Photography* – 314 photographs were taken during the day.

APRIL 21

Artillery Co-operation – Thirty-two targets were dealt with by aeroplane observation. Capt Mowcock & Lt McCartney, 9 Squadron, observed an MT convoy on a road and sent down a zone call. Artillery destroyed the road in front of the convoy, then shelled and completely destroyed the convoy.

COMMUNIQUÉ No.85

22 - 28 April 1917

The intensity of aerial activity by the opposing air forces is partly reflected here by the greatly increasing details being included in communiqués. Prominent space is given to air combats, and mention made of particularly successful pilots, such as Albert Ball, 'Billy' Bishop, and especially the RNAS pilots still attached to the RFC. Of the latter, Roderick Dallas, C D Booker, and L S Breadner were to achieve high scores eventually, while Hubert Broad, 3 Squadron RNAS, was to become test pilot for the De Havilland aircraft company in the post-war years. Nevertheless, the daily essential tasks of the reconnaissance, bomber, and kite balloon crews continued apace.

APRIL 22

Artillery Co-operation – 100 targets were dealt with by artillery with aeroplane observation, and 14 by kite balloon observation.

Hostile Aircraft – Evening of the 21st – Flight Sub-Lt R A Little, 8 Squadron RNAS, observed five hostile machines attacking an FE of 25 Squadron. He at once dived at a scout attacking the FE from behind. The HA fell completely out of control. 2nd Lt R G Malcolm & 2nd Lt J B Weir, 25 Squadron, dived at a formation of five hostile scouts. Flight Cdr A R Arnold, 8 Squadron RNAS, came to the assistance of the FE. One hostile machine, after being badly hit, fell to pieces in the air and crashed in our lines. 2nd Lt L L Morgan, 40 Squadron, drove down a hostile machine. 2nd Lt R Stocken, 23 Squadron, attacked a two-seater near Sauchy Lestree. He followed it down to 800 feet and fired 200 rounds into it. This HA was seen to disappear into a small wood. A German machine was driven down completely out of control by Lt R I Keller, 23 Squadron. Capt K C McAllum, also of 23 Squadron, drove down a hostile machine, in which the Observer is believed to have been shot. Flight Sub-Lts F D Casey and H S Broad, 3 Squadron RNAS, attacked four Albatros scouts. Flight Sub-Lt Casey fired 80 rounds into one HA, finishing at about 10 yards distance.

The HA was seen to fall out of control. He then attacked and drove down a second HA out of control. Flight Sub-Lt Broad also drove one down which was afterwards seen crashed on the ground. Flight Sub-Lt J J Malone of the same squadron drove down a German aeroplane out of control near Queant, and Flight Lt H G Travers, also of 3 Squadron RNAS, drove down a German machine completely out of control.

On April 22, Flight Cdr A R Arnold, 8 Squadron RNAS, in a Sopwith Triplane, dived at one of several hostile aircraft and fired about 60 rounds at close range. Unfortunately, his gun jammed so he immediately out-climbed the HA, cleared the jam, then re-engaged the hostile aircraft. One HA was seen to fall in flames by other pilots and is believed to have been brought down by Flight Cdr Arnold. 2nd Lt J S Leslie & Lt A R Sortwell, 16 Squadron, while on artillery duty, were attacked by three hostile aircraft. One HA was hit and is believed to have been brought down. Three Sopwith Triplanes of 8 Squadron RNAS attacked three hostile aircraft and a running fight ensued in which one HA was driven down. 2nd Lt W T Walder, 40 Squadron, drove down a hostile machine out of control near Henin-Lietard. It was shortly afterwards seen by another pilot completely wrecked on the ground. While on an

Offensive Patrol, machines of 1 Squadron attacked eight HA south-east of Lille. 2nd Lt E M Wright drove one HA down completely out of control, and Captain E D Atkinson also drove down one out of control. Major A J L Scott, 60 Squadron, when on photographic duty, was attacked by five HA. An Offensive Patrol of 60 Squadron dived to his assistance and one HA was driven down out of control by Lt W A Bishop. Later, Lt Bishop engaged five HA and drove them off east. A hostile machine was destroyed by 2nd Lt C Patteson, and one was driven down out of control by Lt W E Molesworth, both of the Offensive Patrol of 60 Squadron. Lts G A H Pidcock and N D Henderson of 60 Squadron dived to the assistance of FEs that were engaging a number of HA. They drove two HA down. Flight Cdr R S Dallas and Flight Lt T G Culling, 1 Squadron RNAS, attacked about eight HA over Douai. One HA was destroyed and another driven down enveloped in flames by Flight Cdr Dallas, while a third was driven down completely out of control by Flight Lt Culling. A patrol of 48 Squadron (Bristol Fighters) engaged a formation of 14 HA. One HA was driven down out of control by Capt A M Wilkinson & Lt L W Allen, while two others were driven down by the patrol. Captain C E M Pickthorn, 32 Squadron, saw a German machine diving at a BE on artillery work. He at once flew at the HA which was driven off after being hit. Lt W E Reid, 19 Squadron, while on an Offensive Patrol, observed an HA approaching from the east. He secured a favourable position between the sun and the German machine and then dived at it. About 200 rounds were fired at the HA which fell completely out of control and in flames. A hostile machine dived at a Sopwith Scout of 66 Squadron but was itself attacked from behind by Lt J T Collier. The pilot was hit and seen to fall forward, and the machine fell completely out of control. The German pilot appeared to manoeuvre his machine with more than the average skill shown by the enemy.

Balloons – Lt D de Burgh, 40 Squadron, attacked a hostile balloon with Le Prieur rockets. The balloon did not burst into flames but was hauled down emitting a large amount of smoke. 2nd Lt E S T Cole, 1 Squadron, destroyed a hostile balloon when about 20 feet from the ground. The engine of his Nieuport was hit and he crossed the lines considerably under 50 feet, while on more than one occasion his machine actually touched the ground on the enemy's side of the lines. Captain E F Elderton, 29 Squadron, brought down a balloon in flames. 2nd Lt H G Ross, 60 Squadron, destroyed a balloon, and Lt W E Molesworth, 2nd Lts A R Penny, and G L Lloyd, all of 60 Squadron, also attacked balloons which were seen to be hit and from which smoke issued. The balloons of Nos.3 and 14 Sections were destroyed by hostile aircraft.

Photography – 700 photographs were taken during the day.

APRIL 23

Artillery Co-operation – Eighty-eight targets were dealt with by aeroplane and 56 with kite balloon observation.

Hostile Aircraft – 2nd Lt C E de Berigny & 2/AM E Bowen, 43 Squadron, drove down an Albatros which landed in a ploughed field, turned over, and crashed. Lt K MacKenzie and Lt H E O Ellis, both of 40 Squadron, attacked a German two-seater and drove it down out of control. Flight Sub-Lt R A Little, 8 Squadron RNAS, drove down an Albatros two-seater in damaged condition. Flight Cdr R S Dallas and Flight Sub-Lt T G F Culling, 1 Squadron RNAS, each engaged and drove down a German aeroplane out of control. Four German aeroplanes were driven down out of control; one by Lt R N Upson, two by Lt A G Jones-Williams, and one by Lt Rutherford, all of

29 Squadron. Lt W A Bishop, 60 Squadron, drove down a hostile machine which landed. He continued attacking the machine and believes that both the pilot and Observer were killed or wounded. He then destroyed a hostile scout which was attacking a Nieuport from behind. Capt E R Manning & Lt Duncan, 11 Squadron, shot down an HA out of control. A patrol of 48 Squadron engaged ten HA over Vitry and Lt F P Holliday & Capt A H Wall in one Bristol Fighter destroyed a hostile machine, while a second HA was brought down out of control by the patrol, and a third driven down severely damaged. Lt C A Parker, 11 Squadron,was attacked by eleven hostile aircraft and his FE was brought down in flames. The controls had been nearly all shot away, and the Observer – seriously wounded – had fallen partly out of the machine, but was held from falling out by Lt Parker, who landed safely and took his Observer out of the burning FE and carried him to safety while under heavy shell fire. On the evening of the 22nd, Flight Cdr R S Dallas and Flight Sub-Lt T G F Culling, 1 Squadron RNAS, met about 14 hostile aircraft, composed of scouts and two-seaters, flying from the east. The HA were unable to keep formation owing to the two Triplanes continually diving at the formation and firing short bursts as they passed. For about three-quarters of an hour, owing to the superior climbing powers and speed of the Triplanes, they were able to continue such tactics as suited their purpose. After two HA had been destroyed by Flight Cdr Dallas, and one driven down out of control by Flight Sub-Lt Culling, the German formation was thoroughly disorganised, gave up its attempt to reach the lines and retired eastwards. Flight Lt L S Breadner, 3 Squadron, RNAS, engaged and brought down in our lines a double-engined pusher machine carrying a pilot and two Observers. The officers were taken prisoners, but burnt the machine before being captured.
(Editor's note: This was a Gotha G IV, 610/16 from KG 111/15).

Flight Sub-Lt J J Malone, 3 Squadron RNAS, engaged a hostile machine and shot the pilot, and the HA crashed. He drove down a second HA out of control and attacked a third. He then ran out of ammunition, and so returned to an aerodrome, obtained more ammunition, recrossed the lines, and drove down another HA out of control, while still another was forced down. Capt K C Patrick, 23 Squadron, drove down two hostile machines and then attacked a third which fell out of control. A hostile machine was driven down by each of the following pilots of 3 Squadron RNAS – Flight Sub-Lts E T Pierce, H F Beamish, and Anderson. Captain A Ball, DSO, MC, 56 Squadron, attacked two Albatros two-seaters, one of which soon dived away east. After considerable manoeuvring, Captain Ball obtained a favourable position under the second HA and fired about half a drum. The HA, which was painted with many colours, was destroyed. Later in the day, Captain Ball observed five Albatros scouts over Cambrai. He dived at the nearest and fired about 150 rounds at close range, and the HA fell in flames; while the remaining four HA broke off the combat. Captain Ball had two other combats and on each occasion the HA dived away east. Lt J M Child, 19 Squadron, drove down an Albatros two-seater out of control. A hostile machine was driven down out of control by 2nd Lt F A Handley & 2nd Lt E Percival, 57 Squadron. Bombing machines of 55 Squadron, when returning to the aerodrome, were dived at by nine hostile aircraft. 2nd Lt I Pyott, DSO & 2nd Lt Taylor, on a De Havilland 4, drove down one of the attacking machines out of control as it passed. Major H D Harvey-Kelly, 19 Squadron, destroyed an Albatros scout near Cambrai.
Photography – 573 photographs were taken during the day.

APRIL 24

Artillery Co-operation – Ninety-three targets were dealt with by aeroplane observation and 43 by kite balloon observation.

Hostile Aircraft – Flight Sub-Lt G G Simpson, 8 Squadron RNAS, drove down a hostile machine out of control. 2nd Lt C S Hall, 40 Squadron, attacked a two-seater at very close range and shot the Observer, and the HA dived away. Lt J G Brewis and I P R Napier, 40 Squadron, encountered a two-seat DFW at 17,000 feet. They attacked and drove it downwards in a westerly direction. Flight Sub-Lt R A Little, 8 Squadron RNAS, also joined the chase and the HA was forced to land in our lines in an undamaged condition and the occupants were taken prisoners. Lt T F Hazell, 1 Squadron, shot down a hostile machine in flames. An escort of machines of 20 Squadron engaged 12 HA near Roulers. One HA was destroyed and one driven down out of control. Flight Cdrs T F N Gerrard and R S Dallas, 1 Squadron RNAS, each drove down a hostile machine out of control. Lt F P Holliday & Capt J H Wall, 48 Squadron, destroyed an HA near Cagnicourt and drove another down out of control. Three pilots of 3 Squadron RNAS attacked a DFW two-seater over Queant. The HA endeavoured to fly east but the wind was against it and the Naval pilots intercepted it and drove it west. Two of the pilots' guns jammed but the third, Flight Lt J J Malone, continued to engage the HA and drove it down in our lines. The Observer was killed and the pilot wounded. Sergt J Whiteman & 2nd Lt K Fearnside-Speed, 18 Squadron, brought down an Albatros scout completely enveloped in flames. Two Halberstadt scouts were seen to collide in the air and break to pieces. Flight Sub-Lt A W Carter, 3 Squadron RNAS had several encounters during the day. In one with an Albatros scout he eventually succeeded in hitting and driving the machine down, then followed behind firing at it until it reached the ground and crashed. On regaining height he engaged another HA and drove it down completely out of control. Flight Sub-Lts A T Whealy, J S T Fall, F C Armstrong, F D Casey and Flight Lt L S Breadner, all of 3 Squadron RNAS, had decisive combats. Captain C E Bryant & 2nd Lt D Couve, 18 Squadron, observing an HA attacking an FE, at once opened fire at it from behind and drove it down out of control. Lt V H Huston & Lt Foord, 18 Squadron, drove down two hostile aircraft, one of which was seen crashed on the ground shortly after the fight. A German machine was driven down out of control by 2nd Lt E L Zink & 2nd Lt B D Bate, 18 Squadron. 2nd Lt K J Knaggs, 56 Squadron, on an SE5, drove down an Albatros painted red and green out of control. A reconnaissance of 70 Squadron met six Halberstadt scouts and drove three of them down, two falling out of control. One of these was shot down by Lt Gotch & Lt Kiburz, and the other by Sergt Thomson & 2/AM Impey. Lt L M Barlow, 56 Squadron, engaged an HA at about 10,000 feet. The fighting continued until the machines had gone down to within 1000 feet of the ground when the HA fell and crashed.

Photography – 1368 photographs were taken during the day.

Balloons – A hostile balloon was brought down by Lt W E Molesworth, 60 Squadron, and Lts Legallis and L M S Essell, both of 29 Squadron.

APRIL 25

Artillery Co-operation – Forty-eight targets were dealt with by aeroplane observation and 66 by observation from balloons.

Hostile Aircraft – On the evening of the 24th, 2nd Lt A Roulstone & 2nd Lt E G Green, 25 Squadron, were attacked while taking photographs by three Albatros scouts. One hostile scout was severely hit, the wing broke off, and the machine crashed. On the 25th Lt C R O'Brien & Lt J L Dickson, 43 Squadron, engaged four Albatros scouts which were painted red. One HA was driven down out of control and was seen by AA observers to crash. A patrol of 25 Squadron engaged ten hostile scouts. None of the HA were seen by the patrol to fall, but AA observers report that one HA fell in flames and one crashed. Lts W T Price & M A Benjamin, 48 Squadron, destroyed a German aeroplane.

APRIL 26

Artillery Co-operation – Eighty-nine targets were dealt with by aeroplane observation and 15 with observation by balloon.

Hostile Aircraft – A hostile scout made three determined attacks on No.8 Section's balloon and set it on fire at a height of 500 feet. A hostile machine was destroyed by a patrol of 41 Squadron and a hostile balloon was brought down in flames by 1 Squadron. 2nd Lt E B W Bartlett, 41 Squadron, engaged two HA, one of which he drove down and it is reported by artillery to have crashed. Captain A Ball, 56 Squadron, on an SE5, while on patrol at 13,000 feet, observed a number of hostile machines leaving an aerodrome at Cambrai, so he waited for them to get up. When the HA were about 6000 feet he dived at the nearest one, firing at it with both his Lewis and Vickers guns at a range of about 20 yards. The HA crashed. He then found that five HA had got between him and the lines. He endeavoured to get through this formation but, finding it difficult, turned south-east and was followed by the HA, one of which was far in advance of the others. Captain Ball turned round and engaged this machine which burst into flames and crashed. He then finished firing what ammunition he had left and crossed the lines at dusk.

APRIL 27

Artillery Co-operation – Fifty-nine targets were dealt with by aeroplane observation and 26 by balloons.

Hostile Aircraft – Six FEs of 25 Squadron, while taking photographs and escorted by six Sopwith Triplanes of 8 Squadron RNAS, were heavily attacked by 12 hostile machines. As the result of the combat, one HA was destroyed by Lt C Dunlop & 2nd Lt J B Weir, and two were driven down out of control – one by Sergt J H R Green & 2nd Lt H E Freeman-Smith, and the other by Flight Lt C D Booker of 8 Squadron RNAS. Lt H E O Ellis, 40 Squadron, proceeded to attack a hostile balloon but was attacked by four hostile aircraft. He succeeded in destroying one of these machines. Flight Sub-Lts R Thornely and G G Simpson, 8 Squadron RNAS, each drove down a hostile machine apparently out of control. Lts W T Price & M A Benjamin, 48 Squadron, drove down a two-seater which crashed in the River Scarpe, near Vitry. Lt W A Bishop, 60 Squadron, attacked a balloon into which he fired 60 rounds. The balloon was seen to emit a great deal of smoke. On the 26th bombing machines of 20 Squadron destroyed one HA, and a second was driven down out of control by Lt D Y Hay & AM T E Allum. Captain F N Hudson & 2nd Lt R M Charley, 54 Squadron, each drove down an HA out of control, and Lt S G Rome of the same Squadron drove one down. A hostile machine was driven down out of control by each of the following pilots; Captain K C Patrick, 2nd Lt R I Keller, 2nd Lt G C Stead and Sergt T Evans, all of 23 Squadron. Flight Sub-Lt J J Malone, 3 Squadron RNAS, attacked a hostile machine over Cambrai. Three other HA joined in the engagement which took place at a height of 7000 feet. Flight Sub-Lt Malone followed one machine down to 3000 feet, firing at it, and was in turn followed by the three HA. Eventually the first machine was destroyed. When at a height of 1000 feet Flight Sub-Lt Malone turned west, but finding it impossible to evade the attacking HA, he pretended to land. As soon as his wheels touched the ground he saw that the HA were also just about to land and at once put on his engine and flew off, and though he was pursued by the three HA they were unable to overtake him and were driven off east by heavy fire from our trenches.

APRIL 28

Artillery Co-operation – Thirty-three targets were dealt with by aeroplane observation and eight with observation by balloon.

Hostile Aircraft – Lt H E O Ellis, 40 Squadron, engaged a two-seater Aviatik from underneath. The HA fell over and went down completely out of control. 2nd Lt D S Kennedy & Capt J A le Royer, 11 Squadron, on the evening of the 27th, drove down an HA in flames, while they destroyed a second south-west of Vitry, and drove down another apparently out of control. Captain A Ball, 56 Squadron, on an SE5, drove down a hostile machine near Noyelles. He then destroyed an Albatros two-seater west of Cambrai. After this he waited above the clouds for any hostile machine that might come up. Finally, he saw a two-seater Albatros which he promptly pursued. The HA put its nose down and fled. When at about 500 feet from the ground Captain Ball's machine was hit by anti-aircraft and his controls – with the exception of a thread on the left elevator – were all shot away and the fuselage was very severely damaged. The machine got into a spin but the pilot cleverly pulled it out again and returned to the aerodrome where he made a perfect landing.

COMMUNIQUÉ No.86

29 April – 4 May 1917

With improved weather conditions, Allied aircraft were able to provide low-level support to the ground troops with contact patrols and trench-strafing sorties, apart from their unceasing co-operation with the artillery. Opposition by the German fighter units also intensified, claiming among other victories Major H D Harvey-Kelly, DSO, commander of 19 Squadron, who had been the first RFC pilot to land in France after war had been declared, a victim of Leutnant Kurt Wolff of Jagdstaffel 11, on April 29. That same day, Rittmeister Manfred von Richthofen, commander of Jagdstaffel 11, claimed four victims to bring his tally to 52 Luftsiege.

APRIL 29

Artillery Co-operation – Eighty-one targets were dealt with by aeroplane observation and 27 by observation by balloons.

Hostile Aircraft – Flight Sub-Lt R A Little destroyed a two-seater Aviatik. In the evening Triplanes of 8 Squadron RNAS drove off a scout which was attacking a BE. When over Monchy-le-Preux five more hostile scouts were encountered and a fight ensued which took the Naval machines over Douai aerodrome. Flight Sub-Lt R P Minifie of 1 Squadron RNAS who had joined in the fighting destroyed one HA which crashed on Douai aerodrome from a height of 2000 feet. Capt F H Thayre & Capt F R Cubbon, 20 Squadron, shot down two HA in flames. Hostile aircraft were driven down out of control by Lt Knight & F/Sgt Cardno, 6 Squadron; 2nd Lts Smart & T A M S Lewis, 20 Squadron 2nd Lts F E Conder & H G Neville, also 20 Squadron; and 2nd Lt Cole, 1 Squadron. A patrol of 1 Squadron RNAS engaged about 12 hostile aircraft over Epinoy aerodrome. Flight Cdr T F N Gerrard and Flight Lts C B Ridley and J S Rowley drove down two HA out of control, and Flight Sub-Lt Minifie destroyed one. Captain W A Bishop, 60 Squadron, destroyed a German aeroplane east of Epinoy. Flight Cdr E W Norton and Flight Sub-Lt A H Fletcher, 6 Squadron RNAS, drove down an HA out of control. Flight Cdr E W Norton, 6 Squadron RNAS, shot down an enemy machine which fell in flames, and then hit the pilot of another machine which fell apparently out of control. Flight Sub-Lt F D Casey, 3 Squadron RNAS, drove down an HA which burst into flames and fell, and Flight Sub-Lt J S T Fall drove one down out of control. 2nd Lts G Dinsmore & B D Bate, 18 Squadron, while on escort duty, attacked three hostile aircraft and drove one down in flames. They then attacked and crippled a second HA which dropped out of the combat. The third HA, however, shot Lt Bate and hit the FE badly. The pilot just succeeded in crossing the lines while followed closely by the German aviator, and landed. A patrol of 57 Squadron observed several hostile aircraft engaging two SE5s of 56 Squadron. The FEs joined in the combat and the pilot of one HA which was engaged by Capt N G McNaughton & 2nd Lt H G Downing was seen to fall from his machine, which crashed. Lt J H Ryan & 2nd Lt B Soutten drove down another HA out of control. An encounter took place between six Albatros scouts and three SE5s of 56 Squadron. One SE had both guns jammed, so outclimbed the HA in order to rectify the trouble, while the other two SE pilots continued the fight. One SE temporarily got into a spin and was followed by two HA scouts. Seeing this, Captain H Meintjes immediately dived and drove them off, and one fell completely out of control and was undoubtedly destroyed. A second patrol of 56 Squadron, led by Captain A Ball, had two combats and in each case the HA were driven down. Captain C M Crowe, Lt J O Leach and 2nd Lt M A Kay, 56 Squadron, engaged seven hostile machines and drove two down out of control. These pilots then patrolled over Douai aerodrome at a very low altitude and although enemy machines were seen on the aerodrome, no endeavour was made to interfere with their patrol.

Photography – 1080 photographs were taken during the day.

APRIL 30

Artillery Co-operation – Seventy-nine targets were dealt with by aeroplane observation and 30 by balloon observation.

Hostile Aircraft – Flight Sub-Lt R A Little, 8 Squadron RNAS, drove down a German aeroplane out of control, then attacked and drove down a second. Flight Lt R Compston, 8 Squadron RNAS, drove down an Albatros scout out of control, then attacked and drove down another in a spinning nose-dive. Flight Lt C D Booker and Flight Sub-Lt A R Knight, of the same squadron drove down two HA in badly damaged conditions. Capt C J Q Brand, 1 Squadron, destroyed an Albatros two-seater in our lines. 2nd Lt M G Cole, 1 Squadron, drove down an HA out of control, then he and Capt E D Atkinson of the same squadron drove down two more out of control. Flight Lts F H M Maynard, A P Haywood, and J S Rowley, 1 Squadron RNAS, each drove down an HA out of control, and Flight Cdr R S Dallas of the same squadron, who had about seven combats while on patrol, destroyed a two-seater Rumpler and drove down a hostile scout completely out of control. A reconnaissance of 48 Squadron had many combats. Lts F W Game & C A Malcolmson drove down one HA out of control, while Lts T P Middleton & C G Clay, who had six different fights, also drove down an enemy machine out of control. A photographic reconnaissance of 18 Squadron, led by Captain C E Bryant & 2nd Lt D Couve, engaged about 20 HA. In the fight that ensued one HA was driven down out of control, four were driven down damaged, and one was destroyed by 2nd Lt M M Kaizer & Sergt F Russell. It is probable that one HA reported as damaged was actually destroyed for the pilot was seen to fall forward. In spite of hard fighting 24 photographs were taken. Captain K C Patrick, 23 Squadron, engaged a two-seater and shot the Observer. He then engaged a two-seater Albatros and, assisted by 2nd Lt G C Stead of the same squadron, drove down the enemy machine which landed in a field apparently much damaged. Capt Patrick and his patrol then engaged four HA and one was hit by Capt Patrick and fell completely out of control and on fire, 2nd Lt S C O'Grady of the same squadron also drove down one HA out of control. Captain C M Crowe, Lt J O Leach, and 2nd Lt M A Kay, 56 Squadron, saw a formation of eight HA east of Douai which were about to attack some FEs. The FEs immediately dived and intercepted the German scouts and, in a very hard fight Capt Crowe finally succeeded in destroying one HA. Lt Leach observed 2nd Lt Kay's machine going down in a spiral with an HA on its tail and he immediately dived and opened fire on the hostile scout which crashed and was seen to burst into flames. Major L A Pattinson & Lt A H Mearns, 57 Squadron, saw a formation of their FEs fighting with German machines and immediately joined in the combat. They drove down one HA in damaged condition, while a second was driven down out of control by Lt C S Morice & Lt F Leathley.

Photography – 948 photographs were taken during the day.

MAY 1

Reconnaissance – A special reconnaissance was carried out by Lts O'Brien & Jones, 43 Squadron, at very-low altitude and much useful information obtained. An armoured BE of 53 Squadron flew at 500 feet and successfully co-operated with an infantry raiding party.

Artillery Co-operation – 111 targets were dealt with by aeroplane observation and 11 by balloon observation.

Hostile Aircraft – Six FEs of 25 Squadron engaged about 15 HA scouts near Douai. 2nd Lt R G Malcolm & Cpl L Emsden destroyed one and drove down a second, while 2nd Lt B King & Lt G M A Hobart-Hampden drove down another out of control. Captain C J Q Brand, 1 Squadron, destroyed an Albatros two-seater near Warneton, and Capt E D Atkinson of the same squadron destroyed one near Zonnebeke. 2nd Lt R G Dalziel & L/Cpl R Bradley, 20 Squadron, shot down an Albatros two-seater which crashed near Messines. An Albatros scout which was engaged by 2nd Lt M G Cole, 1 Squadron, was brought down in our lines near Elverdinghe. An Albatros two-seater was driven down out of control by 2nd Lt L M Mansbridge, 1 Squadron, and another of the same type was driven down out of control by Capts F H Thayre & F R Cubbon, 20 Squadron. Anti-aircraft gunners of the Third Army brought down a DFW two-seater in our lines. A photographic reconnaissance of 18 Squadron attacked 10 HA near Epinoy. Flight Sub-Lt J S T Fall, 8 Squadron RNAS, one of the escort to the FEs, assisted by 2nd Lt M M Kaizer & Sergt F Russell, 18 Squadron, drove down one HA completely out of control. Three other HA were driven down out of control. Capt Taylor & Lt C G Eccles, both of 32 Squadron, attacked two Albatros two-seaters and drove them down. A green-coloured machine was seen shortly after destroyed on the ground and is believed to be the one which they drove down which was painted that colour. A patrol of three SEs of 56 Squadron saw six HA near Cambrai at 13,000 feet. The SEs immediately attacked and one HA was destroyed by Captain A Ball, while a second was driven down out of control by this pilot. 2nd Lt K J Knaggs, 56 Squadron, drove down an Albatros two-seater which is believed to have fallen into the River Scarpe. Lt F S Wilkins, 19 Squadron, drove down an Albatros two-seater which fell south-east of Arras. 2nd Lt D J Bell, 27 Squadron, drove down a single-seat German machine in a spin.

Photography – 1117 photographs were taken during the day.

Bombing – During the night of 30 April/1 May, bombing raids were made against Carvin, Bauvin, Quiery-la-Motte, Rumbeke aerodrome, St Sauveur, Haubourdin, Le Catelet, and Epinoy aerodrome.

MAY 2

Artillery Co-operation – 145 targets were dealt with by aeroplane observation and 45 by balloon observation.

Hostile Aircraft – On the evening of May 1, Flight Sub-Lt D M Shields, 8 Squadron RNAS, drove down an Albatros scout out of control. He was then attacked by seven more scouts and was forced down; his controls were shot away and the machine crashed and was immediately shelled by the Germans. The pilot, who was injured, crept into a shell hole and remained there until rescued the next morning. A formation of nine Albatros scouts attacked six FEs of 25 Squadron which were

48

returning from a bomb raid. Captain C H C Woollven & Sergt J H Brown destroyed one scout, and 2nd Lt Malcolm & Sergt L Emsden destroyed a second. Lt K Mackenzie, 40 Squadron, attacked five HA and destroyed one near Quiery-la-Motte. Two German machines were driven down out of control by Flight Lt R J O Compston and Flight Sub-Lt G G Simpson, 8 Squadron RNAS. Lt D C Cunnell & 2/AM E H Sayers, 20 Squadron, drove down a German machine out of control near Comines. 2nd Lts H C Farnes & Davis, 48 Squadron, drove down a two-seater Albatros completely out of control. A very keen engagement took place between ten red Albatros scouts and Bristol Fighters of 48 Squadron. One German machine was destroyed by Lts W O D Winkler & E S Moore, and another driven down in flames by Lt O J F Scholte & 2nd Lt F W Game. A fourth was driven down out of control by 2nd Lts Harrison & Richards. Major A J L Scott, 60 Squadron, was attacked by six hostile scouts, one of which he destroyed. Captain W A Bishop, 60 Squadron, had nine combats during the day and destroyed one opponent, drove a second down completely out of control, and forced a third to land in a field. Captain A Ball, 56 Squadron, dived at a German scout and was immediately attacked from behind by four other scouts, one of which shot past Captain Ball. He immediately fired a burst from his Vickers gun into the HA which went down and was followed by Captain Ball who continued to fire until it crashed. He then climbed up in order to join a big fight taking place between hostile two-seaters and scouts, and on our side, Sopwith Scouts, Bristol Fighters and FEs. The fighting drifted to the east and the HA were generally out-manoeuvred. After this combat Captain Ball engaged a white two-seater which he drove down out of control, but owing to the dusk was unable to see what happened to it. Captain H Meintjes, 56 Squadron, dived at one of two Albatros two-seaters and drove it down in a slow spiral; he throttled down and "sat on its tail" until both occupants appeared to be shot, then engaged the other machine. 2nd Lt L M Barlow, also of 56 Squadron, drove down an Albatros two-seater completely out of control. Captain J O Andrews, 66 Squadron, attacked a single-seater HA which was diving at some Martinsydes of 27 Squadron. The HA scout was driven down out of control.

Balloons – Lt K Mackenzie and 2nd Lts W T Walder, B B Lemon, S Thompson, W A Bond, and L L Morgan, 40 Squadron, crossed the line at 50 feet and under in order to attack German balloons. These pilots had practised low flying and had learnt how to use trees, houses and the ground in screening them from infantry and machine gun fire. Artillery co-operated by putting a heavy barrage on the German trenches, leaving the pilots a certain area in which to cross. As a result four German balloons were destroyed.

Photography – 932 photographs were taken during the day.

Bombing – On the night 1st/2nd, bombing raids were carried out on Carvin Station, Marquillies Sugar Factory, Fresnes, Lens, Neuvireuil, Ledeghem Station, Eswars aerodrome, Hendecourt, and Valenciennes Railway Station.

MAY 3

Reconnaissance – Information was received that the Germans were massing for a counter attack, and 13 machines of 43 Squadron went out in order to attack them with machine gun fire and to gather information. These aeroplanes flew at altitudes varying from 50 to 300 feet, attacking German troops, causing many casualties and breaking up formations. The pilots then flew over trenches which were seen to be packed with Germans and fired at them, also attacking transport and machine gun parties. All returned safely after having expended their ammunition.

Artillery Co-operation – Seventy-six targets were dealt with by aeroplane observation and 48 with balloon observation.

Hostile Aircraft – Flight Sub-Lt R A Little, 8 Squadron RNAS, drove down a German scout out of control. On returning from a bomb raid Capt F H Thayre & Capt F R Cubbon, 20 Squadron, attacked and drove down an Albatros two-seater. Our machines were then attacked by about 26 Albatros scouts led by a machine painted bright scarlet. As a result of the combat that ensued two of the HA were destroyed by Capt Thayre & Capt Cubbon, and another driven down out of control by Lt F D Stevens & 2nd Lt H R Wilkinson, 20 Squadron. Lt Porter and 2nd Lt MacKay, 41 Squadron, each drove down an HA out of control after very heavy fighting between seven of our machines and 18 Albatros scouts. Captain Tolhurst & Lt E N Blennerhassett, 18 Squadron, engaged four HA and drove one down completely out of control. Two German machines were destroyed by machine gun and rifle fire from our trenches.

Photography – 416 photographs were taken during the day.

Bombing – On the night of the 2nd/3rd bombing raids were made on Carvin, Harnes, Provin, Avion, Wigres, Lichtervelde Station, La Goulee Station, Valenciennes, Somain, Estrees, Iwuy, Hendecourt, Don Station, Brebieres and Busigny.

MAY 4

Artillery Co-operation – Sixty-seven targets were dealt with by aeroplane observation and 29 by balloon observation.

Hostile Aircraft – Captain W A Bishop and Lt W M Fry, 60 Squadron, dived at one of two HA and destroyed it. Captain J Letts & Lt H Smither, 48 Squadron, destroyed an HA which crashed at Pelves. Captain D A L Davidson, 23 Squadron, drove down an HA out of control east of Havrincourt.

Photography – 676 photographs were taken during the day.

Bombing – On the night of 3rd/4th bombing raids were made on Henin Lietard, Harnes, Courrieres, Annay, Pont-a-Vendin, Carvin, Tourmignies aerodrome, Noyelles, Avion, Billy Montigny, Sallaumines, Wervicq, Chateau-du-Sart aerodrome, Quesnoy, Lens Station, Mericourt Station, Beaumont, Iwuy, Eswars aerodrome, La Brayelle aerodrome.

COMMUNIQUÉ No.87

5 – 11 May 1917

During a week of continuing high activity, men like the Australians Roderick Dallas and Robert Little and the Canadian 'Billy' Bishop added to their mounting tallies of combat victories, but on May 7 the RFC lost its leading fighter, 20-years old Albert Ball. Paradoxically, on the same day 2nd Lt Edward Mannock, 40 Squadron, claimed his first accredited victory and would later be acknowledged as the leading British fighter 'ace' of the entire war.

MAY 5

Artillery Co-operation – Eighty-nine targets were dealt with by aeroplane observation and 16 by observation by balloons.

Hostile Aircraft – Lt H E O Ellis, 40 Squadron, observed three Albatros scouts south of Douai and dived at them, but all three immediately dived away, and at 500 feet one of them side-slipped and crashed. A second landed on its nose on Douai aerodrome and turned completely over, while the third landed safely. Lt Ellis was then attacked by an Albatros scout and after having gained position his gun jammed, so he dived away, rectified it, and re-engaged the HA. He then ran out of ammunition, so got as close as possible and fired seven rounds from his Colt automatic pistol, and the HA went down and was seen to break up in the air and crash. Three HA were driven down out of control; one by 2nd Lt W T Walder, 40 Squadron, one by 2nd Lts C S Richmond & E W Pritchard, 43 Squadron, and one by Lt J D Belgrave & 2nd Lt C G Stewart, 45 Squadron. 2nd Lt R W Farquhar and Lt R I Keller, 23 Squadron, each drove down an HA out of control. Captain A Ball, 56 Squadron, when on patrol, saw two HA coming towards Carvin from the direction of Douai. He climbed steadily and when the Germans had got quite near his tail he did a sharp turn and got underneath one HA and opened fire. This machine fell out of control, and Captain Ball then manoeuvred to get into a favourable position to attack the second HA. The German, however, simply flew straight at him firing hard, so the SE returned fire and the machines almost collided, then the HA went down. The SE's engine was hit and the pilot was covered in oil. Captain Ball went down and saw both HA lying within 400 yards of each other completely wrecked on the ground. On his way home he met two more HA but as he had practically run out of ammunition and his sights were covered in oil he put his nose down and returned to his aerodrome. Lt C A Lewis and 2nd Lt R T C Hoidge, 56 Squadron, each drove down an HA out of control.

Balloons – On May 4, No.29 Balloon was brought down by an HA. It was repaired and sent up again, but was brought down a second time. It was again repaired and went up a third time and did useful work during the night. The same Observer, 24107 Flight Sgt G G L Blake, was in the balloon each time it was brought down and made successful parachute descents on each occasion.

Bombing – Bombing raids on the 4th/5th were made on Izel-les-Equerchin, Brebieres, Beaumont, Quiery-la-Motte, Rauvroy, Avion, Neuvereuil, Recklem aerodrome, Coucou aerodrome, Poelcapelle Station, Dury, Etaing, Iwuy and Hendecourt.

MAY 6

Artillery Co-operation – Eighty-three targets were dealt with by aeroplane observation and 22 with balloon observation.

Hostile Aircraft – 2nd Lt L L Morgan, 40 Squadron, drove down a hostile scout in flames, and Captain R W Gregory of the same squadron drove one down out of control. 2nd Lt F Libby & Lt J L Dickson, 43 Squadron, destroyed a German machine which crashed near Petit Vimy. While on Offensive Patrol five FEs of 20 Squadron engaged two Albatros two-seaters. The Germans were soon reinforced by three formations of Albatros scouts, composed of eight or nine machines each, coming from different directions. A general engagement commenced at about 5 pm at a height of 11,000 feet. Captain F H Thayre & Captain F R Cubbon shot one HA from which the wings were seen to fall before it crashed. 2nd Lt R E Conder & 2/AM J J Cowell hit another HA which fell out of control, and a third which had been engaged at the same time was driven down in a spinning nose-dive by Lt A N Solly & 2/AM C Bemister. 2nd Lt Conder's engine stopped and he had to leave the formation and was followed down by HA. Lt Solly immediately dived to his assistance and one HA was sent down in a vertical nose-dive. Lt Conder's engine picked up and he at once returned to the fighting. Just after this Capt Thayre & Capt Cubbon set one HA on fire and then dived and destroyed an HA that was following closely an FE going down temporarily out of control. At the same time 2nd Lt Heseltine & 2nd Lt F J Kydd drove down a hostile scout out of control, and Lt Solly & 2/AM Bemister hit another HA which fell in flames, while 2nd Lt F F Babbage & 2/AM B Aldred shot down one German scout which fell on our side of the lines. The FEs all returned safely. Captain A Ball, 56 Squadron, flying a Nieuport Scout at 11,000 feet, observed four red Albatros scouts going towards Cambrai at 10,000 feet. He dived into the centre of the formation which broke up, then got underneath the nearest machine into which he fired and which lost control and crashed. The remaining three avoided combat and were easily out-manoeuvred.

Photography – 335 photographs were taken during the day.

MAY 7

Artillery Co-operation – Ninety-three targets were dealt with by aeroplane observation and 24 with balloon observation.

Hostile Aircraft – Flight Sub-Lt H A Pailthorpe, 8 Squadron RNAS, was suddenly attacked by a hostile scout which he engaged and finally destroyed. An Offensive Patrol of 45 Squadron engaged seven HA near Lille. Lt J D Belgrave & 2nd Lt C G Stewart shot down one in flames, and two were driven down out of control – one by 2nd Lt G H Cock & Lt J T G Murison, and the other by 2nd Lts Carleton & J A Vessey. A bomb raid by 20 Squadron engaged about ten HA and one was destroyed by 2nd Lt F F Babbage & 2/AM B Aldred. Captain W A Bishop, 60 Squadron, while escorting FEs of 11 Squadron, drove down two HA out of control, while a third was driven down out of control by Lt Parker & 2/AM Mee, 11 Squadron. A great deal of fighting took place during the day between SE5s of 56 Squadron and HA formations. During these combats Captain H Meintjes and Lt R T C Hoidge each destroyed an HA, while two others were driven down out of control by Lt C A Lewis and the other by an SE5 formation.

(Editor's note: See Communiqué No. 87 for more details of these actions).

Balloons – An attack on German balloons was carried out by seven Nieuports of 40 Squadron. The pilots crossed the lines at about 20 feet and, as on a previous occasion, artillery put a barrage on the German trenches, while 12 other aeroplanes crossed the lines at the same time at a considerable height in order to draw the attention of anti-aircraft gunners. Seven German balloons were destroyed; three caught fire high up, two burst into flames when near the ground, and two when on the ground. The names of the pilots who took part in the attack are; 2nd Lts L L Morgan, C S Hall, C W Cudemore, H B Redler, E Mannock, J Parry, and Captain W Nixon who failed to return.

Bombing – Bomb raids were carried out on the night of 6th/7th on Pont-a-Vendin, Quiery-la-Motte, Brebieres, Izel, Hellemmes, La Madelaine Station, Beaumont Station, and Dorignies aerodrome.

MAY 8

Artillery Co-operation – Forty-nine targets were dealt with by aeroplane observation and 68 by balloon observation.

MAY 9

Artillery Co-operation – Sixty-five targets were dealt with by aeroplane observation and seven with balloon observation.

Hostile Aircraft – Three Triplanes of 8 Squadron RNAS attacked a large formation of hostile scouts. One Naval pilot had to withdraw owing to his gun having jammed, while Flight Sub-Lt L E A Wimbush, after having fought well, had to break off the engagement as he had been wounded and his engine was hit. Flight Sub-Lt R A Little continued the fight and drove down one scout. After considerable fighting another Triplane and some De Havillands came to his assistance and the HA withdrew. A little later a report was received that enemy artillery aircraft were working west of Lens, and Flight Sub-Lt Little immediately went to look for them and found LVGs working at 8000 feet. He drove one down out of control. He was then attacked by six more HA, one of which shot past him and was immediately attacked from behind and driven down damaged. He then ran out of ammunition and returned to his aerodrome. An Offensive Patrol of 45 Squadron engaged about 15 HA near Lille. 2nd Lt G H Cock & Lt J T G Murison engaged two HA at long range and one fell out of control. The pilot then manoeuvred his machine to enable his Observer to use his gun on three HA diving at them. A burst of about 80 rounds hit one HA in the centre section and it immediately collapsed and fell, one of its wings being seen to fall off. 2nd Lts W A Wright & E T Caulfield-Kelly also brought down one HA which broke in the air and crashed. A patrol of 48 Squadron encountered eight HA near Vitry and Lt F P Holliday & Captain A H Wall drove down two of them out of control. Lt Holliday & Capt Wall on one machine and 2nd Lts G W T Price & E S Moore on another machine of 48 Squadron engaged two HA near Vitry and drove one down in a field where they continued attacking it and both passengers are believed to have been killed. A photographic reconnaissance of 22 Squadron, with an escort of 54 Squadron, had a big fight with seven German machines. Capt C M Clement & Lt M K Parlee, 22 Squadron, drove down one HA out of control and then dived at three others that were following our Sopwiths down. They were unable to get there in time, however, and the Sopwith Scout was forced to land in a field, but they succeeded in engaging one HA which crashed quite near to the Sopwith. 2nd Lt M B Cole, 54 Squadron, fired at a large white two-seater which was seen to crash by other pilots. Lt E J Y Grevelink, 54 Squadron, drove down a black and white German scout which was also seen to crash. A third HA was destroyed by Lt M D G Scott of the same squadron. On the evening of the 7th, Captain H Meintjes, 56 Squadron, with three other SE5s of the same squadron, dived at a German aeroplane which they riddled with bullets and drove down. They then saw four red Albatros scouts and Capt Meintjes engaged one at close range. Eventually the HA got into a favourable position and Capt Meintjes put his machine into a spin. On shaking off this HA, he gained height and dived at another scout with which he fought for a considerable time and eventually the HA crashed. Shortly afterwards he engaged another machine of the same type but he was shot through the wrist and the top of his control lever was carried away. Although suffering considerable pain and flying under great disadvantage he succeeded in landing his machine undamaged on our side of the lines, and then fainted. Captain Albert Ball, DSO, MC, failed to return from this patrol. On the 9th a reconnaissance of 70 Squadron was attacked by 15 HA while taking photographs. Lts Griffith & Allen fired at close range into one HA which immediately fell out of control. One Albatros scout dived on Lt Crang's machine but his Observer, Lt Sully, fired a burst at the attacking Albatros which burst into flames and fell.

Bombing – Bomb raids were carried out on Izel-les-Equerchin, Quiery-la-Motte, Courtrai goods yard, Hendecourt, Queue de Bone, La Briquette aerodrome.

MAY 10

Artillery Co-operation – Seventy-nine targets were dealt with by aeroplane observation and 54 with balloon observation.

Hostile Aircraft – Lt T P Middleton & 2nd Lt C A Malcolmson, 48 Squadron, engaged ten hostile scouts and after considerable fighting one HA was observed to crash. A photographic reconnaissance of 55 Squadron had heavy fighting during the whole time they were over the lines. As a result, one German machine was destroyed by Lt Pitt & 2nd Lt Holroyde, and two were driven down out of control; one by Capt Rice & 2nd Lt Clarke, and the other by 2nd Lt Webb & 1/AM Bond.

Photography – 662 photographs were taken during the day.

Bombing – On the night of 9th/10th, bomb raids were made on Meurchin, Pont-a-Vendin, Henin-Lietard, Annay, Izel-les-Equerchin, Bois du Biez, Dorignies aerodrome, Fontaine-Notre-Dame, Sauchy-Cauchy, while on the 10th, made on Recklem aerodrome and Hendicourt.

MAY 11

Artillery Co-operation – 149 targets were dealt with by aeroplane observation and 34 by balloon observation.

Hostile Aircraft – A formation of 29 Squadron encountered eight Albatros scouts and Lt A S Shepherd drove one down which crashed, and two others were driven down out of control by Capt C M B Chapman and Lt W B Wood. No.48 Squadron met 12 Albatros scouts and Lt F P Holliday & Capt A H Wall destroyed one and drove down a second out of control. 2nd Lt Messenger & Pte A Jee, 59 Squadron, destroyed one HA. While on patrol Capt R G H Pixley, 54 Squadron, met a hostile two-seater and fought it for 15 minutes, and the HA was seen to crash into a house in a village. Captain K C Patrick, 23 Squadron, encountered an HA scout which he hit and from which the wings broke off as it fell in flames.

(Editor's note: His victim was the 15-victory ace, Offstvtr. Edmund Nathanael of Jagdstaffel 5.).

Photography – 548 photographs were taken during the day.

COMMUNIQUÉ No.88

12 – 19 May 1917

Further reinforcement for the RFC in France came on May 15 when No.10 Squadron RNAS (Sopwith Triplanes) was attached and was to remain so until November 1917. Of its 15 pilots, 13 were Canadians, including five in B Flight, led by Flight Cdr Ray Collishaw, which became famed as the 'Black Flight' from its aircraft Flight markings. Of the various airmen mentioned this week, Captain J O Andrews, 66 Squadron, and 2nd Lt D F Stevenson, 12 Squadron, were both destined to become Air Vice-Marshals in the RAF.

MAY 12
Artillery Co-operation – 123 targets were dealt with by aeroplane observation and 125 by balloon observation.

Hostile Aircraft – Capt A W Keen, 40 Squadron, drove down out of control an Albatros two-seater which was seen by anti-aircraft observers to crash. On the evening of the 11th a formation of five Sopwith Triplanes of 8 Squadron RNAS encountered nine Albatros scouts which they engaged. Flight Lt G G Simpson drove one down out of control, then dived on another scout which burst into flames and fell. He then attacked two more and drove them down. A bomb raid of 20 Squadron, escorted by Nieuports of 1 Squadron, engaged 12 HA and two were driven down out of control. A patrol of 45 Squadron shot down a German machine in flames near Lille. An Offensive Patrol of 54 Squadron, led by Capt W V Strugnell, dived at a large two-seater crossing the lines and all pilots opened fire at the HA, which crashed in a field. Shortly afterwards Capt Strugnell drove down another HA which crashed in a pond. 2nd Lt M B Cole, of the same squadron, while escorting FEs, drove down an HA out of control; his gun jammed but he followed it down until he saw it crash.

Photography – 424 photographs were taken during the day.

MAY 13
Artillery Co-operation – 120 targets were dealt with by aeroplane observation and 91 by balloon observation. 2nd Lt D F Stevenson, 12 Squadron, observing for the 61st Siege Battery, obtained four OKs, 16 Ys, and three Zs on a hostile battery.

Hostile Aircraft – When returning from a bomb raid on Recklem aerodrome FEs of 20 Squadron were attacked by 12 Albatros scouts which were kept out of range by long distance firing. Near Courtrai the German formation had increased to 30 machines, four of which dived on the tail of an FE piloted by Capt F H Thayre, who immediately turned and dived in the same direction, and his Observer, Capt H R Cubbon, fired half a drum into one HA which had dived past them. The HA went straight down and burst into flames. Immediately afterwards three more HA were attacked and by stalling and firing both guns Capts Thayre and Cubbon shot down a second machine which crashed. 2nd Lt W P Scott & 2/AM J J Cowell of the same squadron also shot down an HA which was seen to crash. A patrol of 29 Squadron met eight Albatros scouts. Lt A M Wray attacked one at close range and followed it down, firing until it crashed. Lt W M Fry, 60 Squadron, attacked an Albatros scout which fell out of control. 2nd Lts D U McGregor & S C O'Grady, 23 Squadron, drove down an HA which was seen to fall in flames, and Capt K C Patrick and Lt Stead of the same squadron also shot down an HA which fell in flames. Lts V H Huston & Foord, 18 Squadron, drove down a Halberstadt scout which was seen to crash. Captain J O Andrews, 66 Squadron, drove down an Albatros scout out of control.

Photography – 592 photographs were taken during the day.

Bombing – Bomb raids were made on Quiery-la-Motte, Harnes, Lens, Recklem aerodrome, Hendicourt.

MAY 14

Artillery Co-operation – 121 targets were dealt with by aeroplane observation and 90 by balloon observation.

Hostile Aircraft – 2nd Lt W C Campbell, 1 Squadron, while on special duty, shot down a Roland two-seater which crashed near Zonnebeke. Capt W G S Curphey and 2nd Lts St C Tayler and Wright, 32 Squadron, attacked German balloons. The Observers descended by parachute and the balloons were hauled down. The De Havillands were then engaged by six Albatros scouts, one of which was destroyed by 2nd Lt Tayler. Captain Curphey was driven down and his machine was seen to turn over on landing.

Photography – 182 photographs were taken during the day.

MAY 15

Artillery Co-operation – Thirty targets were dealt with by aeroplane observation and 66 by balloon observation.

Hostile Aircraft – While on line patrol, machines of 20 Squadron engaged seven HA near Quesnoy and 2nd Lt Grout & 2/AM Tyrell destroyed one HA, while a second was driven down out of control by Lt A N Solly & 2/AM C Bemister.

MAY 16, MAY 17

The weather was very bad and flying was practically impossible.

MAY 18

Artillery Co-operation – Fifty-nine targets were dealt with by aeroplane observation.

Hostile Aircraft – Flight Lt R A Little, 8 Squadron RNAS, saw a German aircraft and engaged it at 10,000 feet north-east of Lens. During the fight the German Observer was seen to fall. Finally the HA went down followed by Flight Lt Little and was seen to crash by artillery.

MAY 19

Artillery Co-operation – Seventy-one targets were dealt with by aeroplane observation and 12 by balloon observation.

Hostile Aircraft – At about 10 am an Albatros scout was seen over Le Hameau aerodrome and was immediately pursued by Lt W M Fry, 60 Squadron, who brought it down near St Pol. The pilot was taken prisoner. A patrol of 19 Squadron engaged a number of HA and one was destroyed by Captain W J Cairnes.

Balloons – On the evening of the 18th six machines of 1 Squadron crossed the lines at about 20 feet and attacked German balloons. Two were brought down in flames; one by Lt H J Duncan and one by 2nd Lt T H Lines. 2nd Lt W C Campbell, 1 Squadron, while on patrol, attacked a German balloon and brought it down in flames.

Photography – 186 photographs were taken during the day.

COMMUNIQUÉ No. 89

20 – 25 May 1917

In addition to their many specific duties, RFC and attached RNAS squadrons paid great attention to strafing enemy troops and trenches at very low altitudes at every opportunity.

MAY 20

Reconnaissance – A patrol of six Nieuports of 60 Squadron attacked enemy troops and other objectives with machine gun fire from 500 feet, while seven FEs of 11 Squadron dropped bombs on trenches and then attacked the occupants with gun fire. Aeroplanes of 54 Squadron attacked a machine gun party from a height of 20 feet.

Artillery Co-operation – 128 targets were dealt with by aeroplane observation and 87 by balloon observation.

Hostile Aircraft – An Offensive Patrol of 20 Squadron engaged ten HA near Menin and drove one down out of control by 2nd Lt R E Conder & 2/AM J J Cowell. Ten HA were also engaged by 45 Squadron and two of the HA were shot down in flames by Sgt Cook & Lt G W Blacklock. A third was destroyed by Capt Jenkins & Lt P C Eglington. On the evening of the 19th an engagement lasting three-quarters of an hour took place between 12 Triplanes of 1 Squadron RNAS and a large formation of HA. Flight Sub-Lt O B Ellis shot down one HA from which the wings were seen to break. On the 20th Flight Lt T G Culling, 1 Squadron RNAS, attacked an Albatros into which he fired 100 rounds at close range and it fell out of control. While on escort duty, 2nd Lt A M Wray, 29 Squadron, attacked an Albatros which was seen to break up in the air. 2nd Lt A S Shepherd of the same squadron attacked a second HA which burst into flames and fell. An escort composed of machines of 48 Squadron had several engagements and 2nd Lt Fraser & Pte J H Muscott drove down one HA with its tail apparently broken. 2nd Lt H J Pratt & Lt H Owen in one Bristol Fighter and Captain B E Baker & Lt Jeff in another drove down two HA out of control after fighting superior numbers.

Captain Pither & Lt Isles, 3 Squadron, engaged a DFW two-seater which was last seen going down very steeply just over Havrincourt Wood. Information has now been received from the 1st Anzac Corps that this HA crashed in Havrincourt Wood and the pilot taken prisoner. Capt K C Patrick and 2nd Lts G C Stead and S C O'Grady, 23 Squadron, saw three HA attacking an RE8 over Queant and dived to the assistance of our machine. A long engagement took place between one HA and Capt Patrick at heights varying from 1000 to 200 feet, and the HA fell temporarily out of control but on flattening out crossed the trenches and was seen to crash.

Photography – 880 photographs were taken during the day.

MAY 21

Artillery Co-operation – Sixty-seven targets were dealt with by aeroplane observation and 51 by balloon observation.

Hostile Aircraft – Four machines of 25 Squadron while on photography were attacked by hostile scouts. Sgt J H R Green & Pte H Else fired three drums into one scout which fell out of control, while a second HA was driven down out of control by Lts A Roulstone & H Cotton. One HA is reported to have crashed. Lt W C Campbell, 1 Squadron, destroyed an HA near Capinghem.

MAY 22
Artillery Co-operation – Forty-seven targets were dealt with by aeroplane observation and 71 by balloon observation.

MAY 23
Artillery Co-operation – 122 targets were dealt with by aeroplane observation and 58 by balloon observation.
Hostile Aircraft – Flight Lt R A Little, 8 Squadron RNAS, attacked three two-seater machines but was immediately attacked by four hostile scouts. He hit and drove down two of these when the Germans broke off the combat. While on patrol, 2nd Lt W J Mussared, 1 Squadron, shot down an Albatros two-seater. An Offensive Patrol of 20 Squadron engaged seven Albatros scouts and one was sent down out of control by Capt H G White & 2nd Lt T A M S Lewis. A second Offensive Patrol of 20 Squadron, while over the enemy lines, observed ten Albatros scouts, so turned and flew towards our lines. When near the lines the FEs quickly turned and attacked these HA, and one was destroyed by Capt F H Thayre & Capt F R Cubbon. After driving off all HA the FEs continued their patrol. An escort of machines of 18 Squadron was attacked by seven Albatros scouts and one HA, into which a drum was fired by 2nd Lts Marshall & G N Blennerhassett, fell and crashed. Five Spads of 19 Squadron engaged four Albatros scouts, and Lt A H Orlebar shot one down in flames.
Photography – 522 photographs were taken during the day.

MAY 24
Artillery Co-operation – Sixty-seven targets were dealt with by aeroplane observation and 90 by balloon observation.
Hostile Aircraft – A patrol of six Sopwiths of 43 Squadron met nine hostile scouts. Capt K L Gopsill & 2nd Lt E H Jones drove down one scout but were then attacked by two others, and 2nd Lt Jones was wounded. He continued fighting and after firing 20 rounds one attacking scout burst into flames and fell. 2nd Lt C H Harriman & 2/AM O'Shea hit another scout in which the pilot was believed to have been killed and the machine fell out of control; while still another was sent down out of control by 2nd Lt L Gedge & CSM L M Lava. Flight Cdr C D Booker, 8 Squadron RNAS, observed the combat from his aerodrome and immediately left and joined the fighting, driving down one scout which fell in flames and crashed. Shortly after Flight Cdr Booker and Flight Sub-Lt R Macdonald engaged two HA and drove both down out of control. One was observed on the ground completely crashed. Capt J H Letts & Lt L W Allen, 48 Squadron, engaged four two-seater HA. One was driven down out of control and a second badly damaged. The other two fled. A patrol of 29 Squadron attacked a formation of nine HA which were fighting FEs of 11 Squadron, and 2nd Lt A S Shepherd drove one down in flames and saw it crash. Lt O M Sutton, 54 Squadron, engaged a German single-seater which flew straight at him, and it was only by a quick turn that Lt Sutton avoided crashing into the HA. As it was, his right-hand top plane hit the HA which broke to pieces in the air and fell. Although his top plane was badly broken, he succeeded in landing safely. Lt O Stewart of the same squadron drove down an Albatros scout in a spin and followed it down. This was seen to crash by anti-aircraft gunners. Offensive Patrols by 56 Squadron met several HA formations but the German machines always broke off the combat and, in some cases, refused to fight. Two were

destroyed – one by 2nd Lts R T C Hoidge and A P F Rhys Davids, which fell in flames, and the second, which had a wing shot off, was destroyed by 2nd Lt F Williams. Two others were driven down out of control, one by the SE5 formation and the other by 2nd Lts Hoidge and Rhys Davids, and this HA fell enveloped in flames and its Observer seen to fall.

Photography – 520 photographs were taken during the day.

MAY 25

Artillery Co-operation – 114 targets were dealt with by aeroplane observation and 111 by balloon observation.

Hostile Aircraft – An Offensive Patrol of 20 Squadron engaged nine Albatros scouts just after crossing the lines, and one scout, attacked by Capts F H Thayre & F R Cubbon, broke up in the air and fell. Shortly afterwards this pilot and Observer shot down a second scout in flames. During the engagement 2nd Lts R E Conder & J J Cowell drove down one HA out of control. An Offensive Patrol of 45 Squadron encountered nine HA. 2nd Lt W A Wright & E T Caulfield-Kelly opened fire at one HA which was diving at them from behind and this HA fell, burst into flames and was seen to crash. Three other Albatros scouts were driven down out of control – one by Lt P T Newling & 2nd Lt Holland, and one by Lt J D Belgrave & 2nd Lt C G Stewart. In a later engagement between three machines of 45 Squadron and a large formation of Albatros scouts, Capt G Mountford & 2nd Lt J A Vessey drove down two of their opponents out of control. An Offensive Patrol of 24 Squadron met a formation of Albatros scouts and one attacked Lt H W Woollett from behind but Lt S Cockerell drove it off and succeeded in destroying it. Machines of 56, 66, and 19 Squadrons had considerable fighting. 2nd Lt A P F Rhys Davids, 56 Squadron, destroyed a two-seater Aviatik, while Capt C M Crowe of the same squadron drove one HA down out of control. Lt J M Child, 19 Squadron, and 2nd Lt F A Smith, 66 Squadron, each drove down an HA out of control.

Photography – 1355 photographs were taken during the day.

COMMUNIQUÉ No.90

26 – 31 May 1917

MAY 26

Artillery Co-operation – 120 targets were dealt with by aeroplane observation and 130 by balloon observation.

Hostile Aircraft – An engagement took place between eight machines of 20 Squadron and ten of 1 Squadron with 15 Albatros scouts. One HA, attacked by Lts H L Satchell & Jenks, 20 Squadron, was seen to loop backwards, its pilot fell out, and it crashed. Lts D C Cunnell & W T Gilson of the same squadron obtained a favourable position on one Albatros scout's tail and followed it down firing until the HA crashed. The following pilots and Observers succeeded in driving down one HA each out of control; Capt H G White & 2nd Lt T A M S Lewis, 20 Squadron; Lts A Boucher & W Birkett, 20 Squadron; 2nd Lt R E Conder & 2/AM J J Cowell, 20 Squadron; Capt R H Cronyn, Lt F Sharpe, 2nd Lt P F Fullard, and 2nd Lt W J Mussared, all of 1 Squadron. Two HA were driven down out of control by 2nd Lt A P F Rhys-Davids and Capt E W Broadberry of 56 Squadron. Captain W A Bishop, 60 Squadron, drove down an HA near Izel-les-Equerchin.

Photography – 1027 photographs were taken during the day.

MAY 27

Artillery Co-operation – 110 targets were dealt with by aeroplane observation and 106 by balloon observation.

Hostile Aircraft – Capt R W Gregory, 40 Squadron, engaged a hostile scout at 19,000 feet and it was hit and fell out of control. An Offensive Patrol of 20 Squadron engaged eight Albatros scouts near Ypres, and one was destroyed by 2nd Lt R E Conder & 2/AM J J Cowell. Capts F H Thayre & F R Cubbon, 20 Squadron, observed an Albatros two-seater doing artillery work and destroyed it. They then attacked an Albatros scout and drove it down. An Offensive Patrol of 41 Squadron flew in two formations. One formation observed an Albatros two-seater being fired at by anti-aircraft and so dived in the direction of the shell bursts. The patrol leader fired a Very Light in order to draw the attention of the other patrol. This light was seen by the German machine which immediately dived away but found itself in the middle of the second patrol, which opened fire and the HA was driven down and seen to crash. A patrol of 45 Squadron engaged ten Albatros scouts and two were driven down out of control – one by Lt J D Belgrave & 2nd Lt G A H Davies, and the other by 2nd Lts G H Cock & E T C Kelly. A second Offensive Patrol of 45 Squadron engaged seven Albatros scouts and one was destroyed by 2nd Lts H E R Fitchat & R Hayes, while Capt G Mountford & 2nd Lt J A Vessey in one machine and 2nd Lt E A Cook & 2/AM H V Shaw in another each drove down a scout out of control. Whilst on artillery work, 2nd Lts Blofeld & Hunter, 45 Squadron, were attacked and both wounded by five Albatros scouts but they succeeded in destroying one of their opponents. 2nd Lts T P Middleton & A W Merchant, 48 Squadron, destroyed one of three Albatros scouts which they engaged. Shortly afterwards they engaged a two-seater machine and drove it down out of control. Captain W A Bishop, 60 Squadron, destroyed a German two-seater, while 2nd Lt W H Gunner of the same squadron engaged an enemy two-seater and shot the wings off before it crashed. 2nd Lt R V Phelan, also of 60 Squadron, destroyed a two-seater Albatros near Biache. Flight Sub-Lt D W Ramsey, 1 Squadron RNAS, attacked a German machine near Bapaume and followed it down to 2000 feet when it was hit by anti-aircraft fire and fell in the German lines. In the evening a patrol of 48 Squadron engaged an HA formation south of Douai, and one HA was destroyed by Capt B E Baker & Lt Jeff. Four other HA were driven down out of control. Flight Sub-Lt J A Glen, 3 Squadron RNAS, attacked an HA which was about to attack an FE and followed it down until it crashed. Lts V H Huston & Foord of 18 Squadron, while returning from a reconnaissance engaged an Albatros scout which was hit and crashed. 2nd Lt West-White & Sergt Cumberland, 18 Squadron, had their service tank shot through by HA and their machine caught fire. However, the flames were put out and, after finishing their patrol, the pilot landed safely. An Offensive Patrol of 56 Squadron engaged a formation of hostile two-seaters and scouts, and 2nd Lt L M Barlow got within close range of one machine and riddled it with bullets. The HA fell out of control, then the wings were seen to break off and it went down like an arrow. After destroying this HA 2nd Lt Barlow turned quickly to engage another HA that was following him down, and after a short engagement the HA fell out of control. 2nd Lt Barlow then flew round and saw the first HA in flames on the ground and the second one crashed within half a mile of the first. Captain C M Crowe, 56 Squadron, observed a fight between some of our machines and a hostile formation, and he took his patrol to join in the fighting. He had a long engagement with a skilful opponent but eventually succeeded in driving him down and saw his machine crash. A second patrol of 56 Squadron engaged a formation of hostile scouts, three of which were driven down out of control by Capt P B Prothero, Lt R T C Hoidge and Lt C A Lewis.

Photography – 1213 photographs were taken during the day.

Miscellaneous – 2nd Lt L L Morgan, 40 Squadron, when returning from pursuing an artillery HA from the lines on the 24th inst., was hit when at 4000 feet by one of our own shells. The shell exploded on the engine and carried away two cylinders, most of the engine bearers, the whole of the bottom right-hand longeron to behind the pilot's seat, and caused a compound fracture of the pilot's leg. 2nd Lt Morgan, however, succeeded in bringing his machine back, and is progressing favourably.

MAY 28

Artillery Co-operation – 127 targets were dealt with by aeroplane observation and 102 by balloon observation.

Hostile Aircraft – An Offensive Patrol of 45 Squadron observed a large formation of Albatros scouts which were being engaged by their own anti-aircraft guns – presumably as a ruse. The Sopwiths engaged the HA and two were destroyed, one by 2nd Lt W A Wright & Lt E T C Kelly, and the other by 2nd Lts G H Cock & W G Corner. Both HA fell in flames.

Photography – 702 photographs were taken during the day.

MAY 29

Artillery Co-operation – Fifty-eight targets were dealt with by aeroplane observation and 145 by balloon observation.

MAY 30

Artillery Co-operation – Eighty-two targets were dealt with by aeroplane observation and 65 by balloon observation.

Hostile Aircraft – Major C E Sutcliffe and Lt E J Y Grevelink, 54 Squadron, each drove down a German machine out of control.

Miscellaneous – 2nd Lts A S Shepherd & J M Leach and Lt A W B Miller, 29 Squadron, crossed the lines east of Bullecourt at about 20 feet and attacked German troops. Lt Miller observed a party of Germans in two ranks and opened fire at 200 yards. A number of men were seen to fall and the rest fled in all directions. 2nd Lt Shepherd saw eight field guns near which was a fire where about 20 gunners were seated. He fired into their midst and continued firing until the wheels of his undercarriage almost touched them.

MAY 31

Artillery Co-operation – Sixty-nine targets were dealt with by aeroplane observation and 25 by balloon observation.

Hostile Aircraft – Captain W A Bishop, 60 Squadron, destroyed one hostile machine.

COMMUNIQUÉ No.91

1 – 7 June 1917

This first week in June saw a build-up in aerial activity by the RFC and RNAS prior to the battle of Messines, which commenced on June 7 and lasted until the 14th. June also saw the operational debut of the Sopwith Camel fighter; the first unit to be equipped being No.4 Squadron RNAS, while the first RFC squadron to receive the type, No.70, replaced its now obsolescent Sopwith 1½ Strutters. Captain W A Bishop's solo exploit on June 2 resulted in his being awarded a Victoria Cross.

JUNE 1

Artillery Co-operation – 187 targets were dealt with by aeroplane observation and 54 by balloon observation.

Hostile Aircraft – Two German two-seater machines were engaged by Capt W T L Allcocks, 40 Squadron, and he drove one down out of control, while 2nd Lt A E Godfrey of the same squadron drove down an HA which infantry confirmed as crashed. A fierce contested combat took place between eight machines of 20 Squadron and 17 Albatros scouts. Lt D C Cunnell & 2nd Lt W C Cambray shot down one scout which was seen to break to pieces in the air, while a second was sent down out of control by 2nd Lts M Hindley & G W Blacklock. Flight Sub-Lt R Collishaw, 10 Squadron RNAS, shot down an Albatros scout which fell in flames before it crashed. Sergt G P Olley, 1 Squadron, drove down a two-seater out of control. At least nine other HA were reported as driven down out of control by other pilots.

Photography – 542 photographs were taken during the day.

Bombing – On the night 31 May/1 June, a very successful raid was carried out by 100 Squadron. One 230lb bomb was dropped on Orchies ammunition depot and partly destroyed the depot, while 25 112lb and 20lb bombs were also dropped on the objective with good results.

JUNE 2

Artillery Co-operation – 185 targets were dealt with by aeroplane observation and 130 by balloon observation.

Hostile Aircraft – An Offensive Patrol of 20 Squadron engaged eight Albatros scouts, and Lt R M Trevethan & 2/AM J J Cowell picked out the leader whose machine burst into flames and crashed. Captain W A Bishop, 60 Squadron, when 17 miles over the lines, saw seven machines, some of which had their engines running, on an aerodrome. He waited and then engaged the first one that left the ground from a height of 60 feet and the HA crashed. Another left the ground and Capt Bishop, who was hovering around immediately dived at it and after 30 rounds had been fired the HA crashed into a tree. Just after that two more left the ground at the same time, so Capt Bishop climbed to 1000 feet and then engaged one of them and it fell and crashed within 300 yards of the aerodrome. The fourth was driven down after a whole drum had been fired into it. After this exploit Capt Bishop returned safely, but with his aeroplane considerably shot about by machine gun fire from the ground. Flight Lt G G MacLennan, 6 Squadron RNAS, while leading a patrol drove down an Albatros scout out of control which is reported by anti-aircraft as having crashed.

Photography – 495 photographs were taken during the day.

JUNE 3
Artillery Co-operation – 193 targets were dealt with by aeroplane observation and 107 by balloon observation.

Hostile Aircraft – Lt A T Rickards & CSM L M Lava, 43 Squadron, engaged an enemy two-seater which burst into flames and fell. 2nd Lt W C Campbell, 1 Squadron, observed an Aviatik two-seater flying towards our lines and immediately dived at it and opened fire at about 20 yards range. The HA went straight down and crashed. Flight Sub-Lt R Collishaw, 10 Squadron RNAS, attacked an Albatros scout which fell out of control and was seen to be on fire. Flight Sub-Lt L H Parker of the same squadron, in an engagement with four HA, shot one down which was seen to crash. A third HA was destroyed by Flight Sub-Lt E V Reid, also of 10 Squadron RNAS. Lt A W Hogg, 41 Squadron, dived at a German machine which immediately flew east. He, however, succeeded in getting in front of it and forced it to fight. The HA crashed. In a fight between an Offensive Patrol of 45 Squadron and about 25 HA, one HA was driven down and seen to break in the air after being engaged by 2nd Lt R Watt & Cpl T M Harries. Lt F P Holliday & Capt A H Wall, 48 Squadron, opened fire on an Albatros at about 20 yards range and, after about 200 rounds, the tail of the German machine was seen to fall off.

Photography – 975 photographs were taken during the day.

Bombing – Bomb raids were carried out on La Bassée, Marquillies, Dourges Station, Phalempin aerodrome, Provin aerodrome, Comines, La Madeline, Menin Station, Wervicq, Hendecourt.

JUNE 4
Artillery Co-operation – 214 targets were dealt with by aeroplane observation and 164 by balloon observation.

Hostile Aircraft – An Offensive Patrol of 1 Squadron engaged nine Albatros scouts east of Hollebeke and Lt T F Hazell fired half a drum into one of them when its left wing was seen to break off after which it crashed. He then turned and fired the remainder of the drum into another HA at about 60 yards and this machine went down in a spin and one wing was seen to break off by other pilots of the patrol. Shortly after Lt Hazell engaged four more HA and drove two down, one of which was forced to land. 2nd Lt P F Fullard of the same squadron dived at one of four HA and this machine, which was painted in many colours, fell completely out of control. He then joined a big fight between 15 HA and a number of our machines, but one HA obtained a favourable position on his tail so he put his machine into a spin. An SE5 of 56 Squadron dived at the attacking scout and drove it down out of control. 2nd Lt Fullard then attacked a black and white Albatros scout from underneath and about 30 shots were seen to go into the HA which flew straight on, then went into a spin, turned completely over, and eventually crashed in a field. Flight Cdr T F N Gerrard, with other machines of 1 Squadron RNAS, took part in the general engagement already referred to and fired 50 rounds at point-blank range into an HA which had driven a Nieuport down in a spin, and the HA fell completely out of control. Flight Cdr Gerrard and a Nieuport Scout then attacked an Albatros scout which had hit one of our machines. The Nieuport attacked from above and the Triplane from below, and the HA fell and crashed. In other engagements 2nd Lt W C Campbell, 1 Squadron, destroyed a two-seater LVG. 2nd Lt F L Luxmoore, 46 Squadron, became separated from the rest of his patrol and was attacked by three Albatros scouts. He secured a favourable position on the tail of one scout which he drove down and it

crashed. The other two continued to attack so he put his machine into a spin and thus evaded them. Lt F Sharpe, 1 Squadron, dived at a Rumpler two-seater and observed his tracers entering the pilot's and the Observer s seats, and the FA fell out of control and crashed. A Roland two-seater which had been engaged by 2nd Lt W J Mussared, 1 Squadron, turned completely on its back and fell out of control with its engine full on. Anti-aircraft report that this HA eventually caught fire.
(Editor's note: Mussared had lied about his age to join the RFC, being just 16 years old, and celebrated his17th birthday after being made a prisoner of war on June 9th).

Captain C M B Chapman, 29 Squadron, engaged an Albatros scout and brought it down on our side of the lines, and the pilot was taken prisoner. *(This was Leutnant Georg Simon, of Jagdstaffel 11).* A bombing raid of 27 Squadron engaged nine Albatros scouts and had hard fighting during the whole of their time over the lines. In spite of this, the pilots dropped their bombs on the objective, St Denis Westrem aerodrome. Capt D J Bell and Lt D V D Marshall attacked one Albatros and one of the HA's wings was shot off. Capt Bell then engaged another HA in which the pilot is believed to have been shot and it fell out of control. Three others were sent down out of control. Bombing machines of 55 Squadron, when over Moorslede, were attacked by about ten HA. One HA dived at a De Havilland in which were Lts C C Knight & J C Trulock, and the latter fired two drums into the attacker which fell out of control and crashed. After dropping the bombs this machine became detached from the rest of the formation and was cut off by six HA, but the pilot succeeded in evading and one HA was shot down attempting to attack the De Havilland from behind.
Photography – 1156 photographs were taken during the day.

JUNE 5
Artillery Co-operation – 180 targets were dealt with by aeroplane observation and 208 by balloon observation.
Hostile Aircraft – An Offensive Patrol of 20 Squadron attacked four HA and Lt D C Cunnell & Sgt Sayers shot one down in flames. A little later our formation again engaged a number of HA and Capts F H Thayre & F R Cubbon drove one down which crashed on Coucou aerodrome. Pilots of 10 Squadron RNAS had a general engagement with a number of Albatros two-seaters and one HA was shot down in flames. While over Menin a patrol of 45 Squadron was attacked by 18 HA scouts, led by a red machine with black wheels. The leader of the German formation showed great pluck and skill, and the fight lasted for 23 minutes. Lts M B Frew & Dalton shot down one HA in flames, then dived on another which had secured a favourable position on the tail of one of ours, and after a burst of fire the HA fell completely out of control. In a fight between 15 HA, led by a red machine, and seven FEs of 20 Squadron, one of our FEs was driven down and followed by the red HA. Lt H L Satchell & 2nd Lt T A M S Lewis at once dived to the assistance of the FE and a fight lasting about 15 minutes ensued in which the German pilot showed great skill and persistence. Eventually, however, after a burst of fire at very close range, the HA burst into flames and its wings were seen to fall off before it crashed.
(Editor's note: This was the 30-victory ace, Leutnant Karl Emil Schafer, commander of Jagdstaffel 28).

Flight Sub-Lt H Taylor, 10 Squadron RNAS, shot down a two-seater HA in flames. Continuous fighting took place between 40 HA and machines of 22, 54 and 6 Squadron RNAS, resulting in at least three HA seen to fall out of control, one of which was seen completely wrecked on the ground. In the evening Lt W A Bond, 40 Squadron, drove one HA down out of control, and then attacked another which crashed. Major A J L Scott, 60 Squadron, observed an Albatros scout diving at a machine of 29 Squadron, and dived at it. After firing about five rounds the HA caught fire and crashed.

Photography – 677 photographs were taken during the day.

JUNE 6

Artillery Co-operation – 161 targets were dealt with by aeroplane observation and 135 by balloon observation.

Hostile Aircraft – In an engagement between 13 of our machines and 15 to 20 HA, Flight Sub-Lt R Collishaw, 10 Squadron RNAS, shot down two Albatros scouts in flames and a third out of control, while Flight Sub-Lt G E Nash destroyed a two-seater Albatros and drove down an Albatros scout out of control. During this encounter Flight Sub-Lt E V Reid destroyed a Halberstadt scout, and Flight Sub-Lt J A Page shot down an Albatros scout, while three others were driven down out of control by Flight Sub-Lts J H Keens, J E Sharman and W M Alexander. All our machines returned safely. A general engagement took place between about 30 of our machines and from 30 to 40 HA, and after about 30 minutes close fighting three of the Germans were seen crashed on the ground, and it is believed at least five others driven down out of control by pilots of 54 Squadron, while several more are claimed by pilots of 6 Squadron RNAS who also took part in the fighting.

Photography – 675 photographs were taken during the day.

JUNE 7

Artillery Co-operation – 247 targets were dealt with by aeroplane observation and 27 by balloon observation.

Hostile Aircraft – Six Spads of 23 Squadron encountered a formation of HA and in the ensuing combat Captains D A L Davidson and A B Wright drove down one HA and Captain Wright fired into it as it fell from close range and the HA crashed. 2nd Lts A E Godfrey and E Mannock, 40 Squadron, each destroyed an HA. Lt C T Lally & 2nd Lt Williams, 25 Squadron, drove down one HA out of control and assisted in the destruction of another. Lts F Sharpe and L F Jenkin, 1 Squadron, dived at an Albatros scout which they destroyed. An Offensive Patrol of 10 Squadron RNAS engaged 15 to 20 HA. Two HA were destroyed and three driven down out of control. Flight Sub-Lt E V Reid shot down one, Flight Sub-Lt J E Sharman destroyed a second and drove one down out of control, while the other two were driven down out of control by Flight Sub-Lts R Collishaw and G E Nash. An Offensive Patrol of 20 Squadron drove down an HA which was seen to crash, and Lt V Joske, 46 Squadron, also destroyed an HA. While on photography, Lt Anderson & 1/AM Kirwan, 42 Squadron, were attacked by three HA but succeeded in destroying one HA and driving the other two away. Considerable fighting took place between machines of 9th Wing and HA formations, and as a result of combats Captain E W Broadberry, 56 Squadron, Lt J M Child, 19 Squadron, and Captain J O Andrews, 66 Squadron, each destroyed an HA, while four others were driven down out of control; one by each of the following; 2nd Lts A P F Rhys Davids and H Rogerson and Captain Broadberry, all of 56 Squadron, and 2nd Lt Taylor, 66 Squadron. Lt F Sharpe, 1 Squadron, destroyed a hostile balloon.

NOTE: In future the following abbreviation will be used for hostile aircraft in place of that (ie HA) now in use; EA – denoting Enemy Aircraft or Aeroplane.

COMMUNIQUÉ No.92

8 – 15 June 1917

All squadrons in support of the Messines battle flew low-level attacks against enemy troops, transport, and other ground targets from dawn to dusk, in addition to Offensive Patrols seeking enemy aircraft. On June 13, No.11 Squadron commenced operations with its replacement Bristol F2b Fighters, while on the 15th, No.9 Squadron, RNAS (Sopwith Triplanes) was officially attached to the RFC.

JUNE 8
Artillery Co-operation – 154 targets were dealt with by aeroplane observation and 53 by balloon observation.
Hostile Aircraft – Major A S W Dore, 43 Squadron, drove down one EA which landed in a field. Flight Sub-Lt J Walder, 1 Squadron RNAS, in an encounter with two EA was wounded but succeeded in destroying one EA. An Offensive Patrol of 1 Squadron engaged six Albatros scouts near Becelaere and 2nd Lt P F Fullard shot down one in flames, while a second was driven down out of control by Lt T F Hazell. Another patrol of this squadron engaged eight Albatros scouts in the same locality and one was destroyed by Lt W J Mussared. An Offensive Patrol of 20 Squadron encountered a large formation of EA and 2nd Lt W Durrand & Sergt E H Sayers drove one EA down which caught fire and fell to pieces before reaching the ground. Captain W A Bishop, 60 Squadron, encountered a number of hostile scouts and drove one down out of control. During this engagement he had fights with eight EA.
Photography – 705 photographs were taken during the day.
Bombing – Bomb raids were made on Haubourdin, La Pouillerie aerodrome, Menin Station, Warneton and Courtrai Stations, Wervicq, Comines, Houthem, Dadizeele, Proville aerodrome.

JUNE 9
Artillery Co-operation – 112 targets were dealt with by aeroplane observation and 13 by balloon observation.
Hostile Aircraft – 2nd Lt J L Barlow, 40 Squadron, while attacking a German balloon saw a two-seater Aviatik below him and dived at it, but was then attacked by eight Albatros scouts from above and other Aviatiks from below. One Aviatik dived past him and after being hit fell out of control and crashed. 2nd Lt Barlow continued fighting and saw another EA turn over and fall out of control, after which he broke off the combat and recrossed the trenches at 80 feet. An Offensive Patrol of seven machines of 1 Squadron encountered about 18 Albatros Scouts and very severe fighting took place. 2nd Lt W C Campbell destroyed one EA and drove down two others completely out of control, and 2nd Lt L F Jenkin shot down an EA which crashed, then attacked an Albatros scout which fell in flames. 2nd Lts R M Trevethan & Dudbridge, 20 Squadron, shot down an Albatros scout in flames during an encounter between 20 Squadron and 12 Albatros scouts.
Photography – 372 photographs were taken during the day.

JUNE 10
Artillery Co-operation – Thirty-one targets were dealt with by aeroplane observation and 15 by balloon observation.

Photography – 155 photographs were taken during the day.

JUNE 11
Artillery Co-operation – Thirty-five targets were dealt with by aeroplane observation and 18 by balloon observation.

JUNE 12
Artillery Co-operation – 164 targets were dealt with by aeroplane observation and 10 by balloon observation.

Hostile Aircraft – An Offensive Patrol of four Triplanes of 8 Squadron RNAS encountered six Albatros scouts. Flight Cdr R Compston shot down one which was seen to crash, and Flight Lt R R Soar drove down an Albatros scout out of control. Later, two enemy two-seaters were attacked and Flight Cdr C D Booker and Flight Sub-Lt C H B Jenner-Parsons drove one down in a spin. This machine, a DFW, was then hit by anti-aircraft and landed in our lines near Arras, and the passengers who were slightly wounded were captured. An EA two-seater was destroyed by Sergeant W J Beadle, 1 Squadron, and an Albatros scout driven down out of control by Sub-Lt R P Minifie, 1 Squadron RNAS. While on a photographic reconnaissance Lts Douglas & Houghton, 59 Squadron, were attacked by an Albatros scout. After a short engagement the EA burst into flames and broke up in the air before it crashed.

JUNE 13
Artillery Co-operation – Eighty-two targets were dealt with by aeroplane observation and 46 by balloon observation. *Hostile Aircraft* – Two Albatros two-seaters were engaged by a patrol of 41 Squadron and one was destroyed by Lt J C MacGowan. *Photography* – 575 photographs were taken during the day.

JUNE 14
Artillery Co-operation – 103 targets were dealt with by aeroplane observation and 11 by balloon observation.

Hostile Aircraft – Lt G S Buck, 19 Squadron, flying a 200hp Spad on Offensive Patrol, observed a German Nieuport climbing above Spads and German machines which were fighting, apparently with the intention of 'scalp hunting' (ie taking no risks but diving at a disabled machine or one wholly unprepared for a sudden attack from above). Lt Buck immediately flew up to him and when the German found that he was unable to outclimb the Spad he put his nose down and fled. The Spad, however, easily followed him and after 70 rounds had been fired from each gun the German machine fell out of control and crashed. In the evening Lts Duff & Judd, 6 Squadron, destroyed a German machine which with others had attacked the RE8. Flight Lt F H M Maynard, 1 Squadron RNAS, destroyed an Albatros scout near Ypres. Lt F P Holliday & Capt A H Wall, 48 Squadron, destroyed a German machine and then drove down another out of control in the vicinity of Arleux.

JUNE 15
Artillery Co-operation – 128 targets were dealt with by aeroplane observation and 130 by balloon observation.

Hostile Aircraft – Flight Lt C A Eyre, 1 Squadron RNAS, pursued an EA which, finding it could not escape, turned and fought. Eventually the EA turned over, fell out of control and crashed. Capt Taylor, Lt Holman and 2nd Lt Barker, 41 Squadron, engaged a DFW which was being driven down by a Sopwith Triplane, and the EA crashed in our lines. Captain P B Prothero and Lt G C Maxwell, 56 Squadron, drove down a two-seater Albatros which was destroyed. 2nd Lt T C Luke, 66 Squadron, destroyed an EA, and Captain J O Andrews forced one to land.

COMMUNIQUÉ No.93

16 – 22 June 1917

German bombing raids on Britain, in daylight, on May 25, June 5 and June 13, plus a night raid by Zeppelins on 16/17 June, created near-panic measures for aerial defences of the United Kingdom, with the result that 56 Squadron (SE5s) was withdrawn from France on June 21 to aerodromes in Kent, while 66 Squadron (Sopwith Pups) was moved to Calais, briefed to intercept any German bombers leaving their Belgian bases bound for the UK. Captain John Slessor, 5 Squadron, mentioned here on June 21, was destined to become Chief of the Air Staff and a Marshal of the RAF.

JUNE 16

Artillery Co-operation – 103 targets were dealt with by aeroplane observation and 61 by balloon observation.

Hostile Aircraft – On the evening of the 15th, Capt A W Keen, 40 Squadron, drove down an EA in flames. Flight Cdr R J O Compston and Flight Sub-Lt R R Thornely, 8 Squadron RNAS, drove down a German DFW two-seater over Lens. This EA fell on our side of the lines and the Observer, who was wounded, was taken prisoner, but the pilot was killed. Flight Lts R A Little and E G Johnstone of the same squadron observed our AA shells bursting near St Eloi, so proceeded in that direction where they saw an EA which they destroyed. 2nd Lt W C Campbell, 1 Squadron, flying a Nieuport Scout, attacked a two-seater Albatros near Houthem at 9 am and destroyed it. Ten minutes afterwards he attacked another two-seater Albatros in the same vicinity and after firing a drum and a half the EA fell and crashed. Immediately afterwards he attacked a third Albatros two-seater but ran out of ammunition, so he returned to his aerodrome and went off again. At 9.40 am he encountered a large two-seater machine and after emptying two drums into the EA it fell out of control and crashed. On the evening of the 15th Lt F P Holliday & Capt A H Wall, 48 Squadron, while on patrol alone, encountered seven EA. They decoyed the EA up to a formation of Bristol Fighters of their squadron which they knew were coming from the north. A keenly contested engagement took place and Lt Holliday & Capt Wall drove down one EA out of control, another was sent down out of control by Lts H Pratt & H Owen and Lts Fraser & A M Benjamin in two machines. Captain B E Baker & Lt H Munro in one machine and Lt J A Binnie & 1/AM V Reed in another drove down one EA in flames, while still another was destroyed by Lt R B Hay & Lt V G Nutkins. On the evening of the 15th an Offensive Patrol of 10 Squadron RNAS engaged a large number of EA and as a result one EA was destroyed, five others driven down out of control, while the Observer in a sixth machine was shot. Flight Lt R Collishaw accounted for three EA, one he shot to pieces in the air and two others fell out of control, while Flight Sub-Lt E V Reid was responsible for two, and Flight Sub-Lt D F FitzGibbon for one.

Photography – 838 photographs were taken during the day.

JUNE 17

Artillery Co-operation – 137 targets were dealt with by aeroplane observation and 120 by balloon observation.

Hostile Aircraft – An Offensive Patrol of 20 Squadron engaged three two-seater Aviatiks near Zonnebeke and one was brought down by 2nd Lt C R Richards & 2nd Lt R E Wear. Lts Douglas & Horton, 59 Squadron, attacked and drove down an EA which burst into flames before it crashed. While on an Offensive Patrol 2nd Lt F J Gibbs and Capt R I Keller, 23 Squadron, saw three two-seater EA employed on artillery work, so manoeuvred for position between the EA and the sun, then dived on them. One EA went straight down and 2nd Lt Gibbs sat on its tail and followed it before it crashed. Captain Keller selected another EA on which he fired and it burst into flames and crashed. Lt W B Hutcheson & Sergt Rose, 59 Squadron, engaged an Albatros scout which opened fire at close range. After considerable manoeuvring the EA nose-dived, attempted to flatten out, but failed and crashed. 2nd Lt R T C Hoidge, 56 Squadron, attacked a number of two-seaters over La Bassée and drove one down which was seen to crash. Capt G H Bowman and Lt C A Lewis of the same patrol each drove down one EA out of control.

JUNE 18
Artillery Co-operation – 99 targets were dealt with by aeroplane observation and 132 by balloon observation.
Hostile Aircraft – On the evening of the 17th an Offensive Patrol of 20 Squadron engaged two formations of eight Albatros scouts in each formation. 2nd Lt C R Alston & Lt W H Chester shot down one, while a second was destroyed by Lt B Strange & 2nd Lt W C Cambray. On the 18th Lt Ballard & 2nd Lt Lees, 6 Squadron, were attacked by nine Albatros scouts over Zandvoorde; they shot down one scout which fell to pieces in the air. An Offensive Patrol of 20 Squadron engaged a number of Albatros scouts and Lt A N Solly & 2nd Lt W C Cambray destroyed one scout which crashed after its wings had broken off in the air. Three machines of 1 Squadron destroyed one of eight Albatros scouts which they encountered. 2nd Lts T P Middleton & A W Merchant, 48 Squadron, while on Offensive Patrol, lost formation and were attacked by seven EA, one of which they destroyed, then returned safely. 2nd Lts W B Wood and D Bird, 29 Squadron, each shot down an EA which burst into flames and crashed. During an Offensive Patrol of three machines of 41 Squadron and three RE8s of 6 Squadron and a formation of Albatros scouts, Capt Taylor and Lt J C MacGowan each drove down an EA, one of which was seen to break to pieces in the air. Capt Harker & Lt Barclay, 57 Squadron, when escorted by a De Havilland 4, were attacked by seven Albatros scouts, one of which was destroyed.
Photography – 533 photographs were taken during the day.

JUNE 19
Artillery Co-operation – 68 targets were dealt with by aeroplane observation and 66 by balloon observation.

JUNE 20
Artillery Co-operation – 59 targets were dealt with by aeroplane observation and four by balloon observation.
Enemy Aircraft – Lt A W Miller, 29 Squadron, brought down an Albatros scout after firing 20 rounds at close range.
Photography – 71 plates were exposed by machines of the 1st Brigade and 57 by the 3rd Brigade.

JUNE 21

Artillery Co-operation – 102 targets were dealt with by aeroplane observation and 27 by balloon observation. On the evening of the 21st Captain J C Slessor & 2nd Lt F Tymms, 5 Squadron, carried out a successful shoot in continuous rain; the following morning these officers took excellent photographs 4000 yards behind the enemy's lines and ranged three of our batteries on to three hostile batteries.

Enemy Aircraft – Very little activity on all fronts except 2nd and 5th Brigades where it was slightly above normal. Flight Lt R A Little, 8 Squadron RNAS, brought down an Albatros scout near Courrieres. Lt A S Shepherd, 29 Squadron, engaged two EA at close range. The pilot of one was seen to collapse, the EA going down completely out of control.

Photography – 110 plates were exposed.

JUNE 22

Artillery Co-operation – 28 targets were dealt with by aeroplane observation and 42 by balloon observation.

Enemy Aircraft – Very slight enemy aircraft activity all day.

COMMUNIQUÉ No.94

23 – 29 June 1917

On June 26, Rittmeister Manfred von Richthofen, commander of Jagdstaffel 11, had three more Staffeln added to his sole command, Nos.4, 6 and 10; the four units having the overall title of Jagdgeschwader Nr.1 – or, as it came to be known by the Allied air crews, "The Circus". Its raison d'etre was to be a mobile formation, able to reinforce any area of the front at short notice, and to achieve aerial superiority there. Temporary combination of units had been tried in the previous April with some success, and Richthofen's "Circus" was to set a pattern in the future. On the same day as Jagdgeschwader Nr 1 came officially into being, a Canadian Bristol Fighter pilot of 11 Squadron RFC, A E McKeever, claimed the first two victories of his eventual tally of 31 combat successes; the highest for any Bristol F2b pilot of the war.

JUNE 23
Artillery Co-operation – 99 targets were dealt with by aeroplane observation and ten by balloon observation.
Enemy Aircraft – 2nd Lt W B Wood, 29 Squadron, engaged two EA and after firing 40 rounds into the first one it went down out of control and crashed. A Rumpler two-seater was brought down in our lines by Second Army anti-aircraft guns.
Photography – 408 photographs were taken during the day.

JUNE 24
Artillery Co-operation – 193 targets were dealt with by aeroplane observation and 87 by balloon observation.
Enemy Aircraft – Enemy aircraft activity was great opposite the Fifth Army but below normal on other Army fronts. Capt W A Bishop, 60 Squadron, fired 20 rounds into an EA at 20 yards range and it burst into flames and fell out of control. Flight Lt R Collishaw, 10 Squadron RNAS, fired 40 rounds into an EA from behind at 25 yards; its wings fell off and it crashed near Moorslede. Flight Lt J E Sharman of the same squadron fired 60 rounds at close range at one of 15 EA which were attacking two De Havilland 4s. The tail plane and right wing of the EA broke off and it crashed. Six EA in two patrols of three machines each attacked six balloons on the Second Army front. Nos.2, 32 and 38 balloons were brought down in flames. The eleven Observers in the six balloons all made successful parachute descents. A subsequent attack was made by an Albatros scout on No.9 Balloon but failed; the EA being brought down in our lines by anti-aircraft fire.
Photography – 419 plates were exposed.

JUNE 25
Artillery Co-operation – 88 targets were dealt with by aeroplane observation and 99 by balloon observation.
Enemy Aircraft – 2nd Lts Fielding & Gardner, 42 Squadron, attacked two EA which were attacking another RE8 and destroyed one while the other was driven down. Lt W B Wood, 29 Squadron, who with others engaged nine EA, drove down an EA which broke up in the air before it crashed. In the evening five Nieuports of 40

Squadron attacked a formation of Albatros scouts. Lt G B Crole and 2nd Lts L B Blaxland and G T Pettigrew each drove one EA down out of control. Capt A W Keen observed a single scout coming towards him so he flew into a cloud and waited. He then dived and secured a favourable position underneath the EA and, after 58 rounds had been fired, the EA fell with pieces of the tail plane and fuselage breaking away. Other EA shot down out of control during various combats were by 2nd Lts A E Godfrey and F W Rook, 40 Squadron; Lts A S Shepherd, W B Wood, 29 Squadron; Capt W A Bishop, Lt W J Rutherford, 60 Squadron; 2nd Lts H Lale & Jeff, 48 Squadron; Capt A G Jones-Williams and 2nd Lt V A Norvill, 29 Squadron.
Photography – 181 plates were exposed.

JUNE 26

Artillery Co-operation – 91 targets were dealt with by aeroplane observation and 123 by balloon observation.

Enemy Aircraft – Capt W A Bishop,60 Squadron, engaged three enemy scouts who were guarding a two-seater. After 25 rounds had been fired the first EA attacked fell in flames, the second was then driven down out of control, while the third fled. In the evening Flight Lt R A Little, 8 Squadron RNAS, observed an Aviatik coming towards his aerodrome so ascended and attacked it east of St Eloi. The EA caught fire and one occupant leaped out while the second crawled down the fuselage but fell off before the machine crashed. A patrol of 11 Squadron Bristol Fighters encountered ten EA, two of which attacked Lt A E McKeever & 2nd Lt E Oaks from behind, but both were driven down and one fell out of control. Immediately after this they attacked another EA which they destroyed. Lt G H Hooper & Cpl Carr destroyed one EA, and 2nd Lt P C Ross & 2/AM Woodward, who engaged four of the EA, destroyed one opponent and drove another down out of control. 2nd Lt Ross was badly wounded but brought back his machine safely, but has since died. Other EA were driven down out of control by 2nd Lt H Reeves and Sgt G Olley, 1 Squadron; Flight Sub-Lt H Taylor, 10 Squadron RNAS.
Photography – 524 photographs were taken during the day.

JUNE 27

Artillery Co-operation – 138 targets were dealt with by aeroplane observation and 105 by balloon observation.

Enemy Aircraft – 2nd Lts A J P Hytch & L A McRobert, 11 Squadron, engaged a large two-seater near Monchy and drove it down out of control, and it was seen to crash by anti-aircraft gunners. Capt F Sowrey, 19 Squadron, when leading a patrol of Spads, encountered six EA, attacked and destroyed one opponent. In the evening a patrol of 29 Squadron engaged six Albatros scouts; Lt A Shepherd destroyed one and drove down a second out of control, while a third was destroyed by Capt C M Chapman.

(Editor's note: One other notable claim not included in this day's communiqué was an Albatros scout flown by the 30-victory ace Leutnant Karl Allmenröder, Jagdstaffel 22 by Flight Lt R Collishaw, though Collishaw made no claim, not having seen its fate).

Photography – 471 photographs were taken during the day.

JUNE 28

Artillery Co-operation – 81 targets were dealt with by aeroplane observation and 86 by balloon observation.

Enemy Aircraft – Captain W A Bishop, 50 Squadron, attacked an EA which fell out of control and broke to pieces before crashing. 2nd Lts C G O McAndrew & A M West, 11 Squadron, drove down two EA out of control near Fresnes.

JUNE 29

Artillery Co-operation – 65 targets were dealt with by aeroplane observation and 43 by balloon observation.

Enemy Aircraft – A patrol of six machines of 20 Squadron engaged about 12 EA. Lt H W Joslyn & Pte Potter drove one down which burst into flames and fell, while a second caught fire and broke to pieces in the air after being engaged by Lt H G E Luchford & 2nd Lt Kennard. Shortly afterwards a third EA was driven down out of control by 2nd Lt R M Makepeace & Lt Waddington. A patrol of seven Nieuports of 29 Squadron encountered 25 Albatros scouts. The EA appeared in three formations and came from different directions and at different heights. The pilots of one formation appeared to be experienced while the other two formations showed little knowledge of fighting and manoeuvring. Our patrol was completely surrounded and split up, but fought their way through, only one Nieuport failing to return. One EA was destroyed by Lt A W Miller who then drove down a second out of control. 2nd Lt A S Shepherd drove down two EA out of control, and Captain A G Jones-Williams, S Simpson and 2nd Lt J D Atkinson each drove down an EA out of control.

COMMUNIQUÉ No.95

30 June – 6 July 1917

On July 5, No.56 Squadron returned to France after two weeks' non-active sojourn in England, while 66 Squadron also returned to front-line operations the following day. Among the four enemy aircraft claimed as 'Out of control' by the 20 Squadron FE2d crew, Captain D C Cunnell & 2nd Lt A E Woodbridge, on July 6 was the Albatros scout flown by Rittmeister Manfred von Richthofen, who received a serious head wound but managed to force-land safely. His wound removed him from operations until July 25. Another German ace from Richthofen's JG1, Leutnant Albert Dossenbach, commander of Jagdstaffel 10, credited with 15 victories, was killed by the 57 Squadron De Havilland 4 crew, Captain L Minot & Lt A F Brown, on July 3.

JUNE 30

Artillery Co-operation – 51 targets were dealt with by aeroplane observation and 52 by balloon observation.

Enemy Aircraft – On the evening of the 29th a formation of six FEs of 20 Squadron engaged about 25 Albatros scouts near Becelaere. Lts Patterson & C A Hoy drove down one EA which broke to pieces in the air, while two others were sent down out of control; one by Capt H L Satchell & Lt A N Jenks, and the other by Lt O H D Vickers & Sgt J J Cowell.

JULY 1

Successful trench reconnaissances were flown by machines of 2 and 5 Squadrons, providing much useful information.

JULY 2

Artillery Co-operation – 87 targets were dealt with by aeroplane observation.

Enemy Aircraft – 2nd Lt A E Godfrey, 40 Squadron, attacked two Albatros scouts near Douai, one of which fell out of control. Lt G B Crole of the same squadron attacked an Albatros scout in the same neighbourhood and shot it down in flames. Lt L F Jenkin, 1 Squadron, dived to the assistance of some RE8s and fired 60 rounds into an Aviatik which fell in flames, and both pilot and Observer of the EA were seen to leap out of the aircraft. Another EA was shot down in flames by Capt H L Satchell & Lt A N Jenks, 20 Squadron, while two others were driven down out of control by 2nd Lt R M Trevethan & Lt C A Hoy and by Sgt W J Beadle, 1 Squadron. Flight Lt R Collishaw, 10 Squadron RNAS, attacked two two-seater Aviatiks over Poelcapelle, one of which fell and crashed. An Albatros scout was brought down by AA fire within our lines at Hendecourt while attempting to attack one of our balloons.

Photography – 966 photographs were taken during the day.

JULY 3

Artillery Co-operation – 61 targets were dealt with by aeroplane observation and 62 by balloon observation.

Enemy Aircraft – An Albatros scout attacked No.12 Balloon when it was at 3000 feet but the EA was shot down by machine guns guarding the balloon. The German pilot was found to have a wrist shattered by a machine gun bullet. Lt K W Macdonald,46 Squadron, attacked a German two-seater which he followed down and it fell completely out of control and is believed to have crashed behind La Bassée. A patrol of 48 Squadron encountered four EA scouts and a two-seater near Queant and 2nd Lt R W Elliott & J W Ferguson shot one down in flames, while two others were sent down out of control; one by 2nd Lts R V Curtis & D P F Uniacke, and the other by Lts A G Riley & W O'Toole. Captain L Minot & Lt A F Brown, 57 Squadron, when on Offensive Patrol with three other DH4s, engaged four Albatros scouts and shot one down out of control. They were then attacked from underneath by one scout into which Lt Brown fired a burst of 30 rounds and the EA fell enveloped in flames. In other combats,EA were claimed as out of control by 2nd Lt J L Barlow,40 Squadron; Flight Lt R A Little, 8 Squadron RNAS; Captain W T Wynn & Cpl Moutrie,43 Squadron; Flight Cdr C A Eyre, 1 Squadron RNAS; Lt F P Holliday & Captain A H Wall, 48 Squadron.

Photography – 518 photographs were taken during the day.

JULY 4

Artillery Co-operation – 59 targets were dealt with by aeroplane observation and 27 by balloon observation.

Enemy Aircraft – An Offensive Patrol of 20 Squadron engaged 15 Albatros scouts in the vicinity of Becelaere. Lt H G E Luchford & 2nd Lt J Tennant opened fire on one EA which banked across their front and the EA spun down through a cloud. It was followed down, attacked again, and seen to crash. Two other EA were driven down out of control; one by Capt F D Stevens & Lt Kydd, and one by 2nd Lts O H D Vickers & S F Thompson. In other combats EA were claimed out of control by Flight Lt R R Soar, 8 Squadron RNAS; Flight Cdr C A Eyre and Flight Sub-Lt C G Brook, both of 1 Squadron RNAS; Captain K L Caldwell and Lt W E Jenkins, both of 60 Squadron.

JULY 5

Artillery Co-operation – Nine targets were dealt with by aeroplane observation and five by balloon observation.

JULY 6

Artillery Co-operation – 57 targets were dealt with by aeroplane observation.

Enemy Aircraft – Flight Lt R A Little, 8 Squadron RNAS, attacked a German two-seater into which he fired 100 rounds. The EA flew straight into the ground and was completely wrecked. An Offensive Patrol of 20 Squadron engaged about 30 Albatros scouts in several formations. The EA came much closer than usual and attacked keenly. Captain D C Cunnell & Lt A E Woodbridge drove down four of their opponents out of control. 2nd Lts C R Richards & R E Wear also drove down one EA scout out of control. All our machines returned safely. A patrol of 48 Squadron encountered six EA and Lts O J F Scholte & A W Merchant destroyed one, while a second was driven down out of control by Capt J T Milne & Lt Tanner. While leading an Offensive Patrol of 23 Squadron, which met 14 Albatros scouts, Captain W K C Patrick opened fire at long range at one EA and this was seen to crash by anti-aircraft gunners. Immediately afterwards he and 2nd Lt G I D Marks and D U McGregor attacked a small EA two-seater and drove it down. 2nd Lt McGregor followed it and continued firing until it crashed. Captain R H G Neville, 23

Squadron, attacked three EA. He attacked one which fell out of control and broke to pieces in the air. In other combats EA were claimed as out of control by Flight Lt R R Soar, 8 Squadron RNAS; 2nd Lts C Ryder & M W Richardson, 2 Squadron; Capt A Harris and 2nd Lt P F Webb, 45 Squadron; Capt M H Findlay & Lt G Moore, 45 Squadron; 2nd Lts C T Warman and D Langlands, 23 Squadron; Flight Lt R Collishaw, 10 Squadron, RNAS; Flight Lt W M Alexander, 10 Squadron RNAS; Flight Sub-Lt E V Reid, 10 Squadron RNAS; Captain J Leacroft, 19 Squadron.

Photography – 914 photographs were taken during the day.

Bombing – On the night of the 5th/6th and during the day of the 6th bomb raids were carried out on Marquillies Sugar Factory, Provin Dump, Houthem, Wervicq, IXth German Army HQ at Escadoeuvres, Ingelmunster aerodrome, Spree Farm Dump, Herenthage Chateau, Kitchener Wood, Proville aerodrome, and Dorignies aerodrome.

COMMUNIQUÉ No.96

7 – 13 July 1917

The month of July brought new types of aircraft to many RNAS and RFC squadrons. Nos. 3, 8, 9, 10 RNAS and 45 RFC all began receiving Sopwith Camels, while 60 Squadron received SE 5s, and 22 Squadron replaced its battle-worn FE 2ds for Bristol F 2b Fighters. On July 10, however, 46 Squadron RFC (Sopwith Pups) returned to England for some Defence duties and eventual re-equipment with Sopwith Camels before returning to France on August 30. Two men mentioned particularly in this week's communiqué, Captain Arthur Harris and Captain Arthur Coningham, were to achieve high rank in the RAF; Harris becoming the commander of RAF Bomber Command, 1942-45, and Coningham an Air Chief Marshal.

JULY 7
Artillery Co-operation – 93 hostile batteries were successfully engaged for destruction by our artillery from aeroplane observation.

Enemy Aircraft – On the evening of the 6th a patrol of 20 Squadron engaged eight Albatros scouts. One was shot down in flames by 2nd Lt M McCall & Lt H L Waddington, while two others were driven down out of control by Capt F D Stevens & Lt A N Jenks and 2nd Lts R P Makepeace & Kennard. During this fight the Albatros scouts were reinforced by 12 more, but after two others had been driven down by Lt H G E Luchford & 2nd Lt J Tennant, the EA broke off the combat and refused to be closely engaged. 2nd Lt G I D Marks, 23 Squadron, engaged three Albatros scouts and shot one down which was seen to crash. On the 7th an Offensive Patrol of 45 Squadron encountered eight Albatros scouts near Comines. One EA attacked Captain A T Harris & 2nd Lt P F Webb from behind. When the German machine was about 100 yards off, Capt Harris did an "Immelman turn" and came out under the EA and fire was opened at very close range. The EA immediately fell out of control and both wings were seen to fall off in the air. Another patrol of 45 Squadron engaged 20 Albatros scouts near Wervicq, and Sgt R A Yeomans & Cpl T Harries shot down one in flames, then drove down two more out of control. 2nd Lts Elliott & Ferguson, 48 Squadron, drove down an EA out of control, while Capt J T Milne & 2nd Lt A D Light of the same squadron shot one down which crashed in a wood. In other combats,EA were claimed shot down out of control by each of the following; Capt G H Cock & Lt Ward, 45 Squadron; 2nd Lts A J Hytch & L A McRobert, 11 Squadron; Capt Blacklock, 45 Squadron; 2nd Lts C R Richards & A E Wear, 20 Squadron; 2nd Lt H Scandrett & Cpl Mee, 11 Squadron; Lt Roadley & 2nd Lt Rushbrooke, 57 Squadron; Flight Lt J A Page, 10 Squadron RNAS; Lt H M Ferreira, 29 Squadron; 2nd Lt R W Farquhar, 23 Squadron; Flight Sub-Lt C Pegler, 10 Squadron RNAS; Capt G H Bowman, 56 Squadron.

Photography – 918 photographs were taken during the day.

JULY 8
Artillery Co-operation – 37 targets were successfully engaged for destruction by artillery with aeroplane observation.

Enemy Aircraft – An Offensive Patrol of 29 Squadron engaged ten Albatros scouts near Wervicq and one EA was brought down by 2nd Lt R M Trevethan and Lt E C Hoy, and another driven down out of control by Lt Joslyn and Pte Potter. Lt A E McKeever & Lt A L Powell, 11 Squadron, while on patrol, dived on an EA which they drove down and saw crash. After this they attacked a second EA which they shot down out of control, then engaged four more, one of which was seen to fall completely out of control. Capt K C Patrick and 2nd Lts D U McGregor and Briggs, 23 Squadron, encountered ten Albatros scouts and three two-seater EA which they attacked. Capt Patrick shot one EA down out of control, then with 2nd Lt McGregor attacked one of the two-seaters and drove it down out of control. 2nd Lt McGregor then attacked another two-seater which he shot down in flames, and the Observer of the EA was seen to leap out as it fell. Other EA claimed as driven down out of control in various combats were by Lt K W Macdonald, 46 Squadron; Lts L F Jenkin, C S T Laver, 2nd Lts P F Fullard, McLaren, and Sgt W J Beadle, all of 1 Squadron; Flight Sub-Lt J C Tanner, 9 Squadron RNAS; Capt R Raymond-Barker & Pte J Mason and 2nd Lts A J Hytch & L A McRobert, all of 11 Squadron.

JULY 9
Very little work was possible owing to rain.

JULY 10
Hostile Aircraft – 2nd Lts F J Foster & H J Day, 11 Squadron, encountered an Albatros scout near Lecluse into which 50 rounds were fired and the EA fell and crashed. Another EA was engaged by 2nd Lt N Sharples & 2/A M Bassenger of the same squadron and this was destroyed near Gouelzin. Other EA were claimed as driven down out of control by Flight Lt R Little, 8 Squadron RNAS; Lt A E McKeever & 2nd Lt W Dodd, 11 Squadron ; Captain W A Bishop, 50 Squadron.

JULY 11
Artillery Co-operation – 44 targets were successfully engaged by aeroplane observation.
Hostile Aircraft – Capt F N Hudson, 54 Squadron, engaged an EA which he drove down and which was seen to crash by the RNAS and Belgian Coastguards. Capt J O Andrews, 54 Squadron, dived on the tail of a two-seater Albatros. He opened fire at about 75 yards range and continued firing until he almost ran into the EA which fell straight down and crashed. In the evening an Offensive Patrol of 20 Squadron engaged two formations of Albatros scouts of about 40 machines in all. Capt D C Cunnell & Lt A G Bill shot down one EA in flames but Captain Cunnell was then killed and his machine was brought back by Lt Bill. Patrols of 32 and 23 Squadrons encountered 15 Albatros scouts. Captain A Coningham, 32 Squadron, attacked three EA in succession and drove one down completely out of control. 2nd Lt D Langlands, 23 Squadron, drove down one EA out of control, then a second in flames. Other EA in this fight claimed driven down out of control were by Lt S R P Walter, 32 Squadron and Capt R H G Neville, 23 Squadron. Further combats saw EA driven down out of control by the following; Capt J F Morris & Lt D L Burgess, 25 Squadron; Lts St C C Taylor and C Turner, 32 Squadron; Capt P B Prothero and E W Broadberry, Lt E Turnbull, all of 56 Squadron; 2nd Lt P F Fullard and Lt C S T Laver, 1 Squadron; Flight Lt R Collishaw, 10 Squadron RNAS; Capt Harker & Lt Barclay, 57 Squadron.
Photography – 650 photographs were taken during the day.

JULY 12

Enemy Aircraft – On the 12th more fighting took place in the air than on any day since the commencement of the war. Flight Lt R A Little, 8 Squadron RNAS and Capt W A Bishop, 60 Squadron, observed a formation of Nieuports engaging Albatros scouts so joined the fight. Capt Bishop shot down one EA which crashed near Vitry-en-Artois, and Flight Lt Little drove one down whose pilot waved a white handkerchief, so Flight Lt Little ceased firing temporarily. The German pilot, however, flew east and escaped. 2nd Lt W MacLanachan, 40 Squadron, drove down an EA out of control, and 2nd Lt E Mannock of the same squadron shot down a DFW two-seater within our lines near Lens, the Observer of which was killed and the pilot taken prisoner. An Offensive Patrol of 1 Squadron RNAS engaged seven Albatros scouts near Quesnoy and Flight Sub-Lt R P Minifie drove one EA down out of control. No.45 Squadron took part in a number of engagements. One patrol observed a very large yellow two-seater Albatros protected by two Albatros scouts. Capt A T Harris & 2nd Lt P F Webb dived at the two-seater and its Observer was seen to collapse in his cockpit. Capt Harris did not cease firing until he was forced to "zoom" in order to avoid flying into the EA which fell completely out of control. One Albatros scout was shot down by Lt J D Musgrave & Cpl A Jex and seen to crash and burst into flames. In other combats by 45 Squadron EA were sent down out of control by Lt G H Walker & 2nd Lt Mullen, and Lt O L McMaking & Lt L M Copeland.

When on photography, Capt J P V Lavarack & Sgt Reeday, 12 Squadron, saw four EA coming towards them. They fired at the nearest one from about 100 yards range and it turned over completely and fell out of control. Six machines of 32 Squadron encountered about 20 Albatros scouts near Polygon Wood. Lt S R P Walter shot down one which lost a wing as it fell, and Lt Taylor drove down another out of control. Pilots of 10 Squadron RNAS engaged a patrol of Albatros scouts near Polygon Wood, and Flight Lt R Collishaw attacked one painted red and saw the pilot collapse and the EA fall out of control. Flight Sub-Lt E V Reid dived into a formation of five EA and destroyed two of them; the wings of one fell off in the air, and the second crashed on a house near Veldhoek. Later in the day machines of this same squadron attacked a number of EA in the same locality, and Flight Cdr J E Sharman attacked one EA which broke to pieces in the air. Seven machines of 29 Squadron met ten Albatros scouts, and Capt A G Jones-Williams drove one down out of control. In response to a warning given by a wireless interception station, 2nd Lts Langlands and Shepperson, 23 Squadron, went up and found a two-seater EA doing artillery work over Polygon Wood. Taking advantage of the sun, they then attacked. 2nd Lt Langlands fired 120 rounds at very close range and the EA fell and crashed. Four machines of 32 Squadron attacked five Albatros scouts and Capt A Coningham secured a position on the tail of one and followed it down from 15,000 feet to 1000 feet and watched it crash. Captain N W Webb, when on a practice flight near Loos on a Sopwith Camel of 70 Squadron, saw anti-aircraft shells bursting at about 17,000 feet. He flew in their direction and observed an Albatros two-seater which he overtook and engaged above Bellevue as it was flying for the lines. After his first burst the enemy Observer appeared to be hit and the EA was finally driven down and landed on Bellevue aerodrome where it turned on its back. 2nd Lt A P F Rhys-Davids, 56 Squadron, when with a patrol of SE5s, observed five EA flying west. He waited until they were nearly over the lines, then dived at them, but the fighting was indecisive. Shortly afterwards he engaged a green EA over Roncq and drove it down out of control. After that he attacked a DFW two-seater on our side of the lines and

drove it down but his machine gave trouble and he was forced to return. However, 2nd Lt K K Muspratt of the same squadron flew in front of this EA which had gone down to 3000 feet and opened fire, forcing it to land north of Armentieres. The occupants were both captured. Capt I H D Henderson, also 56 Squadron, saw 2nd Lt Rhys Davids dive at six EA and immediately followed, attacking an EA on Rhys Davids' tail. The EA turned over and fell out of control. Lt R A Maybery, 56 Squadron, when taking part in a very big fight between a large formation of EA and French and British aircraft, observed an EA diving on the tail of a Sopwith Pup, so he dived at this EA and, despite being attacked himself from behind, destroyed the EA scout he originally attacked. No. 56 Squadron took part in the big fight just referred to and 2nd Lt E H Lascelles drove down one EA which was seen to crash. Seven other EA were driven down out of control by Capt A C Hagon, 19 Squadron; Lt Hunter, 66 Squadron; Lt M H Coote, Capt G H Bowman, Lt G Wilkinson and 2nd Lt R T C Hoidge, all of 56 Squadron. In the evening four Sopwith two-seaters of 43 Squadron engaged seven Albatros scouts, and one, engaged by Lt W Cox & 2nd Lt W Cattell, was attacked and fell in flames and was seen to crash. 2nd Lt L McPherson & Lt W Bell engaged two of the EA, one of which they drove down out of control, and shot a wheel and axle off the other. An Offensive Patrol of 20 Squadron engaged five Albatros scouts near Comines and 2nd Lt O H D Vickers & Sgt J J Cowell shot down one, then drove a second down out of control. The same patrol then attacked three Albatros scouts and 2nd Lt R M Trevethan & Pte Arkley shot down one in flames. Of other combats, at least eight other EA were claimed as driven down out of control.
Photography – 891 photographs were taken during the day.

JULY 13
Artillery Co-operation – 97 targets were successfully engaged by aeroplane observation.
Hostile Aircraft – Activity in the air was above normal and heavy fighting continued all day. Flight Lts R A Little and R R Soar, 8 Squadron RNAS, on Sopwith Camels, drove down a two-seater near Lens, after which they engaged seven Albatros scouts, one of which Flight Lt Little sent down to crash by an anti-aircraft battery. Flight Lts P A Johnston and W L Jordan of the same squadron attacked a Rumpler two-seater which was last seen falling on a house near Montigny. 2nd Lt E Mannock, 40 Squadron, observed three DFW two-seaters and dived at one which then fell completely out of control, falling into a mist. A patrol of 1 Squadron attacked a DFW two-seater over Houthem. Lt L F Jenkin fired a complete drum into it and saw the Observer fall forward, then the EA went into a slow spiral and finally crashed. An Offensive Patrol of 48 Squadron attacked eight Albatros scouts and one was driven down by 2nd Lt J Binnie & Cpl B Reid and was seen to crash. Three others were driven down out of control. While on a practice flight Major W D S Sandy, 19 Squadron, was watching three RE8s doing photography over Messines when he saw an EA at 21,000 feet over Lille. He made a wide circuit in order to intercept the EA and climbed steadily. The EA then came down to 18,000 feet and Major Sanday attacked from underneath. Apparently the occupants were hit by his first burst, and the EA went down and was seen to crash.

Captain I H D Henderson and Lt A P F Rhys Davids of 56 Squadron, flying 200hp SE5s, observed about 20 EA over Roulers, so flew round to the east of them and attacked and each succeeded in driving down one EA out of control.
Photography – 902 photographs were taken during the day.

COMMUNIQUÉ No. 97

14 – 20 July 1917

JULY 14

Artillery Co-operation – 93 targets were dealt with by aeroplane observation and 13 by balloon observation.

Enemy Aircraft – Lt E Cottier & Sgt D Richens, 8 Squadron, engaged six Albatros scouts and, after firing 90 rounds into one, it fell out of control and crashed northeast of Hendecourt. Eight Spads of 23 Squadron engaged 15 Albatros scouts and several two-seaters. The fight began east of Ypres and finished over Menin, by which time only five EA were seen. 2nd Lt Shepperson drove one down out of control, and 2nd Lt R M Smith, who fired 40 rounds into one EA at close range, saw its pilot throw up his hands, then collapse, and his machine fall completely out of control. 2nd Lt D U McGregor also sent one EA down out of control, while a fourth was hit by 2nd Lt A V Hurley and fell apparently out of control. Lt C W Warman who drove down a Rumpler two-seater (in which the Observer was seen to fall), saw it land in a field, run into a hedge and turn over. Captain J T Milne & Lt Tanner, 48 Squadron, destroyed an Albatros scout near Leffinghe. In other combats, EA were claimed as out of control by 2nd Lt H B Redler, 40 Squadron; Capt G H Cock & 2nd Lt V R S White, and 2nd Lt K B Montgomery & Sgt Wickham, both of 45 Squadron; 2nd Lt P F Fullard, 1 Squadron; Lt A E McKeever & 2nd Lt W Dodd, 11 Squadron.

Photography – 142 photographs were taken during the day.

Miscellaneous – After being up for 25 minutes, No.42 Balloon burst while at a height of 2500 feet. The Observer, Lt T B Fraser, was unable to get out of the basket as it had swung on top of the balloon and become entangled in the rigging. The balloon fell very rapidly but fortunately landed in some trees; the basket was held suspended ten feet from the ground and the Observer was unhurt.

JULY 15

Artillery Co-operation – 77 targets were dealt with by aeroplane observation.

Enemy Aircraft – Flight Lt R A Little, 8 Squadron RNAS, dived at six EA over Lens and after firing 100 rounds at the nearest it went into a spin and then fell out of control. Five Sopwith Camels of the same squadron encountered seven Albatros scouts. One of our machines was hit at long range and brought down. On closing with the EA formation Flight Sub-Lt E A Bennetts shot down one in flames. A patrol of 60 Squadron pursued about 12 EA towards Douai. On their return Capt K L Caldwell and Lt W E Jenkins fired on one EA which they drove down completely out of control. Lt F J Morse, 54 Squadron, reported having driven down an EA near Leffinghe, and confirmation has now been received from another pilot that this EA actually crashed.

JULY 16

Artillery Co-operation – 92 hostile batteries were successfully engaged with aeroplane observation.

Enemy Aircraft – Flight Lt R A Little, 8 Squadron RNAS, attacked two Aviatiks and drove one down out of control. While searching for reported EA, three machines of 45 Squadron were attacked by six Albatros scouts near Houthem. 2nd Lts M B Frew & G A Brooke shot down one in flames, and 2nd Lt R H Deakin & Capt Higgins drove another down out of control. In another engagement between this squadron and a formation of Albatros scouts, 2nd Lts K B Montgomery & R C Purvis hit one EA which burst into flames and fell. 2nd Lt W B Wood, 29 Squadron, while on Offensive Patrol, observed eight Albatros scouts below him. He saw one behind the rest, so dived and drove it down out of control.

In the evening two Albatros scouts attacked one of our balloons and 2nd Lt D Langlands, 23 Squadron, succeeded in overtaking them and prevented one from crossing the lines by making it fly west. The EA made frequent attempts to escape but 2nd Lt Langlands followed it closely and continued firing until the German pilot gave in and landed on our side of the lines south-east of Poperinghe and was taken prisoner. An Offensive Patrol of 56 Squadron, when escorting Martinsydes of 27 Squadron, was attacked by four Albatros scouts but these were driven off. Shortly afterwards Capt G H Bowman noticed 15 EA above him, so turned to take his patrol nearer the lines as there was a strong west wind blowing. A number of other machines joined the EA formation and then dived at our SEs who were underneath at 14,000 feet. Our machines were out-numbered and driven down to 4000 feet. Eventually, Captain Bowman secured a favourable position on the tail of one EA which, like all the rest, simply dived past and fired. This machine after being fired at dived straight into the ground, completely crashed. In this fight Lt R G Jardine destroyed one EA, and Lt R A Maybery sent one down completely out of control. In the evening, an Offensive Patrol of 1 Squadron led by Captain W C Campbell encountered eight Albatros scouts which they attacked over Becelaere. Captain Campbell picked out the leader into which he fired a drum and the EA was destroyed. Shortly afterwards he dived at the leader of a formation of 14 EA which the Nieuports attacked, and followed it down until he saw it crash in a field. Sgt G P Olley picked out a scout painted bright green which he shot down and saw crash, and Lt L F Jenkin picked out an EA painted slate-grey and last saw it falling over and over completely out of control. Flight Sub- Lt H Taylor, 10 Squadron RNAS, lost his formation and joined six French machines. When over Polygon Wood they engaged four EA and one, fired on by Flight Sub-Lt Taylor, broke to pieces in the air.

While taking photographs,Lt Carter & 2/AM Farmer, 4 Squadron, were attacked by two Albatros scouts. 2/AM Farmer fired at both in succession and his first opponent was seen by a heavy battery to fall out of control and then break to pieces in the air. During a large encounter which took place over Roulers between ten Albatros scouts and Spads, Sopwith Pups, Camels and SE5s, Captain K C Patrick and 2nd Lt D U McGregor, both of 23 Squadron, each shot down one EA scout completely out of control.

JULY 17

Artillery Co-operation – 90 hostile batteries were successfully engaged for destruction by aeroplane observation, and 24 by balloon observation.

Enemy Aircraft – An Offensive Patrol of 20 Squadron engaged five Albatros scouts shortly after crossing the lines and several were driven down, one falling out of control after being engaged by 2nd Lts W Durrand & F S Thompson. The EA were reinforced by a number of others and during the ensuing heavy fighting Lt D Hoy & 2nd Lt M Tod shot down one EA seen to crash. Immediately after, 2nd Lts

Richards & Wear drove one EA down in a spinning nose-dive and it was seen to crash. A patrol of 11 Squadron met several EA scouts and two-seaters, one of which was driven down by Captain R Raymond-Barker & 2nd Lt E J Price, who immediately attacked another scout which fell in flames. 2nd Lts M S West & F A Adams of the same patrol drove down a two-seater completely out of control. A patrol of 9 Squadron RNAS attacked an EA which crashed north-east of Yser, and another EA was forced to land on the beach after being engaged by Lts R V Curtis and D Uniake. 2nd Lt G I D Marks, 23 Squadron, with seven other Spads, engaged six Albatros scouts over Becelaere and 2nd Lt Marks destroyed one. Flight Sub-Lt C Lowther and flight Lt A W Carter, 10 Squadron RNAS, attacked five Albatros scouts over Polygon Wood and shot a German pilot, whose machine then fell out of control. Five Camels of 70 Squadron encountered a very large formation of about 30 to 40 EA. In the combat two Camels were lost but the other three continued the fight. Capt N Webb drove down two opponents completely out of control, and Lts E C Gribben and J C Smith each drove an EA down out of control.

An Offensive Patrol of six machines of 20 Squadron encountered about 25 Albatros scouts over Polygon Wood. In the engagement which followed 2nd Lts C R Richards & Sgt J J Cowell shot down two EA, both seen to crash, and 2nd Lt R M Trevethan & Lt D Hoy destroyed another. Three other EA were sent down out of control. The fight lasted for about an hour and our machines were reinforced by SE5s, DH5s, Nieuports and Camels. Captain W A Bishop, 60 Squadron, attacked two EA near Havrincourt Wood at 7.40pm. After firing three bursts into one EA it burst into flames and fell. Shortly after he dived on another EA which fell out of control after two bursts and was seen to break up in the air, then crash. 2nd Lt H Scandrett & Cpl Ross, 11 Squadron, drove down one EA, and 2nd Lts M S West & F A Adams of the same squadron shot down one which broke to pieces in the air.

JULY 18
Artillery Co-operation – 34 hostile batteries were successfully engaged for destruction with aeroplane observation and 14 with balloon observation.
Enemy Aircraft – Lt S R P Walter, 32 Squadron, drove down an Albatros scout out of control near Polygon Wood, and Flight Lt A W Carter, 10 Squadron RNAS, drove down an Albatros scout out of control near Roulers.
Miscellaneous – No.24 Balloon burst in the air at a height of 2800 feet. The Observers jumped immediately but their parachutes became entangled and only one opened, but both Observers landed safely by means of this one parachute.

JULY 19
During very bad weather, little work was possible.

JULY 20
Artillery Co-operation – 31 targets were dealt with by aeroplane observation.
Enemy Aircraft – Flight Cdr C D Booker, in a Triplane of 8 Squadron RNAS, engaged an EA two-seater which was attacking our artillery machines. The EA fell completely out of control and was last seen at about 300 feet falling into the mist. Three DH4s of 25 Squadron attacked seven Albatros scouts near Haubourdin, and 2nd Lts L Williams & A Roulstone drove one down completely out of control. Lt J D Musgrave & Cpl A Jex, 45 Squadron, and Lts A E Charlwood & Selby of the same squadron each drove down an EA out of control. Captain W A Bishop, 60

Squadron, attacked two EA eight miles east of Havrincourt Wood and drove one down completely out of control. While taking photographs near Plouvain, Sgt Stanley & 2/AM Wardlow, 13 Squadron, were attacked by five EA. As the German formation leader dived past 2/AM Wardlow succeeded in hitting the machine which was seen to fall completely out of control.   A patrol of 10 Squadron RNAS, led by Flight Cdr R Collishaw, saw 20 EA which they engaged. Flight Lt W M Alexander shot one down in flames, and Flight Sub-Lt E V Reid and Flight Cdr Collishaw each shot down one EA out of control. Captain A Coningham and Lt Wells, 32 Squadron drove down a two-seater out of control, then Capt Coningham drove down an Albatros scout out of control. When over Wervicq he saw an Albatros scout below him. The German dived down while being closely followed and then its left wing folded back and it crashed.   In a fight with some 15 EA east of Ypres, SE5s of 56 Squadron claimed four EA driven down out of control.

Photography – 168 photographs were taken during the day.

COMMUNIQUÉ No.98

21 – 27 July 1917

During a week of relatively heavy air activity, No.101 Squadron, flying a mixture of FE2ds and BE12s, arrived in France on July 25, while the day before saw No.45 Squadron take delivery of its first Sopwith Camel, the start of re-equipment, replacing its two-seat Sopwith 1½ Strutters. Two pilots of 48 Squadron, mentioned this week, Captain Brian Baker and Lt Keith Park, were to rise eventually to Air Marshal and Air Chief Marshal, RAF, respectively; Park achieving particular fame for his command of No.11 Group, RAF Fighter Command during the 1940 Battle of Britain, and later command of the aerial defence of Malta during World War Two.

During the period under review (21st to 27th inclusive) we have claimed officially 31 EA brought down and 35 driven down out of control. As will be seen by the combat reports the number "claimed" is considerably less than those actually brought and driven down. Approximately 20 tons of bombs have been dropped during this period.

JULY 21

Artillery Co-operation – 77 targets were dealt with by aeroplane observation.

Enemy Aircraft – An Offensive Patrol of four Sopwith Camels of 8 Squadron RNAS, led by Flight Lt R A Little, pursued an EA two-seater which went into a spin and then the tail plane was seen to crumble and it crashed into a wood. In later combats two were driven down out of control by pilots of this squadron. Captain W C Campbell, 1 Squadron, while on patrol, saw a balloon near Wervicq just above a bank of cloud, so he attacked it with Buckingham bullets and it fell in flames. On the evening of the 20th, 2nd Lts M S West & F A Adams, 11 Squadron, were attacked from behind but shot it down in flames, while other pilots and Observers of the same squadron claimed two more EA out of control.

Photography – 479 photographs were taken during the day.

JULY 22

Artillery Co-operation – 170 hostile batteries were successfully engaged for destruction by aeroplane observation.

Enemy Aircraft – Activity was very pronounced up till 12 noon, after which it decreased considerably till 6pm, when it again became above normal. An Offensive Patrol of 1 Squadron saw EA endeavouring to stop RE8s from working. Captain W C Campbell shot down one EA which was seen to crash after breaking to pieces in the air, and 2nd Lt R Birkbeck shot the Observer in another. 2nd Lt W Mansell of the same squadron dived at a two-seater EA and was attacked from behind, but out-manoeuvred the attacking scout and shot it down out of control. An Offensive Patrol of 20 Squadron engaged a big formation of Albatros scouts near Menin, and Lts H G E Luchford & H L Waddington drove down one EA out of control. Flight Cdr R Collishaw, 10 Squadron RNAS, while on patrol with three other Triplanes, attacked a formation of about 20 EA scouts and drove down two out of control. Flight Sub-Lt E V Reid of this same patrol destroyed an EA near Becelaere. While taking photographs west of Douai, Lt A Roulstone & 2nd Lt L F Williams, 25 Squadron, attacked an EA into which they fired 300 rounds, after which it crashed in a field. Flight Lt R A Little and Flight Cdr C D Booker, 8 Squadron RNAS, each drove down an EA out of control. The former pilot fought at 500 feet and after his opponent fell, he dived and fired at machine gunners who were firing at him. Flight Lt P A Johnston and R R Thornely of the same squadron engaged five Albatros scouts near Gavrelle, and one into which Flight Lt Johnston fired fell and crashed, while another attacked by Flight Lt Thornely is reported by infantry to have fallen behind the German lines. While on photographic work, Capt J Morris & Lt D Burgess, 25 Squadron, engaged two EA and shot one down in flames. Captain T F Hazell, 1 Squadron, dived at a two-seater EA and continued firing until his machine just touched the German machine, which was shot down and seen to crash near America. Squadron Cdr R Dallas, 1 Squadron RNAS, brought down a two-seater near Lille. Captain P F Fullard, 1 Squadron, dived at two EA, one of which he destroyed, and then drove down the other out of control. During a patrol of this squadron Captain W C Campbell attacked three enemy balloons, and one was seen to burst into flames.

On reports being received that German aircraft were attacking England, a formation of Bristol Fighters of 48 Squadron was sent to intercept them on their return. When about eight miles north-west of Ostend, five enemy Gothas were seen returning at a low altitude. Captain B E Baker & Lt G R Spencer dived from 16,000 feet to 3000 feet and opened fire at one of the EA, which put its nose down and crashed into the sea. Four hours later the tail of this EA was still seen above the surface. During the day Bristol Fighters of 48 Squadron took part in a lot of fighting, resulting in four EA shot down out of control. Four machines of 10 Squadron RNAS encountered a formation of EA; one EA was destroyed and a second sent down out of control. Lt S R P Walter, 32 Squadron, dived at an EA which was attacking one of ours and drove it down out of control.

Photography – 1483 photographs were taken during the day.

JULY 23

Artillery Co-operation – 127 hostile batteries were dealt with by aeroplane observation, and 34 by balloon observation.

Enemy Aircraft – On the evening of the 22nd a photographic formation of 20 Squadron engaged two formations of six and 15 Albatros scouts respectively between Menin and Wervicq. Two EA were destroyed, one by Lt H W Joslyn & Pte Potter, and the other by 2nd Lt R M Trevethan & Lt C A Hoy, while two others were driven down out of control by 2nd Lt O H D Vickers & Lt J J Cowell in one machine, and Lts N V Harrison & Earwaker in another machine. After this combat an Offensive Patrol of 1 Squadron joined the FEs and, over Wervicq, attacked 20 Albatros scouts. Capt H L Satchell & Lt A N Jenks, 20 Squadron, drove one EA down out of control. Another patrol of 1 Squadron engaged three different EA formations – one of 14, one of seven, and one of 12 Albatros scouts in the Wervicq-Houthem area. Lt L F Jenkin destroyed two EA, Captain T F Hazell shot one down which crashed, and drove another down out of control, while 2nd Lt R Birkbeck also drove one down out of control. Lt J G White, 24 Squadron, encountered six EA and dived at a two-seater, at which he continued firing until within ten yards range, when the EA was seen to fall completely out of control. A patrol of 56 Squadron attacked a formation of 20 EA north-east of Ypres. Lt R A Maybery attacked three EA in succession then became detached from his patrol and met three more EA which he drove off. Shortly after, five EA followed him to over Ypres where our anti-aircraft fire broke up the EA formation. As soon as that happened Lt Maybery turned and attacked, and one EA was forced to land in a field and another crashed. Lt R T C Hoidge of the same patrol took part in the fighting against the first 20 EA and shot down one EA which fell completely out of control. Lt H W Woollett, 24 Squadron, attacked a two-seater EA near Havrincourt and after he had fired 35 rounds into it, it fell and crashed. After this he attacked a second EA which he drove down out of control. While on an Offensive Patrol, 2nd Lt W B Wood, 29 Squadron, saw six Triplanes and five SE5s engage a number of EA scouts. He joined the combat and shot down one EA which crashed. Three other EA were shot down out of control by other pilots.

Photography – 843 photographs were taken during the day.

JULY 24

Artillery Co-operation – 82 active hostile batteries were successfully engaged for destruction with aeroplane observation and 70 from balloon observation.

Enemy Aircraft – Activity was considerably below normal during the day.

Photography – 876 photographs were taken during the day.

JULY 25

Enemy Aircraft – Lt K R Park & 2nd Lt A W Merchant, 48 Squadron, while taking photographs, were attacked by three EA, but drove one down apparently out of control.

JULY 26

Artillery Co-operation – 25 hostile batteries were successfully engaged for destruction from aeroplane observation.

Enemy Aircraft – When escorting bombing machines back to the lines, Bristol Fighters of 48 Squadron were attacked by six Albatros scouts. One was hit as it dived by 2nd Lts J Armstrong & P Shone and fell, then burst into flames. SE5s, Sopwith Scouts and Camels of 9th Wing engaged a large enemy formation over Polygon Wood, and in the fighting Captain N Webb, 70 Squadron, shot down one EA which crashed near Zonnebeke, while Capt G C Maxwell and Lt L Barlow, 56 Squadron, and 2nd Lt J C Smith, 70 Squadron, each drove down one EA out of control.

(Editor's note: Captain Webb's victim was Leutnant Otto Brauneck, Jagdstaffel 22, credited with ten combat victories, who was killed. Captain Webb, himself credited eventually with 14 victories, was killed in action on 16 August 1917 by Leutnant Werner Voss of Jagdstaffel 10, the 37th of his ultimate 48 credited victories).

JULY 27

Artillery Co-operation – 115 targets were dealt with by aeroplane observation and 59 by balloon observation.

Enemy Aircraft – Enemy aircraft were inactive until the evening when they came out in large formations and hard fighting took place, resulting in the German machines being literally driven out of the sky. In the 4th Brigade area it was almost impossible to get them to fight, while east of Ypres, where a number of different types of our machines engaged a large EA formation closely, eight were destroyed and at least nine more driven down out of control. No.20 Squadron fought magnificently throughout and lost no machines. Only one of our aeroplanes, an SE5 of 56 Squadron, is missing from this combat. Most of this fighting took place after 6pm, and further details will be included in next week's RFC Communiqué No.99. Flight Cdr R A Little and Flight Sub-Lt R Macdonald, 8 Squadron RNAS, observed an EA two-seater crossing our lines, so took up a position between the EA and the lines, and on its return it was engaged and destroyed. Flight Sub-Lt J H Forman, 6 Squadron RNAS, engaged an EA below him which burst into flames and fell into the sea. Four machines of 32 Squadron engaged ten Albatros scouts and one two-seater near Polygon Wood. A determined attack was made on the two-seater which no enemy scout attempted to protect and it was destroyed. Lt Williams & Sgt Morris, 7 Squadron, were attacked by two EA over Langemarck. When about 100 yards off, one swerved away and Sgt Morris opened fire at the other, with which our machine nearly collided, and the EA fell and was seen to crash.

In other combats, Lt T B Hunter, 56 Squadron, shot down one EA which crashed, while at least seven other EA were claimed as shot down out of control by various pilots. Captain G H Bowman, leading a patrol of 56 Squadron, crossed the lines at Ypres at 7.30pm at 14,000 feet. Nine enemy scouts were observed below so the SE5 formation dived at them. Capt Bowman drove one scout down in a spin and followed it, but was attacked by two more scouts and one of his guns failed to work. He was driven down to 4000 feet but Lt R Maybery who saw his position dived and shot down one of the attacking scouts out of control. Shortly after, when at 3000 feet and a long distance over the lines, Capt Bowman was attacked by an EA which was painted a brilliant red all over and was clearly handled by a skilful pilot and experienced fighter. To quote Capt Bowman: " I still had only my Lewis gun working and was driven down to about 1000 feet by the EA diving on me and zooming away. Each time the German pilot did a climbing turn to dive on my tail again I was able to fly straight towards the sun as I was too low to distinguish landmarks. The enemy pilot noticed that I always made towards our lines while he went round for his next dive, so the third time after his dive he did a straight zoom and stall at the top and dived again as I was flying straight for the line. The next time he dived I throttled back and he over-shot me. He zoomed straight up as usual and I zoomed after him. I got directly below, and with my top gun pulled down, fired about 50 rounds at a range of 20 feet. His machine went down vertically into the ground and crashed about two miles west of Roulers. " After this another EA got on Capt Bowman's tail who found his Lewis gun had also jammed. He had to swerve from right to left and to dive into fields and zoom over hedges to avoid the fire which the German pilot kept up. After a while Capt Bowman got his Vickers gun to work, and at that time the enemy pilot stopped firing, apparently having run out of ammunition, and Capt Bowman turned and fired at him. The fighting was so near the ground that in turning to avoid being shot down, the German pilot flew right into a tree at the edge of a forest and crashed. After this, Capt Bowman flew towards the sun and eventually crossed the trenches at about 50 feet.

COMMUNIQUÉ No.99

28 July - 3 August 1917

The intensive air activity during the last days of July were in the run-up support for the battles of Ypres which commenced on August 1st and were to last until November 10th, 1917.

For the month of July we have claimed officially 122 EA brought down and 120 driven down out of control by aeroplanes. The number actually reported to us far exceeds this. Nearly 67 tons of bombs have been dropped, and over 13,000 photographs taken. 1940 hostile batteries have been successfully engaged for destruction by artillery from aeroplane observation; 345 gun pits have been destroyed, 973 damaged, and 953 explosions caused. During the period under review (28th July to 3rd August inclusive) we have claimed officially 26 EA brought down and 16 driven down out of control.

JULY 28

An EA brought down by Flight Cdr R A Little and Flight Sub-Lt R Macdonald, 8 Squadron RNAS, fell behind the German trenches. The bodies of the aviators were extracted and when about 30 men had gathered round our artillery opened fire and about 12 men were killed. Two officers arrived in a car and one of these was also killed. Flight Cdr Little then attacked enemy troops in their trenches with machine gun fire.

Artillery Co-operation – 128 hostile batteries were successfully engaged for destruction by artillery from aeroplane observation.

Enemy Aircraft – On the evening of the 27th, as reported in RFC Communiqué No.98, very heavy fighting took place, with the result that German aviators were totally beaten and driven east in all the big engagements. This was principally noticeable on the front of the Fourth Army and east of Ypres, where 20 Squadron took part in a fight between many types of our machines and about 20 Albatros scouts. 2nd Lt R M Makepeace & Pte Pilbrow dived on one which fell in flames, and destroyed two others near Polygon Wood. Lts H G E Luchford & M W Waddington drove down one EA out of control and shot down another in flames. 2nd Lts W Birkett & T A M S Lewis engaged one EA which they shot down and which fell to pieces, and then destroyed a second. Lt H W Joslyn & 2/AM Potter in one machine, and 2nd Lt R M Trevethan & Lt C A Hoy in another each drove down one Albatros scout out of control. 2nd Lt A E Godfrey, 40 Squadron, attacked the lowest machine of a formation of 12 Albatros scouts and drove it down out of control. Captain B E Baker & Lt G Spencer, 48 Squadron, drove down an EA on to whose tail a Camel was seen to obtain position at low altitude and this EA burst into flames and crashed into the sea. Capt F Holliday & Lt W O'Toole of the same squadron dived at two DFWs and drove one down out of control. Twelve machines of 10 Squadron RNAS encountered six EA near Tourcoing and Flight Lt A W Carter drove one down out of control. Flight Cdr R Collishaw attacked three Albatros scouts, shot down one which fell to pieces, and a second completely out of control. Flight Sub-Lt E V Reid attacked an Albatros scout which folded up in the air before it crashed, then attacked another which fell out of control. Shortly after he met another EA more skillfully handled but destroyed it. A patrol of 23 Squadron also encountered a large formation of EA and a two-seater attacked by Capt R H G Neville and 2nd Lt F Gibbs was destroyed. 2nd Lt C W Warman shot down one EA out of control. Seven machines of 29 Squadron attacked five Albatros scouts painted red. 2nd Lt J K Campbell shot one down out of control, and Sgt Bathurst destroyed one. 2nd Lt C W Cudmore fired into an Albatros scout at close range and it was seen to break up in the air, then crash. Capt A Coningham, 32 Squadron, attacked and shot down an Albatros scout out of control, while another was crashed by four pilots of his squadron. An Offensive Patrol of 1 Squadron engaged five Albatros two-seaters over Comines. Capt P F Fullard drove one down and followed it for about five minutes, after which the EA fell and crashed. Shortly after, ten EA scouts attacked our patrol and were reinforced by 12 more. Lt L F Jenkin engaged one painted green with black stripes and after 40 rounds it fell in a spin and crashed. Near the end of the patrol Lt Jenkin, and a DH5, dived at an EA two-seater and destroyed it. An Offensive Patrol of 45 Squadron engaged eleven Albatros scouts near Comines, and one was shot down by 2nd Lt M B Frew and Lt G A Brooke. Captain W C Campbell, 1 Squadron, saw five balloons up between Westroosbeke and Gheluwe and attacked the northerly one first, which burst into flames and fell. He attacked a second but his gun jammed and he returned to his aerodrome. On clearing the jam he returned to the lines and attacked another balloon which fell in flames. While escorting bombing machines, 48 Squadron engaged three Albatros scouts. Capt B E Baker & Lt G Spencer fired at one EA which dived away and was then attacked at closer range by 2nd Lt Binnie & Cpl V Reed, and fell in flames. Lts V Curtis & D Uniacke drove down another EA out of control. Flight Sub-Lt N M Macgregor and Flight Lt R R Winter, 6 Squadron RNAS, destroyed one EA. While on Offensive Patrol, 2nd Lts W R Brookes and T A Doran, 23 Squadron, attacked two Aviatiks east of Polygon Wood and destroyed one. When returning from bombing Heule and Bisseghem aerodrome, five machines of 57 Squadron encountered 30 enemy scouts, of which one was seen to break up in the air, and at least six others were claimed as shot down out of control, including one with streamers who was apparently the EA leader. Lt R T C Hoidge, 56 Squadron, saw an EA manoeuvring in circles behind a Sopwith Camel, so followed on the outside of the EA, then throttled back, crossed the circle, and fired at very close range. The EA fell to pieces and crashed. Lt D Wilkinson of the same squadron, when at 14,000 feet, met eight EA over Roulers. He dived and fired at one scout which broke to pieces in the air, then crashed. An Offensive Patrol of 66 Squadron joined other British machines fighting EA and 2nd Lt W A Pritt shot one down which was seen to crash. Lt T C Luke fired 60 rounds into a scout which fell in flames, and two other scouts were claimed shot down out of control. When returning from a bombing raid, Lt Grey & 2nd Lt Rose, 55 Squadron, dived on a two-seater and opened fire, and after two bursts one of the EA's wings crumpled up and it crashed. Machines of 70 Squadron met six EA, and Capt N Webb picked out the leader and fired and it fell straight to the ground in a vertical nose-dive and crashed. When returning from a bombing raid, De Havilland 4s of 57 Squadron met a formation of Albatros scouts. 2nd Lt Biedermann & L/Cpl Clarke shot down one EA in flames, Major E G Joy & 2nd Lt F Leathley shot down two others, one in flames and the other seen to crash, while Capt H Harker & Lt W Barclay shot down one EA out of control. Captain W A Bishop, 60 Squadron, saw three EA in the neighbourhood of Phalempin and shot one down in flames.

Photography – 1022 photographs were taken during the day.

JULY 29
Artillery Co-operation – 76 hostile batteries were successfully engaged with aeroplane observation, and 84 by balloons.
Enemy Aircraft – Captain W A Bishop, 60 Squadron, when leading a patrol, attacked four EA which were soon reinforced by others. In the fighting Capt Bishop shot down one EA out of control. A patrol of 22 Squadron, led by Capt C M Clement, pursued four two-seater EA, one of which turned to fight while the others continued to fly east. This EA eventually burst into flames and crashed. Flight Lt A T Whealy, 9 Squadron RNAS, saw an Albatros scout flying on the edge of a cloud, so dived and opened fire before the EA pilot realised his presence, and the scout burst into flames. Flight Sub-Lt O C Boutillier of the same squadron saw several EA near Leke, and dived at one which had secured a position on the tail of a Triplane, and destroyed it. While on patrol, Capt Williams and Lts Taylor, Turner and Pearson of 32 Squadron saw an EA two-seater doing artillery work in the vicinity of Langemarck, so dived – taking care to keep well on the east side of it – and forced the pilot to cross the lines and land on our side. Both occupants were captured, the Observer being wounded.
Photography – 311 photographs were taken during the day.

JULY 30
Bombing – Bomb raids were made on Cuerne, Heule, and Moorslede aerodromes by 27 Squadron.

JULY 31
Rain fell most of the day and clouds were seldom above 1000 feet. In spite of this machines of the 2nd Brigade carried out 14 contact patrols, and the 5th Brigade, 44 (15 by 4 Squadron, ten by 9 Squadron, nine by 21 Squadron, and ten by 7 Squadron). All these were done at a very low altitude and the machines were heavily fired at by rifle and machine gun fire. Every opportunity was seized to harass enemy troops, transport, and to bomb aerodromes, and by firing at low altitudes. Aeroplanes fired 11,258 rounds with machine guns and 15 with revolvers. A few low-flying EA were encountered, and fighting took place generally under 200 feet, resulting in destruction of six EA and one balloon. The following is a brief resume of some of the work:

NO.1 SQUADRON – When over Terhand, at a height of 2000 feet, 2nd Lt H G Reeves was attacked by two EA. He went into a spin; the EA followed him down, and one dived past him, so he flattened out at about 200 feet, fired a burst at close range, shot the EA down and saw it crash. Lt L F Jenkin flew to Herseaux aerodrome and fired into the hangars and at EA on the ground from 200 feet. One scout was set on fire. 2nd Lt Maclaren fired 80 rounds from 500 feet into a column of horse and motor transport two miles long on the Gheluwe-Menin road and caused great confusion. Captain T F Hazell fired 90 rounds from 800 feet into a battalion of infantry in close formation in Tenbrielen, then fired 50 rounds from 600 feet into some transport on the Wervicq-Becelaere road. Captain W C Campbell went down to 50 feet over Mouveaux aerodrome and fired 300 rounds into 12 two-seaters which were lined up. He was then attacked by three EA and slightly wounded.
NO.45 SQUADRON – Lt J C B Firth and 2nd Lt V R S White fired 300 rounds at transport and two cars on the Becelaere-Zonnebeke road from 500 feet. Lts A E

Charlwood and Ward pursued a hostile anti-aircraft gun mounted on a lorry along the Warneton-Comines road and fired 800 rounds. 2nd Lts K B Montgomery and R C Purvis fired 400 rounds from 400 feet into enemy troops on a canal bank. 2nd Lt M B Frew and Lt G A Brooke, when flying at 1000 feet, saw two companies of infantry on the Comines-Deulemont road and fired 800 rounds into them. 2nd Lts N Macmillan and L M Copeland fired 300 rounds from 800 feet into hutments and stationary transport at Korentje.

NO.1 SQUADRON RNAS – Flight Sub-Lt J S de Wilde went down to 400 feet at Coucou aerodrome and fired 180 rounds into the hangars. Flight Sub-Lt C B Ridley went down to 150 feet and fired 200 rounds into the hangars of Recklem aerodrome. Flight Cdr F H M Maynard fired 250 rounds into a convoy a quarter of a mile long just north of Menin from 200 feet. He returned for more ammunition and went out again. Flight Sub-Lts E Anthony and A G A Spence each fired 100 rounds from 400 feet into the German trenches at the junction of the 9th and 10th Corps. Flight Sub-Lt Everitt fired 100 rounds from 300 feet into 12 tents just west of Menin. Flight Sub-Lt R P Minifie flew out to Gheluwe and fired into a number of huts from 200 feet. He then flew up and down the Menin-Ypres road at 200 feet, engaging parties of troops, firing 150 rounds. Flight Sub-Lt S W Rosevear fired into a mass of huts from 200 feet at Gheluwe. Flight Sub-Lts J S Rowley and C B Ridley each fired 250 rounds from 300 feet into gun-pits south-east of Armentieres. Flight Sub-Lt C G Brooke fired 200 rounds on a camp west of Menin from 300 feet.

NO.4 SQUADRON – 2nd Lts Lewis & Stevens, Lt Thomas & 2nd Lt Hodgson, and Lt Corbould & 2nd Lt Robson, all attacked hostile troops from low altitudes.

NO.32 SQUADRON – Lt Taylor attacked and scattered an enemy party from 500 feet. Lts Salt, St Clair, and H J Edwards fired into trenches near Langemarck from 100 feet.

NO.9 SQUADRON – 2nd Lts G N Moore & Dumbell attacked transport in Poelcappelle from 200 feet, then attacked enemy troops in shell holes.

NO.10 SQUADRON RNAS – Lt G L Trapp engaged infantry on the Menin-Gheluvelt road from 1000 feet.

NO.23 SQUADRON – Lt C W Warman engaged an EA at 200 feet and fought it down to 50 feet, from where it fell and crashed. 2nd Lt F Gibbs fired 250 rounds from 300 feet on troop parties. He then engaged a field battery east of Polygon Wood. Lt T A Doran fired 100 rounds from 200 feet on German troops. Lt G I D Marks went down to 100 feet and fired 300 rounds at troops near Westroosbeke. He then attacked a field battery from the same height near Polygon Wood. 2nd Lt C K Smith fired 50 rounds into lorries north-east of Houlthulst Forest from 600 feet.

NO.29 SQUADRON – Lt D F Hilton met an EA over Westhoek at a low altitude and destroyed it. Subsequently, when flying at 500 feet he observed a gun, carriages and horses, and fired 50 rounds into them. Lt W B Wood encountered two EA east of Polygon Wood and fought both, destroying both of them. Later, at a height of 100 feet east of Polygon Wood, he emptied a drum into a machine gun emplacement which had fired at him. 2nd Lt H M Ferreira, when at 1000 feet near Gheluvelt, saw 50 infantry on the road and fired into them.

NO.66 SQUADRON – 2nd Lt C L Morley flew to Abeelhoek aerodrome and dropped three 20lb bombs, then fired at some mechanics in a shed and at a machine gun firing at him. Lts W Pritt and Huxley flew across the lines at low altitude and machine-gunned enemy vehicles, and some troops crossing a bridge over Heulebeke stream.

NO.70 SQUADRON – Lt F H Bickerton saw men leading horses on the Roulers-Iseghem road and fired 140 rounds into them at 200 feet.

NO.27 SQUADRON – Lt S Campbell dropped one 230lb bomb on Herinnes (east of Roulers) which burst on the railway line and caused a large explosion. Captain R B Bourdillon went down to 100 feet and dropped one 230lb bomb on Grammene (between Thielt and Deynze). Captain H Rushford dropped one 230lb bomb from 600 feet on a railway track at Ingelmunster. It missed the target by a few feet. 2nd Lt Schoones dropped eight 20lb bombs on Heule aerodrome from 2000 feet. 2nd Lt G Smith dropped eight 20lb bombs on Ingelmunster aerodrome from 1800 feet. 2nd Lt R H Ayre dropped seven 20lb bombs from 700 feet on a railway station between Courtrai and Audenarde. Lt R H S Hunter dropped eight 20lb bombs on Marcke aerodrome from 200 feet and then fired into the hangars.

NO.56 SQUADRON – Lt E Turnbull attacked parties of troops on the Ypres-Menin road from 200 feet, and on going further east saw some machine gun emplacements with troops, so went down to 100 feet and fired 140 rounds into them. The following is an account given by Lt R A Maybery who went out with 20lb bombs: "Left Estree Blanche at 4.45am. Crossed the lines over Ypres at 500 feet just underneath very thick clouds. Got into the smoke from the artillery barrage and found it impossible to see ahead at all. Went south-east and found myself over Wervicq at 200 feet. Dived down to about 30 feet and flew straight along the road to Gheluwe. From there I went due east to Bisseghem. I could then see Courtrai and went north-east to strike Heule, but two EA scouts appeared from over Courtrai and attacked me. I manoeuvred to try to throw them off, pulling down my Lewis gun and firing short bursts to try to frighten them away, but they would not be shaken off, so I made west again. Both EA followed until I reached the lines south of Armentieres, when they turned south-east towards Lille. I then turned north, striking the canal at Comines, and again followed the same route to Bisseghem, when I saw a Spad just south of me firing at something on the ground and flying west. It was now getting a little clearer and I could see Courtrai more easily though the clouds were still at 500 feet. From Bisseghem I went north-east and immediately saw Heule aerodrome. I zoomed up to just under 200 feet. Circling round the aerodrome, the only sign of activity I could see was one man lighting two smoke fires at the Heule end of the aerodrome. This man looked at me but did not seem to take any particular notice. I then flew east, turned and came back along the line of the southernmost sheds and dropped my first bomb, which hit the third shed from the east and exploded. This caused enormous excitement and I could see people running about all round the sheds. Turning sharp to the left, I flew north along the line of the eastern most sheds and dropped another bomb which hit the first shed from the south and exploded. Turning sharp to the west, I flew straight at the sheds at the Heule end of the aerodrome and dropped my third bomb which hit the second shed from the east, and either went through the roof or in at the front, as I could see smoke coming out of the front and heard and felt the explosion, but could not see it. Turned north, again flew down the line of the easternmost sheds from the north. As I came near, a machine gun opened fire from the back of these sheds. I pulled the bomb release but nothing happened. Flying straight on and still watching for the explosion, I found myself approaching Courtrai Station, so pulled the bomb release again. The bomb fell and exploded between a goods train and a big shed. Turned north again to Heule aerodrome and the same machine gun and another, which I could not locate, opened fire. I dived at the former, shooting with both guns, and the crew dispersed. Turning to try and locate the second gun, it suddenly stopped. I then flew straight across the aerodrome at the southernmost sheds, firing both guns into the sheds from 20 feet. Changed Lewis drum and flew straight across the aerodrome from the west, firing both guns at the sheds in front, and at one time actually touched the ground. Zoomed over the sheds and flew straight on to Cuerne aerodrome, again attacking the sheds with both guns, driving back a machine which was just being got out. Leaving the aerodrome, saw two horsemen who looked like officers. Attacked them and their horses bolted. Turned west and attacked a goods train going from Courtrai to Menin via Bisseghem. Saw a column of infantry about 200 strong on the road just west of Wevelghem marching towards Menin, and attacked them with both guns. They scattered to both sides of the road, changed drums, turned back east, and attacked infantry again. Looking up, saw one EA two-seater at about 500 feet just below the clouds making east. Zoomed up and got very close under EA's tail without being observed. Pulled down Lewis gun and fired half a drum into EA which started going down in a steep left-handed turn. EA straightened out again and I followed, firing Vickers gun. EA crashed just north of the railway, south of the G in Wevelghem. Only one man got out. A small crowd started to collect and I dived firing both guns. The crowd either ran or lay down flat. Saw a passenger train coming (towards Courtrai) and attacked, but Lewis gun ran out of ammunition, and the Vickers gun stopped. Flew west, recrossed the lines south of Messines and returned."

(Editor's note: Heule and Cuerne aerodromes were at the time the bases for Jagdstaffel 10 and 4 respectively, both units of the "Richthofen Circus". Captain Richard Aveline Maybery, MC & Bar, credited with 21 combat victories, was killed in action on 19 December 1917 by Vizefeldwebel Artur Weber of Jagdstaffel 5).

AUGUST 1ST, 2ND AND 3RD – No service flying was possible owing to unfavourable weather conditions.

COMMUNIQUÉ No.100

4 – 10 August 1917

AUGUST 4

Very little flying was possible owing to the low clouds and rain all day. Lts Finch & Sleep, 9 Squadron, while on artillery work, attacked enemy transport in Langemarck from 900 feet. Lt Curtis & A M Bell of the same squadron also attacked targets from the same height, and Lt Fish, 32 Squadron, fired at enemy troops in trenches. Captain R B Bourdillon, 27 Squadron, dropped one 230lb and four 20lb bombs from 5700 feet on Cortemarck Station.

AUGUST 5

Enemy Aircraft – While dropping bombs on Mouveaux aerodrome, DH4s of 25 Squadron engaged five Albatros scouts, and one was shot down in flames by Capt Morris & Lt Burgess, and another seen to crash after having been engaged by Lts C T Lally & Blackett. 2nd Lt E Mannock, 40 Squadron, engaged five Albatros scouts near Henin-Lietard. He shot one down out of control but was unable to see it crash owing to the presence of other EA. 2nd Lt L M Barlow, 56 Squadron, in an engagement between SE5s and about ten enemy scouts, destroyed one EA, and Capt C F Collett, 70 Squadron, shot one down out of control. 2nd Lts M Allport & W C MacMurray, 5 Squadron, engaged an enemy two-seater which got into a spin and crashed in our lines. The EA pilot and Observer were both injured and the former died from his injuries. Lt A McKeever & 2nd Lt L A Powell, 11 Squadron, attacked an Albatros scout which they shot down out of control. Immediately after this, another Albatros scout came out of the clouds and was shot down in flames by the same pilot and Observer, who had several indecisive combats but succeeded in shooting down a third Albatros scout which fell out of control. Captain W A Bishop, 60 Squadron, flying an SE5, when with his patrol which engaged eight EA, shot down one of his opponents in flames, then attacked a second which he drove down out of control. During the same combat, Capt W E Molesworth and Lt C S Hall, also of 60 Squadron, shot down another EA in flames. 2nd Lt Mitchell, 29 Squadron, saw an EA two-seater below him and drove it down completely out of control after firing 70 rounds at close range.

AUGUST 6

Artillery Co-operation – 33 hostile batteries were successfully engaged from aeroplane observation.

Enemy Aircraft – Captain W A Bishop, 60 Squadron, saw three EA below him when near Vis-en-Artois, so flew over a cloud using it as a cover, then dived through and opened fire at the EA. As they did not return fire he suspected a trap so zoomed up through the cloud and found that three other EA scouts were diving to attack him. He opened fire at the nearest one which fell out of control and crashed. After this, Captain Bishop was joined by Capt C M Clement & Lt Carter in a Bristol Fighter of 11 Squadron, and the two machines then attacked the EA and dispersed them.

Photography – 230 photographs were taken during the day.

Miscellaneous – Owing to a heavy ground mist Lts A W Little & J G Sharpe, 34

Squadron, went a long way over the enemy's lines in order to locate hostile batteries. They were heavily fired at with machine gun fire, but not by anti-aircraft until they turned west, when both "Archie" and machine gun fire was very severe. One machine gun was observed on top of a house, so the pilot dived at it and it was temporarily silenced. He returned to Middelkerke and the RE8 was hit by anti-aircraft fire and its engine damaged. The pilot glided in a westerly direction, while heavily fired at the whole time, and landed 300 yards the other side of the canal. The machine turned over and the Observer was thrown clear, but the pilot had to be helped out. They both ran along the beach under heavy fire from rifle and machine guns, then threw off their heavier garments and dived into the canal. Barbed wire greatly retarded their progress, but eventually they reached the opposite side, and after further exciting experiences, were taken in charge by a sentry and finally taken to the HQ of the Manchester Regiment. While running along the opposite bank eight Germans pursued them to the edge of the canal, and then two of the enemy took shelter in a barrel in the remains of an old bridge. This barrel was riddled with bullets from our front. Lt Little got the gunners to open fire on his RE8 and it was soon destroyed.

AUGUST 7

Artillery work was attempted at intervals. Twelve machines of 27 Squadron went out independently carrying a 230lb bomb each, and Captain R B Bourdillon carrying four additional 20lb bombs. Lt S J Stewart released his from 500 feet and it fell on the line half-a-mile south-west Gyseghem (half-way between Termonde and Alost) and a tremendous hole was made in the embankment and the rails were seen to be all twisted. Lt Aire dropped his bomb from 500 feet one mile east of Schoonaerde (between Termond and Wetteren) and it blew one truck of a moving train completely off the line, and the pilot then opened fire at the engine. Scores of troops leapt out of the train and ran to a wood, then opened fire at the aeroplane. Captain R B Bourdillon lost his way, so came down very low and read the name on a station platform which proved to be Lede (north-east of Alost). He dropped a 20lb bomb from 800 feet and it fell 50 yards from a train, and a second one fell 12 yards from a small shed which he believed contained ammunition. He dropped his 230lb bomb from 500 feet on a train loaded with pit-props in Melle Station and two of the trucks containing props went right up into the air. After this he dropped two 20lb bombs on new sidings north-west of Melle. One exploded near a train carrying a wagon, and the other apparently failed to explode. Captain H Rushford saw his bomb burst on the line about 100 yards north of Menin Station, while Sgt S Clinch hit the embankment north of Menin.

AUGUST 8

Five hundred rounds were fired from 1500 feet into trenches by machines of 54 Squadron. Lt Webster, 23 Squadron, fired 50 rounds into Staden Station and also attacked a wagon drawn by horses and two lorries, while Lt Howes of the same squadron attacked German infantry from 100 feet. Lt Fish, 32 Squadron, fired at German troops and into trenches from a low altitude, and Lts Thorowgood and Wells opened fire from 200 feet into trenches which were closely packed with enemy troops. Captain R M Williams and Lts W R G Pearson and Wells also attacked other trenches. Machines of 7 and 9 Squadrons also used their machine guns against German troops. *Photography* – 356 photographs were taken during the day.

Enemy Aircraft – Flight Lt R P Minifie and Flight Sub-Lt C G Brook, 1 Squadron RNAS, attacked five Albatros scouts, and the former pilot shot one down in flames, while Flight Sub-Lt Brook drove one down out of control. An engagement took place between 20 Squadron and about 25 EA, and in the fighting 2nd Lt R M Trevethan & Lt C A Hoy shot down two completely out of control. 2nd Lts H Scandrett & Herron, in a Bristol Fighter of 11 Squadron, dived at six Albatros scouts and drove one down out of control. Captain R M Williams, 32 Squadron, attacked two Albatros scouts and drove one down out of control. 2nd Lt D U McGregor, 23 Squadron, attacked an Albatros scout into which he fired 170 rounds at close range and it fell out of control.

AUGUST 9

Artillery Co-operation – 43 targets were successfully engaged from aeroplane observation.

Enemy Aircraft – While engaged on artillery work, 2nd Lt Hutchison & Lt Williams, in an RE8 of 16 Squadron, observed an Albatros scout flying at about 1000 feet, apparently co-operating with infantry. When fire was opened at the EA it fired a white Very Light and was joined by another Albatros scout. The RE8 continued firing from a range of 400 yards and shot down one Albatros which crashed. 2nd Lts R Dawson & E Williams, in an Armstrong Whitworth FK8 of 2 Squadron, were attacked by an Albatros scout but drove it down completely out of control. 2nd Lts F Woollett & D McKerron of the same squadron were attacked by two EA and drove one down out of control. Captain P F Fullard and 2nd Lt W Rooper, 1 Squadron, destroyed a two-seater EA near Houthulst Forest. A patrol of Bristol Fighters of 11 Squadron engaged six Albatros scouts and 2nd Lt C G O McAndrew & Lt McKinney shot one down which was seen to break to pieces in the air, then crash. After this they drove down another scout completely out of control. SE5s of 60 Squadron engaged eight Albatros scouts over Cagnicourt and Captain W Molesworth destroyed one EA, while Lt S B Horn shot down another completely out of control. Captain W A Bishop, 60 Squadron, engaged a scout which was very skillfully handled and drove it down under control. He then attacked a two-seater which he followed down to 6000 feet after which the EA crashed. In other combats, EA were claimed as out of control by 1 Squadron RNAS (3 EA), 3 Squadron (1 EA), and 23 Squadron (1 EA).

Balloons – Machines of 40 Squadron attacked six German balloons. One was shot down in flames by Sgt L A Herbert, and three were seen to be smoking, and the other two hit. 2nd Lt J H Tudhope hit some German telegraph wires with his undercarriage before attacking a balloon . 2nd Lt W Maclanachan flew over a troop of cavalry and his undercarriage hit the officer leading.

Machines of the 5th Brigade also attacked German balloons, and one was brought down in flames by Lt C W Warman, 23 Squadron, who used Buckingham ammunition.

Photography – 658 photographs were taken during the day.

AUGUST 10

Artillery Co-operation – 95 targets were successfully engaged from aeroplane observation.

Enemy Aircraft – 2nd Lt J Barlow, 40 Squadron, dived at an Albatros scout but was then attacked from behind, so he turned sharply and drove his opponent down out of control. Capt A W Keen of the same squadron drove down another Albatros scout which he believed fell out of control. 20 Squadron engaged eight Albatros scouts near Polygon Wood and Capt A N Solly & Lt C Hoy drove down one EA out of control. Later in the day Capt Solly & 2nd Lt Cawley as Observer shot down an EA two-seater artillery machine in flames. A patrol of 1 Squadron encountered six Albatros scouts over Becelaere and Capt P F Fullard and 2nd Lt McLaren each drove one down out of control. Another patrol of this squadron fought four Albatros scouts and Capt T F Hazell drove one down out of control and Lt R Birkbeck also drove one down out of control. A formation of Albatros scouts was engaged by 45 Squadron and one was shot down by Capt M Findlay & 2nd Lt Mullen. The same patrol next engaged seven more EA scouts and 2nd Lt M B Frew & Lt G A Brooke drove one down out of control. Flight Cdr F H M Maynard, 1 Squadron RNAS, also drove down an Albatros scout out of control. A patrol of 29 Squadron encountered eight EA and 2nd Lt D F Hilton attacked one which fell out of control, while 2nd Lt W B Wood of this squadron saw three two-seater EA, one of which he sent down out of control. While on artillery work, Capt Robbins & 2nd Lt Davies, 4 Squadron, were attacked by three Albatros scouts. One attacked the RE8 from behind and then the enemy's gun appeared to be jammed for he ceased firing, and after several bursts from the RE8 the EA crashed. 2nd Lt G I D Marks, 23 Squadron, joined in a fight between Spads and a German formation, and destroyed one EA. 2nd Lt C K Smith of the same squadron attacked a two-seater DFW which he destroyed. A patrol of 23 Squadron attacked five DFWs escorted by ten scouts, and 2nd Lt T A Doran shot down one DFW completely out of control.

In a fight between a large EA formation and SE5s of 56 Squadron and Sopwith Camels of 70 Squadron, Lt R A Maybery destroyed one EA, and then he and Lt V Cronyn, also 56 Squadron, shot down another EA which crashed. Lt E Gribben, 70 Squadron, got on the tail of one EA which spun down and crashed, while Capt C Collett of the same squadron engaged one EA which anti-aircraft reported to have crashed.

Miscellaneous – While on a night bombing raid 2nd Lt D Gordon, 10 Squadron, went down to 200 feet and fired at a convoy of motor lorries, and the leading lorry crashed into a tree. Four FE2bs of 18 Squadron and three DH5s of 41 Squadron co-operated in an attack by the 17th Corps by shooting at German infantry, anti-aircraft guns, machine guns and batteries. 4000 rounds were fired. Six machines of 32 Squadron harassed the enemy by dropping bombs and using their machine guns. 2nd Lt Edwards dropped two bombs from 500 feet on an enemy strong point, hitting his objective. He then dived and fired from 100 feet at the panic-stricken troops. After this, he attacked gunners at a battery from the same altitude and pursued an enemy machine which was attacking an RE8. 2nd Lt Wilson dropped two bombs from 700 feet, one of which burst among a party of infantry moving towards the line. He then fired 100 rounds from 100 feet at German troops on the march. Subsequently, he drove down an EA two-seater, and fired 100 rounds at German infantry in trenches and shell holes. 2nd Lt Wells fired on enemy strong points from a height of 200 feet but had his petrol tank shot through, so returned to his aerodrome, then went out again on another machine and continued firing at German troops from about 200 feet.

Photography – 565 photographs were taken during the day.

COMMUNIQUÉ No.101

11 – 16 August 1917

During this period German aerial activity was particularly aggressive against Allied troops, observation balloons, and front-line trenches. No.20 Squadron's doughty FE2ds began being replaced by Bristol F2b Fighters during this month, while on the German side the notorious Fokker Dr1 Triplane was introduced to Jagdgeschwader Nr 1 ("Richthofen Circus") by the end of August, although the Albatros D.V. remained the main type of fighter ("scout") in first-line units.

During the period under review (11th to 16th August inclusive) we have claimed officially 54 EA brought down and 36 driven down out of control by aeroplanes, and we have dropped 25½ tons of bombs.

AUGUST 11

Artillery Co-operation – 89 hostile batteries were engaged successfully from aeroplane observation and 23 by balloon observation.

Enemy Aircraft – On the evening of the 10th, while searching for reported EA, Captain P F Fullard, 1 Squadron, fought an EA two-seater which he destroyed. An Offensive Patrol of 45 Squadron engaged three Albatros scouts and one was shot down out of control by Lt O L McMaking & Cpl A Jex. A patrol of Bristol Fighters of 22 Squadron encountered six Albatros scouts north-east of Douai, and one was shot down in flames by Sgts C L Randell & Lambert. Capt C M Clement & Pte Clement attacked one Albatros which they followed down until it fell out of control, but were unable to watch it crash owing to the severity of the fighting. Lts G A Wells & H J Edwards, 32 Squadron, observed a two-seater Albatros below them and shot it down in flames, and it was seen to crash.

Photography – 506 photographs were taken during the day.

Bombing – On the night of 10th/11th, bomb raids were made on Henin-Lietard, Harnes, Carvin, Estevilles, Mouveaux aerodrome, Wervicq Station, Comines, Menin Town & Station, Linselles, Ledeghem Station.

AUGUST 12

Artillery Co-operation – 113 targets were successfully engaged from aeroplane observation and 11 by balloon observation.

Enemy Aircraft – The following narrative of fights by machines of 45 Squadron has been sent by the Officer Commanding that squadron and is of considerable interest: "While on north line patrol Lt O L McMaking and Capt I Mc A M Pender crossed the lines at 6.35pm (on the 11th instant) under the clouds at 4500 feet over Deulemont. While passing a gap in the cloud two Albatros scouts dived at them from the clouds, firing continuously. Cpl A Jex (Lt McMaking's Observer) got in a full drum at the enemy scout from very close quarters. The EA crashed in flames on the canal immediately to the left of Deulemont. The second EA attacked Capt Pender's machine from the side and one bullet passed through both the main petrol tanks and wounded Capt Pender seriously in the back. Pioneer W T Smith (Capt Pender's Observer) got in a full double drum at the EA from close

quarters and it crashed four fields to the left of the first machine. Capt Pender then fainted and his machine got into a spin. As Pioneer Smith could not make him hear, he climbed over the side and forward along the plane to the pilot's cockpit and found the stick wedged between Capt Pender's legs. He pulled Capt Pender back and pushed the stick forward. The machine came out of the spin and Capt Pender almost immediately recovered. Capt Pender then brought the machine and landed his Observer safely near Poperinghe. Members of the 16th Divisional Ammunition Column, where Capt Pender came down, saw Pioneer Smith standing on the side of the machine and heard him encouraging Capt Pender, saying 'Pull her up, sir' as they were about to crash into some hop poles. Capt Pender did pull her up and landed on the other side with very little damage.". Capt A W Keen, 40 Squadron, when patrolling east of Oppy, saw three EA two-seaters at which he dived. One EA turned and flew towards Nieuport, so Capt Keen looped over the EA and opened fire when diving down, and the right-hand planes of the EA folded back, after which it fell and crashed. 2nd Lt E Mannock, 40 Squadron, observed an Albatros scout attacking one of our balloons, so engaged it and brought it down within our lines.
(Editor's note: Leutnant Joachim von Bertrab, Jagdstaffel 30, credited with five victories).

Flight Cdr R Dallas, 1 Squadron RNAS, saw our anti-aircraft bursts so at once left the aerodrome in search of the object of the gunfire, and found an Albatros scout, which he followed over the lines and eventually shot down and saw crash in a field. While searching for reported EA, Capt P F Fullard, 1 Squadron, found a two-seater DFW which he drove down out of control, while Sgt G Olley of the same squadron drove down another two-seater out of control. While escorting DH4s, Bristol Fighters of 48 Squadron engaged four Albatros scouts, three of which dived at Lt A D Coath & 2/AM Walker. The Observer opened fire at one which turned completely over and fell out of control. Another Albatros got on the tail of this Bristol Fighter and was also shot down out of control by 2/AM Walker, and burst into flames before reaching the ground. When on an Offensive Patrol, 2nd Lts S C O'Grady and C W Warman, 23 Squadron, attacked several two-seater Albatros but eventually centred their attention on one, which was shot down out of control and, after falling through cloud, was seen by Lt Gibbes, who was underneath the cloud, to crash. Later in the day Lt Warman destroyed another Albatros. 2nd Lt J D Payne, 29 Squadron, in a fight between his patrol and three Albatros scouts, drove one EA down and followed until he saw it crash. In other combats the following each claimed EA shot down out of control; 2nd Lts K Park & A R Noss, 48 Squadron; Lts G Hyde and Gibbes, 54 Squadron; 2nd Lt H Maddocks, 54 Squadron; Capt T A Oliver, 2nd Lt C W Cudemore, Lt Wilson, and 2nd Lt D F Hilton, all of 29 Squadron; Flight Sub-Lts H Day and G L Trapp, 10 Squadron RNAS; 2nd Lt Briggs, 25 Squadron; 2nd Lts P Kirk & G Fullalove, 55 Squadron.
Photography – 901 photographs were taken during the day.

AUGUST 13
Artillery Co-operation – 120 hostile batteries were successfully engaged from aeroplane observation and 136 by balloon observation.
Enemy Aircraft – A patrol of 40 Squadron engaged an EA formation and Capt A W Keen attacked one which went down in a spin and crashed behind Lens, while

2nd Lt A E Godfrey and Capt G Lloyd each drove an EA down out of control. While searching for reported EA, Capt T F Hazell, 1 Squadron, fought a Rumpler two- seater and a DFW. He dived and fired at the Rumpler which he destroyed. Later in the day, with 2nd Lt H Reeves of the same squadron he attacked a two-seater Albatros and drove it down out of control. An Offensive Patrol of Bristol Fighters of 22 Squadron engaged seven Albatros scouts. Capt C M Clement & Lt R Carter engaged the foremost EA which they shot down out of control. During the latter part of the patrol an enemy scout followed the formation and got fairly close to the rear Bristol, so Capt Clement dived under the Bristol Fighter and then zoomed up and attacked the EA which immediately dived away and was followed by Capt Clement, who continued firing, and the EA burst into flames and crashed. After this, another EA of a bright red colour attempted to get between the Bristol Fighters and the lines. It came straight for the formation and then went off at right angles. Capt Clement and two other machines opened fire at it and it fell out of control. They then observed an EA formation being engaged by SE5s and joined the fight, and Lts J Bush & W M Turner shot one EA down out of control. When flying above the clouds, Captain W A Bishop, 60 Squadron – who has just been awarded the VC (in addition to the DSO and MC previously conferred upon him) – saw three EA diving on him. At 300 yards distance he opened fire, then swerved, but continued firing, and one EA burst into flames. The other two continued to attack so Capt Bishop out-manoeuvred one and engaged the other at close range, and it also burst into flames and fell, and the third EA flew away, but was followed by Capt Bishop who, on looking round, saw both the others still falling in flames near the ground. On the evening of the 12th, Lts Green & Fairweather, 7 Squadron, while on artillery work, were attacked by an Albatros scout. Lt Green put his machine into a spin and his Observer fired a drum into the EA which went into a spin, burst into flames and crashed. 2nd Lts Sayers & Tobin-Willis of the same squadron when on artillery work attacked a two-seater EA which they drove away, but it came back again and was re-engaged and destroyed. Capt G H Morton, 23 Squadron, when taking part in a fight between a patrol of that squadron and six Albatros scouts, shot down one which fell out of control and is reported by a balloon section to have burst into flames. 2nd Lt F J Gibbs, 23 Squadron, attacked a DFW which he destroyed. When on an Offensive Patrol, Camels of 70 Squadron engaged a number of two-seater EA. Capt N Webb dived at one but overshot it, so zoomed up and opened fire from underneath, and this EA fell into a cloud. Shortly after he dived at another which fell into marshy ground in which the whole engine was buried. Captain C Collett of the same squadron dived into a cloud when at 18,000 feet and came out at 7000 feet, saw a two-seater EA, attacked and destroyed it. DH4s of 55 Squadron, when bombing Deynze railway junction, were attacked by EA scouts and in the fighting Capt F Turner & 2nd Lt R Bett destroyed one EA and drove down another in a vertical nose-dive with its engine full on, apparently out of control. Lt C Waters & 2nd Lt G Smith succeeded in destroying one EA and one out of control, while three others were driven down out of control by 2nd Lts A White & A Castle; Lt A Whitehead & 2nd Lt H McDonald and the third by Lt Cook & 2nd Lt Davies. Lt F E Barker, on a Spad of 19 Squadron, succeeded in driving down one EA completely out of control. Lt R A Maybery, 56 Squadron, engaged an EA which was very ably handled. The fight lasted for a long time and, in the end, the EA's propeller stopped and it landed in a field. In the evening 2nd Lt A E Godfrey, 40 Squadron, flying a Nieuport, attacked an Albatros scout which crashed and burst into flames on the ground. At 6.15pm on the 12th, Flight Cdr Simpson and Flight Sub-Lts J W Pinder and R Mellersh, 2 Squadron RNAS, saw three EA between Ostende and Zeebrugge. They followed them to England and pursued them up the Thames, but were unable to reach the height of the EA.

Photography – 498 photographs were taken during the day.

Balloons – Lt R Greenwell stayed in his balloon (No.10) while under heavy shell fire for 50 minutes, as he had registered three guns of the 5th Siege Battery on to a hostile battery and wished to observe the shooting. When the balloon had been badly holed, he threw his maps overboard and descended safely by parachute.

AUGUST 14

A violent storm came at about 7pm when a number of our machines were out, and two failed to return. Lts C A Youdale & A D Ashcroft, 9 Squadron, obtained valuable information from a reconnaissance over enemy lines at a very low altitude, and fired 350 rounds, causing many casualties among German troops from a height of 800 feet. Capt B E Sutton & Lt W F Leach of the same squadron carried out two very extensive contact patrols at a very low altitude. This pilot and Observer fired 200 rounds from 150 feet at shell holes full of German infantry, causing several casualties. On another occasion they attacked 40 enemy troops, then fired into trenches from 200 feet.

Artillery Co-operation – 91 hostile batteries were successfully engaged from aeroplane observation, while 13 batteries and 41 other targets were dealt with from balloon observation.

Enemy Aircraft – Enemy aircraft were active and endeavoured to stop our artillery machines from working, while a number of our balloons were attacked, and they fired at our infantry and batteries from low altitude. After having taken photographs of Phalempin, Capt J Morris & Lt D Burgess on a DH4 of 25 Squadron were attacked by ten Albatros scouts. The DH4 returned safely after destroying one EA and driven another down apparently out of control. An Offensive Patrol of 20 Squadron attacked a two-seater DFW as it was crossing the lines and shot it down in flames. While on patrol, Flight Lt C B Ridley and Flight Sub-Lt S W Rosevear, 1 Squadron RNAS, engaged six EA and each drove one down out of control. Bristol Fighters of 11 Squadron met six Albatros scouts over Brebieres and one EA was shot down in flames by Lt R F S Mauduit & Pte J Mason. Two machines of 10 Squadron RNAS attacked three Albatros scouts which were reinforced by five more. One EA was shot down in flames by Flight Lt J S T Saint. 2nd Lt C R Smith, 23 Squadron, attacked two DFWs and shot one down completely out of control. After this he was wounded and fainted and on recovering found his Spad upside down at 4000 feet with EA still firing at him. He evaded the EA and returned. Capt A T Lloyd, 32 Squadron, saw an Albatros attacking an RE8 so dived to the assistance of the RE and shot the EA down out of control. Lt L M Barlow and 2nd Lt K Muspratt, 56 Squadron, attacked three two-seater EA of an old type, and each drove one EA down to crash.

Photography – 261 plates were exposed during the day.

Bombing – Bomb raids were carried out on the night 13th/14th on Oignies, Berelau, Carvin, Ascq, Somain, Dorignies aerodrome, Phalempin aerodrome, and Abeelhoek aerodrome.

AUGUST 15

Artillery Co-operation – 91 hostile batteries were successfully engaged from aeroplane observation and 23 batteries and 27 other targets from balloon observation.

Enemy Aircraft – Enemy aircraft were active and continually attacked our balloons and fired at our infantry. 2nd Lt A E Godfrey, 40 Squadron, engaged an EA over Lens and drove it down out of control. After bombing Dorignies aerodrome, five DH4s of 25 Squadron engaged a large formation of Albatros scouts, one of which was shot down in flames by 2nd Lts D Jardine & G Bliss. Three machines of 1 Squadron engaged seven Albatros scouts and Capt T F Hazell shot down one in flames, then drove down another out of control, while two other EA were driven down out of control each by Lt C Laver and 2nd Lt H Reeves. When returning from a bomb raid four DH4s of 25 Squadron were attacked by 12 Albatros scouts, and in the fighting Captain J Morris & Lt D Burgess shot one down in flames. Three of the Albatros scouts remained above the clouds, evidently with the intention of diving when a favourable opportunity offered, but Lts C T Lally & J Blacket flew up and kept them engaged and so prevented their diving down. A patrol of six Nieuports of 40 Squadron engaged seven Albatros scouts and Captain A W Keen shot one down in flames and it fell through the centre of the German formation, scattering them, and then he dived at another and shot it down out of control. 2nd Lt R Hall, also 40 Squadron, attacked an Albatros scout near Lens and shot it down out of control, and it was seen to crash on the roofs of houses in Lens. Captain E Mannock of the same squadron drove down an EA out of control near Lens. Three two-seater EA attacked 2nd Lt A Maplestone & Pte Watson,43 Squadron, when they were flying over Bois Dixhuit, but they returned safely after destroying one of these EA. Captains W McClatchie & A Pickering, also 43 Squadron, were attacked by six EA over Lens, but drove one down and evaded the rest. Flight Lt R P Minifie, 1 Squadron RNAS, attacked and shot down an Albatros scout out of control east of Ypres. While on Offensive Patrol Captain W A Bishop, 60 Squadron, dived at three EA and opened fire at one which turned completely over and fell out of control. Flight Sub-Lt F Strathy, 6 Squadron RNAS, observed a large German biplane and, after considerable manoeuvring and firing by both pilots, the EA fell vertically and then broke to pieces in the air. An Offensive Patrol of 54 Squadron noticed a disc out in Sector 2, so flew in the direction indicated and encountered two EA two-seaters. The patrol attacked and Captain O Stewart, assisted by Lts C G Wood and G Clapham, shot down one EA which crashed.

Photography – 235 photographs were taken during the day.

AUGUST 16

The weather was fine and an exceptionally large amount of work was carried out, especially by our low-flying aeroplanes. Enemy aircraft were active and aggressive until the evening and attacked our infantry and artillery machines. In the evening, however, their aggressiveness ceased and they avoided fighting, and apparently attempted to draw our machines east in order to benefit by a very strong west wind which was blowing. The following is a resume of special work and fighting done by our aeroplanes during the day. A patrol of 1 Squadron saw from 50 to 60 enemy scouts in various formations and had a number of engagements. In one instance Captain P F Fullard saw a Spad attacking two EA scouts and watched one of the scouts waiting to get on the Spad's tail, so he dived on this scout which he shot down and saw crash. Shortly after, he took part in another fight and destroyed a second EA. When on patrol after 6pm on the evening of the 15th, Captain Fullard dived at four EA which were attacking an FE from behind but he in turn was attacked by enemy scouts from the rear, but succeeded in out-manoeuvring these scouts and shot one down which crashed. In another fight later he shot down an EA which rolled over and over and was last seen near the ground out of control. On the 16th Lt R Birkbeck of the same squadron drove down a German scout and saw it falling completely out of control into a cloud. Flight Sub-Lt S W Rosevear, 1 Squadron RNAS, joined with a French Spad and attacked four EA, one of which he destroyed. Squadron Cdr R Dallas of the same squadron destroyed an Albatros scout which was attacking an RE8.2nd Lt G Nicholas & Lt W Ferguson, 6 Squadron, while on counter-battery patrol, were attacked by five EA but destroyed one of the Germans, and with the assistance of a Spad which came to help, the other EA were dispersed. Capt F D Stevens & 2nd Lt W C Cambray, 20 Squadron, drove down out of control one of nine Albatros scouts which their patrol encountered. In another engagement between a patrol of this squadron, assisted by Nieuports and Sopwiths, and about 25 Albatros scouts, 2nd Lt O H D Vickers & Lt J A Hone shot down one EA and drove down another out of control, while three others were driven down out of control by 2nd Lt C R Richards & A E Wear, the second by 2nd Lt R M Makepeace & Lt H L Waddington, and the third by 2nd Lts A G V Taylor & M Todd. Captain W A Bishop, 60 Squadron, while pursuing two enemy scouts, saw a two-seater approaching the lines slightly above him, so fired a short burst at this EA which immediately turned on him, and after another burst the EA fell and two planes came off; then the whole machine collapsed and crashed. After this he saw two more scouts which he followed and attacked, and one went into a spin and crashed, but the other succeeded in escaping.

NO.70 SQUADRON
Lt Crang flew to Bisseghem aerodrome where he saw seven hangars, so dropped two bombs from 100 feet, but just missed the hangars. He again flew over the aerodrome and fired into the hangars, but as there was no sign of life he left, and crossed the Courtrai- Ypres railway line where he saw a train in the siding at which he fired. He then turned south and saw an aerodrome (probably Rumbeke) with five hangars into which he fired from 20 feet. He then fired at a two-seater which was out on the aerodrome and, on turning round, saw one of the hangars in flames and a two-seater in flames inside the wrecked hangar. He afterwards fired at an engine on the Courtrai-Tourcoing line, then returned.

NO.66 SQUADRON
Lt C L Morley flew to Abeelhoek aerodrome in the dark and on coming out of the clouds was very heavily fired at by anti-aircraft and had to go up again. He then came out over Harlebeke Station and dropped two 20lb bombs on the railway line, and one each side of the track. Lt W A Pritt flew to Marcke aerodrome in the dark and dropped one 20lb bomb from 100 feet right in the middle of a group of machines on the aerodrome. He dropped a second which fell in a road, and a third which just missed the machines, then dropped a fourth on Herelbout siding

which was full of troops. Just as he was doing this he saw an Albatros scout getting off the aerodrome so attacked it, and saw it crash on the houses north-east of the aerodrome. On turning round he saw another machine getting off the aerodrome. This he also attacked and it made a half-turn, side-slipped, then crashed on the aerodrome. He then silenced a machine gun which was firing at him and returned home. Lt E H Lascelles flew over the lines through the clouds and when he came down he saw a two-seater aeroplane on its nose completely wrecked on an aerodrome which he recognised as Chateau du Sart. He fired 200 rounds into a party of mechanics collected around the wreck and scattered them from a height of 200 feet, then went lower and fired into the hangars.

NO.29 SQUADRON

Lt F W Wilson descended to between 1000 and 500 feet and fired tracers up the main street of Zonnebeke and men were seen to scatter. He then attacked the railway siding where men were working from between 800 and 400 feet. He also attacked a battery position, then fired 50 rounds into the enemy trenches from low altitude. 2nd Lt E Holdsworth attacked troops in reserve in Polygon Wood and Racecourse, firing one drum from between 600 and 300 feet. He then fired 50 rounds at a gun in action from 250 feet and 40 rounds at Iron Cross Redoubt, and a further 40 rounds at two lorries. 2nd Lt E S Meek fired two drums into Polygon Wood and Racecourse from 800 to 500 feet, and half a drum into a house north-east of the Wood from 400 feet; troops were seen to come out and scatter. 2nd Lt P De Fontenay fired a drum at troops in a shell hole from 200 feet, and another drum into a hostile trench full of men north of Polygon Wood. He then fired 70 rounds at enemy troops in shell holes east of Polygon Wood and also engaged several machine gunners who were firing at him. 2nd Lt D F Hilton fired 85 rounds from 400 feet at troops in shell holes and troops on the Westroosebeke – Zonnebeke road, firing about 100 rounds from 100 feet. 2nd Lt J Machaffie fired several bursts from 600 feet into shell holes containing troops on the east bank of the Hansbeke, then attacked two Albatros scouts and drove them both off. He then fired the remainder of his ammunition into enemy trenches from 200 feet. 2nd Lt C Salmond fired one drum at an active hostile battery from 1000 to 500 feet, half a drum into a trench, and the remainder into a railway siding. He also fired half a drum from 200 feet into a wood where there were infantry, and two drums into trenches from a height of 900 to 200 feet. 2nd Lt F J Williams fired three drums into Polygon Wood from 600 feet; 2nd Lt J D Payne two drums from 600 to 50 feet range; 2nd Lt J Collier three drums into Iron Cross Redoubt and Polygon Wood from 800 feet; 2nd Lt J Gilmour about 100 rounds from 200 feet along the Menin road. Lt F Rose dived down to 100 feet and fired at troops in shell holes north of Polygon Wood. 2nd Lt A Colin fired about 65 rounds into a wood occupied by infantry, and also attacked troops on the Westroosbeke – Menin road, firing 20 rounds from 500 feet. While engaged on this work he was attacked from behind by an Albatros scout but out-manoeuvred the EA and, after firing a burst at close range, the EA fell completely out of control. When over Zonnebeke, 2nd Lts D F Hilton and J Machaffie were attacked by three Albatros scouts. 2nd Lt Hilton shot down one scout which was last seen falling through our barrage completely out of control. After this they drove down another Albatros scout out of control.

NO.1 SQUADRON

Lt W S Mansell flew to Mouveaux aerodrome and fired into three machines on the ground from 400 feet, then fired 97 rounds into the hangars from the same height, and on his return journey fired 80 rounds into a train on the Wasquehal – Lille line from 200 feet.

NO.1 SQUADRON RNAS

Flight Sub-Lt R P Minifie went to Chateau du Sart aerodrome and had a combat at a height of 1000 feet. Reports received from other pilots show that the EA was destroyed. He flew on to Mouveaux aerodrome where he fired into the hangars from 500 feet, then fired into Mouveaux Square and into various villages. Flight Sub-Lt Cole and Flight Cdr W M Alexander attacked and drove down an enemy scout out of control.

NO.32 SQUADRON

Capt Phillips fired about 200 rounds into Langemarck from 800 feet. Lt Wilson fired about 200 rounds into strong points from about 200 feet, and also fired into shell holes from the same altitude. Lts Wilson and Simpson attacked enemy troops in shell holes and small trenches about 50 yards west of the Langemarck-Zonnebeke road. Other small bodies of troops coming up from the east, and some lying in shell holes were attacked from about 200 feet.

NO.23 SQUADRON

2nd Lt C W Warman went out to attack Beveren aerodrome. On approaching the aerodrome a white light was fired, whereupon he glided down to 1000 feet and dropped two 20lb bombs on buildings and hangars on either side of the aerodrome. A two-seater DFW was getting off the ground, so he dived at it, firing a long burst from 100 feet, and it crashed. On his way home he saw a hostile battery in action, so glided down to 200 feet and fired a long burst along the line of guns. The battery ceased firing and 2nd Lt Warman sat over it for five minutes, but they did not start firing again. In addition to this he attacked an enemy kite balloon near Passchendaele and shot it down in flames. On the evening of the 15th, when with a patrol of three Spads, he saw two Albatros scouts over Houthulst Forest. He fired into one at close range and it went down and crashed. After this his engine gave trouble so he returned to his aerodrome, and went out again in a new machine. When over Zonnebeke he met an Albatros scout which dived away, but he followed closely and sat on its tail firing until the EA crashed. *(Editor's note: Captain Clive Wilson Warman, DSO, MC, an American, credited with 12 combat victories, died in Canada in a flying accident on 12 June 1919).*

Lt Webster set out to attack Abeele aerodrome and fired from 600 feet into the aerodrome and attacked tents around it. 2nd Lt W R Brookes went out at dawn to bomb Ingelmunster aerodrome and dropped two 20lb bombs which exploded just outside some hangars. He flew up and down the line of hangars at a height of 50 feet, three times. He was fired at by machine guns from the ground which he silenced with a burst of 30 rounds. On the return journey he attacked bodies of troops on the Roulers road, and then attacked an active hostile battery from 900 feet, and fired 50 rounds into a train from 800 feet, and 50 rounds into enemy trenches. 2nd Lt D U McGregor attacked an Albatros scout which was diving on an RE8 and shot it down out of control. Subsequently, in an engagement between his patrol and seven Albatros scouts, he shot down one scout in flames and it was seen to crash. Lt L D Baker observed a battery firing, so dived, fired, and silenced it. He had several indecisive combats, then shot the Observer in a two-seater EA, but was unable to destroy this EA as he was attacked by Albatros scouts, one of which he shot down out of control.

4 SQUADRON
2nd Lt Starley & Lt Grinwood during a counter attack patrol had two longerons, a main spar, a centre-section strut, two fuselage struts and an aileron balance wire cut through by a shell, whilst the wireless transmitter was destroyed and the Observer wounded. Before returning, however, they wrote out the information they had gained and dropped the message to the Divisional HQ, then returned in an almost uncontrollable machine.

7 SQUADRON
2nd Lts N Sharples & O'Callaghan while on counter attack patrol in the vicinity of Poelcappelle attacked and dispersed several parties of enemy troops, firing over 700 rounds in all. 2nd Lts I A Johnson-Gilbert & C Lillieran engaged enemy troops on the ground with machine gun fire north of Poelcappelle. While engaged on counter attack patrol they were attacked by eight Albatros scouts but shot down one which crashed. 2nd Lts L M Isitt & W E V Richards were attacked by two Albatros scouts while on patrol. They shot one down out of control, and on reconnoitring the ground from low altitude an EA was seen on the ground.

NO.21 SQUADRON
Sgt A A L Moir & 2nd Lt M L Hatch, while on flash reconnaissance, were attacked by nine EA, but shot down one out of control, and were engaging an Albatros when they were hit by AA fire and forced to return.

NO.9 SQUADRON
Lts C A Youdale & A B Ashcroft attacked Au-bon-Cite with machine gun fire from 400 feet in the semi-darkness, as the infantry attacked, going through the 18-pdr barrage several times to do so. Lt J Hood & 2nd Lt J MacDaniel met an Albatros scout over Menin and shot it down out of control.

NO.19 SQUADRON
Lt J Manley, when with a French Spad, attacked a formation of 12 enemy scouts over Roulers. He selected one at which he dived and shot it down completely out of control. Lt H L Waite shot down an Albatros scout out of control just when it was firing at an RE8 from behind. Lts A A N Pentland and A R Boeree attacked enemy transport on the Ypres-Menin road.

NO.52 SQUADRON
Lts Wills, Hill, and Sgt Smith each attacked hostile batteries from heights between 1000 and 800 feet.

NO.43 SQUADRON
Lt C L Veitch and 2nd Lt S H Lewis fired 200 rounds at about 100 men in trenches

from a low altitude. On the evening of the 15th, a patrol of Sopwith Camels of 8 Squadron RNAS engaged four Albatros scouts, and Flight Lt R R Thornely drove one down out of control. In encounters between EA and Nieuports of 40 Squadron, Lts G Crole, H Kennedy, and 2nd Lt E Mannock each drove down an EA out of control. Lt H Joslyn & 2nd Lt J Adams, 20 Squadron, in a fight between 20 Albatros scouts and FE2ds, destroyed one EA just as it got on the tail of an FE. Capt A L Gordon-Kidd, 19 Squadron, attacked an Albatros scout, east of Ypres and shot it down out of control.

Bombing – On the night of the 15th/16th, No.100 Squadron dropped eight 230lb, 58 25lb, and four 112lb bombs on Roulers Station, Lichtervelde, Wervicq, Houthem and Lille Goods Station. Capt W J Tempest & Lt R S Greenslade saw a great deal of traffic on the Gares de Fives, which was well lit up, so dropped one 230lb and five 25lb bombs in the centre, then flew up and down the station and fired machine guns. Other targets, bombed on the 16th, included Dorignies aerodrome, Carvin, Raimbeaucourt, and Auby (all by 25 Squadron); Heule aerodrome, Recklem aerodrome, Ingelmunster Railway Siding, Courtrai Station (all by 57 Squadron); Heule aerodrome, Courtrai rail sidings, and Seclin Railway Station (55 Squadron).

COMMUNIQUÉ No.102

17 – 23 August 1917

In a week of high aerial activity by both opposing air forces, two RFC squadrons began to finally replace their obsolete BE2c/d aircraft; No.8 Squadron re-equipping gradually with Armstrong Whitworth FK8s, and No.12 Squadron with RE8s (known by RFC crews as "Harry Tates" after a popular music hall comedian of the time). On the ground the so-termed Battle of Hill 70 (just one of the battles of Ypres) was in progress, necessitating greater efforts by the RFC crews.

During the period under review (17th to 23rd August inclusive), we have claimed officially 51 EA brought down by aeroplane and 45 driven down out of control. Over 36 tons of bombs have been dropped during this period.

AUGUST 17
Artillery Co-operation – Artillery with aeroplane observation successfully engaged 126 hostile batteries for destruction and 14 by balloon observation.
Enemy Aircraft – On the evening of the 16th, when on a bomb raid, five DH4s of 25 Squadron were attacked by eight Albatros scouts, and in the fighting Lt Stubbington & 2/AM Leach shot down one scout in flames, while 2nd Lts Hancock & Algie shot down another out of control. A DFW was destroyed by Capt E Mannock, 40 Squadron, and an Albatros scout shot down out of control by 2nd Lt Gedge & 2/AM Blatherwick. An Offensive Patrol of 20 Squadron engaged eight Albatros two-seaters near Menin, and one was driven down out of control by Lt H G E Luchford & 2nd Lt J Tennant. Captain P F Fullard and Capt T F Hazell, 1 Squadron, each drove down an EA out of control. 2nd Lts R V Curtis & D Uniacke, 48 Squadron, dived at a hostile two-seater but lost sight of it and found themselves in the midst of Albatros scouts, while several more were lower down. One which they attacked crashed in a field and burst into flames. When on a reconnaissance, Major E G Joy & Lt F Leathley, 57 Squadron, shot down an Albatros scout out of control.
   On the 17th a patrol of 48 Squadron fought several formations of EA. In one big fight 2nd Lts K Park & A R Noss saw three EA attacking a Camel, so dived at them, but were immediately attacked by two more from behind. 2nd Lt Noss fired a drum at one and it fell out of control. Two EA dived past the Bristol Fighter, so they followed one EA down and destroyed it. After this, seven more EA scouts attacked but one was hit by the Observer's first burst and turned on its back and fell out of control. The Bristol's front gun then jammed and the pilot turned west, and one of three Albatros scouts which continued to attack from behind was shot down completely out of control. 2nd Lts A Simpson & K Tanner in one machine, and Capt J H Letts & Lt J Jameson in another machine attacked one Albatros scout which was seen to break to pieces in the air and to crash. Sgt W Roebuck & 2/AM W Walker shot down another of the EA which crashed near Ostend. When pursuing two German scouts at 14,000 feet over Harnes, Captain W A Bishop, 60 Squadron, saw a two-seater approaching the lines, so dived past it, firing as he went, and then zoomed up from underneath, fired another burst, and the planes of the EA fell off. Shortly afterwards he attacked two EA scouts (apparently the two which he had

previously pursued) but they would not fight and flew away, so he opened fire on one of them and it went into a spin and crashed. Lt C S I Laver, 1 Squadron, shot down a two-seater DFW out of control. Patrols of 20 Squadron engaged several EA formations at different times, during which 2nd Lt O H D Vickers & Lt J A Hone drove down four out of control, and Lt H G E Luchford & 2nd Lt J Tennant drove down one out of control. When escorting photographic machines, 2nd Lts M West & F Herron, 11 Squadron, attacked two EA. One was driven off and the other shot down in flames and seen to crash. Captain H Woollett, 24 Squadron, drove down a two-seater out of control. Flight Sub-Lt R F P Abbott, 6 Squadron RNAS, was attacked by a Fokker and an Albatros scout, and shot down the Fokker out of control. Lts H J Edwards and Johnston, 32 Squadron, attacked four two-seater Albatros in the vicinity of Zonnebeke. Lt Edwards fired 200 rounds into one at close range after which it fell and crashed and the others flew away. When returning from a bomb raid, Major E G Joy & Lt F Leathley, 57 Squadron, were attacked by four EA who dived on them from behind. Lt Leathley shot down three of these in turn out of control. Sgt Bousher & 2nd Lt Heffer of the same raid also shot an EA down out of control. An Albatros scout which was engaged by Flight Sub-Lt G L Trapp, 10 Squadron RNAS, was driven down out of control. Spads of 19 Squadron had considerable fighting, and Captain A L Gordon-Kidd, Lt F Sowery, and Lt J Manley each shot down an EA out of control. 2nd Lt L M Barlow, 56 Squadron, saw two large EA scout formations which were diving towards our lines in order to protect some of their two-seaters which were being attacked by our Triplanes. He dived at these scouts and destroyed one and drove another down out of control. While escorting bombing machines, 2nd Lt A Gilbert & 2/AM Boxall, 22 Squadron, shot down in flames one of two EA attempting to interfere with the bombing aeroplanes. In other combats, EA were claimed out of control by the following; Captain G H Bowman, 56 Squadron; Capt A Bell Irving and Lt E H Lascelles, both 66 Squadron; Lt J Butler & Flight Sgt W Organ, 22 Squadron; Lt F M Kitto & 1/AM A Cant, 43 Squadron; 2nd Lt R M Makepeace & Gunner J McMechan, and 2nd Lts A G V Taylor M Todd, 20 Squadron.

Photography – 1223 photographs were taken during the day.

Bombing – On the night of the 16th/17th, No.100 Squadron went out three times with bombs, and dropped in all 21 230lb, six 112lb, and 159 25lb bombs on Mouveaux aerodrome, Menin, Courtrai, Comines and Roulers Station. On the 17th bomb raids were made on Raimbeaucourt, Tourmignies aerodrome, Baralle, Courtrai, Cortemarck, Ingelmunster Station.

AUGUST 18

With Aeroplane Observation – Artillery successfully engaged 154 hostile batteries for destruction.

With Balloon Observation – 36 hostile batteries were successfully engaged for destruction, 15 neutralised, and 68 other targets dealt with.

Enemy Aircraft – Hostile activity close to the lines was very much less than on previous days, but large formations were engaged by our long distance bombing and photographic machines. Capt G L Lloyd, 40 Squadron, attacked an Albatros two-seater which he drove down out of control. A formation of eight Bristol Fighters of 11 Squadron encountered a formation of Albatros scouts near Douai. These EA attacked extraordinarily well and persistently, and it was not until they had all been hit and driven down that the combat ceased. Three of our machines failed to return, one having been seen to land under control. One Albatros scout engaged by 2nd Lt C G O McAndrew & Pte Long crashed, while two more were shot down out of control by Lts A J Hytch & I H McRobert in one Bristol, and Capt G H Hooper & Lt H G Kent in another. Another EA was seen to be hit and land in a field by Capt Barnet & Pte Mason. Lts H Thom & R Gaisford, 34 Squadron, when on trench registration, were attacked by an EA scout but destroyed it and continued working. When returning from a bomb raid six DH4s of 57 Squadron engaged 15 EA scouts. Fighting was very severe and one EA was destroyed by 2nd Lts Cook & Bullock. 2nd Lt B A Powers, 19 Squadron, attacked a Rumpler two-seater which fell out of control. 2nd Lt K Muspratt, 56 Squadron, and Capt C Collett, 70 Squadron, each destroyed one EA, while Captains G C Maxwell and J T B McCudden both of 56 Squadron, each drove one EA down out of control.

Photography – 950 photographs were taken during the day.

AUGUST 19

Artillery Co-operation – With aeroplane observation, artillery successfully engaged 89 hostile batteries for destruction, and neutralised 40. With balloon observation, 19 hostile batteries were successfully engaged, and 37 other targets dealt with.

Enemy Aircraft – Enemy aircraft displayed little activity near the front lines, but moved about in large formations a long way back. A patrol of 8 Squadron RNAS attacked a DFW which was shot down out of control by Flight Lt R R Thornely. No.20 Squadron engaged six Albatros scouts near Menin, and one was destroyed by 2nd Lt C B Simpson & Lt R F Hill, and another driven down out of control by 2nd Lt G L Boles & L/Cpl Harrop. In an engagement between Nieuports of 1 Squadron and six EA scouts, Capt P F Fullard got very close to one of his opponents and, after emptying three-quarters of a drum into it, it fell and crashed. When returning from a bomb raid, machines of 57 Squadron were attacked by about 20 EA scouts, one of which was shot down completely out of control by 2nd Lt A Drinkwater & Lt F T S Menendez. Lt C W Warman, 23 Squadron, got within 50 yards of an EA, then opened fire, and it turned completely over and was seen to crash. Captain J T B McCudden, 56 Squadron, whilst leading a patrol, got above an EA formation then dived and selected one painted red with yellow stripes and drove it down out of control. Lt A Pratt, 70 Squadron, also shot down one EA completely out of control. A Rumpler two-seater was shot down over Oosttaverne Wood by anti-aircraft of the 2nd Army. The pilot and Observer were both wounded and taken prisoners.

Photography – 498 photographs were taken during the day.

Aeroplane Co-operation with Infantry Attack – Machines of the Army Wing of the 3rd Brigade fired 9290 rounds from low altitudes at various targets (living) during the course of the successful attacks by the III Corps.

NO.24 SQUADRON

Captain H W Woollett fired at four different large bodies of troop and dispersed them all, and also attacked a wagon which ran off the road. Lt J G White observed troops marching in artillery formation, so dived to 100 feet and attacked, scattering the lot and causing casualties. After this he saw a trench strongly manned so flew up and down it eight times, firing 200 rounds. He then attacked several parties of men. Lt W Statham scattered troops then attacked a trench full of soldiers. Lt A J Brown caused troops marching towards Bony to scatter and fired into trenches.

After this he attacked a machine gun, then flew to Vendhuille where he fired at troops standing on a pavement with their kit. Lt S L Blofeld fired at a trench strongly held and then attacked troops on the march, after which he finished his ammunition at enemy in trenches. Lt C E Woodhams caused troops to disperse by firing at them from 300 feet. Lt J H Jephson kept diving at trenches strongly held by the enemy north of Bony, and then dispersed 40 men on the march. Lt McDonald dispersed troops from 200 feet and inflicted casualties, firing 500 rounds. Lt D Sutherland fired a drum at a lorry on the road. He circled Bony looking for reinforcements but observed a trench to be very strongly manned so dived and fired at these men until his ammunition had been expended.

NO.60 SQUADRON
Lt W E Jenkins observed German reinforcements coming up, so fired 300 rounds at them from low altitude. Lt R B Steele fired 350 rounds at enemy trenches and at troops on the road. Lt Thompson fired 160 rounds at infantry in trenches. Lt W J Rutherford attacked infantry in trenches and on roads from 400 feet. Sgt Bancroft silenced a machine gun and fired 350 rounds into trenches.

NO.41 SQUADRON
Lt Thomas fired 450 rounds into trenches from 500 feet. Lt R Winnicott and 2nd Lt Taylor fired 500 rounds each into trenches. 2nd Lt Chapman fired 230 rounds. Captain Martin attacked trenches and gun emplacements and fired 500 rounds after diving from 20 to 25 times to a low altitude.

NO.18 SQUADRON
Lts Byron & Foord dropped eight bombs and shot several men in trenches during firing 400 rounds, and silenced a machine gun. 42 bullets pierced their machine but both were uninjured. 2nd Lts Bell & Robinson fired 50 rounds into trenches and 250 at machine guns which they silenced, after which they fired 300 rounds at bodies of infantry. They also dropped eight bombs on suitable targets. 2nd Lts Pearman & Moir fired over 200 rounds into communication trenches, and 380 at parties of German troops, in addition to dropping eight bombs. Aeroplanes of the 4th Brigade fired 1150 rounds into trenches.

AUGUST 20
Artillery Co-operation – 105 hostile batteries were successfully engaged for destruction with aeroplane observation.
Enemy Aircraft – In the morning more EA than usual crossed our lines, but otherwise activity was normal. Three Armstrong Whitworths of 10 Squadron were attacked by six EA and Major G B Ward & 2nd Lt E Wilson shot one down completely out of control. 2nd Lt W A MacLanachan, 40 Squadron, went up after an EA artillery machine and shot it down out of control. Flight Sub-Lt M Findlay, 6 Squadron RNAS, dived at two EA, one of which he shot down out of control. Another EA engaged by 2nd Lts H Lale & G Waters, 48 Squadron, is believed to have fallen out of control. When returning from bombing Ledeghem Dump, six machines of 57 Squadron encountered a large formation of Albatros scouts. 2nd Lts Mackay & Halliwell fired 100 rounds into one which dived past them and it fell into a cloud. Lts Hutcheson & Godwin engaged four of their attackers at the same time. One EA pilot did an Immelmann turn but he was shot down out of control. A

second EA then attacked from the rear and 2nd Lt Godwin shot it down out of control. A third EA was shot down in flames after 2nd Lt Godwin had fired 150 rounds into it. Two others were shot down completely out of control; one by Major Joy & Lt F Leathley, and the other by 2nd Lt A Drinkwater & Lt F T S Menendez. When returning from a bomb raid, Sgt W Weare & 2/AM Moreman, 55 Squadron, who were just about to cross the lines, saw an EA coming up underneath the leading DH4, so fired 30 rounds into it and it turned over and crashed in a field. Captain J T B McCudden, 56 Squadron, when leading a patrol of SE5s, dived and opened fire at an EA which burst into flames and crashed. Shortly after, he saw an SE being closely engaged by two EA so dived and assisted the other SE. One EA went down, then zoomed up and, when about to flatten out, Capt McCudden opened fire and only just avoided running into the enemy which fell completely out of control. 2nd Lt L M Barlow of the same squadron dived with his formation at six EA scouts over Polygon Wood, but then saw ten more preparing to dive at the SEs. He at once climbed and fired into one EA scout which fell out of control and crashed. He then shot down a second scout out of control. 2nd Lt R H Sloley, also of 56 Squadron, climbed with other SEs to attack six EA, and one EA dived at him, but he swerved avoiding its fire, then followed it and shot it down out of control. 2nd Lt H Layfield, 70 Squadron, was attacked from underneath and behind by an Albatros scout. He turned to engage and so lost the rest of his formation. The fight continued until the two machines had gone from 16,000 feet to 500 feet. Finally 2nd Lt Layfield stalled his machine and at the same time fired a burst into the EA which went down in a spin and crashed. A patrol of Sopwith Scouts of 66 Squadron were returning to their aerodrome when they observed two Rumpler two-seater EA going west over Ypres, so the Sopwiths climbed to attack these EA which were above them. Capt P G Taylor fired 50 rounds into one Rumpler which burst into flames and crashed in our lines two miles north-west of Ypres.

Sixteen Albatros scouts were met at 17,000 feet by Bristol Fighters of 48 Squadron. One engaged by Capt J Milne & 2nd Lt W O'Toole crashed near Ghistelles aerodrome, and the same pilot and Observer drove down a second EA out of control and on fire. 2nd Lts R V Curtis & D Uniacke drove down a third EA out of control. 2nd Lt S C O'Grady, 23 Squadron, saw a fight taking place between Allied and German aircraft so joined in and drove one EA off a Nieuport's tail. He then saw a black and white EA firing into a Spad from behind. He drove it away from the Spad and finally shot it down out of control, and it crashed and burned on the ground.
Photography – 1912 photographs were taken during the day.

AUGUST 21
Artillery Co-operation – 138 hostile batteries were successfully engaged with aeroplane observation, while 40 hostile batteries were engaged, ten neutralised, and 54 other targets dealt with from balloon observation.
Enemy Aircraft – Enemy aircraft were very active until the evening. During the day they fired into trenches and attacked our artillery machines. When taking photographs west of Douai, an Albatros scout dived at a DH4 of 25 Squadron in which were 2nd Lts S Simpson & R Butler. The latter immediately opened fire and the EA burst into flames and crashed. An Offensive Patrol of 45 Squadron engaged an Albatros scout and two DFW two-seaters. Lt Smith & Pte Grenner shot down the Albatros which broke to pieces and crashed. 2nd Lts N MacMillan & R Morris also 45 Squadron dived to attack several EA which were fighting our Triplanes, and shot

down one EA which fell out of control and when near the ground burst into flames, then crashed. Flight Lt S T Edwards, 9 Squadron RNAS, shot an EA down out of control and it burst into flames, but before reaching the ground the flames were seen to go out and the EA regained control and flew east. Flight Lt H J T Saint, 10 Squadron RNAS, attacked an EA two-seater south of Roulers and shot it down out of control. When taking photographs Lt N Sharples & 2nd Lt M O'Callaghan, 7 Squadron, were attacked by four Albatros scouts. 2nd Lt O'Callaghan opened fire at the nearest which burst into flames and crashed. The other three were driven off by Spads of 19 Squadron which had arrived on the scene.
(Editor's note: O'Callaghan's victim was the 26-victory ace, Oberleutnant Edouard Ritter von Dostler, commander of Jagdstaffel 6 of JG1, the "Richthofen Circus").

Three Albatros scouts were attacked by Capt A Macdonald & Lt I Wodehouse, 9 Squadron, when engaged on artillery work. After a burst by the Observer, one EA fell and crashed. A patrol of 56 Squadron noticed a fight between Bristol Fighters and an EA formation so joined in, and Captain G C Maxwell noticed two EA attacking an SE5, so at once dived from 14,000 feet to 5000 feet and shot down one EA painted black and white and saw it crash. Twenty EA were engaged by ten Bristol Fighters of 48 Squadron. Captain J T Milne & Lt W O'Toole shot one down which crashed, while a second EA was driven down in flames by Lts R D Coath & A D Light. Capt H Dean, 70 Squadron, shot down one EA out of control. A patrol of 10 Squadron RNAS joined in a fight between DH4s of 57 Squadron returning from bombing Ledeghem Dump and Albatros scouts. Flight Sub-Lt J G Manuel shot one EA down which crashed, and another which fell out of control. Flight Lt G L Trapp and Flight Cdr W M Alexander each drove an EA down out of control, while another EA scout was shot down in flames by Capts Barker & Barclay, 57 Squadron.
Bombing – On the night of the 20th/21st, No.100 Squadron dropped 38 25lb and eleven 230lb bombs on Lezennes aerodrome. An enemy machine was attacked by Lt A H Thompson who fired three drums into it while taking part in this night raid. 2nd Lts J F Bush & L A Colbert saw all the lights put out when they arrived at Lezennes aerodrome, so waited above, and on the return of the enemy machines which were also out bombing, a number of lights were fired by the EA and the aerodrome was then lit up. Taking advantage of this, bombs were then dropped and direct hits obtained. This squadron carried out three separate raids. Other enemy targets attacked by other squadrons included Courrieres, Oignies, Pont-a-Vendin, Harnes, Ledeghem Dump, Ramegnies Chin aerodrome, Aulnoye Ammunition Dump, while Lezennes aerodrome was also bombed by 27 Squadron.

AUGUST 22
Artillery Co-operation – 111 hostile batteries were successfully engaged for destruction from aeroplane observation, and 55 by balloon observation.
Enemy Aircraft – Enemy aircraft activity was great, but not as marked as on the last few days, and the Germans seemed disinclined to fight near the lines. A formation of 25 Squadron whilst on a bomb raid met 15 Albatros scouts which attempted to stop our machines from recrossing the lines, and Capt A Roulstone & 2nd Lt Fox shot one EA down in flames. All our aeroplanes returned safely. 2nd Lt A E Godfrey, 40 Squadron, shot down an EA artillery machine out of control. A patrol of six Nieuports of 1 Squadron encountered 17 EA scouts near Houthulst. Captain P F Fullard shot down one out of control, but then had engine trouble and turned for

the lines but was attacked by five EA. 2nd Lt H Reeves saw his position and skillfully kept the EA off Capt Fullard's tail, and shot one down which fell out of control. 2nd Lt W Mansell drove down another EA with its engine full on. Ground observers state that one EA fell in flames and two crashed as the result of this fighting.

Lt A E McKeever & 2nd Lt L Ebbutt, 11 Squadron, shot down an EA which fell and broke to pieces in the air. Five Bristol Fighters of 48 Squadron engaged 20 EA over Ghistelles aerodrome and in the ensuing fighting two EA were seen to crash, one was shot down in flames, one was forced to land near the aerodrome, and three others were shot down out of control. 2nd Lt J Binnie & Cpl V Reed shot the EA down in flames; Lt A D Coath & Lt A D Light destroyed one and drove one down out of control, while 2nd Lts R V Curtis & D Uniacke destroyed the third. Three EA were engaged by 6 Squadron RNAS, and Flight Sub-Lt N MacGregor shot down one which broke to pieces in the air. 2nd Lt F Gibbs, 23 Squadron, attacked three DFWs over Wervicq and destroyed one, and on his way home he attacked a balloon and drove down an Albatros scout which was guarding it. Lt W R G Pearson, 32 Squadron, attacked an Albatros scout which he shot down out of control. Pilots of the 9th Wing had a very great deal of fighting during the day with the result that four EA were destroyed, six driven down out of control, and three badly shot about and forced down. The four destroyed were by Capt G C Maxwell, Lts R Maybery, K Muspratt and C H Jeffs. The EA shot down by Lt Muspratt fell in our lines. Each of the following shot down EA out of control; Capts G C Maxwell and G Bowman, Lts R T C Hoidge and R Sloley, all of 56 Squadron, and Capt C Collett and Lt F H Bickerton, 70 Squadron. In the evening a patrol of 40 Squadron engaged seven Albatros scouts and 2nd Lt W McLanachan drove one down out of control. Capt P F Fullard, 1 Squadron, dived at a two-seater and fired 75 rounds at close range and the EA was seen to crash by anti-aircraft observers of the Second Army. Lt R L Graham, 19 Squadron, attacked a two-seater EA north of Houlthulst Forest and shot it down out of control. 2nd Lt H Rothery, 29 Squadron, shot down an enemy balloon north of Houlthulst Forest. Lt V Cronyn, 56 Squadron, reported having shot down an EA out of control, and confirmation has been received from the Fifth Army anti-aircraft that this EA crashed. Anti-aircraft of the Second Army shot down a two-seater DFW which fell near Houthem.

Photography – 782 photographs were taken during the day.

AUGUST 23

Artillery Co-operation – 120 hostile batteries were successfully engaged with aeroplane observation, and 21 from balloons.

Enemy Aircraft – Enemy aircraft activity was slight all day, probably due to unfavourable weather. A patrol of four Nieuports of 40 Squadron observed a two-seater DFW east of Lens so dived at it, and Lt G Crole shot it down in flames. Lt A E McKeever & 2nd Lt Ebbut, 11 Squadron, attacked eight Albatros scouts, and one EA was shot to pieces and crashed. 2nd Lt C G Wood, 54 Squadron, saw an Albatros scout attacking an RE8, so dived at it, opened fire, and the Albatros burst into flames and crashed. Lt H Crocker & Sgt H Lindfield, 48 Squadron, drove down one of eight Albatros scouts out of control.

COMMUNIQUÉ No.103

24 – 31 August 1917

In a week of bad weather conditions aerial activities were sporadic, though the RFC's artillery and reconnaissance squadrons continued their unglamorous duties faithfully whenever possible. No.6 Squadron RNAS (Nieuport Scouts) was officially disbanded on August 26, but was to be reformed as a day bomber squadron later; while on August 30, No.46 Squadron (Sopwith Pups) returned to France from England.

During the period under review (24th to 31 August) the weather has been unfavourable for aerial work. For the month of August we claim 135 EA brought down and 103 driven down out of control by aeroplanes; approximately 79 tons of bombs have been dropped, and over 11,000 photographs taken. 1860 hostile batteries have been successfully engaged for destruction with aeroplane observation, 304 gun pits destroyed, 803 damaged, 764 explosions and 302 fires caused.

AUGUST 24
Very little work was possible owing to unfavourable weather.

AUGUST 25
The weather was unsettled. Trench reconnaissances and contact patrols were carried out by machines of the 4th and 5th Brigades.
Enemy Aircraft – A patrol of DH5s of 24 Squadron engaged five two-seater EA near Bellenglise. Lt W B Ives drove down one in which its propeller was seen to stop, and then attacked another with which he fought for five minutes when Captain B P G Beanlands came to his assistance and the latter pilot followed the EA down, firing from close range until it fell completely out of control. Ground observers who witnessed the fighting say that one EA fell in flames and one fell out of control. An Offensive Patrol of 48 Squadron attacked four Albatros scouts near Westkerke and in the fighting 2nd Lts H Pratt & H Owen shot one down out of control, and another was shot down out of control by Capt J Milne & 2nd Lt W O'Toole. While on low patrol, Lts Thorowgood & W R Jones, 32 Squadron, attacked a DFW two-seater near Polygon Wood, which burst into flames and crashed. Flight Lt H J T Saint, 10 Squadron RNAS, in a fight with Albatros scouts, shot down one EA out of control. In the evening, Lt N McMillan, 45 Squadron, on a Sopwith Camel, encountered 10 Albatros scouts over Polygon Wood and drove one down out of control. A patrol of 48 Squadron encountered 25 EA south of Slype, and two EA were shot down in flames; one by Lts Armstrong & P Shone, and the other by 2nd Lts K Park & A R Noss. Lt O C Bryson, 19 Squadron, attacked a two-seater EA into which he fired 90 rounds and it fell completely out of control, and Flight Lt D F Fitz-Gibbon, of 10 Squadron RNAS, shot down an Albatros scout out of control.

AUGUST 26
Low clouds interfered with work considerably. Twelve DH5s of Nos 24 and 41 Squadrons attacked infantry in trenches and motor transport on roads on the front of the III Corps by firing over 4000 rounds from their machine guns. This was done in conjunction with a successful attack by that Corps. Over 2000 rounds were fired at similar targets by aeroplanes of the 4th Brigade.

Artillery Co-operation – 149 hostile batteries were successfully engaged with aeroplane observation, and 18 by balloons.

Enemy Aircraft – During the fine intervals enemy aircraft displayed a considerable amount of activity. Flight Sub-Lts J S Rowley and S W Rosevear, 1 Squadron RNAS, when searching for reported EA, engaged two DFW two-seaters and drove one down out of control. Lt S B Horn, 60 Squadron, flying an SE5 on a special patrol, saw a two-seater firing red and green lights about two miles over the line, so dived and shot it down out of control. This EA was seen by anti-aircraft gunners to burst into flames. Three Bristol Fighters of 48 Squadron encountered 28 EA between Westende and Middelkerke and engaged 12 of them. One EA was shot down and seen to crash by Lt J Binnie & Cpl V Reed, who also drove another down completely out of control. While escorting machines attacking enemy aerodromes, Capt J Leacroft, 19 Squadron, fired at several EA which left Bisseghem and Heule aerodromes, and one into which he fired at long range fell and was seen to crash. Another patrol of this squadron, consisting of Lts H Ainger, G Pentland, A R Boeree, R L Graham and T G Candy, attacked several EA concentrated on a two-seater which fell out of control and crashed. Lt B McEntegart of the same squadron attacked an Albatros scout near Courtrai and shot it down out of control. After this, the whole patrol attacked a two-seater EA and shot it down in flames. 2nd Lts S O'Grady and D U McGregor, 23 Squadron, each shot down an Albatros scout out of control. Later in the day, Captain G B A Baker of the same squadron attacked a DFW north of Zonnebeke which was seen by anti-aircraft to crash.

Photography – 401 photographs were taken during the day.

AUGUST 27

Rain and strong wind interfered with work considerably.

Artillery Co-operation – 26 hostile batteries were successfully engaged with aeroplane observation.

Enemy Aircraft – An Offensive Patrol of 45 Squadron engaged seven Albatros scouts near Moorslede and Captain A Harris drove one EA down out of control.

AUGUST 28

Owing to heavy rain and strong wind no work was possible until the evening.

AUGUST 29

No work was possible owing to strong wind and rain.

AUGUST 30

Strong wind and rain again interfered with work in the air. Information has been received from the French that an Albatros scout was shot down in flames on the 25th inst. by 2nd Lt F E Barker, 19 Squadron, who was seriously wounded.

AUGUST 31

Low clouds and rain again interfered with work, though a little was accomplished in the evening when the weather cleared. Enemy aircraft activity was very inactive until the evening. Lt M H Coote, 56 Squadron, saw two Spads engaging several EA, so joined the fight and shot down one EA out of control. 2nd Lt G Wilkinson of the same squadron observed a single-seater EA diving at the tail of an SE5 so at once attacked it from behind and shot it down completely out of control.

COMMUNIQUÉ NO. 104

1 – 7 September 1917

Continuing bad weather conditions hindered but did not prevent the daily routine for the army co-operation squadrons, while the "scout" squadrons maintained their unceasing offensive patrols into German air space. On September 3, No.43 Squadron received its first Sopwith Camel as the start of re-equipment from its two-seat Sopwith 1½ Strutters, and flew its first Camel sorties just two days later.

During the period under review (1st to 7th September inclusive) we have claimed 27 EA brought down, and 22 driven down out of control and have destroyed an enemy balloon. Approximately 26 tons of bombs have been dropped.

SEPTEMBER 1
Low clouds and rain hindered aerial work.
Artillery Co-operation – 27 hostile batteries were successfully engaged with aeroplane observation.
Enemy Aircraft – Activity was normal in the early morning but very slight the rest of the day. On the evening of August 31, EA scouts were claimed as shot down out of control by Lts H Pratt & H Owen, 48 Squadron, and one by Lt A A N Pentland, 19 Squadron. On the 1st, 2nd Lt McLeod, 19 Squadron, shot down one EA scout which he is convinced fell out of control, and Capt J Leacroft shot down another which also fell apparently out of control. Anti-aircraft report that they saw one EA crash. A Rumpler two-seater (G.66) landed near Elverdinghe (5th Brigade) and pilot and Observer were both captured.
Bombing – On the night 31 August/1 September, 25 machines of 100 Squadron bombed Lezennes aerodrome, Heule aerodrome, Mouveaux aerodrome, Moorslede aerodrome, Ascq aerodrome, Tournai Station. Menin Station, and Hellemes. After bombing Tournai Station, Captain V E Schweitzer attacked the station with his Pom-pom (37mm) and fired 30-1lb shells.

SEPTEMBER 2
Low clouds, strong wind and rain greatly interfered with aerial work. Aeroplanes continued to fire into enemy trenches.
Artillery Co-operation – 74 hostile batteries were successfully engaged with aeroplane observation.
Enemy Aircraft – Enemy aircraft activity was more pronounced than it has been for some days, and his aircraft were exceptionally active at night, bombing various places behind our lines. During the day a considerable amount of fighting took place. Lts C Lally & B Blackett, 25 Squadron, were taking photographs when an EA scout dived at them, but they succeeded in shooting it down out of control. While on an Offensive Patrol, Sopwith Camels of 45 Squadron engaged 14 Albatros scouts flown by pilots who appeared to be more experienced than the majority. Captain A T Harris dived at one EA which was attacking the rear Camel and shot it down in flames. Another EA, however, followed Capt Harris, so Lt W C Moore dived at it and shot it down out of control. Lt O L McMaking also drove one EA down out of

control. After the fight three EA were seen wrecked and burning on the ground. Another patrol of this squadron encountered 11 EA and in the fighting 2nd Lt E D Clarke shot down an Albatros scout which fell in flames, and 2nd Lt M B Frew shot down one out of control. In an engagement earlier in the day, 2nd Lt N Macmillan of the same squadron flew to the assistance of some RE8s being attacked by Albatros scouts. He shot down one Albatros which was seen by an RE pilot to burst into flames. When on photographic work, four FE2ds of 20 Squadron were attacked by about 12 EA. The FEs were soon reinforced by four Bristol Fighters of the same squadron, and 2nd Lt R M Makepeace & Lt H L Waddington in one Bristol Fighter destroyed an EA scout. Sopwiths of 46 Squadron also joined in this fight and Lt V Joske shot down one EA which was seen to crash. Sgt R Taylor & Lt Steel, 13 Squadron, while taking photographs, were attacked by seven EA, six of which dived from behind. The Observer, Lt Steel, opened fire at one EA scout which turned completely over and was seen to crash, while a second was driven down in a spin. After the RE8 crossed the lines the other EA ceased to attack. When escorting bombing machines, Lt R Dodds & 2nd Lt T Suffield, 48 Squadron, were attacked by two Albatros scouts. One scout was shot down apparently out of control, and the second which attacked from behind was out-manoeuvred and shot down in flames. 2nd Lt C W Cudemore, 29 Squadron, fired 100 rounds into an Albatros scout which turned on its back and fell out of control. Eight Spads of 19 Squadron attacked a large patrol of Albatros scouts and Captain J Leacroft shot one down out of control. Lt B McEntegart, also 19 Squadron, shot down one EA apparently out of control. In the evening four SE5s of 56 Squadron engaged eight EA. One EA became detached from the rest and was destroyed by Lt R Maybery and 2nd Lt A P F Rhys Davids. Two others were shot down out of control by 56 Squadron, one by 2nd Lt E Turnbull and the other by Lt W Potts. Bristol Fighters of 22 Squadron were attacked by ten EA, three of which dived at 2nd Lts R Boby & A Smith, but they shot down one EA out of control. In other engagements Lt T V Hunter, 66 Squadron, and Capt H P Dean, 70 Squadron, each shot down one EA out of control. In the evening Lts C T Lallay & B Blackett, 25 Squadron, observed two EA coming from the direction of Lens, and drove one down apparently out of control. 2nd Lt W S Mansell, 1 Squadron, when diving to assist SE5s, was attacked by four EA scouts. He turned round and shot one down which crashed. Flight Cdr J S T Fall, Flight Lt Scott, and Flight Sub-Lts A W Wood and H Stackard, 9 Squadron RNAS, saw a signal showing EA working in Sector 3. They cleared this area of EA, then went to Dixmude where they drove away an EA formation. Later they saw an Allied machine being driven down by EA, so attacked and destroyed one EA.

Photography – 895 photographs were taken during the day.

Bombing – On the night of the 2nd/3rd, No.100 Squadron made two trips and bombed aerodromes at Ramegnies Chin, Ascq, Chateau du Sart, and Lezennes, while Nos 10 and 25 Squadrons bombed Hantay, Marquillies, Bauvin, Provin, Mangre, and Nos 18 and 55 Squadrons bombed aerodromes at Carnieres and Heule respectively.

SEPTEMBER 4

Photography – 102 photographic flights were carried out and a record number of photographs – 1805 – were taken.

Artillery Co-operation – 100 hostile batteries were successfully engaged with aeroplane observation, and 27 by balloons.

Enemy Aircraft – Enemy aircraft attacked our artillery machines but were less inclined than on the 3rd inst, to engage our scouts unless far east. On the night of the 3rd/4th, however, they were exceptionally active. Captain E Mannock, 40 Squadron, went up in search of a reported German artillery machine which he found and engaged. The Observer was seen to fall back apparently killed but the machine was not destroyed. Later in the day Capt Mannock and Sgt L A Herbert of the same squadron attacked a two- seater DFW which they shot down apparently out of control. In the afternoon Capt Mannock attacked a DFW near Petit Vimy and shot it down in flames within our lines (G.68). Two Camels of 45 Squadron attacked a formation of 11 EA. 2nd Lt M B Frew drove down a two-seater in a spin and followed it, and when it came out of the spin he re-opened fire and shot it down out of control. He then attacked another two-seater which turned over and fell out of control. After the fight one EA was seen wrecked and burning on the ground. Lt W J Potts, 56 Squadron, saw two SE5s diving towards Houlthulst Forest, so followed and saw three EA scouts below. He opened fire at one which fell sideways, burst into flames, and crashed. In the evening a patrol of DH4s of 25 Squadron fought a formation of Albatros scouts near La Bassee and destroyed one. In other combats EA were claimed as shot down out of control by 2nd Lt Armstrong & Lt Farrow, 10 Squadron ; Capt L F Jenkin, 1 Squadron ; Lt A S G Lee, 46 Squadron ;2nd Lt F A Smith,66 Squadron ; Capt J H Letts & 2nd Lt Frost, 2nd Lts Bostock & Collins, Sgt Roebuck & 2/AM Walker, all of 48 Squadron.

SEPTEMBER 5

Artillery Co-operation – 42 hostile batteries were successfully engaged from aeroplane observation, and 17 by balloons.

Enemy Aircraft – A patrol of 45 Squadron met six DFW two-seaters escorted by a number of Albatros scouts and very heavy fighting ensued. Our machines were reinforced by Spads and Triplanes. Lts W A Wright and O L McMaking, 45 Squadron, each drove down one EA out of control. A photographic formation of 20 Squadron engaged ten Albatros scouts near Lille. In the fighting 2nd Lts Campbell & Harrop shot one EA down out of control which broke to pieces in the air, and 2nd Lt R M Makepeace & Lt H L Waddington drove down another out of control. When north of Ostend, Bristol Fighters of 48 Squadron were attacked by Albatros scouts and 2nd Lt K Park & 2/AM H Lindfield shot one down which fell into the sea. Captain C F Collett,70 Squadron, climbed with his formation to attack several EA and were joined by SE5s and Nieuports and Capt Collett shot down one EA which broke to pieces in the air. An Offensive Patrol of 22 Squadron engaged seven EA east of Houthulst Wood. Lts J Bush and W Chapman attacked one EA which they shot down in flames, and Lts H McKenzie & S McLenaghan shot down one out of control. A patrol of SE5s of 56 Squadron encountered 15 EA in three formations near Moorslede. The SEs were reinforced by FE2ds and Bristol Fighters and a determined attack was made against the EA. 2nd Lt A P F Rhys Davids, 56 Squadron, got a good burst at close range into one EA and it fell out of control. He then pulled down his Lewis gun and fired both guns at a red-fuselaged machine above him, and it at once put its nose down and dived. 2nd Lt Rhys Davids followed and continued firing until the EA broke to pieces and its planes went floating down in all directions. After this he and Lt R Maybery found themselves isolated so flew for the lines. On the way there 2nd Lt Rhys Davids saw an EA under some FEs so at once engaged it. The German pilot fought well but having been out-manoeuvred put his machine into a roll and came out in a nose-dive, but before he recovered sufficiently to fight, 2nd Lt Rhys Davids opened fire and the EA fell and crashed in a wood. Lt R Maybery engaged a black and white EA and eventually shot it down out of control. Lt R T C Hoidge, 56 Squadron, took part in this fighting and on his way back to the lines saw an EA below him and shot it down out of control. Lt R Sloley of the same squadron, shot down one of two two-seaters out of control.

When returning from a bomb raid, DH4s of 55 Squadron were attacked by ten EA scouts, two of which were shot down out of control; one by 2nd Lt J Heading & Lt A Sattin, and the other by 2nd Lt J Fox & 2/AM Leyland. In the evening an Albatros scout was seen attacking an RE8 and Lts R V Curtis & Munro, 48 Squadron, shot it down in flames. A two-seater EA landed in the Third Army area on the night of the 3rd/4th, and another landed in the Fourth Army area on the beach. The passengers in the first machine were captured, and those in the second apparently escaped.

SEPTEMBER 6
Low clouds and a little rain prevented the usual amount of aerial work.
Artillery Co-operation – 53 hostile batteries were engaged successfully from aeroplane observation, and 13 by balloons.
Enemy Aircraft – Enemy aircraft activity was below normal. Lt S B Horn, 60 Squadron, was attacked by four EA but succeeded in shooting one down out of control and dispersing the rest. Lt R Winnicott, 41 Squadron, attacked and shot down an Albatros two-seater out of control. While engaged on artillery work, Capt Minchin & 2nd Lt Donald, 21 Squadron, were attacked by an Albatros scout. Fire was opened at long range at the EA and when it got to within 50 yards of the RE8 it suddenly went down out of control and crashed. Lt C H Jeffs, 56 Squadron, saw the leader of his patrol dive at two EA scouts, so at once selected one and after putting a good burst into it the EA fell and crashed. In other combats at least three EA were claimed as shot down out of control by each of the following; Flight Sub-Lt H S Broughall and Flight Sub-Lt W A Curtis, 10 Squadron RNAS, and one each by Sgts J Hamer & G Lambeth, and Capt R Stuart-Wortley & 2nd Lt P V Burton, both of 22 Squadron.

SEPTEMBER 7
Very little flying was possible owing to bad weather.
With Balloon Observation – 21 hostile batteries were successfully engaged for destruction, five neutralised, and 41 other targets dealt with.
Enemy Aircraft – Enemy aircraft were very inactive, and only one decisive engagement took place. Lt R M Charley, 54 Squadron, opened fire at an EA scout which was attacking a Sopwith Scout from behind, and shot it down, and it was seen to crash into the sea.

COMMUNIQUÉ No.105

8 – 16 September 1917

While prominence is normally given in these communiqués to the deeds of the "Scout" (fighter) squadrons, the trojan work of the day and night bombers is acknowledged particularly here, though mainly based on unconfirmed intelligence sources. On September 9, No.69 Squadron (RE8s) arrived in France; the first Australian squadron of the RFC, which would be retitled as No.3 Squadron, Australian Flying Corps (AFC) on 19 January, 1918.

The following reports concerning the results of certain bomb raids have been received from various sources. The accuracy of the statements is not vouched for.

RAIDS CARRIED OUT BY THE RFC

On the 4th of March a British machine dropped bombs on Billy-Montigny. One of them fell on a train full of German soldiers, said to be a Pioneer Company of the Guard, en route to Hem. One report states that all the officers were killed and most of the soldiers, while another report asserts that the whole of eight companies were either killed or wounded, with the exception of one officer and a few NCOs and men. On the 5th of April a troop train in Lille Station was hit by a bomb and fifty soldiers killed. A troop train which was attacked by 6 Squadron on the night of 5th/6th April at Menin was hit, and resulted in casualties amounting to 200 killed and wounded. On the night of the 9th/10th April, the Arsenal at Douai exploded as a result of a raid by 100 Squadron.

On the 7th of April machines of the 2nd Brigade bombed Mouveaux aerodrome. Information states that the raid took place during a military review and about 300 soldiers were killed and wounded. On the 8th of April, 30 Germans were killed at Meurchin by bombs, and many casualties were caused among a working party of the 35th (German) Infantry Regiment. At Chateau-du-Sart aerodrome, 27 Germans were killed and four machines destroyed. A report states that two German Generals were killed at the HQ of the Prince Rupprecht de Baviere by bombs. No date is given. About the 5th/6th June, a German ammunition train was blown up at Menin (No.100 Squadron). At about the same time considerable damage was done at St Denis Westrem aerodrome which was attacked by British machines. During a raid over Bruay (near Valenciennes) about the end of April a bomb fell on an officers' train, another on the railway junction south of Bruay, and two on the camps of the 436th and 328th Regiments of the Bavarian Landsturm. The casualties were heavy. This would probably refer to a raid by 55 Squadron on the 4th of May. On the 9th of May, No.27 Squadron attacked hutments at Bone. Several ammunition huts were blown up, and explosions continued all afternoon.

On Good Friday, April 6th, a troop train coming from the front was hit by bombs and only about 20 men escaped injury (27 Squadron). Reports state that on the 11th/12th July, a 230lb bomb fell about three yards from a large hangar on Ramegnies Chin aerodrome. One report states that the hangar contained 12 machines, while another gives the number at 30. Both reports, however, agree that all the aeroplanes contained within were completely destroyed.(100 Squadron).

The new sidings at Melle were attacked by 55 Squadron on the 28th July, and it appears that 30 German soldiers were killed. The following is an extract:- "On Monday, 23rd July 1917, the population of Brussels was on holiday when seven or eight aeroplanes flew over the town and dropped bombs on the Gare du Midi and on the aviation park at Etterbeck. Two German aeroplanes rose. The first was brought down and its officer killed; the second had to descend hurriedly. The people of Brussels were wild with delight. Even if these raids had no military value, they did immense good. It is inconceivable to what extent the morale of the population rises on these occasions." At the end of July a direct hit was obtained on a hangar at Recklem aerodrome, and on 30th July two two-seater German machines were destroyed at Heule aerodrome, while at Ramegnies Chin aerodrome which was attacked on June 7th by 55 Squadron, ten sheds are said to have been completely burnt with ten machines in them.

The following account of work carried out by No.19 Squadron was omitted from Communiqué No.103:- At dawn on the 26th August, five Spads of 19 Squadron, escorted by seven other Spads of the same squadron, set out to attack Bisseghem and Marcke aerodromes. Although fiercely attacked by EA the work was satisfactorily concluded, with three attacking EA destroyed, and two others driven down out of control. Lt A Boeree led the five attacking Spads and on the way they drove off several EA. He fired 350 rounds into the hangars from 100 feet, drove down two EA scouts, and returned safely. Lt H Ainger saw a train leaving Courtrai, so fired into it. He then flew to Marcke aerodrome where he saw eight Albatros scouts on the ground in front of the sheds, so dived twice and fired into them from 800 feet. He then returned owing to gun trouble. Lt A A N Pentland had an engagement on the way to Marcke aerodrome, then went down to 20 feet and fired into the eight Albatros scouts on the ground, and at mechanics. After leaving Marcke he saw a troop train leaving Courtrai, so, guarded above by Lt R L Graham, he flew right down to the train and riddled it with bullets from end to end. He engaged two EA, then returned. Lt R L Graham, with other Spads, fired at one EA which fell out of control, then fired into hangars at Bisseghem aerodrome from 400 feet. Lt T G Candy helped shoot down an EA out of control. Particulars of the EA destroyed will be seen in RFC Communiqué No.103.

During the period under review (8th to 16th September inclusive), 28 EA have been brought down, 38 driven down out of control, and AA have shot down two, one falling in our lines. Approximately 20 ½ tons of bombs have been dropped.

SEPTEMBER 8
Heavy ground mist and low clouds prevented much aerial work.

SEPTEMBER 9
Heavy mist and clouds again interfered with aerial work. As enemy aircraft were reported flying low over our trenches in the Third Army, DH5s of 24 and 41 Squadrons went out to engage them and succeeded in driving them all away. After this three DH5s of 41 Squadron attacked parties of men in German trenches, and horse transport, firing 750 rounds at them from about 400 feet.

Artillery Co-operation – 19 hostile batteries were successfully engaged from aeroplane observation.

Enemy Aircraft – Enemy aircraft activity was below normal except between 12-noon and 1pm when it was considerable. An Offensive Patrol of 45 Squadron engaged 15

Albatros two-seaters. 2nd Lt E Smith singled out one EA behind the rest and shot it down in flames. After this he shot down a second out of control. 2nd Lt A P F Rhys Davids, 56 Squadron, saw two EA scouts over Houthulst Forest and fired a drum from his Lewis gun into one which fell in a slow spiral and was seen to crash. In the evening Lt H Weightman, 70 Squadron, was severely wounded in a combat with two Albatros scouts. Information has been received that the first one he engaged was driven down out of control and crashed. In the evening a patrol of 70 Squadron engaged several EA between Gheluvelt and Houthulst. Captain C F Collett destroyed two and drove down a third out of control, and then Capt Collett followed a two-seater down from 10,000 feet to 4000 feet, after which it fell and crashed. Shortly after he drove down another EA which landed partially under control and turned over. Capt Collett then went down to 40 feet and fired into the EA which burst into flames. He was then attacked by three Albatros scouts but evaded them and crossed the lines at 30 feet. He was slightly wounded in the hand during the last encounter. In other combats, EA were claimed driven down out of control by 2nd Lt H Reeves and 2nd Lt W S Mansell, 1 Squadron; Lt H G E Luchford & 2nd Lt Hill, 20 Squadron; 2nd Lt K Park & 2/AM Lindfield, and Capt J T Milne & Lt A D Light, 48 Squadron.

SEPTEMBER 10

In spite of unfavourable weather, 15 photographic flights, during which 166 plates were exposed, were carried out.

Artillery Co-operation – 14 hostile batteries were successfully engaged from aeroplane observation.

Enemy Aircraft – Flight Cdr J S T Fall and Flight Lt H Stackard, 9 Squadron RNAS, attacked two Albatros scouts, one of which they drove down out of control, and the other was hit and seen to dive vertically. While on an Offensive Patrol, Lt R A Maybery, 56 Squadron, dived at one of eight EA and shot it down out of control. He next saw two EA scouts over Houthulst Forest, so opened fire with both guns at one which went down in a steep nose-dive and then its wings folded back and it crashed. Lt R T C Hoidge of the same squadron shot one EA down out of control, while another fell out of control after being engaged by Lt C H Jeffs. In the evening Flight Sub-Lt C B Ridley, 1 Squadron RNAS, drove down a DFW two-seater out of control. An Offensive Patrol of 45 Squadron engaged two DFW two-seaters and five Albatros scouts near Houthulst. One EA was shot down in flames by 2nd Lt R J Brownell, and two were driven down out of control; one by 2nd Lt N Macmillan, and one by 2nd Lt Smith.

Bristol Fighters of 11 Squadron engaged eight Albatros scouts over Dury and one was shot down out of control by Lt R F S Mauduit & Lt Dennis. A patrol of 70 Squadron engaged eight Albatros scouts, two Triplanes and a two-seater between Roulers and Staden. 2nd Lt F H Bickerton opened fire at one Triplane which burst into flames and fell out of control. 2nd Lt Waddell & Sgt Fraser, 21 Squadron, when taking photographs, were attacked by seven Albatros scouts near Passchendaele. The Observer, Sgt Fraser, opened fire at the nearest one as it dived at them and shot it down out of control. He then fired at another scout which fell and was seen to crash. After this he engaged a third but it and the other EA flew away.

SEPTEMBER 11

During the day, 96 photographic flights, during which 1294 photographs were taken, were carried out.

Artillery Co-operation – 58 hostile batteries were successfully engaged from aeroplane observation.

Enemy Aircraft – Enemy aircraft were very active and attacked our reconnaissance, bombing and photographic machines with large formations of scouts. Flight Lt R R Thornely, 8 Squadron RNAS, found three EA artillery machines and shot one down completely out of control. Captain E Mannock, 40 Squadron, attacked two two-seater machines over Thelus and shot one down which fell out of control. An Albatros scout was shot down out of control by 2nd Lts Kier & Ross, 16 Squadron. Captain L F Jenkin, flying a Nieuport of 1 Squadron, dived on an Albatros scout and after firing 48 rounds into it, it rolled over and fell completely out of control. Captain Jenkin, who has accounted for 22 enemy machines, failed to return from a patrol later in the day. An Offensive Patrol of 45 Squadron engaged two DFW two-seaters and ten Albatros scouts, and two were shot down out of control; one by 2nd Lt H M Moody and one by 2nd Lt M B Frew. 2nd Lt J E Child in another patrol of this squadron engaged three Albatros scouts near Hooge and drove one down out of control, while a third patrol of this squadron engaged six Triplanes near Langemarck, and 2nd Lt N Macmillan shot one down out of control. Flight Sub-Lt A Binks, 1 Squadron RNAS, drove down an Albatros scout out of control. When in search of German artillery machines reported to be working, 2nd Lt A Pentland, 19 Squadron, met two two-seater EA. He dived at one which flew east, but 2nd Lt Pentland "sat on its tail" down to 2000 feet when the EA fell and crashed. The other two-seater attacked the Spad from behind so 2nd Lt Pentland swung round to engage this EA but his gun jammed and he was driven down while trying to rectify the jam. At this juncture Captain F Sowrey and Lt H Ainger of the same squadron dived to his assistance and Capt Sowrey, who flew right up to within a few feet of the EA, soon destroyed it.

A photographic formation of six Bristol Fighters of 20 Squadron engaged about 25 Albatros scouts near Menin. With their customary vigourousness of attack, they dispersed the EA formation after two had been shot down in flames; one by 2nd Lts F F Babbage & R C Purvis, and one by Lt R K Kirkman & 2nd Lt J P Flynn. Two others were driven down out of control; one by 2nd Lt R M Makepeace & Lt H L Waddington, and one by Lt H G E Luchford & 2nd Lt R F Hill. A second photographic formation of this squadron engaged an enemy scout of an unknown type near Wervicq and it was shot down out of control by 2nd Lt A G V Taylor & 2nd Lt G A Brooke. Four Sopwith Scouts of 46 Squadron saw a German two-seater doing artillery work so dived at it, and Capt M D G Scott, who almost collided with it, fired 50 rounds and shot it down out of control. 2nd Lts J Binnie & Tuffield, 48 Squadron, shot down a DFW two-seater out of control near Dixmude. Captain N Jones, 70 Squadron, followed a two-seater EA down from 10,000 feet to 6000 feet and it was last seen falling upside down. Captain G C Maxwell and Lt R T C Hoidge, 56 Squadron, each drove down an EA out of control, while a third was shot down out of control by Sgt J Bainbridge & 2nd Lt G Dell, 22 Squadron.

SEPTEMBER 12

Mist and low clouds interfered with aerial work.

Artillery Co-operation – 21 hostile batteries were successfully engaged from aeroplane observation, five hostile batteries and 62 other targets from balloon observation.

Enemy Aircraft – An Offensive Patrol of 45 Squadron engaged seven EA two-seaters near Moorslede and Lt W Wright dived at the leader of the formation and shot it down completely out of control. Another patrol of this squadron met six Albatros scouts and three Triplanes east of Langemarck. 2nd Lt N Macmillan dived at a Triplane and after a burst at close range it fell out of control. He then saw another Triplane attacking one of our machines so dived and followed it down from 10,000 to 4000 feet, and it was last seen falling completely out of control. An Offensive Patrol of 1 Squadron attacked nine Albatros scouts near Houthulst Forest and Lt W Rooper, 2nd Lt H G Reeves, and Sgt G P Olley each shot down one EA out of control. Six Bristol Fighters of 11 Squadron met six Albatros scouts over Cagnicourt. Four of the EA were driven off, while two were shot down out of control; one by Capt G H Hooper & Lt L A Powell, and the other by 2nd Lts M S West & F A Herron. Four Camels of 9 Squadron RNAS encountered two formations of eight Albatros scouts near Leke. Flight Cdr J S T Fall and Flight Sub-Lts H Stackard and A W Wood concentrated their attention on one EA which they shot to pieces in the air and various parts were seen to flutter down in all directions. Another EA passed in front of Flight Cdr Fall who fired directly into it, while other Camels attacked from each side, and this machine fell and was seen to crash. The remaining EA then flew away.

Lt R M Charley, 54 Squadron, selected one of eight Albatros scouts which he fought for some time and finally shot down completely out of control. When returning from a bomb raid, 2nd Lt C Halley & 2/AM T Barlow, 57 Squadron, who were slightly behind the rest of the DH4s, were attacked by five EA. The first burst from an EA wounded the pilot in the foot and shot a control wire away. The Observer, 2/AM Barlow, fired at the nearest EA which fell and was seen to crash. Another EA was driven down after a burst of fire, while the others were soon out-distanced.

Bombing – 9th Wing – On the night of the 11th/12th, 100 Squadron dropped three 230lb, six 112lb, sixty 25lb and four 40lb phosphorous bombs on targets at Bisseghem Dump, Ascq sidings and railway lines. Owing to the extreme darkness of the night, 2nd Lt J Bushe & L Colbert flew to Bisseghem Dump at dusk and dropped phosphorous bombs which enabled the other bombing machines to find their objective with ease and to bomb with greater accuracy. Thirty 1-lb Pom-pom shells and 1300 rounds of ammunition were fired at search-lights and traffic during this raid.

SEPTEMBER 13

Low clouds and mist made aerial work very difficult.

Artillery Co-operation – 39 hostile batteries were successfully engaged from aeroplane observation, and five from balloons.

Enemy Aircraft – Enemy aircraft activity was very slight. A formation of Bristol Fighters of 11 Squadron attacked an Albatros scout which was shot down out of control. Lts O J F Scholte & G R Horsfall, in a Bristol Fighter of 48 Squadron, went up on the night of the 12th/13th in pursuit of EA which were bombing Dunkirk. They encountered one machine which was returning towards the lines and into which they fired 40 rounds at close range. Unfortunately, the pilot's gun jammed and the EA was last seen diving away with one engine apparently damaged, as the exhaust which was conspicuous before the attack, ceased to be noticeable.

SEPTEMBER 14

Strong wind, clouds and rain interfered with aerial work to a great extent.

Artillery Co-operation – 45 hostile batteries were successfully engaged from aeroplane observation.

Enemy Aircraft – One EA was driven down out of control by 2nd Lt E D Clarke, 45 Squadron.

(Editor's note: Captain E D Clarke became Managing Director of the Saunders-Roe Aircraft Company from 1945 to 1960).

Eight machines of 10 Squadron RNAS encountered eight EA and three EA were shot down out of control; one each by Flight Lt D F Fitzgibbon and Flight Sub-Lts R E Carroll and W C Johnston. An Offensive Patrol of 56 Squadron patrolled the area north of Ypres-Menin and met eight EA which immediately scattered on being attacked. Captain G H Bowman by keeping under cover in a cloud managed to catch up an EA which he destroyed. 2nd Lt R H Sloley drove down one EA, then shot down another out of control, and Lt C H Jeffs and 2nd Lt F J Horrell each drove down one EA out of control. A photographic formation of 20 Squadron engaged three Albatros scouts and three DFW two-seaters near Lille, and 2nd Lts H F Tomlin & Morris drove one of the DFWs down out of control. While on photographic work, 2nd Lts R V Curtis & D Uniacke, 48 Squadron, were attacked by three EA, one of which they destroyed and drove the others down. Another EA was destroyed by 2nd Lts K Park & Owen of the same squadron. The pilot was seen to be shot, after which his machine burst into flames and crashed in our lines. Two Albatros scouts which were returning from our side of the lines were attacked by machines of 9 Squadron RNAS. Flight Cdr J S T Fall dived after one and by keeping behind it and firing at point-blank range shot it down, and it was seen to crash.

SEPTEMBER 15

Artillery Co-operation – 44 hostile batteries were successfully engaged from aeroplane observation, and 12 by balloons.

Enemy Aircraft – Captain J P Y Lavarack & Lt H Rick, 12 Squadron, while observing results for zone calls, were attacked by three EA. The leading one was shot down out of control and the other two driven off. Later on, they were again attacked and drove one EA down in damaged condition, but then had to return for more ammunition. Flight Sub-Lts A R Brown and E M Knott, 9 Squadron RNAS, each drove down an EA out of control. Flight Sub-Lt N M Macgregor, 10 Squadron RNAS, when with a patrol of seven other Camels, attacked five Albatros scouts and four Triplanes, and drove one of the latter down out of control.

(Editor's note: In fact, Macgregor's victim was Oberleutnant Kurt Wolff, 33-victory ace, commander of Jagdstaffel 11 of the "Richthofen Circus", whose Fokker Triplane exploded as it fell to earth).

2nd Lt J D Payne, 29 Squadron, observed a hostile scout diving at a Camel from behind, so intercepted and destroyed the EA. In the evening Lt W MacLanachan, 40 Squadron, attacked an EA scout south-east of Vimy and shot it down apparently out of control. Bristol Fighters of 48 Squadron encountered seven Albatros scouts. Lts H H Hartley & E Birch were attacked by three of these scouts and one, which passed the Bristol Fighter's tail, was shot down completely out of control and after falling several thousand feet broke to pieces. Captain J H Letts & 2nd Lt J Frost were fighting at a lower altitude and saw the first EA destroyed. They became detached from the rest of their formation, then sighted an EA two-seater which they attacked, but their front gun jammed. On correcting this, they dived in front of the EA and headed it west, then shot it down out of control. After falling some distance, however, the EA righted itself, so was again headed west and this time was shot down and crashed. 2nd Lts E Williams & J Boughton shot another EA which fell completely out of control. 2nd Lt King, 70 Squadron, shot down an Albatros scout near Menin and followed it for 8000 feet, then left it as it was completely out of control falling into the mist. Lt J R Wilson of the same squadron was attacked by four Albatros scouts but had engine trouble so had difficulty in escaping their attack. He eventually stalled his machine and shot down the most aggressive EA completely out of control.

Miscellaneous – Two machines of 35 Squadron collided in the air and one had the right-hand bottom plane broken. As the Armstrong Whitworth FK8 became uncontrollable, the Observer, 2nd Lt Perkins, climbed out of his seat on to the bottom left-hand plane and balanced the machine sufficiently well to enable his pilot to make a successful landing.

SEPTEMBER 16

In spite of unfavourable weather conditions, a considerable amount of work was done. 65 photographic flights – during which 854 photographs were taken – were carried out. Captain D Stevenson & Lt J Webster in one RE8, and Capt J F V Lavarack & Lt H Rick in another machine of 12 Squadron worked in conjunction with the Sixth Corps in an attack on enemy trenches. They flew up and down the trenches at low altitude, taking photographs and making observations, while attracting the fire of enemy machine guns that would have been used against our troop. The former RE fired 272 rounds at Germans in trenches, and the latter fired 742 rounds. Captain J C Slessor & Lt F Tymms, 5 Squadron, fired 350 rounds at enemy in trenches. Spads of 19 Squadron after crossing the lines saw a barrage, so headed in that direction. Lt R L Graham fired at a body of troops from 500 feet, then he and Lt A Pentland took a zig-zag course up the trenches for half an hour at 200 feet firing at the Germans wherever they saw them. Our own troops showed up very plainly and waved a greeting. After this they went further east and flew above roads, attacking any troops and transport they saw. They worked together for a considerable time. During this work, shells were often seen passing in the air. On his way home Lt Pentland shot down a two-seater EA out of control. Lt H Dawson and Capt F Sowrey of the same squadron crossed the lines at Armentieres and Lt Dawson fired at troops from 100 feet, then, when near Mouseron, he saw about 2000 infantry marching along a road, so attacked them. After this he drove down an EA and on his way home continued firing at troops until he got a stoppage. Capt Sowrey fired 50 rounds at enemy in trenches from 100 feet, then flew to La Croix-au-Bois where he scattered a party of troops at a cross roads. After this he flew to Quesnoy and again attacked troops, transport and guns which were going up to the lines. Lt Golding & 1/AM Gadd, 3 Squadron, fired 100 rounds at three motor transport. Lts Sharples & Ryan, 7 Squadron, fired 410 rounds at German troops from 500 feet.

Artillery Co-operation – 59 hostile batteries were successfully engaged from aeroplane observation, and eleven by balloons.

Enemy Aircraft – Enemy aircraft activity was slightly below normal, though large formations were encountered at times. 2nd Lt Balaam & Lt Wallas, 16 Squadron, were taking photographs when they were attacked by two EA scouts which they drove away. They were then attacked by a large Nieuport-type machine which they engaged and hit, and it was last seen falling into mist. Lts C T Lally & B Blackett, 25

Squadron, were also attacked but shot the Observer in the EA which then dived away. Lt A Pentland, 19 Squadron, shot down an Albatros scout out of control. 2nd Lts J Byrom & E Detmold, 18 Squadron, while on photography, were attacked by an Albatros two-seater into which they fired 1½ drums and it fell over and went down out of control.

When on an Offensive Patrol, four Sopwith Scouts of 46 Squadron found an Albatros two-seater through following the direction of an anti-aircraft crew arrow and drove it off. They then met a number of Albatros scouts. Lts V Joske and R L M Ferrie each drove an EA scout down in a spin. The fight was observed by K Battery anti-aircraft and it is thought that both EA fell out of control. 2nd Lt L M Barlow, 56 Squadron, dived with an SE5 formation at a number of EA scouts near Comines, and singled out one which he followed down until it fell out of control and crashed. 2nd Lt R H Sloley of the same squadron saw four EA flying towards Martinsydes of 27 Squadron, so dived and followed one down and shot it out of control. Captain G C Maxwell, 56 Squadron, hit another EA scout which went down badly damaged.

Top left: F/Sgt T Mottershead, VC, DCM.

Top right: Major J T B McCudden, VC, DSO, MC, MM, in SE5a cockpit.

Middle: Captured Albatros D.III Scout of Jagdstaffel Eleven.

Bottom left: FE2d with Observer illustrating his defensive stance.

Bottom right: Lt W G Barker (later, Major, VC, DSO, MC) with his RE8 of 15 Squadron.

Top left: W A Bishop, VC, DSO, MC, DFC, in the cockpit of a Nieuport Scout, 60 Squadron.

Top right: Capt W L Robinson, VC, 48 Squadron.

Middle: 56 Squadron, April 1917. Standing L-R; G C Maxwell; Melville; Lehmann; Knight; Barlow; Knaggs.

Seated: C Lewis; J O Leach; Major Blomfield (OC); Capt A Ball; R T C Hoidge.

Bottom left: Jagdstaffel 11, 23 April 1917. From L; Allmenröder; Hintsch; Festner; Schäfer; Manfred von Richthofen(in cockpit); Kurt Wolff; Simon; Brauneck. Seated; Esser; Lothar von Richthofen; Krefft.

Bottom right: Capt Albert Ball, VC, DSO, MC.

Top: Albert Ball in SE5, A4850, 56 Sqn, in which he was killed.

Middle left: Ltn Lothar von Richthofen, Jagdstaffel 11, credited incorrectly with shooting down Albert Ball on 7 May 1917.

Middle right: Capt R T C Hoidge, 56 Sqn, credited with 28 combat victories.

Bottom left: Major Edward 'Mick' Mannock, VC, DSO, MC, of 40, 74 and 85 Squadrons.

Bottom centre: Major Raymond Collishaw, DSO, DSC, DFC, credited with 60 victories.

Bottom right: Major A E McKeever, DSO, MC, credited with 31 victories.

Top left: Aces of Jagdgeschwader Nr.1, the "Richthofen Circus". L-R: Vzfw Sebastian Festner; Ltn Karl Schäfer; Rittmeister Manfred von Richthofen; Ltn Lothar von Richthofen; Ltn Kurt Wolff. The dog was "Moritz", the Red Baron's pet.

Top right: Major G H Bowman, 32 victories, with a captured Fokker D.VII of Jagdstaffel 16.

Middle: Major B E Baker, DSO, MC, 12 victories, later Air Marshal Sir Brian.

Bottom left: Capt Richard Maybery, MC, 21 victories.

Bottom right: Martinsyde G.102, "Elephant" of 27 Squadron, May 1917.

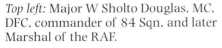

Top left: Major W Sholto Douglas, MC, DFC, commander of 84 Sqn, and later Marshal of the RAF.

Top right: 'Drachen'. German observation kite ballon.

Middle left: Ltn Werner Voss, 48 victories (L) talking to Manfred von Richthofen.

Middle right: De Havilland 4 bombers,

27 Squadron, Serny, 17 February 1918.

Bottom left: Capt Arthur Rhys Davids, DSO, MC, 25 victories, killed in combat on 27 October 1917.

Bottom right: Pilots of 40 Sqn at Bruay, April 1917. L-R: Redfern; Mannock (rear); Barlow (front); Blaxland (with pipe); Napier.

Top: Capt G C Maxwell, MC, DFC, AFC, 26 victories, 56 Sqn.

Middle left: Major Cyril M Crowe, MC, DFC, 15 victories.

Middle right: LVG.C. two-seater.

Bottom centre: Capt Matthew Frew, 23 victories, 45 Sqn, later AVM Sir, KBE, CB, DSO, MC, AFC.

Bottom right: Major D R Maclaren, DSO, MC, DFC, 54 victories, all with 46 Sqn.

Top: Redler, Hall, Bath and W A Bond, of 40 Sqn.

Middle left: Capt A W B Proctor, VC, DSO, MC, DFC, 84 Sqn, 54 victories, killed in a flying accident, 21 June 1921.

Centre: Capts G Lewis, DFC (L) and G E

H McElroy, MC, DFC, 40 Sqn.

Middle right: Hugh Trenchard, commander of the RFC in France, 1917.

Bottom left: Lt A W Hammond, MC (L) and Lt A A McLeod, VC.

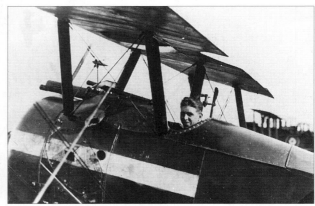

Top left: John Salmond, who succeeded Trenchard as GOC, RFC in France.

Top right: Capt J L Trollope, MC, 43 Sqn.

Middle right: Capt H W Woollett, DSO, MC, of 24 and 43 Sqns, credited with 35 victories, including six in one day.

Bottom left: Capt J Gilmour, 39 victories, 27 and 65 Sqns.

Bottom right: Capt S M Kinkead, DSO, DSC, DFC, 40-plus victories, who was killed in a crash on 12 March 1928 when a member of the RAF High Speed Flight, practising for that year's Schneider Trophy Race.

COMMUNIQUÉ No.106

17 – 23 September 1917

This week saw the arrival of two more fighter squadrons in France: No.68 Squadron, equipped with De Havilland 5s and No.84 Squadron with SE5As, the latter commanded by Major Sholto Douglas, MC, who would eventually retire from the RAF as Marshal of the RAF, Lord Douglas of Kirtleside, GCB, MC, DFC, DL. Another pilot, 2nd Lt P W Bulman, 46 Squadron, mentioned on September 21, was destined to become Chief Test Pilot for the Hawker Aircraft Company in the post-war years. On September 23, the German air force lost its No.2 ace, when Leutnant Werner Voss, credited with 48 victories and leader of Jagdstaffel 10 of the "Richthofen Circus" was killed in an outstanding lone combat with SE5As of 56 Squadron.

During the period under review (17th to 23rd September) we have officially claimed 38 EA and one balloon brought down by aircraft and two by infantry, and 33 driven down out of control. Thirty-nine of our aeroplanes are missing.

SEPTEMBER 17

Artillery Co-operation – 56 hostile batteries have been successfully engaged with aeroplane observation.

Enemy Aircraft – Enemy aircraft activity was slight all day. Captain J Manley, 19 Squadron, pursued one of three EA which his patrol engaged and shot it down out of control. 2nd Lts R V Curtis & D Uniacke, 48 Squadron, dived at a two-seater which they shot down out of control. Major C M B Chapman, 29 Squadron, attacked an Albatros scout but was immediately attacked by several more from behind, so turned round and got underneath one scout which he shot down out of control.

On the Evening of the 16th – Flight Lt R P Minifie, 1 Squadron RNAS, engaged three Albatros scouts which were attacking an RE8 and destroyed one. Captain J Leacroft, 19 Squadron, attacked four Albatros scouts and drove one down out of control. Five Albatros scouts were attacked by an Offensive Patrol of 60 Squadron near Houthem. Capt R Chidlaw-Roberts picked out the leader and after firing 60 rounds the EA burst into flames and spun to earth where it crashed. Capt H Hamersley shot down one EA out of control. Four Albatros scouts attacked two RE8s of 6 Squadron. One RE8 was driven down out of control after hard fighting, and II Battery anti-aircraft report that one EA was shot down and another driven down out of control. 2nd Lt H Maddocks, 54 Squadron, when attacking a two-seater, was attacked from behind by an Albatros scout, so he did a climbing turn and immediately obtained a favourable position and shot it down in flames. Flight Cdr J S T Fall and Flight Sub-Lts A W Wood and Wallace, 9 Squadron RNAS, destroyed a DFW.

SEPTEMBER 18

Artillery Co-operation – 50 hostile batteries were successfully engaged from aeroplane observation, and seven by balloons.

Enemy Aircraft – Lt R Winnicott, 41 Squadron, shot down one EA completely out of control.

131

SEPTEMBER 19
Strong wind and low clouds again interfered with work.

Artillery Co-operation – 78 hostile batteries were successfully engaged from aeroplane observation. During 65 photographic flights, 958 plates were exposed.

Enemy Aircraft – Flight Sub-Lt A R Knight, 8 Squadron RNAS, attacked an Albatros two-seater which he forced to land in a field apparently much damaged. While searching for reported EA, four Spads of 19 Squadron attacked six Albatros scouts near Becelaere. Lt H Dawson observed one scout diving at his tail so stalled his machine with the result that the Albatros scout shot past below, and Lt Dawson immediately dived after him and got in a good burst at close range, and the EA went down and crashed. Another patrol of this squadron engaged ten Albatros scouts near Roulers and Capt J Leacroft drove one down out of control. Later, nine Albatros scouts were met near Moorslede and Capt Leacroft again drove down one EA out of control. Three pilots of 1 Squadron RNAS encountered EA and Flight Sub-Lt S W Rosevear attacked one into which he fired 100 rounds and destroyed it. Another EA, attacked by Flight Sub-Lts J Winn and E Desparats, fell completely out of control and was last seen falling into mist near the ground. Flight Lt R P Minifie, when patrolling with other machines of 1 Squadron RNAS in the evening, dived at an Albatros scout which was diving at a Triplane. After he fired 30 rounds the EA turned over, fell and crashed. Flight Sub-Lt R E McMillan shot down another Albatros scout which fell completely out of control. Eight Albatros scouts were met near Hooge by eight Triplanes of 10 Squadron RNAS. Flight Sub-Lt H B Maund opened fire at one EA which was coming straight at him and shot it down out of control. A second scout attacked by Flight Lt R E Carroll went down with engine full on and was also out of control. Ground observers report that one of these EA crashed. Captain J T B McCudden, 56 Squadron, when at 18,000 feet over Bois de Biez, saw an EA crossing the lines at 14,000 feet and, taking advantage of the sun, obtained a favourable position and shot it down and it crashed just east of the lines. Capt G C Maxwell and 2nd Lt H Sloley of the same squadron drove down one EA in badly damaged condition.

Miscellaneous – A patrol of four Camels of 70 Squadron went out in the morning to attack ground targets with machine gun fire and bombs. 2nd Lt O Stuart attacked a column of about 600 infantry and later dropped two 20lb bombs on targets in Houthulst Forest; 2nd Lt F Quigley attacked several strong points and dropped two 20lb bombs on two of them, and on his way home fired at troops from 200 feet and also shot into communication trenches ; 2nd Lt A H Dalton attacked a column of infantry from 1000 feet and then dispersed a second body of troops from low altitude near Merckem; 2nd Lt J S Michie dropped one 20lb bomb near Stadenreke and one into Clerekem village.

Pilots of 10 Squadron RNAS also did similar work. Flight Cdr H J T Saint dropped two 20lb bombs in Houthulst Forest, then fired 350 rounds into enemy transport on the Staden Road; Flight Sub-Lt N M MacGregor dropped two 20lb bombs in the same locality, then attacked a battery in the forest ; Flight Sub-Lt H S Broughall dropped two 20lb bombs on the crossroads south of Houthulst Forest which disorganised MT transport, then fired 380 rounds at various bodies of troops ; Flight Sub-Lt G L Trapp fired 400 rounds from 500 feet at a battery in the south-east corner of Houthulst Wood. In the evening an Offensive Patrol of 1 Squadron RNAS engaged several Albatros scouts and Flight Lt R P Minifie destroyed one, while a second was driven down out of control by Flight Sub-Lt R E McMillan. Captain W Rooper, 1 Squadron, shot down an Albatros scout in flames. While taking photographs, 2nd Lts A G V

Taylor & H Dandy, 20 Squadron, were suddenly attacked by eight EA. The Observer was badly hit in the leg by one of the first bursts from an EA but kept up a strong fire at one adversary which fell in flames, and then shot down two more in succession out of control.

SEPTEMBER 20

In spite of low clouds, strong wind and rain, a very considerable amount of aerial work was carried out, a special effort being made on account of an attack by the Second and Fifth Armies. Even though the clouds at about 8am were at about 50 feet, machines went out and attacked enemy troops, transport, guns and other targets throughout the day and fired 28,725 rounds. Scouts carried bombs and dropped them on aerodromes and other targets, but space does not permit a detailed account of work by individual machines being given. With the exception of a few cases only, the squadrons, with the numbers of rounds fired, and names of pilots are given. 19,300 rounds were fired by the 5th Brigade and 8450 by the 2nd Brigade. In the Corps Wing of the 2nd Brigade, although a great many contact patrols and much artillery work was done during the day, there were no casualties, and out of 72 combats by machines of this Brigade, only six were by the Corps machines.

Artillery Co-operation – 47 hostile batteries were successfully engaged by aeroplane observation, and eight by balloons.

Enemy Aircraft – No enemy machines were seen before 8am, but after this they were active. In the evening activity decreased and EA encountered were disinclined to fight. 2nd Lt B Poole & 1/AM A J Lea, 16 Squadron, while doing artillery work, were attacked by an Albatros scout which dived on their tail. 1/AM Lea shot the EA down and it was seen to crash. Lt R Strang, 19 Squadron, while flying at 300 feet, saw an EA two-seater doing contact patrol work at 150 feet, so dived and shot it down, and it was seen to be completely wrecked on the ground. An Offensive Patrol of 45 Squadron engaged several EA formations with the result that 2nd Lt E D Clarke destroyed an Albatros scout, 2nd Lt W A Wright shot down a two-seater also destroyed, while 2nd Lts K B Montgomery and P Carpenter each shot down one EA out of control. 2nd Lt L Cummings, 1 Squadron, while on special duty, engaged a DFW two-seater which he destroyed, and Lt F Soden, 60 Squadron, shot down an Albatros scout which crashed. Flight Sub-Lt A Binks, 1 Squadron RNAS, destroyed an EA two-seater, and 2nd Lt J Crompton, 60 Squadron, drove one down out of control. While on artillery work, Capt J P V Lavarack & 2nd Lt J Godfrey, 12 Squadron, were attacked by four Albatros scouts, but they shot one down out of control and drove the rest away. Four Camels of 9 Squadron RNAS attacked five Albatros scouts and shot one down out of control. Captain A G Jones-Williams, 29 Squadron, was attacked by five Albatros but shot one down out of control, while 2nd Lt P de Fontenay of the same squadron who attacked four two-seater EA destroyed one. Flight Sub-Lt J G Manuel, 10 Squadron RNAS, drove down a two-seater EA in which the pilot is believed to have been hit and then fired at it from 200 feet when it landed, and neither of the passengers was seen to get out. 2nd Lt E B Booth, 70 Squadron, shot down an Albatros scout out of control, while Capt G C Maxwell and 2nd Lt R H Sloley, 56 Squadron, each shot down an EA out of control. Lt Cross, 23 Squadron, attacked an enemy balloon south of Houthulst Forest. He was then attacked by EA so dived into a cloud, but the balloon was seen by another pilot to burst into flames. Infantry of the Second Army shot down a low flying EA in flames. In the evening Captain E Mannock, 40 Squadron, observed a two-seater EA east of

Lens so climbed into the sun, then dived and shot it down out of control. 2nd Lts R Brownell and H M Moody, 45 Squadron, dived at a two-seater EA and drove it down, and 2nd Lt E Smith then continued firing at it until it burst into flames. Captain F Sowrey, 19 Squadron, shot down one of several EA which he engaged out of control. Flight Sub-Lt A Binks, 1 Squadron RNAS, shot down a two-seater EA which turned on its nose on reaching the ground, after which he fired 50 rounds into it. A patrol of 60 Squadron dived at five EA and Lt W Jenkins fired 100 rounds into one which turned on its back and fell completely out of control.

Targets engaged by machine gun fire and bombs dropped from low altitudes:
NO.23 SQUADRON – Lt N MacLeod dropped two 20lb bombs on a machine gun emplacement and fired 200 rounds on transport from 500 feet. 2nd Lt J Macrae dropped two bombs on a machine gun emplacement and fired 150 rounds into a party of men. 2nd Lt A Paul dropped two bombs on the Junction of the Ypres-Roulers railway and Zonnebeke-Langemarck road. 2nd Lt H Hiscock dropped two bombs on an active hostile battery, silencing it, and fired 100 rounds from 800 feet.

NO.70 SQUADRON – 2nd Lt J Michie dropped two 20lb bombs on troops in Clereken village from 1000 feet. 2nd Lt C Stewart dropped two 20lb bombs from 1000 feet on some small buildings in a wood, then dived and fired on a body of 600 enemy troops. 2nd Lt F Quigley dropped two 20lb bombs from 800 feet on earthworks and dug-outs at the west end of Houthulst Forest, then fired into a small village from a height of 200 feet. 2nd Lt A H Dalton dropped two 20lb bombs near a house and fired at parties of troops south of Houthulst Forest from 1000 feet.

NO.66 SQUADRON – 2nd Lt Warnock flew along the canal from Armentieres to Menin when clouds were at a height of 50 feet. He came out of the clouds over some railway sidings east of Menin and dropped four 20lb bombs on to 30 or 40 trucks, then fired 70 rounds at transport, motor lorries and a team of six horses drawing a wagon. Lt E H Lascelles crossed the lines at Messines and flew to Roulers at 1000 feet. He came down to 200 feet and fired 100 rounds at a car and motor cycle on the Ypres-Menin road. He then dropped four 20lb bombs from 300 feet on an active battery which stopped firing, then went south and fired 150 rounds from 200 feet on a crowd of men towing a barge on the canal. As his gun then jammed he recrossed the lines, landed at Bailleul where it was rectified, then returned and fired again at the men towing the barge. Forty rounds were then fired from 200 feet into a dump just north of Wervicq.

NO.27 SQUADRON – Lt C Brown flew to Bisseghem aerodrome at a height of 500 feet and dropped two 112lb bombs close to a hangar. Lt R Aire crossed the lines above the clouds and when he came out found himself over Menin. He then flew along the road and canal to Marcke aerodrome where he saw several two-seaters and scouts lined up. He dropped two 112lb bombs from 1000 feet and after the explosions saw the tail plane of one two-seater had been blown off and its fuselage all twisted. Captain E Fawcus dropped two 112lb bombs from 3000 feet on Abeele aerodrome. Lt Hay dropped eight 20lb bombs from 1500 feet on an aerodrome and fired 20 rounds at a machine gun which was engaging him. Lt E C J Elliott crossed the lines in cloud and came out over Abeele where he dropped two 112lb bombs from 2000 feet. Lt H E Darrington dropped two 112lb bombs on Heule aerodrome from 2500 feet.

NO.9 SQUADRON – 2nd Lts C A Youdale & A B Ashcroft in the morning fired 300 rounds into enemy troops in Eagle Trench. In the afternoon they fired 750 rounds from 800 feet at troops in trenches and shell holes. They made a third flight in the evening and fired 950 rounds from 100 feet into troops in Eagle Trench.

NO.19 SQUADRON – Lt O C Bryson left the ground at dawn and on coming out of clouds flew above a good road and saw a dump with huts nearby, so dropped one bomb from 150 feet, then fired 70 rounds at men working. Subsequently he came across hutments on which he dropped a second bomb from 100 feet. Lt A Pentland and Lt C Thompson patrolled together over Polygon Wood, then went to Courtrai and from there to Becelaere, where they fired at infantrymen from 400 feet. They observed a battery firing so Lt Pentland dropped a bomb on it, while Lt Thompson raked the position with gun fire. In another patrol Lt Pentland dropped one bomb on the railway bridge near Comines, and Lt Thompson attacked troops marching towards the lines from 100 feet, scattering them. Captain F Sowrey came down from the clouds at Gheluwe where he saw 100 infantrymen whom he attacked. When near Oosthoek he found an anti-aircraft battery of three guns which he attacked from 100 to 200 feet until his ammunition was finished. He next observed a long range gun firing so dropped a bomb on it, then continued flying east and found rows of sheds on which he dropped another bomb.

The following rounds were fired by pilots from heights ranging from 100 to 800 feet into enemy trenches, troops in shell holes, at transport, troops in villages, hutments and active batteries:

NO. 1 SQUADRON – 1580 rounds by 2nd Lt Baalman, Capt Rooper, 2nd Lts Cummings, Garratt and Baker, Sgts G Olley, 2nd Lts Reeves, Chown, W W Rogers, G Moore, Kelsey, Wilson, and Capt Bath.

NO.4 SQUADRON – 350 rounds by Lts Hunt, Lewis, Golden and 2nd Lt Jones.

NO.45 SQUADRON – 175 rounds by Lt Davis.

NO.1 SQUADRON RNAS – 5950 rounds by Flight Lts Minifie and Rowley, and Flight Sub-Lts Rosevear, Ridley, Guard, Binks, Calvert, Simpson and Burton.

NO.60 SQUADRON – 200 rounds by Lt W J Rutherford.

NO.10 SQUADRON RNAS – 3740 rounds by Flight Cdrs Saint and Alexander, Flight Sub-Lts Bassell, Manuel, Emery, Johnson, Carroll, Fitzgibbon, McGregor, Bowyer, Maund, Broughall, Trapp and Macdonald.

NO.7 SQUADRON – 170 rounds by Lts Watson & O'Callaghan, and 2nd Lts Skinner & Manley.

NO.21 SQUADRON – 120 rounds by 2nd Lts Whitworth-Jones & Wilson, and Lt Zimmer & 2nd Lt Mott.

NO.32 SQUADRON – 750 rounds by Capt Salt, Lts Johnston, Monkhouse and Howson.

NO.23 SQUADRON – 5970 rounds by Lts Bullock-Webster, Baker, 2nd Lts Macrae, Paul and Fielder, Lts Cross and Trudeau, 2nd Lts Drewitt, Smith, Sharland, Fiscock, Lt Gibbs, and Capt D U McGregor.

NO.70 SQUADRON – 2738 rounds by Lt Vinter, 2nd Lts Michie, Wilson, Quigley, Stuart, Layfield, Hobson, Dalton, Runnels-Moss, Lt Gould and Capt Kemsley.

NO.9 SQUADRON – 2000 rounds by 2nd Lts Youdale & Ashcroft.

NO.34 SQUADRON – 20 rounds by Lt Bryson.

NO.52 SQUADRON – 150 rounds by Lt Wells.

SEPTEMBER 21
Over 9000 rounds were fired at ground targets; 1250 by the 1st Brigade, 100 by the 3rd, 660 by the 4th, and 3155 by the 5th, 2400 by 100 Squadron during night work, and 1500 by 101 Squadron also while night bombing.
Artillery Co-operation – 68 hostile batteries were successfully engaged from aeroplane observation, and 20 by balloons.
Enemy Aircraft – Enemy aircraft were very active, especially on the fronts of the Second and Fifth Armies; in the afternoon, however, the activity decreased and EA when met often refused combat. Lt Gordon Duff & 2nd Lt J Ironmonger, 6 Squadron, were attacked by five Albatros scouts. The two nearest EA were fired at in turn and each fell out of control and crashed, after which the other three flew away. Sgt G P Olley, 1 Squadron, attacked three EA two-seaters over Wervicq. He drove one down which he followed and when it flattened out he fired again, and the right-hand wings of the EA folded up, after which he crashed. Captain J Leacroft, 19 Squadron, drove down an Albatros scout out of control. In an engagement between a patrol of 20 Squadron and 18 Albatros scouts, 2nd Lt W Durrand & Lt A N Jenks in one machine, and Lt K R Kirkman & J P Flynn in another machine, drove down two EA out of control. Seeing an arrow on the ground, four pilots of 46 Squadron flew in the direction indicated and found a two-seater EA which they pursued. They then met several enemy scouts, and 2nd Lt P Wilcox shot one down which was seen to crash in water. Capt V Robeson dived at another and shot it down out of control. 2nd Lt P W S Bulman fired about 200 rounds into a third machine which turned on its back, then fell completely out of control, while another was forced to land in a field after being engaged by Lt R S Asher. Another patrol of this squadron engaged an Albatros two-seater, protected by five scouts, and shot the two-seater down out of control. Capt A T Lloyd and Lt Wood, 32 Squadron, attacked four Albatros scouts which fought briefly then dived away. Anti-aircraft observed one of these EA crash. In another patrol of this squadron Capt Lloyd and Lt Packe drove down an EA two-seater out of control. An Offensive Patrol of four DH5s of 24 Squadron, which was reinforced by two Bristol Fighters of 11 Squadron, engaged five Albatros scouts. One EA was destroyed and another driven down out of control. Flight Cdr J S T Saint, 10 Squadron RNAS, attacked one of five Albatros scouts and drove one down completely out of control. When returning from a bomb raid, 2nd Lt A Drinkwater & Lt F T S Menendez, 57 Squadron, were attacked by five EA from underneath. The Observer opened fire at the nearest one and it spun down and crashed. He then fired at a second which turned completely over and fell out of control. Owing to the superior height and speed of the

DH4, the pilot was able to manoeuvre and so afford his Observer opportunities of engaging each EA separately. In hard fighting between EA formations and SE5s of 60 Squadron, two EA were destroyed by Capt R Chidlaw-Roberts and Lt J O Whiting, two by Lt I MacGregor, and two by the patrol. Capt G C Maxwell, 56 Squadron, with other SE5s, pursued six EA scouts, but on seeing four two-seater EA below, turned and attacked one into which he fired a drum from his Lewis gun at about 15 yards range. The German pilot made effort to escape the fire, and the EA broke to pieces in the air and crashed. 2nd Lt Sloley also fired at it. 2nd Lt G M Wilkinson also ceased pursuing the same six EA in order to attack one of the two-seaters and opened fire at about ten yards range at the one he selected, which went down in a slow spin and crashed. Another Offensive Patrol of this squadron observed a fight between Sopwith Scouts, SE5s and about 21 EA, so joined the combat. Lt R T C Hoidge saw one EA on the tail of an SE5,so fired a drum from his Lewis gun, after which the EA fell out of control, then broke to pieces before crashing.

SEPTEMBER 22

The weather was fine but visibility bad, and in the morning clouds interfered with work.

Artillery Co-operation – 54 hostile batteries were engaged successfully with aeroplane observation, and 25 by balloons.

Enemy Aircraft – Enemy aircraft activity was below normal during the whole day. An Offensive Patrol of 40 Squadron engaged four DFWs and four Albatros scouts over Pont-a-Vendin. They drove down the two-seaters and then fought the scouts, and 2nd Lt J H Tudhope attacked one at close range, shot it down out of control, and saw it crash. An Offensive Patrol of 45 Squadron encountered ten Albatros scouts near Tenbrielen which they attacked, and 2nd Lt K B Montgomery drove one down out of control. Capt R L Chidlaw-Roberts, 60 Squadron, also drove an Albatros down out of control. Sopwith Scouts of 46 Squadron attacked an Albatros scout which was destroyed by Capt V Joske and Lt R Ferrie. An EA scout attacking a Bristol Fighter was shot down by Capt M G Scott, 46 Squadron. Lt E D Perney & 2nd Lt C H Jordan,11 Squadron, attacked an Albatros scout which turned completely over and fell out of control into the clouds. 2nd Lt Wallace & Capt Revill, 11 Squadron, shot down one EA out of control. Flight Sub-Lt R Sykes,9 Squadron RNAS, drove down an Albatros scout which he believes fell out of control, but was unable to watch it as he had been wounded and had to return. In a fight between Albatros scouts and Bristol Fighters of 22 Squadron, Capt R Stuart-Wortley & Lt P Burton shot one EA down out of control, and the Observer then shot the propeller off another EA, and shot a third down out of control. Capt J A McKelvie & 2nd Lt G Nelson-Smith, 22 Squadron, also shot down one out of control, and two others badly damaged.

On the evening of the 21st, an Offensive Patrol of 20 Squadron engaged 12 Albatros scouts over Menin, and Lts H G E Luchford & W C Cambray drove one down out of control. No.45 Squadron engaged 20 Albatros scouts over Comines. Lt M B Frew drove one down with its engine stopped, then attacked another which he shot down in flames and saw it crash. 2nd Lt E Smith shot down another out of control. Flight Cdr S T Edwards and Flight Sub-Lt O W Redgate, 9 Squadron RNAS, attacked a two-seater DFW and shot it down out of control.

Bombing – 9th Wing – On the night of the 21st/22nd, 101 Squadron bombed Roulers Station and Menin Station. On the same night, 100 Squadron bombed Ledeghem, Menin, Gheluwe Village, Wervicq. The raids by these two squadrons were carried out with the object of demoralising German troops and transport which were proceeding to counter-attack our troops who had just gained their objective. The pilots threw out parachute flares from time to time which showed the roads to be crowded with vehicles and troops. It was during these raids that the pilots, in addition to dropping bombs, flew up and down firing from a few hundred feet 8220 rounds.

SEPTEMBER 23

Artillery Co-operation – 51 hostile batteries were successfully engaged from aeroplane observation, and 18 by balloons.

Enemy Aircraft – Enemy aircraft activity was normal most of the day but slightly above normal at times. 2nd Lt Ferguson & 2/AM Fry, 16 Squadron, drove down a DFW out of control. 2nd Lt W McLanachan and Captain E Mannock, 40 Squadron, each destroyed an EA. On the evening of the 22nd, Lt J Rutherford,60 Squadron, destroyed a two-seater EA; 2nd Lt H Dawson, 19 Squadron, drove down an Albatros scout out of control, and Capt C Riddle & Lt King, 6 Squadron, drove down a two-seater EA out of control. On the 23rd, 2nd Lts R Strang and A Pentland, 19 Squadron, each drove down an Albatros scout out of control, while 2nd Lt P Wilson, 1 Squadron, drove down another out of control. 2nd Lts F Watts & E Ripley, 53 Squadron, while on photographic work, were attacked by an Albatros scout but shot it down out of control. In a fight between an EA formation and four machines of 11 Squadron, Lt A E McKeever & 2nd Lt L A Powell shot down two Albatros scouts out of control, while Sgt Stevenson & 1/AM Platel shot down a third out of control. Flight Cdr S T Edwards, 9 Squadron RNAS, destroyed two EA, and Flight Sub-Lt J P Hales of the same squadron destroyed one EA. Capt A G Jones-Williams, 29 Squadron, and Flight Cdrs W M Alexander and H J T Saint, 10 Squadron RNAS, each shot down an EA out of control. Lt S Sibley & 2nd Lt P Shone, 48 Squadron, shot down an EA two-seater out of control. Captain J T B McCudden, 56 Squadron, attacked an EA two-seater which he destroyed. He then saw an SE5 fighting an EA Triplane, so with the rest of his patrol dived at it, and for the next ten minutes the Triplane fought the five SE5s with great skill and determination. Eventually, however, it was destroyed by 2nd Lt A P F Rhys Davids, 56 Squadron, who had previously driven down an EA two-seater out of control. The following is part of his report;

" ... The other EA scout now vanished, but the red-nosed Albatros and the Triplane fought magnificently. I got in several bursts at the Triplane without apparent effect, and twice placed a new drum on my Lewis gun. Eventually I got east and slightly above the Triplane and made for it, getting in a whole Lewis drum and a corresponding number of Vickers into him. He made no attempt to turn until I was so close to him I was certain we would collide. He passed my right-hand wing by inches and went down. I zoomed. I saw him next with his engine apparently off, gliding west. I dived again and got one shot out of my Vickers; however, I reloaded and kept in the dive. I got in another good burst and the Triplane did a slight right-hand turn, still going down. I had now overshot him (this was at 1000 feet), zoomed, but never saw him again. Immediately afterwards I met the red-nosed scout who was a short way south-east of me. I started firing at 100 yards. The EA then turned and fired at me. At 30 yards range I finished a Lewis drum and my Vickers stopped, so I dived underneath him and zoomed. When I looked again I saw the EA spiralling down steeply out of control."

The Triplane crashed in our lines and the occupant proved to be Lt Werner Voss who was killed.

COMMUNIQUÉ No.107

24 – 30 September 1917

On September 24th yet another squadron arrived in France from England, No.102 Squadron, flying FE2b/ds, for night bombing duties; a role it was to continue fulfilling, still with FEs, until the Armistice in 1918. In comparison with the figures for enemy aircraft claimed for September, the RFC suffered its highest monthly casualties since the previous April. Commencing with this communiqué, individual gallantry awards were included in these weekly summaries.

During the month of September we have claimed 139 EA brought down by aircraft, and 13 by anti-aircraft, and 122 out of control. 125 tons of bombs have been dropped which is the greatest amount ever dropped in a month by the RFC. Over 16,000 photographs have been taken, and 1372 hostile batteries have been successfully engaged for destruction.

SEPTEMBER 24

Artillery Co-operation – 59 hostile batteries were successfully engaged from aeroplane observation, and eight by balloons.

Enemy Aircraft – Enemy aircraft activity was below normal. 2nd Lt E Morris & 2/AM Dixon, 5 Squadron, were attacked by an EA scout when on artillery work, and shot it down out of control. Six Bristol Fighters of 20 Squadron engaged seven Albatros scouts near Lille. Capt E H Johnston & Lt J Hone, who led the formation, drove down one Albatros out of control and it was seen by anti-aircraft to crash. A patrol of 46 Squadron dived on a DFW two-seater and destroyed it. Capt D Stevenson & Lt P Wood, 12 Squadron, while on photography, shot down an Albatros scout out of control. 2nd Lt C Horsley & Lt A Hahn,18 Squadron, were taking photographs when attacked by about nine EA who dived at the DH4 from all sides. During the fight 700 rounds were fired at the EA and one driven down completely out of control. Flight Sub-Lt A P V Daly, 10 Squadron RNAS, shot down an EA two-seater out of control, and 2nd Lt C N Lomax and Lt W H R Gould, 70 Squadron, attacked an Albatros scout which they believe fell out of control.

Lt L M Barlow,56 Squadron, dived at two two-seaters, one of which zoomed away after being fired at, then went into a spin, and continued spinning until it crashed. 2nd Lt A P F Rhys Davids of the same squadron also dived at two EA two-seaters and selected one which he followed, but was in turn attacked from behind by three more. He continued pursuing the first one and eventually destroyed it. A formation of 27 Squadron, when returning from bombing Ath Railway Station, was heavily attacked and shot down one EA out of control. In the evening, 2nd Lt H Dawson, 19 Squadron, attacked a Rumpler two-seater and shot it down out of control. Capt F Morse and Lt G Hyde, 54 Squadron, drove down two EA scouts, one of which was seen to fall out of control by anti-aircraft observers.

SEPTEMBER 25

The weather was fine and 12 reconnaissances, 63 photographic flights during which 1076 photographs were taken, 42 contact patrols and 12 bomb raids were

carried out, and over 1000 rounds were fired at various ground targets from the air.
Artillery Co-operation – 70 hostile batteries were successfully engaged from
aeroplane observation, and seven by balloons.
Enemy Aircraft – Enemy aircraft were active and in the fighting that took place our
pilots showed marked superiority. We had a single-seater machine missing, two
pilots and an Observer killed, and three others wounded, while 19 EA were seen to
crash and 13 driven down out of control. In addition a large three-seater bombing
EA was brought down in our lines by anti-aircraft of the Fourth Army at night.
(Editor's note; Gotha G.IV 1064/16 of KG 111/15, coded G.74 by the RFC).

Lts R Durno & G Cooke, 5 Squadron, shot down an Albatros scout out of control, and
Captain E Mannock,40 Squadron, drove down another which is also believed to have
fallen out of control. An Offensive Patrol of 60 Squadron engaged an Albatros scout
which was destroyed by 2nd Lts J Crompton and G C Young. 2nd Lt W Jenkins shot
down a two-seater out of control, then his patrol attacked seven EA over St Julien
and Capt K L Caldwell drove one down out of control. Lt J C B Firth,45 Squadron,
drove down a two-seater out of control. 2nd Lt R G Holt, 19 Squadron, attacked a
two-seater and shot it down out of control which was seen an hour later crashed. An
EA dived at Lt J Worstenholme & Lt F C McCreary, 6 Squadron, and the pilot (Lt
Worstenholme) was shot dead. The Observer took the controls, and on two occasions
left them alone in order to fire at the EA. He brought the machine back to within a
mile of his aerodrome where it crashed, but he was not killed. Four Sopwith Scouts
of 46 Squadron attacked a two-seater over Pelves. Lts P Wilcox and G E Thompson
fired 70 rounds each, then 2nd Lt P W S Bulman continued firing and followed it
down until he saw it crash. Lts A E McKeever & W Dodd, 11 Squadron, shot down an
Albatros scout which broke to pieces in the air. When at 12,000 feet a patrol of eight
DH5s of 41 Squadron met ten EA scouts and very severe fighting took place in which
two EA were destroyed and three driven down out of control. Lt R Winnicott and Lt
M Thomas destroyed one each, while 2nd Lts J Haight, T Langford- Sainsbury and R
Anderson shot down one each out of control. A patrol of 54 Squadron attacked
seven Albatros scouts over Middelkerke. Capt O Stewart shot down one which fell in
the sea. 2nd Lt H Maddocks shot down another in flames, and 2nd Lt M Gonne shot
down one which broke to pieces in the air.

2nd Lt R M Smith, 23 Squadron, attacked a two-seater from behind but it got
away. He then attacked another which he followed down until it turned over, fell out
of control, then crashed in flames. Lt F Gibbs of the same squadron saw a two-
seater above him flying west, so climbed up to 20,000 feet, then dived at the EA as
it returned and followed it down to about 4000 feet from where it fell and crashed.
Lt W Gould and 2nd Lt C Runnels-Moss, both of 70 Squadron, shot down an EA
two-seater in flames despite being attacked by its protecting scouts. 2nd Lt A Dalton
and Lt F Hobson,70 Squadron, attacked two EA both of which went into spinning
nose-dives apparently out of control. 2nd Lts Cook & Coppard,57 Squadron, when
returning from bombing, were attacked by four EA and shot one down out of
control. The following account is given by 2nd Lt L M Barlow, 56 Squadron, who
destroyed three EA while on Offensive Patrol in the evening :

"As we were climbing towards the lines I saw an enemy two-seater over east end
of Nieppe Forest at about 18,000 feet being engaged by anti-aircraft which was
bursting at about 11,000 feet. I immediately signalled to the rest of the formation
and opened my engine full out but was unable to catch the EA up, he then being

about 5000 feet above us on reaching the lines. I next saw about ten EA scouts coming south at about 16,000 feet, so led the SE5 formation under the EA hoping to decoy them so that C Flight could engage them. The EA did not want to fight and immediately dived off east. I then turned west to regain height but lost the rest of the patrol for the time being. I then attacked slightly from above, at about 12 to 13,000 feet over Houthulst Forest, four EA scouts (two ordinary yellow fuselage V-Strutters and two Fokker biplanes). I met the middle machine, a V-Strutter, end on firing a big burst from both guns at him until only a few yards away. I zoomed and saw the EA going down in pieces and then burst into flames (this is confirmed by Capt G H Bowman and Lt R Maybery). At the top of the zoom I did a right-angle turn, then dived and finally met end on the Fokker biplane. I fired a good burst at him and he went down in a very slow but steep spiral, with smoke issuing from his tail. This EA was seen to crash by Lt Maybery. I then dived at the other V-Strutter which was diving away east and fired a good burst at the EA from both guns at about 150 yards, but zoomed away as I saw more EA scouts diving on me from the east and above. The EA was seen to fall out of control and crash into the ground half a mile from the north-west corner of Houthulst Forest by Captain Bowman".

(Editor's note: Two of Barlow's victims were from Jagdstaffel 10 of the "Richthofen Circus"; Oberleutnant Weigand and Uffz. Werkmeister).

In the evening a patrol of 19 Squadron engaged two Albatros scouts near Houthem and Lt O C Bryson destroyed one. Capt W Rooper, 1 Squadron, drove down an Albatros scout out of control. A patrol of 20 Squadron fought six Albatros scouts over Becelaere and Lt H G E Luchford & 2nd Lt R F Hill destroyed one; 2nd Lt Harrison & Lt White shot down another in flames, while Lt Dally & Sgt A N Benger, and Sgt Hopper & Capt L W Burbidge each shot down an EA out of control. 2nd Lts C A Youdale & 2nd Lt Wilson, 21 Squadron, were attacked by three EA scouts and shot one down, and were then attacked by two two-seaters, one of which they destroyed. Lt Caswell & 2nd Lt Manley, 7 Squadron, were attacked by EA scouts and drove two away, then shot down a third out of control.

SEPTEMBER 26
Mist and low clouds greatly interfered with work. In spite of this, over 30,000 rounds were fired at enemy troops, transport, guns and other targets by our low-flying aeroplanes in co-operation with an attack by infantry. A few extracts taken at random from the list compiled are given here. Lt A Pentland, 19 Squadron, crossed the lines at 2000 feet and attacked a two-seater, but was driven back by EA scouts. On avoiding them he recrossed the lines and fired at scattered troops from low altitude. He then found an ammunition dump so dropped a 20lb bomb and blew up the dump. He was again attacked by EA so dived into the barrage to escape, and a shell went through his fuselage, cutting the elevator controls and one side of the rudder controls. His machine fell out of control and he only regained control when a few feet from the ground. He crossed the lines and crashed just on our side. Infantry ran to his assistance but unfortunately one was killed and another wounded, and Lt Pentland was also hit. Others then came and carried him away. On the way to safety a shell knocked the party down but no one was hurt.

Capt A T Harris, 45 Squadron, fired 200 rounds at three gun teams and went down to ten feet. He then fired 100 rounds at troops. Flight Sub-Lt J S Rowley, 1 Squadron RNAS, attacked men in shell holes and trenches from 100 feet and fired

300 rounds. Capt Kemsley and Lts Michie, E B Booth and F Quigley, 70 Squadron, dropped nine bombs on and near Westroosebeke, and fired 760 rounds. Lt N Macleod, 23 Squadron, flew up and down Zonnebeke-Moorslede road, firing 500 rounds at various targets.

Flight Sub-Lt J G Manuel, 10 Squadron RNAS, dropped two bombs on Abeele aerodrome and one fell among four EA machines standing outside the sheds, then dived and attacked a machine gun firing at him, after which he scattered some 500 men, firing in all 230 rounds. Flight Cdr W M Alexander, 10 Squadron RNAS, attacked a body of men about 1000 strong from 300 feet, firing 350 rounds.

Artillery Co-operation – 39 hostile batteries were successfully engaged with aeroplane observation, and three by balloons.

Enemy Aircraft – Lt R Strang, 19 Squadron, dived at two EA two-seaters and shot one down which was seen to crash by ground observers, while Capt J Leacroft and 2nd Lt W Jones of the same squadron each shot down a two-seater out of control. An Offensive Patrol of 45 Squadron attacked an Albatros two-seater and Lt E D Clarke destroyed it, while an Albatros scout was destroyed by Lt J Firth. Capt H M Ferreira, 29 Squadron, shot one EA down out of control, while Lt J H Wilson and 2nd Lt A H Dalton, 70 Squadron, shot down a two-seater out of control. Three EA dived at 2nd Lts D H Sessions & Alexander, 21 Squadron, and the pilot immediately put his machine down, then opened fire from underneath at one EA and shot a wing off, after which it crashed. Flight Sub-Lt A P V Daly, 10 Squadron RNAS, destroyed an EA near Houthulst Forest, and Flight Lt D Fitzgibbon drove down an Albatros scout out of control. Capt D U McGregor, 23 Squadron, shot down an EA out of control and saw it crash. Infantry of the Second Army shot down five enemy low flying machines, two of which, an LVG and a Rumpler, fell in our lines (coded G.76 and G.77 respectively).

SEPTEMBER 27

Artillery Co-operation – 20 hostile batteries were successfully engaged from aeroplane observation.

Enemy aircraft – Enemy aircraft were disinclined to fight, but his scouts attacked our infantry from low altitudes. Flight Lt R P Minifie, 1 Squadron RNAS, destroyed a two-seater near St Julien. A photographic formation of 20 Squadron fought eight Albatros scouts near Moorslede. 2nd Lt Dalley & Lt Rowan in one machine, and 2nd Lt W Durrand & Sgt W Benger in another machine each shot down one EA in flames, while 2nd Lts F F Babbage & R C Purvis drove one down out of control. 2nd Lt N McLeod, 19 Squadron, shot down an Albatros scout out of control. Flight Sub-Lt W A Curtis, 10 Squadron RNAS, shot down an EA scout out of control which was seen to crash by another pilot. Flight Lt D F Fitzgibbon and Flight Sub-Lt S A Bowyer of the same squadron patrol each shot down an EA out of control. Lt L M Barlow, 56 Squadron, engaged six EA and shot one down out of control. Captain J T B McCudden of the same squadron went up to test his engine and saw a two-seater EA coming south over Langemarck. He manoeuvred for position, then dived and shot it down within our lines. Infantry of the Second Army shot down one EA.

HONOURS AND AWARDS

Bar to the Military Cross – Capt J P V Lavarack, MC; Capt D F Stevenson, MC.
The Military Cross – 2nd Lt M B Frew, 45 Squadron.
The Distinguished Service Cross – Flight Lt R P Minifie, RN.

SEPTEMBER 28

Artillery Co-operation – 49 hostile batteries were successfully engaged from aeroplane observation, and 31 targets by balloons.

Enemy Aircraft – On the evening of the 27th an Albatros scout which brought down one of our balloons was attacked and shot down in our lines by Flight Cdr C D Booker, 8 Squadron RNAS, and 2nd Lt J H Tudhope, 40 Squadron. The EA pilot was slightly wounded and taken prisoner. An Offensive Patrol of 20 Squadron engaged 25 Albatros scouts between Menin and Wervicq. A very severe fight ensued and Lt H G E Luchford & 2nd Lt R F Hill destroyed two EA, one of which fell in flames. Capt Ridley & Lt King, 6 Squadron, while on artillery work, were attacked by a number of EA scouts but returned safely after shooting one down out of control. Bristol Fighters of 11 Squadron and DH5s of 41 Squadron met nine Albatros scouts over Bugnicourt. The enemy fought well but were completely beaten. Lt A E McKeever & 1/AM Hewitt, 11 Squadron, shot one down out of control, then dived on another which they destroyed, then dived on three more, drove two away and shot the third down in flames and saw it crash. 2nd Lts Stanley & Le Fernie of the same squadron dived at a scout but another EA scout dived at the Bristol Fighter's tail and was engaged by the Observer, while the pilot engaged the one beneath. Both EA were shot simultaneously out of control. Lt M Thomas on a DH5 of 41 Squadron destroyed one EA scout, while Lt E Weiss and Lt R Winnicott, both 41 Squadron, each shot down one EA out of control. A patrol of 48 Squadron attacked six Albatros scouts. 2nd Lts W Bostock & V Collins destroyed one, then attacked another which broke to pieces in the air before it crashed. During this combat our machines fired 1845 rounds. A patrol of 9 Squadron RNAS, led by Flight Cdr S T Edwards, destroyed an Albatros scout. Flight Sub-Lt G L Trapp, 10 Squadron RNAS, destroyed an EA, and Flight Cdr W M Alexander drove one down which broke up on landing. Lts J H Wilson and N O Vinter, 70 Squadron, each shot down an EA out of control. Captain J T B McCudden, 56 Squadron, dived with his formation at EA and selected one which he destroyed. The wings were seen to fall off this EA before it reached the ground, and the pilot fell out at about 8000 feet. Lt L M Barlow dived at another which was seen to crash, while Capt G H Bowman and Lt R T C Hoidge each destroyed an EA. Lt A P F Rhys Davids shot one down out of control, and it has since been reported by French infantry to have crashed.

Bombing – On the night of the 27th/28th, bomb raids were carried out by machines of 2, 8, 10, 12, 13, 15, 25, 18 and 57 Squadrons against targets at Hantay, Lambres, Annoeullin, Carvin, Marquillies, Fournes, Sainghin, Courrieres, Pont-a-Vendin, Corbehem, Arleux, Rumilly, Gouy le Catelet, Oisy le Verger. On the 28th raids were made by 18, 55, 57, 100 and 101 Squadrons against targets at Carnieres aerodrome, Moorslede, Hooglede, Ledeghem, Menin, Wevelghem, Dadizeele, Rumbeke railway, Beythem Railway Station, Gontrode aerodrome. Machines of 10 Squadron RNAS carried bombs which they dropped on Rumbeke aerodrome and fired 1420 rounds into the sheds and at EA on the aerodrome.

SEPTEMBER 29

A very thick mist allowed only a little aerial work to be accomplished.

Artillery Co-operation – 21 hostile batteries were successfully engaged from aeroplane observation, and ten targets by balloons.

Enemy Aircraft – Enemy aircraft were very inactive and when encountered generally refused combat and flew away. Captain T S Wynn, 43 Squadron, engaged an EA and drove it down but had his machine hit and only just managed to return. Ground observers report that this EA fell in flames. Lt L Baker, 23 Squadron, shot down an Albatros scout apparently out of control. A patrol of 56 Squadron attacked EA near Staden, and Capt G C Maxwell drove one down and followed up behind shooting until the EA broke up in the air and crashed. Two others were driven down out of control; one by Lt H Johnston and the other by the SE5 patrol.

HONOURS AND AWARDS

Bar to the Military Cross – Captain G H Bowman, MC; Lt R T C Hoidge, MC; 2nd Lt A C Youdale, MC; 2nd Lt R B Ashcroft, MC; 2nd Lt K R Park, MC.

The Military Cross – Captain W Smith; Lt C A Brewster-Joske; Lt F L McCrearsy.

SEPTEMBER 30

Artillery Co-operation – 90 hostile batteries were successfully engaged from aeroplane observation.

Enemy Aircraft – Capt F Sowrey, 19 Squadron, shot down an Albatros two-seater out of control. Patrols of Bristol Fighters of 11 Squadron, and DH5s of 41 Squadron met an EA formation and hard fighting ensued, resulting in nine EA being driven down out of control without any casualties to our pilots or Observers. The following pilots and Observers shot down these EA;

11 Squadron – 2nd Lts C Pern & P J Cayley – 2 machines
2nd Lts A Brown & C Jordan – 2 machines
2nd Lts H Scandrett & Lt Watson – 2 machines

41 Squadron – 2nd Lt R Winnicott – 2 machines
2nd Lt R M Whitehead – 1 machine

A patrol of 66 Squadron were pursuing a hostile two-seater when they were dived on by an EA formation. The pilots, though at a disadvantage, fought well and one EA was destroyed by Capt T Bayetto, while another was driven down out of control by Lt W A Pritt. Two of our machines were lost on the other side, and two were forced to land on our side, while the other machines were much shot about, one coming back with a cylinder completely shattered. No.56 Squadron encountered a large formation which they completely routed. Lt R Maybery destroyed one EA, while Capt G C Maxwell shot down another out of control. This brings the number of EA accounted for by this squadron to 200 since their arrival in April. This beats the record claimed by the German Circus. Bombing machines of 55 Squadron (DH4s) had hard fighting on their way back to the lines and were ably assisted by Bristol Fighters who met them. All our machines returned safely, while the enemy lost three destroyed and two out of control. Of these, Capt J Burd & Lt F Singleton, 55 Squadron, destroyed one EA, drove two down out of control, and one down in badly damaged condition. Another was destroyed by 2nd Lt E F van der Riet & 2/AM S Groves. A third was destroyed by Sgt M J Weare & 2/AM Moreman, 55 Squadron, and by Capt J McKelvie & 2nd Lt G F Dell, 22 Squadron.

Miscellaneous – On the 29th, Lt White & 2nd Lt Preston, 16 Squadron, dived on a party of 40 men who were unloading an ammunition train, and fired 250 rounds from 1000 feet. A hostile kite balloon landed in our lines in the morning. The balloon was intact with its parachutes, but no trace of the Observers could be found.

COMMUNIQUÉ No.108

1 – 7 October 1917

On October 6, No. 3 Squadron flew its first operations with Sopwith Camels, having finally exchanged its out-dated Morane Parasol two-seaters, while No.66 Squadron commenced replacement of its Sopwith Scouts ("Pups") with Camels. Despite prolonged bad weather conditions, air operations were maintained in the gradual build-up of support for the forthcoming Battle of Passchendaele, due to commence on October 12. Flight Lt A R Brown, 9 Squadron RNAS, mentioned in Honours and awards, would gain fame in April 1918 for his involvement in the death of Germany's "Ace of Aces", Rittmeister Manfred von Richthofen.

During the period under review (1st to 7th October inclusive) the weather has made aerial work difficult. In air fighting we have brought down 17 of his machines and have driven down 14 out of control. Approximately 312 tons of bombs have been dropped.

OCTOBER 1
Artillery Co-operation – 83 hostile batteries have been successfully engaged from aeroplane observation, and 22 by balloons.
Enemy Aircraft – An Offensive Patrol of 1 Squadron attacked a two-seater which was destroyed by 2nd Lt L Cummings. The patrol then engaged another two-seater and shot it down out of control. An Offensive Patrol of 45 Squadron met eight Albatros scouts near Quesnoy and 2nd Lt R J Brownell drove one down out of control. Capt W A Wright, 45 Squadron, and Lt Reeder & Cpl Holmes, 53 Squadron, attacked an Albatros scout which they shot down in our lines near Hooge. Another EA was driven down apparently out of control by 2nd Lt E Smith,45 Squadron. Lt H G E Luchford & 2nd Lt R Hill, 20 Squadron, destroyed an Albatros scout. A photographic formation of 4 Squadron met four Albatros scouts two of which were driven down out of control; one by 2nd Lt Mitchell & Lt Barrington, and the other by 2nd Lt E Jackson Lt T Flanaghan. In a fight between Sopwith Scouts of 46 Squadron and Albatros scouts, Capt M D G Scott shot one down out of control, but was attacked himself from behind, so turned and shot this EA down out of control. Lt A S G Lee saw an EA two-seater below the Sopwiths so dived and shot it down out of control. A Bristol Fighter of 11 Squadron, Lt A E McKeever & H Kent, attacked a two-seater into which they fired 25 rounds and the EA fell out of control and crashed. Flight Sub-Lt W A Curtis, 10 Squadron RNAS, attacked an Albatros scout into which he fired 150 rounds at close range and it went into a spin and fell out of control. A patrol of Bristol Fighters of 22 Squadron dived at six EA and Lts J Bush & W Chapman shot down one out of control. An SE5 formation of 56 Squadron met a large formation of EA and one was driven down out of control by 2nd Lt A P F Rhys Davids, and another by the SE5 formation.
Bombing – ***9th Wing*** – On the night of 30th September/1st October, No.100 Squadron dropped two 230lb, two 112lb, two 25lb and two phosphorous bombs on Gontrode Airship Shed. Both the 230lb, one phosphorous, and one 25lb bomb hit the shed from which volumes of smoke were seen ascending. Thirty 1lb Pom-pom shells were also fired into it. Courtrai Station and trains in the vicinity were also

attacked. A large fire was started among the rolling stock in the station. Twelve 25lb bombs were dropped on Bisseghem Dump, and one 230lb and two 25lb bombs on Wervicq. During this raid 1035 rounds were fired at searchlights and other objectives. The same night, No. 101 Squadron carried out a raid on Gontrode Airship Shed and dropped two 230lb, six 112lb and four 20lb bombs. One 230lb was dropped on Heule aerodrome, two on Beythem Station, one on transport, and one 230lb and two 112lb bombs on other targets. 1330 rounds were fired on various objectives. On 1st October, 55 Squadron dropped twelve 112lb, 32 20lb, and 199 1lb bombs on Gontrode Airship Shed. Direct hits were obtained on aeroplanes in front of the sheds, and a fire started near the large shed.
(Editor's note: Gontrode aerodrome was the base for four squadrons of Gotha bombers responsible for day and night raids on England).

HONOURS AND AWARDS
The Distinguished Service Order – 2nd Lt A P F Rhys Davids.
The Military Cross – Lt F T S Menendez.

OCTOBER 2
Artillery Co-operation – 95 hostile batteries were successfully engaged from aeroplane observation, and 37 targets by balloons.
Enemy Aircraft – Enemy aircraft generally avoided our fighting machines, but attacked our long-distance bombers vigorously when far east. In the 2nd Brigade five EA were driven down out of control, one being a two-seater attacked by 2nd Lts E Moore and H Hamilton, 1 Squadron. Two were by Sgt Hopper & Capt Burbidge, 20 Squadron, one by Lts Dalley & Rowan of the same squadron, while the remaining one – a two-seater – was driven own by 2nd Lt Lothan and Sgt G Olley, 1 Squadron. Lt F Gibbs, 23 Squadron, drove down a two-seater out of control and saw it crash in a shell hole. When returning from a bomb raid on Abeele aerodrome, five DH4s of 57 Squadron were attacked by about 15 Albatros scouts. In the combat that followed 2nd Lt F Martin & Lt J O'Neill were attacked by three scouts and the Observer shot one down in flames. Capt D Hall & 2nd Lt E Hartigan engaged a large number of scouts. One attacked from the side but after 2nd Lt Hartigan had fired 90 rounds into it the struts were seen to be shot away on one side, the main planes came together, and the EA broke up. Another EA passed in front of the DH4 and the pilot fired 50 rounds into it when it immediately dived, broke into flames, then crashed. The pilot then fired into another EA which went completely over and fell out of control. One Albatros scout continued to follow the DH4, firing at long range, and so when getting nearer the lines the DH4 throttled back and allowed the Albatros to approach. When within about 200 yards the DH4 pilot turned his machine and 2nd Lt Hartigan, the Observer, fired a burst into the EA which turned over and over, then fell out of control.

A two-seater EA was attacked by Lt J Bush & 1/AM A Whitehouse, 22 Squadron, and after the Observer had fired into it, it fell out of control and crashed. Lt R Maybery, 56 Squadron, destroyed one EA, and Capt G H Bowman of the same squadron drove down one out of control. 2/AM S Leyland, Observer in a DH4 of 55 Squadron, piloted by Lt M Jones, shot down an EA apparently out of control. In the evening, 2nd Lt S Gilray & Lt H Smith, 53 Squadron, while on flash reconnaissance, were attacked by an Albatros scout, and the Observer was immediately wounded but opened fire and shot down the Albatros in flames. 2nd Lt G Jooste & Cpt J

Johnstone, 20 Squadron, engaged four Albatros scouts and shot one down out of control. A formation of Bristol Fighters of 11 Squadron engaged seven Albatros scouts, and Lt A E McKeever & 2nd Lt L A Powell attacked one which 2nd Lt Powell shot down in flames. Lt R H Rivers & 2nd Lt Fosse fought three scouts and shot one down out of control. 2nd Lts G Armstrong & H Pughe-Evans, 57 Squadron, when returning from a reconnaissance, met five EA which they attacked and drove one down out of control. Sgt F Legge & 1/AM J Clarke of the same squadron met a large formation of Albatros scouts, and after 70 rounds had been fired one EA was shot down and crashed and the others flew off.

OCTOBER 3
Only a little work was possible owing to unsettled weather.
Artillery Co-operation – 23 hostile batteries were successfully engaged from aeroplane observation.
Enemy Aircraft – An Offensive Patrol of 20 Squadron engaged six Albatros scouts and one was shot down out of control by 2nd Lt Taylor & Sgt W Benger.

HONOURS AND AWARDS
The Military Cross – 2nd Lt C A Stevens; Captain A Gray.
The Distinguished Conduct Medal – No.2105 Sgt S J Clinch.
The Military Medal – No. P/13891 2/AM S L Leyland; P/286 1/AM A Walters;
                    94089 2/AM S Moreman.

OCTOBER 4
The weather was very bad indeed.

OCTOBER 5
The weather continued unsettled and stormy. Despite this quite a lot of work was done.
Artillery Co-operation – 17 hostile batteries were successfully engaged from aeroplane observation.
Enemy Aircraft – When returning from a bomb raid on Chateau du Sart aerodrome, three DH4s of 25 Squadron were attacked by eight Albatros scouts. Five of these attacked 2nd Lt Main & 1/AM Leach from behind and the Observer shot down one out of control. 2nd Lt Wright & Lt Plamondon shot down another out of control, while a third was shot down out of control by 2nd Lt Pfeiffer. 2nd Lt G Ferguson & 2/AM Fry, 16 Squadron, were attacked by an Albatros scout when doing artillery work and succeeded in shooting it down out of control. A patrol of 1 Squadron attacked four EA near Zandvoorde and Capt W Rooper destroyed one of these. A fight took place between Bristol Fighters of 20 Squadron and Albatros scouts near Becelaere, and Capt J Johnston & Lt J A Hone shot down one completely out of control. Another fight took place between 1 Squadron and several EA two-seaters. Three EA were destroyed; one by Sgt G Olley; one by Capt F Fullard; and the third by 2nd Lt G Moore which burst into flames and crashed. A fourth EA was driven down out of control by 2nd Lt Baalman.

OCTOBER 6
The weather did not improve at all and little work was possible.
Artillery Co-operation – 33 hostile batteries were successfully engaged from aeroplane observation, and 43 targets by balloons.

HONOURS AND AWARDS
The Distinguished Service Cross – A/Flight Cdr S T Edwards, RNAS;
A/Flight Lt A R Brown, RNAS.

OCTOBER 7
On the 7th work was only possible in the morning, as during the greater portion of the day heavy rain fell.
Artillery Co-operation – 42 hostile batteries were successfully engaged from aeroplane observation.
Enemy Aircraft – Capt G Lloyd, 40 Squadron, attacked an EA artillery machine guarded by three scouts and shot down one scout out of control. An Offensive Patrol of 1 Squadron engaged two DFW two-seaters and Capt P F Fullard shot down one out of control. In another fight with three Albatros scouts 2nd Lt M Peacock shot down one scout out of control, and in a fight between this squadron and 13 Albatros scouts near Menin, 2nd Lt W W Rogers and G Moore each shot down one EA out of control. Capt F Sowrey, 19 Squadron, went up with two other Spads in search of EA wireless machines and found a two-seater which they engaged. They were driven away by a large formation of EA but returned, and Capt Sowrey attacked one of two EA which were engaging an RE8 and destroyed it. 2nd Lt H R Hicks engaged an EA two-seater which fell completely out of control. When bombing Courtrai Railway Station and sidings, DH4s of 55 Squadron were strongly attacked by EA. All our machines returned safely, while two of the EA were shot down in flames and two out of control. Capt D Owen & Gunner W Osborne shot down one in flames and another fell completely out of control. Another was shot down in flames by Sgt P O'Lieff & Cpl A Walters, and Sgt M J Weare & Gunner S Moreman shot one down out of control. Lt G E H McElroy, 40 Squadron, attacked a hostile balloon south-east of Lens and saw it smoking, but owing to anti-aircraft fire could not see further result. Anti-aircraft observers report that at this time a hostile balloon was seen to break loose.

COMMUNIQUÉ No.109

8 – 15 October 1917

This week saw the arrival in France of No.28 Squadron (Sopwith Camels) on October 8, and No.64 Squadron (De Havilland 5s) on October 14; while on October 11, a newly created 41st Wing, RFC came into existence officially, comprised of Nos.55 (DH4s), and 100 (FE2bs) Squadrons, RFC, and No.'A' Squadron RNAS (Handley Page 0/100s), under the overall command of Lt-Colonel C L N Newall. This new Wing's brief was to carry out strategic bombing raids on German industrial centres; all three squadrons being based initially at Ochey.

During the period under review (8th to 15th October inclusive) the weather has not been good for aerial work. Eighteen EA have been brought down, and eighteen out of control. Approximately 10 tons of bombs have been dropped.

OCTOBER 8
The weather was worse than it has been during the last few days.
Artillery Co-operation – 32 hostile batteries have been engaged successfully from aeroplane observation.
Enemy Aircraft – A few EA were encountered and four were driven down out of control by 1 Squadron; one each by Capt P F Fullard, and 2nd Lts Moore, Rogers and Wilson. 2nd Lt Smith, 23 Squadron, shot down an EA out of control.

HONOURS AND AWARDS
The Military Cross – 2nd Lt C F Horsley; 2nd Lt R Winnicott;
2nd Lt G W Ferguson.
The Distinguished Service Cross – Flight Sub-Lt D F Fitzgibbon, RNAS;
Flight Lt (A/Flt Cd) H J T Saint.

OCTOBER 9
Owing to a very strong wind and low clouds very little work was done.
Artillery Co-operation – 21 hostile batteries were successfully engaged from aeroplane observation.
Enemy Aircraft – A patrol of Nieuports of 1 Squadron engaged about nine EA scouts and one was driven down out of control by 2nd Lt W W Rogers. 2nd Lt G Moore observed an EA scout sitting on Lt Rogers' tail and drove it off, then saw two others attacking a Nieuport from behind, so drove them off, following one down until it fell out of control and crashed. Another patrol of this squadron attacked five EA which were pursuing two RE8s. 2nd Lt H Reeves fired a drum into one at close range and it burst into flames and fell out of control, and the pilot was seen to fall out before it crashed. 2nd Lt R Birkbeck attacked one of the other EA and shot the pilot, after which the EA went down out of control with engine full on. Another scout passed in front of him was shot into flames and in this also the pilot was seen to fall out. 2nd Lt F Baker shot down another EA out of control.
　　2nd Lt Chattaway & Lt Ward, 6 Squadron, were in one of the RE8s being pursued and the Observer fired into one EA scout and by doing so probably assisted in the

destruction of one which fell in flames. The EA brought down today by No.1 Squadron bring the squadron's total of EA shot down and driven down out of control since commencing work as a scout squadron on 15th February 1917, to 200 machines. A fight took place between Spads of 19 Squadron and an EA formation, and Capt F Sowrey shot down a two-seater out of control. When on an Offensive Patrol, 2nd Lt F H Hobson, 70 Squadron, attacked an EA scout near Staden, and after shooting it down out of control, watched it crash.

OCTOBER 10

Little flying was possible, except in the early morning and the evening owing to wind and rain.

Artillery Co-operation – 52 hostile batteries were successfully engaged from aeroplane observation, and 14 targets by balloons.

Enemy Aircraft – A patrol of 45 Squadron met and attacked seven EA and 2nd Lt M B Frew shot down two out of control. 2nd Lt F Quigley, 70 Squadron attacked an Albatros scout and shot it down in flames. He was then attacked by six more but escaped, and believes one EA into which he fired fell out of control. In the evening a patrol of eight Camels of this squadron engaged five EA. Lt Cook shot one EA down which fell in flames, while Capt C N Jones and Lt J R Wilson followed one EA down until it fell completely out of control. When returning after having dropped bombs, Lts Dixie & Rissen, 57 Squadron, shot down an Albatros scout completely out of control.

HONOURS AND AWARDS

The Military Cross – Capt J Leacroft: Lt H G E Luchford: 2nd Lt R F Hill.

OCTOBER 11

Artillery Co-operation – 58 batteries were successfully engaged from aeroplane observation, and 63 targets by balloons.

Enemy Aircraft – A patrol of 20 Squadron met about 16 EA and Lt H G E Luchford & Sgt W Benger shot down one EA and drove down another out of control. Sgt Johnson & Lt Sanders also shot one EA down out of control. SE5s of 56 Squadron had a certain amount of fighting and 2nd Lt A P F Rhys Davids shot one EA down out of control. Lt W Meggitt & Capt F Durrand in a Bristol Fighter of 22 Squadron took part in fighting against six EA and the Observer shot down one apparently out of control.

HONOURS AND AWARDS

Bar to the Military Gross – Lt A E McKeever, MC.
The Military Cross – Capt M D G Scott.

OCTOBER 12

Low clouds and rain made aerial work very difficult.

Artillery Co-operation – 26 hostile batteries were successfully engaged from aeroplane observation.

Enemy Aircraft – 2nd Lt R Birkbeck, 1 Squadron, saw an EA two-seater west of Comines and shot it down, seeing it crash in a street in the town. A fight took place between seven Sopwith Camels of 45 Squadron and about 20 EA scouts, one of which Lt J Firth shot down out of control. 2nd Lt J Crompton, 60 Squadron, was fired at from below by an enemy scout, so dived at it and, after 20 rounds, the EA spun down and crashed. 2nd Lt E B Booth, 70 Squadron, joined in a fight with EA scouts and shot one down out of control. 2nd Lt Grant & 2nd Lt H Attwater, 57 Squadron, were attacked by EA scouts and drove one down which they believe fell out of control.

9th Wing – 2nd Lt G L Dore and 2nd Lt F D C Gore, 66 Squadron, fired at several bodies of infantry, mounted troops and transport. The former brought down an EA from a height of 60 feet on to its aerodrome and then fired into hangars. Over 10,000 rounds were fired by pilots from low altitudes at enemy troops, transport, guns etc.

HONOURS AND AWARDS
The Military Medal – No.540041 Pte W A Fraser.

OCTOBER 13
Rain and strong wind prevented much aerial work being done.
Artillery Co-operation – 23 hostile batteries were successfully engaged from aeroplane observation, and 38 targets by balloons.
Enemy Aircraft – Enemy aircraft activity was slight all day. When on patrol, Lt W Sherwood, 60 Squadron, attacked an EA two-seater and drove it down out of control. 2nd Lts Dreschfield & Moore, 21 Squadron, were on flash reconnaissance when they met an EA scout which they attacked and destroyed. Their RE8 was shot through the petrol tank and landed in "No Man's Land". A patrol of six machines of 54 Squadron engaged a large number of EA scouts. French pilots state that they saw several machines of unknown nationality fall out of control. Only two of ours returned and it is not known if any EA were shot down by the missing pilots.

OCTOBER 14
The weather improved but visibility was bad.
Artillery Co-operation – 34 hostile batteries were successfully engaged from aeroplane observation.
Enemy Aircraft – Capt P F Fullard, 1 Squadron, saw an EA two-seater flying up and down between Wervicq and Houthem, so waited until it was underneath him, then dived and shot it down out of control, but was attacked by scouts and unable to watch it crash. Sgt G Olley of the same patrol attacked another two-seater which fell out of control. Capt J Leacroft, 19 Squadron, shot down an EA scout out of control, and Capt F Sowrey saw it crash. A patrol of 32 Squadron saw about ten EA scouts attacking an RE8, so dived at the EA, and Lt W R Jones fired 300 rounds into one which broke to pieces in the air and crashed into our lines west of Poelcappelle.

OCTOBER 15
Artillery Co-operation – 53 hostile batteries were successfully engaged from aeroplane observation.
Enemy Aircraft – On the 14th, whilst on Offensive Patrol, Lt C R J Thompson, 19 Squadron, brought down a hostile machine. This was confirmed by a pilot of 84 Squadron who saw the EA crash near Menin. On the 15th, Capt F Sowrey, 19 Squadron, when leading his patrol against five Albatros scouts, shot one down which was seen to fall in flames. 2nd Lt K B Montgomery, 45 Squadron, shot down an EA two-seater which he, with four other pilots, saw crash. 2nd Lt E O Krohn, 84

Squadron, when on Offensive Patrol, had to leave the formation owing to engine trouble. He was attacked all the way back to the lines by EA, one of which he managed to get several bursts into, and which was observed to crash by the infantry of the IX Corps. Hostile machines were driven down out of control by 2nd Lt H G Reeves,1 Squadron; Lt J C Kirkpatrick & 2nd Lt N Couve, 20 Squadron; Capt N Macmillan, 45 Squadron; Flight Sub-Lt W A Curtis, 10 Squadron RNAS.

HONOURS AND AWARDS
Meritorious Service Medal (without Pension) - No.69380 2/AM A H Norris, RFC.

COMMUNIQUÉ No.110

16 – 22 October 1917

No. 40 Squadron began exchanging its Nieuport Scouts for SE5As during this month, and would fly its first SE operations on October 29th.

During the period under review (16th to 22nd October inclusive) the weather was unfavourable for aerial work. Activity on the enemy's part was not very marked. In air fighting we have brought down 44 of his machines and have driven 19 down out of control. 293 hostile batteries have been engaged for destruction and 523 zone calls sent. A total of 23,851 rounds were fired at ground targets, and 4530 photographs taken. Approximately 232 tons of bombs have been dropped with good results.

OCTOBER 16

Artillery Co-operation – 59 hostile batteries have been engaged successfully from aeroplane observation, and 25 by balloons.

Enemy Aircraft – While on photographic reconnaissance, four machines of 11 Squadron engaged two two-seater EA escorted by six Albatros scouts. Lt A E McKeever & 2nd Lt L A Powell shot down two EA which were both seen to crash. 2nd Lts Prout & Bird, 4 Squadron, whilst doing artillery work, were attacked by an Albatros scout which they drove down out of control. Anti-aircraft of the Third Army brought down an EA.

Miscellaneous – Machines of the 1st Wing fired 1250 rounds into troops in trenches and on roads. 1300 rounds were fired into enemy trenches by machines of the 4th Brigade. Lts Young & Davey, 15 Squadron, silenced an active anti-aircraft battery by firing 200 rounds from 1200 feet.

OCTOBER 17

1210 photographs were taken, and 3120 rounds fired at the enemy in his trenches and in the open.

Artillery Co-operation – 96 hostile batteries were successfully engaged from aeroplane observation and 14 neutralised.

Enemy Aircraft – EA were particularly active and aggressive during the morning. Several flights were made by single machines over our lines at a great height. Capt P F Fullard, 1 Squadron, when leading an Offensive Patrol, brought down one EA and drove two others down out of control. Flight Cdr R P Minifie, DSC, fired 350 rounds into a two-seater EA at a height of 16,000 feet over our lines. The EA finally crashed within our lines. At about the same time, Flight Sub-Lt S W Rosevear, 1 Squadron RNAS, fired 200 rounds into a two-seater which fell completely out of control. He followed it down but lost sight of it near the ground. Infantry state that this machine crashed in our lines close to the one brought down by Flight Cdr Minifie. A photographic reconnaissance of three machines of 20 Squadron was attacked by eight EA. 2nd Lt G D Jooste & Capt E H Johnston drove one down in flames, and Lts H G E Luchford & V R S White shot another down. Both were confirmed by Anti-Aircraft. An Offensive Patrol of 20 Squadron met nine Albatros scouts. Three of these dived on the tail of 2nd Lt French & Gunner Veale, who fired at one which fell out of control and was seen to crash. 2nd Lt R M Makepeace & Lt M W Waddington of the same patrol drove another EA down out of control. 2nd Lt Reeves, 2 Squadron, and Flight Lt S M Kinkead, 1 Squadron RNAS, each drove down an EA completely out of control.

An Offensive Patrol of 11 Squadron was attacked by 20 Albatros scouts, one of which was driven down out of control by 2nd Lt Stanley & 2nd Lt Fosse, and two by Lt R F S Mauduit & 2nd Lt L A McRobert. Capt H M Ferreira, 29 Squadron, and 2nd Lt H F S Drewitt, 23 Squadron, each brought down a two-seater EA which was observed to crash by other pilots. Capt J T B McCudden, 56 Squadron, observed our AA shells bursting over Bailleul when at a low altitude. He climbed with his patrol to 13,000 feet and found two two-seater EA. One EA disappeared east, but the other Capt McCudden managed to surprise from behind and fire a burst into it which sent it down in a steep dive. The EA then burst into flames and one wing came off, the pieces falling north-west of Dickebush. This machine is numbered G.81. Capt R Stuart-Wortley & Lt McGrath, 22 Squadron, saw a formation of 12 EA over our lines. These were engaged and the EA made off towards their lines. Lt McGrath opened fire at one at close range and the EA got into a spin, then burst into flames, and was seen to break to pieces and crash near Ypres. This machine is numbered G.80. The total for the day was 11 EA brought down (three falling in our own lines and one EA brought down by AA fire), and 11 driven out of control.

OCTOBER 18
Artillery Co-operation – 37 hostile batteries were successfully engaged from aeroplane observation, and 11, plus 18 other targets by balloons.
Enemy Aircraft – There was a decided decrease in EA activity from the 17th inst., though several large formations were encountered in the vicinity of the Roulers-Menin Railway. While on Offensive Patrol, Bristol Fighters of 20 Squadron engaged several EA formations. Capt H G E Luchford & Lt V R S White attacked three which were diving on an RE8. Two went east diving steeply, but they fired 200 rounds at a range of 20 yards into the third EA which fell and was observed to crash. Shortly afterwards they attacked another EA firing 200 rounds at point-blank range. This EA fell and crashed. Another patrol of 20 Squadron engaged six or seven EA. 2nd Lt T Colville-Jones & Lt L H Phelps drove one down completely out of control which was seen to crash by an anti-aircraft battery. Fifteen Gothas, escorted by ten scouts, were met by a patrol of 1 Squadron RNAS, and Flight Cdr R P Minifie fired 250 rounds into one Gotha which nose-dived vertically for over 2000 feet into the clouds and was lost to sight. A DFW two-seater was driven down out of control by Flight Lt S M Kinkead and Flight Sub-Lt J H Forman, 1 Squadron RNAS, after it had received 400 rounds at close range. During a combat between eight machines of 41 Squadron and ten Albatros scouts, Lt R Winnicott and 2nd Lt R Whitehead each drove down an EA out of control. Lt G Hyde and 2nd Lt M Gonne, 54 Squadron, attacked an EA at close range and it fell away and was seen to crash by a Belgian aviator. 2nd Lt J D Payne, 29 Squadron, fired 60 rounds into a two-seater EA which turned on its back and went down completely out of control. 2nd Lt J Highman & 1/AM S Hookway, of the Detached Flight of 5 Squadron, whilst on photography, were attacked by an EA into which they fired bursts from a range varying from 200 to 400 yards, and the EA burst into flames and was seen to crash. Lt R T C Hoidge, 56 Squadron, with his formation, attacked four two-seater EA, along with two

Spads. One he brought down between the road and river east of Comines, then drove down another two-seater out of control.

OCTOBER 19
Clouds and thick mist.
Enemy Aircraft – Enemy aircraft activity was practically nil, only a few EA being seen in the afternoon.
Miscellaneous – 3450 rounds were fired at ground targets.

OCTOBER 20
Weather was fine but thick haze which continued all day prevented observation for the artillery.
Enemy Aircraft – An Offensive Patrol of 20 Squadron engaged 15 EA scouts, and 2nd Lt Boles & Lt Rowan drove down one out of control. Four Bristol Fighters of 11 Squadron engaged seven Albatros scouts, one of which was shot down in flames by 2nd Lt A E McKeever & Lt H G Kent. Two others were driven down out of control by Sgt F Stephenson & Lt S Plater. Nine Albatros scouts were met by a patrol of 10 Squadron RNAS at a height of 16,000 feet. One EA was shot down by Flight Cdr J S T Saint and was seen to crash. During an attack on Rumbeke aerodrome with bombs by 70 Squadron, the escort consisting of machines of 70 and 28 Squadrons shot down EA as follows; 2nd Lt E B Booth, 70 Squadron, fired about 150 rounds into an EA which dived into a field, ran into a hedge and overturned. 2nd Lt J S Michie, 70 Squadron, engaged a two-seater EA taking off; it tried to turn, stalled, and dived straight into the ground. 2nd Lt F Quigley, 70 Squadron, attacked a two-seater EA whose wings folded up in the air. 2nd Lt P G Mulholland, Lt J Mitchell, and Capt W G Barker – all of 28 Squadron – each shot down an EA which were either seen to crash or broke up in the air. One EA was driven down out of control in various combats by each of the following; 2nd Lt W W Rogers, 1 Squadron; Flight Cdr R P Minifie, 1 Squadron RNAS; Capt N Macmillan, Lt E D C1arke, 2nd Lt Davies, and 2nd Lt R Brownell, all of 45 Squadron; Capt F H Lawrence, Capt J G Smith-Grant, and 2nd Lt A Koch, all of 70 Squadron.
Miscellaneous – A successful attack was carried out during the day by the 22nd Wing on Rumbeke aerodrome. A patrol of 70 Squadron carrying 25lb bombs flew out at a height of 400 feet, with a close escort of eight Camels from the same squadron. High patrols of 23 and 28 Squadrons operated in the same neighbourhood at the same time. Twenty-two 25lb bombs were dropped from below 400 feet. 2nd Lt J S Michie dropped his three bombs on machines lined up on the aerodrome, one of which was blown to pieces. Another bomb was seen to go right through a hangar, and several fell within 20 feet of the sheds. After dropping their bombs the pilots fired at personnel on the aerodrome and into the hangars from a height of about 20 feet; two of the pilots' undercarriages actually hitting the ground, and another sustaining a bent axle. During this attack the patrols brought down seven EA and drove one down out of control in full view of the aerodrome. A total of 4874 rounds were fired at ground targets, including 3724 fired by 70 Squadron during their attack on Rumbeke aerodrome. On his way home 2nd Lt F Quigley fired at some troops playing football and at horse transport on the road, while trains were attacked by Lt C W Primeau and 2nd Lt F E Hobson, 70 Squadron, from a height of 50 feet.

OCTOBER 21

Artillery Co-operation – 67 hostile batteries were successfully engaged from aeroplane observation.

Enemy Aircraft – Enemy aircraft were active and aggressive well east of the lines. Capt J Leacroft, 19 Squadron, saw two RE8s and four Spads being attacked by 12 EA. He joined in the fight and drove one EA down out of control which was seen to crash by an AA Section. Capt H G E Luchford & Lt V White, 20 Squadron, while on patrol with eight others, engaged nine EA consisting of seven scouts and two two-seaters. They poured 250 rounds into one two-seater which fell out of control and crashed. A patrol of 45 Squadron dived on four two-seater EA over Lille and were in turn attacked by seven EA scouts. 2nd Lt P Carpenter shot down one scout in flames, while 2nd Lt M B Frew pursued another scout, firing 300 rounds into it from a range of 30 feet. The EA went down out of control with engine full on. Lt W J Rutherford, 60 Squadron, attacked several two-seater EA, one of which he drove down and saw it crash into the ground. Flight Sub-Lt A G A Spence, 1 Squadron RNAS, and Capt H A Hamersley, 60 Squadron, each drove down an EA out of control. Four Bristol Fighters of 11 Squadron engaged two two-seater EA, escorted by ten scouts. Lt R F S Mauduit & Cpl Mason drove one EA down in flames, then drove down another which was seen to crash, and drove down a third EA completely out of control. One of the EA attacked by 2nd Lts Nixon & Johnson turned over and fell upside down completely out of control. Lts Davies & Tubbs each fired over 200 rounds into an EA which went down and crashed in the Belgian trenches. Three pilots of 10 Squadron RNAS attacked three two-seater EA, one of which was brought down in flames. One EA was driven down out of control over Ostend by Capt B E Baker & Lt E F Dixon, 48 Squadron. A patrol of eight machines of 29 Squadron attacked seven two-seater EA, one of which was brought down by Lt J D Payne, and three driven down out of control by the same pilot assisted by 2nd Lts J Leach and C Hamilton. Four pilots of 32 Squadron attacked three Albatros scouts which were bothering an RE8. A large number of rounds were fired by all pilots into the EA which fell and crashed. Capt F H Lawrence, 70 Squadron, drove down one EA out of control, and Lts Monkhouse and Lane, 32 Squadron, one between them. On a report that EA were flying west of the lines, three pilots of 56 Squadron went up in pursuit. Capt J T B McCudden got close up to one EA and fired a good burst from both guns, and the EA crashed in our lines (G.84). A patrol of 84 Squadron became involved in a fight with a large number of EA scouts lasting for 40 minutes, and Capt K Leask, Capt R M Child, and Lt P J Moloney each claimed one EA driven down out of control.

Bombing – Bomb raids were made against Annay, Noyelles, Fouquieres, Abeele aerodrome, Ingelmunster, Heule aerodrome, Bisseghem aerodrome.

41st Wing – During the afternoon a second raid into Germany was made by 12 DH4s of 55 Squadron. 2464lb of bombs were dropped with excellent results on factories and an important railway junction about ten miles north-west of Saarbrucken. Bursts were seen in Bous Station and at the glass works at Wadgassen. Ten EA were encountered over the objective, four of which were driven down out of control.

OCTOBER 22

Artillery Co-operation – 24 hostile batteries were successfully engaged from aeroplane observation, and nine targets by balloons.

Enemy Aircraft – Few EA were seen throughout the day. Machines of 57 Squadron when returning from bombing Hooglede were attacked from below by three Albatros scouts. The first zoomed up under the tail of 2nd Lt J Orrell's machine and opened fire from about 20 yards. 2nd Lt Orrell banked his machine, allowing his Observer, 1/AM Spicer, to fire about 60 rounds into the EA which burst into flames. Another scout opened fire from about 100 feet below the DH 4; 1/AM Spicer fired one drum into this EA which spun down about 500 feet then burst into flames. 2nd Lt J D Payne, 29 Squadron, saw seven EA over Menin and out-climbed them, then dived at one firing a drum from about 70 yards without effect. After climbing again, he dived at the same EA firing about 50 rounds from 30 yards, and the EA dived down vertically out of control.

Bombing – When the moon was out, the night bombing squadrons concentrated their efforts on hostile aerodromes, and later in the night attacked railway stations. Six tons of bombs were dropped.

9th Wing – 5947 rounds were fired at ground targets, including machine gun emplacements, active anti-aircraft batteries, enemy troops in shell holes, in trenches, on roads and in villages.

COMMUNIQUÉ No.111

23 – 29 October 1917

This week saw No.27 Squadron receive its first De Havilland 4 on October 29, the start of re-equipment from its now out-dated Martinsyde G.102 "Elephants". The day before, however, No.28 Squadron (Sopwith Camels) moved to the Candas depot prior to its intended posting to the Italian – Austro-Hungarian front. Air Mechanic 1st Class A G Whitehouse, awarded a Military Medal, was an aerial gunner with 22 Squadron (Bristol Fighters), and as "Arch" Whitehouse, became well known in postwar years for his prolific writings on aviation subjects. Captain Henry Luchford, a pilot with No.20 Squadron, was eventually credited with 24 combat victories before being killed in action on 2nd December 1917 by Leutnant Walter von Bulow, Jagdstaffel 36, himself a 28-victory "ace".

During the period under review (23rd to 29th October inclusive) the weather for the most part was unfavourable for much aerial work owing to mist, thick haze and clouds. We have brought down 24 enemy machines and have driven down 13 out of control. 252 hostile batteries have been engaged for destruction, and 779 zone calls sent. A total of 38,834 rounds were fired at ground targets, and 1600 photographs taken. Approximately 32¾ tons of bombs have been dropped.

OCTOBER 23
Rain and mist prevented much flying being done.
Artillery Co-operation – 15 hostile batteries were successfully engaged from aeroplane observation, and 34 reported by zone call.
Bombing – 9th Wing – During the night of 22nd/23rd, 101 Squadron bombed Lichtervelde aerodrome, Moorslede aerodrome, Rumbeke aerodrome, Ingelmunster aerodrome, and Roulers, while 102 Squadron bombed Marcke aerodrome, Bisseghem aerodrome, Cuerne aerodrome, Ingelmunster aerodrome, Tourcoing, Ledeghem, and Courtrai Railway Station. Flight Cdr R M Munday, 8 Squadron RNAS, flew out to Moncheaux aerodrome just after dark and dropped four 25lb bombs on the sheds which were lit up, then fired several bursts from 50 feet into the hangars. On his way back he fired a burst into the Cambrai Railway Station.

HONOURS AND AWARDS
Bar to the Military Cross – Capt H G E Luchford, MC; Lt V R S White,MC.
Military Medal – No.78563 1/AM A G Whitehouse.

OCTOBER 24
A total of 374 photographs were taken, and 2100 rounds fired at ground targets.
Artillery Co-operation – 67 hostile batteries were successfully engaged from aeroplane observation.
Enemy Aircraft – Lt J H G Womersley, 43 Squadron, attacked a two-seater Aviatik over Lens. He continued firing at it till within 800 feet of the ground when it fell completely out of control. This was confirmed by anti-aircraft observers. Capt P F Fullard, 1 Squadron, drove down a two-seater EA out of control from 2000 feet after firing 100 rounds into it at a range of ten yards. 2nd Lt T Williams, 45 Squadron,

whilst on patrol with four others, was attacked from behind by one of seven Albatros scouts. He made a sharp turn behind the EA, fired 150 rounds into the cockpit at close range, and the EA went down in a slow spin, then crashed. Flight Sub-Lt S W Rosevear, 1 Squadron RNAS, fired 100 rounds into an EA attacking one of our Triplanes. The EA turned over, caught fire, and crashed near Comines. Flight Lt S M Kinkead of the same squadron fired 300 rounds at point-blank range into a two-seater EA which dived vertically for 2000 feet and crashed after the left-hand planes had broken off. A patrol of 19 Squadron met nine Albatros scouts over Menin, and three were driven down out of control by Capts J Leacroft and P Huskinson, and Lt O C Bryson. Six EA were met by a patrol of 48 Squadron. One EA dived on the tail of the Bristol Fighter of 2nd Lt H Jenkins & 1/AM E Dunford, and was shot down in flames. 2nd Lt J D Payne, 29 Squadron, fired 50 rounds into one of five Albatros scouts which he attacked over Roulers. The EA got into a spin, turned over, then went down completely out of control.

Bombing – During the day 3½ tons of bombs were dropped.

HONOURS AND AWARDS
The Military Cross – Capt H C W Hill, RFC(SR).
Military Medal – 7443 1/AM F A Biscoe, RFC; 8009 1/AM R Johnson, RFC.

OCTOBER 25
Weather – Rain, with a violent gale. No service flying was done except by the 1st and 2nd Brigades.
Artillery Co-operation – Ten hostile batteries were engaged for destruction and four neutralised from aeroplane observation, and 79 targets were registered by balloons, and 52 active enemy batteries located.
Bombing – The first night raid into Germany was carried out on the night of the 24th/25th by machines of Naval Squadron 'A' and 100 Squadron. Four and a half tons of bombs were dropped on the town and works at Burbach, north-west of Saarbrucken. Many fires were started and explosions caused. Over 50 bombs fell on the works and 20 in the town. A further 12 tons were dropped on railway communications south-west of Saarbrucken, good results being obtained. One train was hit by a 230lb bomb and completely demolished.

OCTOBER 26
In spite of heavy rain which continued most of the day, a good deal of low flying and artillery work was carried out. The following are descriptions of attacks on ground targets during which a total of 8780 rounds were fired. 2nd Lt E Olivier, 19 Squadron, fired 300 rounds from 150 feet at troops marching along the Ypres-Gheluwe road, and then attacked a two-seater EA which he shot down out of control. Lt M R N Jennings, also 19 Squadron, fired 70 rounds from 600 feet at machine guns which were silenced. 2nd Lts K Montgomery and M B Frew, 45 Squadron, fired 700 rounds from 500 feet at troops loading railway trucks, and also fired at troops and transport on roads. The same two pilots subsequently saw two EA, dived at the rear one and, after firing about 15 rounds each, saw it fall out of control and crash. Flight Lt S M Kinkead, 1 Squadron RNAS, fired 300 rounds from 500 feet at groups of men on roads, while Flight Sub-Lt W M Clapperton of the same squadron fired 250 rounds from 400 feet at men behind a house. Flight Sub-Lt J S de Wilde, also 1 Squadron RNAS, fired 50 rounds from 600 feet at troops in trenches.

Capt Roberts, 60 Squadron, fired 250 rounds at 200 feet at 12 pack mules, and 70 rounds by Capt H A Hamersley of the same squadron at 50 feet at men repairing wire. Lt Hewitt and 2nd Lt R F S Drewitt, 23 Squadron, fired 1150 rounds from 800 feet at parties of men on roads, while stationary MT were engaged by Lt Trudeau and 2nd Lt Allen of the same squadron, who fired 150 rounds from 300 feet. Capt McAlery, 23 Squadron, fired 30 rounds at transport from 500 feet.

Lt J D Payne, 29 Squadron, fired 50 rounds at two lorries and 15 men from 1000 feet, while 2nd Lt D F Hilton fired 40 rounds into an occupied trench, then silenced two hostile batteries. 100 rounds were fired from 100 feet by 2nd Lt J B Fenton, 28 Squadron, at transport on roads, as a result of which two lorries were set on fire.

Active hostile batteries were attacked by 2nd Lt Tyrrel, 32 Squadron, who fired 100 rounds from 1000 feet. Parties of enemy troops and various ground targets were attacked with good effect by Capt O J Mackay, Lts W H Rothwell, A S Pearce and G D Gillie, and Capt W F Anderson and Lt R B Ashcroft – all of 9 Squadron – by whom a total of 1700 rounds were fired from altitudes varying between 150 feet and 800 feet.

Lts R A Hewat and J de Pencier, 19 Squadron, attacked about 20 men on a road south of Moorslede, and then went to Moorslede. Seeing troops in the main street, they flew down it practically between the house-tops at a height no greater than 50 feet. Lt de Pencier stated that he himself was lower than the church spire, and Lt Hewat was below him. Lt Hewat fired 200 rounds at these troops and Lt de Pencier 80 rounds, when he had a stoppage. Both pilots then flew to Gheluwe and when just north of the town Lt Hewat saw a two-seater EA at 800 feet; he attacked it at very close range and, despite heavy fire from the ground, followed it down to 400 feet; while correcting a stoppage he was hit in the face by a bullet and was badly cut over the eye and mouth and had his glasses broken, but returned safely to his aerodrome. The EA was seen to be going down completely out of control when not more than 200 feet up.

Flight Sub-Lt A G A Spence, 1 Squadron RNAS, attacked a two-seater EA which he shot down out of control.

Capt W G Barker, 28 Squadron, attacked a German scout west of Roulers and after fighting for 15 minutes shot it down in flames and saw it crash. He was then attacked by another scout and succeeded in destroying this one also.

2nd Lt F J Williams, 29 Squadron, and 2nd Lt H S Malik, 28 Squadron, each shot down an EA out of control.

BOMBING

41st Wing – On the 24th "A" Naval Squadron dropped 54 112lb bombs on the Burbach Works, on the western side of Saarbrucken, and all hit the objective. Sixteen 112lb bombs were also dropped on the town of Saarbrucken. On the night 24th/25th, No.100 Squadron dropped twelve 230lb and twenty-three 25lb bombs on trains, railway junctions, stations and sidings on the line between Falkenberg and Saarbrucken. Bombs were seen bursting on buildings around Saarbrucken Station, others were seen to burst on the railway line, while one 230lb bomb dropped from 400 feet fell on a train near Wallersberg Junction. A parachute flare showed the front portion of the train to be considerably damaged.

During this raid 1200 rounds were fired at various targets.

OCTOBER 27

Artillery Co-operation – 95 hostile batteries were engaged for destruction and 21 neutralised.

Photography – A total of 848 photographs were taken during the day.

Enemy Aircraft – Capt A H Fellowes, 43 Squadron, attacked a DFW which he drove down out of control. He then attacked an Albatros scout and drove it down in flames. Capt P F Fullard, 1 Squadron, fired 35 rounds into a DFW two-seater doing artillery work and saw it crash into some trees. Then, with his patrol, he attacked a formation of 14 EA, composed of Gothas and DFWs. Into one DFW he fired 70 rounds at close range and drove it down out of control. This EA was seen to crash by personnel of an anti-aircraft battery. Flight Cdr R P Minifie, 1 Squadron RNAS, brought down an EA which was attacking one of our artillery machines. A patrol of 45 Squadron saw an EA formation attacking three RE8s. 2nd Lt M B Frew engaged the rear EA which broke to pieces in the air. Lt J C B Firth shot one EA down in flames. 2nd Lt Frew then noticed a Camel 3-4000 feet below him going down smoking, pursued by three EA scouts. One of these he singled out and fired 20 rounds into it at about 15 yards range, and the EA burst into flames and was seen to crash east of Moorslede.

Capt P Huskinson, 19 Squadron, fired three bursts into a two-seater EA which went down completely out of control. A reconnaissance of 20 Squadron engaged ten EA over Comines. 2nd Lt W Durrand & 2nd Lt A E Woodbridge shot down one seen to crash by our anti-aircraft, and 2nd Lts McGouan & D Couve drove one EA down out of control. Another EA was driven down out of control by 2nd Lt F F Babbage & Gunner McMechan, 20 Squadron while on an Offensive Patrol. Four Bristol Fighters of 11 Squadron engaged five EA Albatros scouts from a range of 500 yards. One of these was driven down out of control by Lt D Coath & 2nd Lt Jones. One of six Albatros scouts attacked by Flight Sub-Lt W A Curtis and Flight Sub-Lt K V Stratton, 10 Squadron RNAS, was driven down out of control and one other by a patrol of 24 Squadron. A patrol of 13 Camels of 28 Squadron engaged a formation of 14 Albatros scouts. One was shot down in flames by Lt J Mitchell, and another shot down and seen to crash by the same pilot. 2nd Lt A G Cooper of the same patrol drove down one Albatros completely out of control. A patrol of 70 Squadron then joined the fight and drove another EA down out of control. In other combats 2nd Lt R F S Drewitt, 23 Squadron, and Capt H Lawrence, 70 Squadron, each drove an EA down out of control. Five other EA were driven down out of control by: Capt G H Bowman, 56 Squadron; Lt R S P Boby, 22 Squadron; 2nd Lt Pfeiffer & 1/AM Harris, 25 Squadron.

HONOURS AND AWARDS

The Distinguished Service Order – Capt P F Fullard, MC, RFC.
The Distinguished Service Cross – Flight Sub-Lt S W Rosevear, RNAS.
The Military Cross – Capt F Sowrey, DSO, Royal Fusiliers & RFC.

OCTOBER 28

Artillery Co-operation – 25 hostile batteries were engaged for destruction and 13 neutralised from aeroplane observation, and 78 targets registered and 75 active hostile batteries located by balloons.

Enemy Aircraft – An Offensive Patrol of 60 Squadron engaged nine Albatros scouts, one of which was driven down out of control by Lt W J Rutherford. 2nd Lts

Jones & Watson, 4 Squadron, engaged a formation of two Gothas and eleven Albatros scouts. One Gotha was driven down out of control. Four Sopwith Scouts of 46 Squadron met four Albatros scouts. A stiff engagement followed in which one EA was shot down completely out of control, and another driven down vertically by Lts R L M Ferrie and J H Cooper; a third was damaged by Lt Robinson. Capt D Hall & Lt E Hartigan, 57 Squadron, while engaging two Albatros scouts, shot one down out of control. Lt R Maybery and Capt G H Bowman, 56 Squadron, were attacked by one EA scout which was above with 14 others in the clouds. Lt Maybery attacked this EA which he drove down out of control and it was seen to crash by pilots of the 2nd Brigade.

Bombing – On the night of 27th/28th, bombing raids were made on Meurchin, Estevillers, Carvin, Courrieres, Beaumont, Vitry, Chateau du Sart aerodrome, Quiery la Motte, Gontrode aerodrome, Rumbeke, Moorslede, Abeele and Bisseghem aerodromes, Harlebeke, Courtrai Railway Station, and Marcke aerodrome.

OCTOBER 29

A total of 245 photographs were taken, and 13,414 rounds fired at ground targets.
Artillery Co-operation – 36 active hostile batteries were engaged for destruction from aeroplane observation.
Enemy Aircraft – Flight Lt S M Kinkead, 1 Squadron RNAS, attacked an EA scout in the semi-darkness at 15 yards range and it was hit and fell out of control. 2nd Lts E G H C Williams & G W Croft, 48 Squadron, when on Offensive Patrol, met a large EA formation at 16,500 feet. One EA was attacked at 150 yards range, burst into flames, and crashed. 2nd Lts H H Hartley & E C Birch of the same patrol attacked another EA which crashed. 2nd Lts W Ives and A Cooper, 24 Squadron, while on Offensive Patrol, saw an Albatros scout attacking a Camel and drove the EA down out of control. An Offensive Patrol of 23 Squadron engaged 12 EA which appeared unwilling to close with them. Capt J M McAlery, who was leading, attacked one EA which turned on its back and fell out of control. Lt Baker of the same squadron singled out one of four EA and in a short encounter fired a burst from 25 yards range. The EA went down out of control, crashed, and burst into flames. Capt G H Bowman, 56 Squadron, while on Offensive Patrol, attacked an EA Nieuport type which went down in a steep spiral and crashed badly. Later the same patrol clashed with other EA at 11,000 feet and Lt K Muspratt singled out the leader and drove it down out of control. During the same fight Lt M H Coote drove one EA down out of control.

COMMUNIQUÉ No.112

30 October – 5 November 1917

During the coming month of November, No.19 Squadron began receiving Sopwith Dolphins to replace their Spads, while No.41 Squadron began exchanging their De Havilland 5 scouts for SE5As. Captain Matthew Frew, 45 Squadron, mentioned in Honours and Awards, retired from the RAF eventually as Air Vice-Marshal, Sir Matthew, KBE, CB, DSO, MC, AFC.

During the month of October 149 bomb raids were carried out and 113 tons of explosives dropped. Many of the objectives have been in Germany and results have often been most satisfactory. 108 EA were brought down and 60 driven down out of control. Over 11,000 photographs were taken and 1189 hostile batteries successfully engaged for destruction with aeroplane observation, and 491 targets dealt with by balloon observation.

OCTOBER 30
The weather was unfavourable for aerial work.
Artillery Co-operation – 18 hostile batteries were successfully engaged for destruction, 44 neutralised, and seven other targets dealt with, and 26 targets by balloons.
Enemy Aircraft – Capt P F Fullard, 1 Squadron, destroyed one EA. Machines of the 5th Brigade took part in 19 combats, and Lts D Robertson and D F Hilton, 29 Squadron, each drove down one EA out of control.
Bombing – 41st Wing – On the night of the 29th/30th, No.100 Squadron dropped one 230lb and three 25lb bombs on Saarbrucken; one 230lb and three 25lb bombs on St Avold Station, and one 230lb and three 25lb bombs on Falkenberg. During this raid 400 rounds were fired into searchlights and at trains and sheds along the railway. On the 30th, 12 machines of 55 Squadron dropped 2712lbs of bombs on the munitions factories and town of Pirmasens, 80 miles distant from their aerodrome. One pilot obtained a direct hit on the gas works.

OCTOBER 31
Artillery Co-operation – 38 hostile batteries were successfully engaged and 12 neutralised from aeroplane observation. No work was possible with balloons owing to mist.
Enemy Aircraft – During the day 389 Offensive Patrols were done, during which seven EA were brought down and 16 driven down out of control. 2nd Lts B D Bate & Broadhurst, 18 Squadron, when on photography, met four EA and turned on one, a two-seater, and fired 200 rounds at close range and drove it down completely out of control. In response to a wireless call, Lt J H G Womersley, 43 Squadron, pursued an EA which he attacked at close range and drove down out of control. An Offensive Patrol of 19 Squadron engaged six Albatros scouts which were dispersed, one being driven down out of control by Lt O C Bryson. They next met a formation of four EA – one a two-seater – this being driven down by Lt E Olivier. Major A D Carter attacked an Albatros at 10,000 feet and fired two short bursts at close range.

It dived steeply but was followed closely by Major Carter who got several more bursts into it. Finally, the EA turned over several times, nose-dived and crashed near the lines. An Offensive Patrol of 1 Squadron engaged two EA, one of which was brought down by 2nd Lt R Birkbeck and seen to crash. Flight Cdr R P Minifie, 1 Squadron RNAS, met an EA firing into our trenches in the semi-darkness and attacked it at point-blank range. The EA crashed. On various Offensive Patrols, four other machines, piloted respectively by Lt J C B Firth, 45 Squadron; Lt F Gartside-Tippinge, 19 Squadron; Major A D Carter, 19 Squadron; and Lt A P Warnum, 20 Squadron each drove down one EA out of control. While on Offensive Patrol, eight machines of 11 Squadron met 11 EA scouts. A general engagement at close range ensued during which one EA, attacked by Lt A E McKeever & 2nd Lt L A Powell, after a burst of 50 rounds at 50 yards range, was driven down completely out of control. The Observer then attacked another EA at 75 yards range, which nose-dived, burst into flames, then fell to earth. A third he attacked at 50 yards range; it turned over and fell out of control but was not seen to crash owing to clouds.

An RE8 of 5 Squadron, when taking photographs, was attacked by two two-seater EA. The first was driven down apparently out of control; the second was driven away east and the photographs were then taken. The pilot and Observer were Lt Griffen & AM Hookway respectively. Capt K Leask, when leading an Offensive Patrol of 84 Squadron, was attacked from above by nine EA. A fight lasting ten minutes ensued, during which one EA was sent down out of control by Lt J Ralston. A fight with another EA formation during the same patrol resulted in another Albatros sent down out of control by Capt Leask.

Lt R Maybery, 56 Squadron, drove down one EA out of control, and Lt K Muspratt of the same squadron destroyed one.

Bombing – On the night 30th/31st, bomb raids were made on Henin-Lietard, Esquerchin, Pont-a-Vendin, Wingles, Benifontaine, Roulers Station, Ingelmunster Station, Bisseghem aerodrome, Carvin.

41st Wing – On the night 30th/31st, No.100 Squadron carried out another raid into Germany despite very bad weather. Seven 230lb and 22 25lb bombs were dropped on Volklingen Steel Works, situated a few miles west of Saarbrucken. The works were so brilliantly illuminated that the pilots had no difficulty in placing their bombs on main gas boiler range, central power house, and blowing engines. 1150 rounds were also fired into the works, at the station, and at trains and searchlights.

NOVEMBER 1

Artillery Co-operation – During the day exceptionally good work was done by balloons, especially by those of the 2nd Brigade. In all, eleven hostile batteries were engaged for destruction, six neutralised and 33 registrations carried out by this Brigade.

Enemy Aircraft – Two EA were driven down out of control by Lt G C Young, 60 Squadron and Lt W J Rutherford of the same squadron, while on Offensive Patrol. In the latter case, Lt F O Soden, 60 Squadron, contributed in bringing down the EA.

Bombing – 1st Brigade – On the night 31 October/1 November,10 Squadron dropped 67 25lb bombs on Chateau de la Vallee.

9th Wing – Machines of 101 Squadron bombed Roulers Station, Thourout Station, Beythem Station, and Staden, while 102 Squadron bombed Gontrode, Heule and Marcke aerodromes, and attacked Courtrai Station, Iseghem, and trains near

Ghent. At 2pm on the 1st, when clouds were at a height of about 200 feet, four Martinsydes of 27 Squadron left to bomb Gontrode aerodrome. Sgt S Clinch climbed through the clouds and flew for 40 minutes and, on diving down through the clouds, found himself over Ghent. He followed the canal at low height and dropped his bombs on the aerodrome, then returned and landed at 4.25 pm. The other three pilots became completely lost and returned with their bombs after a flight of two hours.

41st Wing – On the 1st instant, 12 machines of 55 Squadron set out two formations of six DH4s each to bomb works at Kaiserlautern, a distance of 100 miles from their aerodrome. One formation reached the objective and dropped three 230lb and six 112lb bombs from 15,000 feet. The other formation met seven EA, so dropped their bombs behind the German lines to enable them to fight. One EA was shot to pieces and fell. All our machines returned.

NOVEMBER 2
During the night 1st/2nd and the following day, low clouds and heavy ground mist almost entirely prevented aerial work.

NOVEMBER 3
Owing to low clouds and mist there were few flying operations during the day.

HONOURS AND AWARDS
Bar to the Military Cross – 2nd Lt M B Frew, MC.

NOVEMBER 4
Artillery Co-operation – 15 hostile batteries were successfully engaged for destruction. The balloons were unable to work owing to the mist.

Enemy Aircraft – A patrol of 54 Squadron attacked five EA scouts, one of which was out-manoeuvred by 2nd Lts S J Schooley and H H Maddocks, and it fell and was seen to crash. Flight Sub-Lt W A Curtis, 10 Squadron RNAS, engaged two EA. Into the first he fired 150 rounds at close range and drove it down quite out of control. An RE8 of 5 Squadron Detached Flight, while on photography with two scouts as escort, was attacked by six EA. Capt Douglas & Lt Whitehead in the RE8, with the help of their escorts, drove off the EA, one of which went down in a nose-dive. The Observer in the RE8 was wounded in the foot and the machine riddled with bullets.

NOVEMBER 5
Enemy Aircraft – Capt H Hamersley, 60 Squadron, attacked one of six EA with a yellow fuselage and drove it down where it crashed in a forest. A patrol of 45 Squadron met seven EA scouts and Capt J C B Firth shot down one completely out of control. Infantry of the Second Army shot down an EA which fell in our lines (G.86).

HONOURS AND AWARDS
Military Cross – Lt E D Clarke, RFC (SR).

COMMUNIQUÉ No.113

6 – 12 November 1917

On November 7, No.28 Squadron (Sopwith Camels) left Candas depot on its journey to Italy, arriving in Milan five days later. On the day of its departure, 46 Squadron received its first Sopwith Camel as the start of re-equipment from Sopwith Pups. On November 12, a fresh addition to the RFC's bombing force was No.49 Squadron's arrival at La Bellevue (De Havilland 4s).

During the period under review (6th to 12th inclusive) the weather has been persistently bad for aerial work. Six EA have been brought down and 17 driven down out of control. Approximately 13 tons of bombs have been dropped, and over 55,000 rounds fired from low altitudes at ground targets.

NOVEMBER 6
Enemy Aircraft – A two-seater was driven down out of control by Lts F O Soden and W J Rutherford, 60 Squadron, while Lt W Duncan of the same squadron destroyed a two-seater near Polygon Wood. Lt R Holt, 19 Squadron, drove down an EA scout out of control. Flight Sub-Lt A A Cameron, 10 Squadron RNAS, drove down a single-seat scout which he followed, firing at close range until it fell into clouds completely out of control.

NOVEMBER 7
Enemy aircraft were not active and only one EA, which was attacked by 2nd Lt F Gorringe, 70 Squadron, was driven down out of control. Flight Cdr R M Munday, 8 Squadron RNAS, crossed the lines at dawn and attacked a balloon north of Meurchin. He opened fire at 100 yards range and the balloon burst into flames. He then attacked the shed, but machine gun fire was too active so he left, and on his return flight fired into the Metallurgique Works.

HONOURS AND AWARDS
Bar to the Distinguished Service Cross – Acting Flight Cdr R P Minifie.
Bar to the Military Cross – Lt R A Maybery, Lancers and RFC.
The Military Cross – 2nd Lt W Durrand, RFC General List.

NOVEMBER 8
With aeroplane observation, 56 hostile batteries were successfully engaged for destruction and 33 neutralised.
Enemy Aircraft – A considerable amount of fighting took place this day. Flight Cdr R Compston, 8 Squadron RNAS, shot down an EA scout in the vicinity of Oppy and it was seen to crash. While engaged on photographic work, 2nd Lt Jackson & Pte J Reid, 4 Squadron, were attacked by seven scouts and drove one down out of control. 2nd Lt B Starfield & Lt A Hutchinson, 20 Squadron, shot down one EA which was seen by ground observers to crash. Two other EA were driven down out of control; one by Lts J Kirkpatrick & G Brooke, and the other by Capt W Durrand & 2nd Lt A E Woodbridge, 20 Squadron. Major A D Carter, 19

Squadron, shot down an EA two-seater, seen to crash. A fight between nine EA and a patrol of 45 Squadron resulted in Lt J Child destroying one EA, while a two-seater was driven down out of control by 2nd Lt P Carpenter. In another patrol pilots of this squadron dived at an Albatros scout which 2nd Lt T Williams shot down in flames, after which he and Capt J C B Firth sent another down out of control. A patrol of 60 Squadron found an EA two-seater near Zillebeke and Capt F H B Selous shot it down in our lines (G.88). A second patrol of this squadron engaged a two-seater near Houthem which was destroyed by 2nd Lt S L G Pope, who shortly after destroyed a second two-seater. Capt H Hamersley of the same squadron destroyed an Albatros scout, and Lt W J Rutherford drove one down out of control. Captain E W Molesworth, 29 Squadron, when leading his patrol, attacked the rear machine of a formation of 15 EA and shot it down in flames. Shortly after he attacked one of two reconnaissance EA and also shot this down in flames. Lt J G Coombe attacked the other two-seater and drove it down out of control. 2nd Lt A Koch, 70 Squadron, shot down an EA out of control, and Capt Cook & Lt Drudge, 57 Squadron, shot down an Albatros scout which attacked them out of control. A formation of 22 Squadron met and fought eight EA scouts, and Lts H McKenzie & S McClenaghan dived at one which was attacking a Bristol Fighter and shot it down in flames. Another was shot down out of control by Capt J Butler & 2nd Lt H Johnstone. In other fighting by the 9th Wing Capt R M Child and Lt F Brown, 84 Squadron, shot down an EA out of control, while another fell out of control after being engaged by Capt T Hunter, 66 Squadron. Anti-aircraft of the Second Army shot down an EA which fell in our lines (G.87).

Bombing – 9th Wing – On the night of the 7th/8th. No 101 Squadron bombed Gontrode aerodrome, Roulers and Ingelmunster Railway Stations, while No.102 Squadron bombed the Gontrode, St Denis Westrem, Bisseghem, Moorseele, and Marcke aerodromes, and Courtrai Dump and sidings.

NOVEMBER 9

Artillery Co-operation – 50 hostile batteries were successfully engaged for destruction from aeroplane observation, and five, plus 20 other targets by balloons.

Enemy Aircraft – A patrol of 19 Squadron engaged five EA scouts near Zuidhoek and Lt C R J Thompson destroyed one which was attacking another Spad from behind. The patrol then engaged a scout which was interfering with two RE8s, and Lt Thompson drove it down out of control. Shortly after, the patrol attacked a two-seater EA and it fell out of control after Major A D Carter fired into it at close range. 2nd Lt K B Montgomery, 45 Squadron, and 2nd Lts P Kelsey and R Birkbeck, both of 1 Squadron, each drove down an EA out of control. Four other EA are believed to have been driven down out of control; one by 2nd Lt J D Payne, 29 Squadron; one by 2nd Lt C Runnels-Moss, one by 2nd Lt E B Booth, and the fourth by Lt J Aldred, all of 70 Squadron. 2nd Lts J Macauley & G Bliss, 25 Squadron, were on an instructional flight when they were attacked by three EA scouts, and they shot down one scout completely out of control.

HONOURS AND AWARDS

Bar to the Military Cross – 2nd Lt L A Powell, MC, Gloucester Regiment and RFC.

NOVEMBER 10

Rain fell all day on the 10th and very little work was accomplished.

NOVEMBER 11

Low clouds and rain still interfered with work.

Enemy Aircraft – 2nd Lt S Pope, 60 Squadron, shot down an EA scout which fell and crashed. Lts T Candy and G Rice, 19 Squadron, drove down an EA apparently out of control. Lts A E McKeever & L Pogson, 11 Squadron, attacked one of two two-seater EA and drove it down completely out of control. A patrol of 48 Squadron met a formation of four large bombing machines, escorted by about 30 EA scouts. During a fight with 15 of these, Capt B E Baker & 2/AM B Jackman drove down two scouts completely out of control, both of which are believed to have crashed. In another fight with six EA scouts, Lt N Millman and 2nd Lt T Tuffield drove down one EA scout out of control.

NOVEMBER 12

Artillery Co-operation – 30 hostile batteries were successfully engaged for destruction from aeroplane observation, and eight by balloons. Nearly 12,000 rounds were fired at ground targets.

Enemy Aircraft – Enemy aircraft activity was normal, but a large number of combats took place. A patrol of Sopwith Camels of 43 Squadron saw four Albatros scouts about to attack some of our Corps machines, so immediately engaged the EA. Major A S W Dore shot one down out of control. The same patrol attacked another scout and 2nd Lt C King, assisted by Lt W MacLanachan, 40 Squadron, shot it down out of control. A patrol of five machines of 20 Squadron attacked seven EA scouts. Two were driven down by Capts Knight & Wornum, and later a third fell out of control after being engaged by 2nd Lts Boles & Wallis. Another EA was driven down out of control by Lt O C Bryson, 19 Squadron, who attacked it when it was interfering with RE8s. Lt Balmford & Cpl Elliott, 6 Squadron, were taking photographs when they were attacked by a formation of EA scouts. The Observer, who was wounded, shot down one EA out of control. A patrol of 10 Squadron RNAS attacked a two-seater EA and Flight Lt G L Trapp and Flight Sub-Lt A S Beattie shot it down out of control, and it was seen by the French to crash. Another EA was shot down out of control by Capt B P G Beanlands, 24 Squadron. 2nd Lt F Quigley, 70 Squadron, and 2nd Lt P de Fontenay, 29 Squadron, each drove down an EA apparently out of control. A reconnaissance of 57 Squadron met about ten EA over Staden and 2nd Lts O McOustra & A Flavell shot one down out of control. 2nd Lt A Drinkwater & Lt F T S Menendez of the same squadron fought three EA, two of which fell apparently out of control.

COMMUNIQUÉ No. 114

13 – 19 November 1917

On November 17 yet another fresh squadron arrived in France when No.82 Squadron (Armstrong Whitworth FK8s) flew from England to St Omer, then three days later settled in to its new base, Savy. 2nd Lt K B Montgomery's victim on November 15 was the 21-victory commander of Jagdstaffel 6 of the "Richthofen Circus", Leutnant Hans Ritter von Adam.

During the period under review (13th to 19th inclusive) the weather has been unfavourable for aerial work. Ten EA have been brought down by aeroplanes and six driven down out of control. Over 33,000 rounds were fired from low altitudes at ground targets.

NOVEMBER 13
Enemy Aircraft – Capt P Huskinson, 19 Squadron, saw a formation of 12 EA bombing machines coming west, so dived at one and, after 150 rounds had been fired, the EA went down in a slow glide to about 3000 feet, then went into a spin and crashed. Two other EA were driven down out of control; one by Major A D Carter, and the other by 2nd Lt T Candy of the same squadron. Lt Trudeau, 23 Squadron and 2nd Lts T Williams and H M Moody, both 45 Squadron, also drove an EA down out of control. 2nd Lts W Beaver & C J Agelasto, 20 Squadron, destroyed an Albatros scout near Houthulst, and another was driven down out of control by Lt R K Kirkman & Capt Burbidge, east of Passchendaele. A patrol of 24 Squadron attacked eight EA scouts and Capt B P G Beanlands shot one down out of control, and in another fight drove one down which fell into a cloud and was seen by ground observers to crash. Lt E Williams & 2/AM T Jones, 48 Squadron, shot down an EA scout apparently out of control. 2nd Lt D F Hilton, 29 Squadron, shot down an EA scout apparently out of control. One EA was brought down by aeroplanes in the 4th Brigade area, and another forced to land within our lines, after being hit by anti-aircraft of the Second Army. The EA was slightly damaged and the pilot unhurt (G.90).

NOVEMBER 14
A thick ground mist prevented work.

NOVEMBER 15
Enemy Aircraft – A fight took place between EA scouts and 65 Squadron over Dadizeele and Lt F Symons shot one down out of control, while Lt G Cox shot down another badly damaged. 2nd Lt J Leach, 29 Squadron, dived at four EA scouts which were attacking Camels and, after firing 30 rounds at close range, sent one down in flames which crashed. A patrol of 45 Squadron attacked a two-seater EA which was destroyed by 2nd Lt P Carpenter. Shortly after this patrol engaged another EA formation of scouts and 2nd Lt K B Montgomery shot one down in flames which broke to pieces before reaching the ground. Another was shot down in flames by 2nd Lt E Hand, while Capt J C B Firth shot one down out of control.

Major A D Carter and 2nd Lt E Olivier, 19 Squadron, attacked and destroyed an EA two-seater near Zandvoorde. Capt P F Fullard, 1 Squadron, dived at an EA scout on the tail of a Nieuport and destroyed it. Meanwhile another EA scout was getting on his tail, but he outmanoeuvred it and after firing three-quarters of a drum into it, the EA fell out of control and was seen breaking up before reaching the ground. 2nd Lt L Cummings of the same squadron shot down one EA out of control during this fight. 2nd Lts R M Makepeace & W T V Harmer, 20 Squadron, shot down a hostile scout out of control. A fight took place south-east of Dixmude between an Offensive Patrol of 24 Squadron and EA scouts. Lt J Jephson and 2nd Lts E Macdonald and P MacDougall each drove down one EA scout out of control, while another was driven down damaged by 2nd Lt J Jackson. Flight Sub-Lt H B Maund, 10 Squadron RNAS, attacked a two-seater EA which fell out of control. Flight Sub-Lt J G Manuel attacked an Albatros scout which he drove down and followed until it fell out of control and crashed. Flight Sub-Lt F V Hall shot an Albatros scout down apparently out of control.

NOVEMBER 16
Very little flying possible owing to low clouds and mist.

NOVEMBER 17
Low clouds and mist prevented much flying being done.

NOVEMBER 18
Low clouds and mist again interfered with aerial work.
Enemy Aircraft – While on an Offensive Patrol, Major A D Carter and 2nd Lt E Olivier, 19 Squadron, drove down a two-seater out of control, while two other two-seaters were driven down out of control; one by Capt H G Reeves, 1 Squadron, and the other by 2nd Lt J Macrae, 23 Squadron. Capt R Chidlaw-Roberts and H Hamersley, 60 Squadron, saw two EA two-seaters at work so attacked and destroyed one. When on line patrol, SE5s of 56 Squadron observed a two-seater EA flying west, so Capt J T B McCudden dived on its tail and after a burst from both guns the German gunner was seen to collapse. The EA went down and was completely wrecked in a trench in the German lines. A patrol of 48 Squadron engaged six EA scouts. Lt J Cordes & 1/AM E Dunford shot down one which crashed and burst into flames. Two others were shot down apparently out of control; one by Capt A Field & 2nd Lt G Horsfall, and the other by Capt Beanlands & 2nd Lt D Sutherland. Infantry of the Second Army shot down one EA which was destroyed.

NOVEMBER 19
Not much work was possible on account of low clouds and mist.
Enemy Aircraft – Capt A E Mackay, 23 Squadron, saw two EA two-seaters patrolling south-west of Moorslede, so attacked the lower one which fell apparently out of control. He was unable to watch its fate, being attacked by the other EA which he then destroyed. Lt W Jenkins, 60 Squadron, and 2nd Lt J Allen, 23 Squadron, each drove down one EA which was hit and fell possibly out of control.

COMMUNIQUÉ No.115

20 – 26 November 1917

On November 20 the Battle of Cambrai commenced and aerial support for the Allied infantry overall was primarily low level attacks on enemy troops, transport, communications etc, despite very bad weather conditions, as exemplified in this week's reports.

During the period under review (20th to 26th November inclusive) the weather has been very bad for flying. In air fighting ten EA have been brought down and six driven down out of control, and an enemy balloon shot down in flames. 52,673 rounds have been fired at ground targets.

NOVEMBER 20
On the 20th low clouds and mist again made aerial work very difficult, but quite a considerable amount was carried out on account of the attack by the First and Third Armies south and south-west of Cambrai.

NO.3 SQUADRON – Lt R Brown dropped four 25lb bombs on Caudry aerodrome from 150 feet. A hangar was hit and wrecked, and the pilot then fired 200 rounds at five machines and several mechanics on the ground. He then attacked three wagons carrying road material. 2nd Lt D Chamberlain also dropped four bombs on this aerodrome and destroyed a small hut. Another bomb damaged an EA on the ground. Lt H Brokensha dropped four bombs on Carnieres aerodrome and destroyed a hangar. Lt J McCash dropped four 25lb bombs from 150 feet on Estourmel aerodrome where three sheds were hit and one bomb exploded on an Albatros two-seater on the ground.

NO.46 SQUADRON – 2nd Lt J Cooper, after firing 200 rounds into transport, dropped a bomb on a wagon which blew up. He then scattered infantry but had his machine badly hit and the spar of the bottom plane collapsed, but he managed to return safely by putting on full aileron control. He also dropped a bomb from 100 feet on a small factory at Noyelles which appeared to be wrecked. 2nd Lts R L M Ferrie, E Macleod and J Cooper dropped bombs from 150 feet on a shed at Awoingt aerodrome which was wrecked. 2nd Lt W Robinson dropped two bombs from 50 feet on a battery and obtained a direct hit which damaged a gun. 2nd Lt A S G Lee dropped four bombs on a battery but was then driven away by three EA. Subsequently he attacked a party of German cavalry and other bodies of troops.

NO.64 SQUADRON – Capt R St C McClintock, when flying at 100 feet, saw a gun team galloping along a road, so dropped three 25lb bombs, one of which killed four horses. He fired 200 rounds at other targets. Captain J Slater obtained a direct hit on a gun with a bomb and dispersed troops. Lt I Harris silenced a battery on which he dropped bombs, then attacked a train, after which he dropped a bomb on a large dump at Marcoing. Lt A Duffus dropped two bombs on fortified shell holes in which were many troops, and one bomb burst directly in the hole. He then fired 350 rounds at troops in trenches. 2nd Lt E Ashton dropped bombs and attacked troops. 2nd Lt L Williams also attacked troops but his machine was hit and he had to land in "No Man's Land". Capt E Tempest obtained direct hits on two gun emplacements with bombs, then attacked troops with machine gun fire, after which he returned to his aerodrome for more bombs and ammunition and went out again. Capt St C Morford and Lt J McRae also dropped bombs and engaged ground targets.

NO.68 SQUADRON – Lt H Taylor, while engaging troops at 30 feet, had his machine hit, so landed in "No Man's Land". On crawling out of his machine he was fired at by German snipers, so took up a German rifle with which he fired at the enemy and then crawled back. On the way he picked up a wounded man and carried him until reaching one of our patrols. He then found another British machine which had landed owing to its pilot being wounded, so he got in it and tried to fly off, but could not start it. 2nd Lt F Huxley dropped bombs on a gun and horses,obtaining a direct hit. He also obtained a direct hit on a G.S. wagon which was destroyed and two personnel killed, then attacked 300 troops marching in fours and shot about 14 of them.

2nd Lt M Clark & Lt Westerby, 15 Squadron, and 2nd Lts R Bentley & C Nathan, 59 Squadron, and Capt J B Solomon & Lt B Morgan, 15 Squadron carried out contact patrols from 50 to 300 feet. Four reconnaissances were done by Bristol Fighters of 11 Squadron. Four 25lb bombs were dropped on Oppy by 5 Squadron, and two on Auchy by 2 Squadron. One machine of 57 Squadron dropped two 112lb bombs on Courtrai sidings from 300 feet. Two other machines of this squadron attacked Menin on which one 230lb and two 112lb bombs were dropped. Eighteen 25lb bombs were dropped by 7, 9, and 69 Squadrons on various targets. *Enemy Aircraft* – Only a few were encountered during the day, and two were driven down apparently out of control; one by 2nd Lt A L Cuffe, 32 Squadron, and one by Capt W M Fry, 23 Squadron.

HONOURS AND AWARDS
The Distinguished Service Cross – Flight Sub-Lt W A Curtis, RNAS.
The Military Cross – Lt A Mann, ASC & RFC.

NOVEMBER 21
Practically no work was done owing to rain and low clouds. Nine successful reconnaissances were carried out by machines of 11, 15 and 59 Squadrons. 2nd Lt C Brown, 27 Squadron, dropped two 112lb bombs from 200 feet on Brebieres Station and two bursts were seen among trucks in the station.

NOVEMBER 22
Low clouds and thick ground mist again considerably hindered aerial work. In spite of the weather, machines went out in order to interfere with the enemy's movements and to gain information. In all, 32 successful reconnaissances were carried out, gaining valuable information.
No.3 Squadron – Lt L Nixon dropped a bomb on a train which hit and wrecked a house beside the track. Lt R Brown dropped three 25lb bombs on two guns and 12 limbers on a road, then fired 300 rounds and disorganised traffic. 2nd Lt D Chamberlain engaged the same convoy with machine gun fire and obtained a direct hit with one bomb.

NO.64 SQUADRON – Capt E Tempest obtained a direct hit on enemy troops in trenches with a 25lb bomb, and dropped another which exploded in a machine gun pit. Capts St Clair Morford and Fox-Russell, Lt Barrett, and 2nd Lts Burge and Thompson all fired at various targets from low altitudes and dropped bombs.

NO.46 SQUADRON – Capt V Robeson fired at troops in Bourlon Wood and dropped four bombs. Lts P W S Bulman and Wilcox also dropped bombs on troops.

NO.68 SQUADRON – Lt F Huxley dropped two 25lb bombs on enemy in close formation and obtained direct hits. Capt R C Phillips fired 300 rounds at gun crews, then dropped bombs which fell in the middle of a machine gun crew. After this he attacked transport. Lts R W Howard and A Griggs also dropped bombs and fired at troops.

Enemy Aircraft – Flight Cdr R Compston, 8 Squadron RNAS, and 2nd Lt L Herbert, 40 Squadron, each drove down an EA apparently out of control. Capt J M Child, 84 Squadron, met an EA east of Bourlon Wood and engaged it at close range and shot it down completely out of control. It was seen to crash by other pilots. He then saw two EA two-seaters approaching the lines from the east, so climbed into the clouds and waited until they crossed the lines, then attacked one and hit the engine which stopped. The enemy pilot tried to fly east but was prevented by Capt Child, so the EA landed within our lines. Both pilot and Observer were unhurt and were captured (G.91). Lt F Huxley, 68 Squadron, destroyed an EA scout.

NOVEMBER 23

There was a slight improvement in the weather and machines were out during the day co-operating with the successful attack on Bourlon Wood and Village. With aeroplane observation 26 hostile batteries were successfully engaged for destruction. Scouts were employed in dropping bombs and firing machine guns at troops, transport, batteries and other ground targets, and a total of 24,175 rounds were fired during this work, and 120 25lb bombs dropped. Lt F Huxley, 68 Squadron, saw three tanks held up in Bourlon Wood so dropped four bombs from 100 feet, one by one, upon two anti-tank guns which were holding them up. The guns were silenced and the tanks then advanced into the wood. He then saw a strong point preventing the advance of our infantry, so dived on a number of occasions and fired 500 rounds. This caused great confusion and so assisted in the taking of the strong point which soon occurred. In all, 325 25lb, 46 112lb, and one 230lb bombs were dropped during the course of the day.

Enemy Aircraft – Enemy aircraft were more active than on previous days and attacked our bombing and low flying machines. When returning from a bomb raid on Dechy, 2nd Lts C Evans & 1/AM K Gellan, 18 Squadron, were attacked by four Albatros scouts, but the DH4 succeeded in shooting down one scout which crashed on a house south of Douai. Capt R Chidlaw-Roberts, 60 Squadron, destroyed an EA scout east of Passchendaele. Major A D Carter, 19 Squadron, Capt A E McKay, 23 Squadron, and 2nd Lt F H Hobson, 70 Squadron, each drove an EA down out of control. Capt J T B McCudden, 56 Squadron, saw two Albatros scouts attacking a Bristol Fighter so joined the fight and destroyed one EA. Two other EA were destroyed by pilots of 56 Squadron; one by Capt G H Bowman, and one by Lt B Harmon. 2nd Lt L A Rivers & Lt L V J Podgson, 11 Squadron, shot down an EA completely out of control. This makes the 100th EA accounted for by the squadron since changing FE2bs for Bristol Fighters in June 1917. 2nd Lt J McF Stewart & Lt W Borthistle, 25 Squadron, were attacked by four EA scouts just after having dropped bombs, and the Observer, Lt Borthistle fired 80 rounds into one EA scout which burst into flames and fell out of control.

HONOURS AND AWARDS
The Military Cross – Lt J H G Womersley, RGA (TF) and RFC.

NOVEMBER 24
A little flying was done up to 11am, after which it was impossible owing to a gale. 1488 rounds were fired at ground targets, and eighty-two 25lb and fourteen 112lb bombs were dropped. Practically no EA were encountered and no decisive combats took place.

NOVEMBER 25
A strong west wind and low clouds made work almost impossible. The following additional work, which took place on the 23rd instant, is interesting; Lt A Duffus, 64 Squadron, engaged enemy infantry in the open north of Bourlon Wood by machine gun fire. He dropped four bombs on dug-outs and the R.R. embankments and fired 100 rounds at long range at four EA which retired. Being then hit in the engine and petrol tanks, Lt Duffus just managed to clear Bourlon Wood, landing in some barbed wire. Capt Fox-Russell, 64 Squadron, dropped three bombs from 100 feet on enemy trenches north-east of Bourlon Wood, then attacked troops retiring from the wood. He was then hit by a shell and was forced to land in front of our line. Capt A S G Lee, 46 Squadron, assisted in driving down an EA two-seater north of Bourlon. He dropped four bombs into the wood, then fired at troops in Fontaine. While retiring temporarily to correct jams in his guns a shell burst underneath him and brought his machine down so close to the Germans that he had to run 100 yards under machine gun fire and was unable to destroy his machine. While walking back to Cantaing with a guide a shell burst in a house he was passing and blew him across the road.

HONOURS AND AWARDS
The Military Cross – Lt F H Holmes; 2nd Lt C G Fenton; Lt G R Hunter; 2nd Lt D H Sessions; 2nd Lt A J Tyler; Capt J L Vachell.

NOVEMBER 26
A total of 5660 rounds were fired from low altitudes at ground targets.
Enemy Aircraft – Four EA were shot down out of control; two by Capt J D Payne, one by Lt J Coombe, and the fourth by Capt E W Molesworth, all of 29 Squadron, who fought and dispersed twelve EA scouts. Lt H Taylor, 68 Squadron, shot down a two-seater EA which crashed into the ground, and 2nd Lt W Brown and Lt J Larson, flying SE5s of 84 Squadron, each shot down an EA scout out of control.

COMMUNIQUÉ No.116

27 November – 3 December 1917

During December Nos 24 and 32 Squadrons would exchange their De Havilland 5 scouts for SE5As, while No.46 Squadron replaced its Sopwith Scouts ("Pups") for Sopwith Camels. On November 29 the Air Force (Constitution) Act came into force with royal assent; the legal prelude to the eventual creation of the Royal Air Force on 1 April 1918 when the RFC and RNAS were amalgamated into the Third Service. The Albatros scout destroyed by 2nd Lts J Pattern & P Leycester, 10 Squadron, on November 29 was flown by the 24-victory commander of Jagdstaffel 2, "Boelcke", Leutnant Erwin Böhme.

During the month of November 49 EA were brought down and 37 were driven down out of control. 55½ tons of bombs were dropped, and 5000 photographs taken, while 177,000 rounds were fired from low altitudes at ground targets. The weather throughout the month was bad for flying and most of the work done at extraordinarily low altitudes.

NOVEMBER 27
During the night of 26th/27th, No.102 Squadron bombed Douai, Vitry and Somain railway stations. Lt H Hammond was wounded while dropping his bombs on Douai Station from a height of 500 feet. On recrossing the lines he fainted and fell forward on his control lever. His Observer, Lt H Howard, managed to pull the lever back and landed the machine near Bethune. 2nd Lt T Colville-Jones and Capt Speakman, 20 Squadron, drove an EA down out of control. On the 22nd, 2nd Lt P J Moloney, 84 Squadron, became separated from his patrol and was attacked by six EA. He was hit almost at once in the thigh, but continued to fight for ten minutes during which his machine was very badly shot about. One EA was driven down in a spin completely out of control and the rest disappeared. As his compass had been hit he steered back to our lines by the sun and made a good landing close to an anti-aircraft battery,in spite of feeling very weak from loss of blood and the damaged condition of his machine.

NOVEMBER 28
Low clouds and a strong west wind hindered aerial work most of the day. Twenty-two hostile batteries were engaged for destruction and seven neutralised from aeroplane observation, and 173 batteries reported by zone call. A total of 420 photographs were taken during the day.
Enemy Aircraft – While on Offensive Patrol over Gheluvelt, Capt A H Dalton, 70 Squadron, fired 50 rounds into a two-seater EA from 100 feet, driving it down completely out of control. Capt H Smith and 2nd Lt Hill, 27 Squadron,drove down one of four EA which attacked their bombing formation.

NOVEMBER 29
With aeroplane observation, 39 hostile batteries were successfully engaged for destruction. Low flying machines fired 4748 rounds at ground targets, and 746 photographs were taken during the day.

Enemy Aircraft – 2nd Lts J Pattern & P Leycester, 10 Squadron, were taking photographs when they were attacked by three Albatros scouts. The pilot opened fire with his forward gun, then manoeuvred in order to give his Observer a free field of fire, and after a short burst the leading EA burst into flames and crashed. Capt W W Rogers, 1 Squadron, dived at a two-seater EA which he shot down out of control, while another was driven down out of control by 2nd Lt French & Lt Keith, 20 Squadron. Capt J T B McCudden when leading a patrol of 56 Squadron got on the tail of a two-seater EA which he shot to pieces in the air. Another patrol of 56 Squadron observed three two-seater EA through a gap in the clouds, so dived at them, and Capt McCudden followed one down to 500 feet when all its wings folded up. Capt McCudden was almost forced to land owing to loss of air pressure, and was only a few feet from the ground when he was able to get his engine to work again. 2nd Lt H Walkerdine drove down one of the other two-seaters out of control which was seen by AA to crash. Lt E Turnbull, 56 Squadron, and Lt D A Macgregor, 41 Squadron, each drove an EA down completely out of control. A patrol of 48 Squadron engaged nine EA scouts. One was forced to land having been engaged by Capt B E Baker & 2/AM Jackman who drove down another out of control. 2nd Lts W Pudney & G Hayward, 22 Squadron, left their patrol with engine trouble and were attacked by five EA. The Observer, Lt Hayward, shot one down which was seen to crash.

NOVEMBER 30

Very hard fighting took place on the ground all day, and machines of 3rd Brigade co-operated with our troops by reconnaissances, contact patrols, bombing and firing at ground targets all day. In many instances the pilots fired all the ammunition they had and dropped their bombs, then returned to advanced landing grounds for more bombs and ammunition and went out again and continued the same work. In all, 20,000 rounds were fired and 111 bombs dropped.

Enemy Aircraft – Enemy aircraft were active on the battle front and a great deal of fighting took place. Sixteen EA were brought down, two falling within our lines, and six driven down out of control. Pilots of 56 Squadron accounted for five of the EA that were destroyed. Capt J T B McCudden with other pilots drove away EA from over Bourlon, then attacked two two-seater EA. He secured a good position behind one which he hit in the engine with his first burst and forced it to glide west and land in our lines.(G.94). Capt R A Maybery attacked a large formation of EA with his patrol and singled out one which turned to fight, but on turning offered a good target, and was shot down and destroyed. After this he saw another scout dive out of the clouds, so flew to close range, opened fire with both guns, and the EA completely crumpled up and the pieces fell to earth. Lt M Mealing shot one EA down out of control near Lesdain, then turned and drove another away, after which he watched the first one crash. Capt G H Bowman saw an EA scout flying west, so got on its tail, opened fire at long range with both guns, and the EA continued straight down and crashed. Capt A E McKeever & 2nd Lt L A Powell, 11 Squadron, were on line patrol in the morning when they met nine EA which they attacked. The pilot and Observer each destroyed two EA. The first, engaged by the pilot at 15 yards range, crashed and burst into flames; the next two were shot down by the Observer, Lt Powell, and crashed; and the fourth, which overshot the Bristol, was destroyed by the pilot. During the fighting the Observer's gun had a stoppage and the pilot fought the EA to within 20 feet of the ground, then as the EA were still attacking, he pretended to land. This deception enabled him suddenly to put on his engine, zoom up, and get away before the remaining EA realised his intention.

Capt G C Wilson, 68 AFC, was engaging one EA when he was attacked by another, so turned, got underneath this EA and shot him down out of control, and saw it crash on landing, so then dropped a bomb which exploded right on the EA. He had expended all his ammunition in firing at ground targets and at this EA, and when flying towards the lines was cut off by two EA, so manoeuvred and pretended to attack the EA who flew away.

Capt M Thomas and Lt R Winnicott, 41 Squadron, each destroyed an EA, while a third was destroyed by Capt L J MacLean and Lt D McGregor. Another was driven down out of control by Capts Thomas and MacLean, and Lts Winnicott and F H Taylor. Lt G Thomson, 46 Squadron, attacked one of three EA flying west and shot one down in our lines. He drove another down out of control after it had recrossed the lines. Capt R M Child, 84 Squadron, saw a large EA formation so climbed within the clouds, and on coming out again saw six EA underneath. He dived at the rear machine and destroyed it. One EA was driven down and fell in a field after being engaged by Capt K Leask of the same squadron. In other combats, EA driven down out of control were claimed by Capt E R Pennell, 84 Squadron; Capt J Slater and E Tempest, both of 64 Squadron; 2nd Lt L Nixon, 3 Squadron; 2nd Lt C T Travers, 84 Squadron.

DECEMBER 1

Over 4000 rounds were fired at infantry in the trenches and in the open, and sixty-three 25lb bombs dropped at the same targets. During the night of 30 November/1 December, Nos 101 and 102 Squadrons went out all through the night and dropped approximately five tons of bombs.

Enemy Aircraft – Enemy aircraft activity was very slight and only five combats took place. Lt F G Huxley, 68 Squadron AFC, shot down one EA which crashed, and Lt R W McKenzie of the same squadron drove down an EA which attempted to land but ran into a shell hole.

HONOURS AND AWARDS

The Distinguished Service Cross – Flight Sub-Lt J G Manuel, RNAS.
The Military Cross – Capt B P G Beanlands; Capt R M Charley; Capt C T Lally.

DECEMBER 2

Squalls and very strong wind prevented much flying being done. With aeroplane observation, 16 hostile batteries were successfully engaged for destruction. 363 photographs were taken, and approximately 2200 rounds were fired at ground targets from low altitudes, and over two tons of bombs dropped. Enemy aircraft activity was very slight. Three Bristol Fighters of 20 Squadron dived at an EA two-seater near Passchendaele, and 2nd Lt W Beaver & 1/AM M Mather shot it down out of control, and it was seen to crash.

DECEMBER 3

With aeroplane observation, 29 hostile batteries were successfully engaged for destruction. Over 3000 rounds were fired from low altitudes at ground targets, and 887 plates were exposed.

Enemy Aircraft – EA activity was below normal except on the Third Army front where it was great. Sgt F Johnson & 2nd Lt S Masding, 20 Squadron, met eight EA over Wervicq when with the rest of their patrol. They shot down one EA completely out of control. Capt P Huskinson, 19 Squadron, fought an Albatros scout and shot it down out of control.

HONOURS AND AWARDS
The Military Cross – Capt J B Solomon.

COMMUNIQUÉ No.117

4 – 11 December 1917

During the period under review (4th to 11th December) we have claimed officially 13 EA brought down, ten driven down out of control, and one enemy balloon destroyed. Approximately 36,000 rounds have been fired at ground targets, and nearly 20 tons of bombs dropped.

DECEMBER 4

Weather was fine but thick ground mist, and in the 2nd Brigade area snow prevented our machines from working freely. With aeroplane observation nine hostile batteries were successfully engaged for destruction, while low flying aeroplanes fired approximately 6000 rounds at ground targets. On the night of the 3rd/4th, Nos. 101 and 102 Squadrons bombed Sains-lez-Marquion, Honnecourt, Malincourt, and fired 300 rounds at ground targets. The majority of pilots of these squadrons made two trips, and some three, during the night.

Enemy Aircraft – One EA was driven down out of control by Capt Pearson & 2nd Lt G R Howsam, 22 Squadron.

DECEMBER 5

With aeroplane observation 44 hostile batteries were successfully engaged for destruction, while balloons engaged seven targets. During the day 1229 photographs were taken and 7982 rounds fired.

Enemy Aircraft – Flight Cdr G W Price and Flight Sub-Lt W H Sneath, 8 Squadron RNAS, drove an Albatros scout down out of control. Lt J C Kirkpatrick & 2nd Lt Hamer, 20 Squadron, destroyed an Albatros scout near Dadizelle, and three others were driven down out of control by machines of this squadron; a two-seater by Sgt F Johnson & Capt J H Hedley, another by 2nd Lt W Beaver & 1/AM Mather, and the third by Lt R K Kirkman & Capt L W Burbidge. Capt W R G Pearson and 2nd Lt W A Tyrrell, 32 Squadron, attacked a two-seater, shot the Observer, then shot the EA down out of control. 2nd Lt F Quigley, 70 Squadron, attacked two EA scouts and destroyed one. Lts A Paul and J F N Macrae, 23 Squadron, and Capt C W Hamilton, 29 Squadron, each drove down an EA out of control. Capt J T B McCudden, 56 Squadron, was testing a new engine at a height of 19,000 feet over Havrincourt Wood when he saw a two- seater EA flying west over Bourlon. He waited until the EA was well over the lines, then secured a good position and attacked. After firing with both guns the EA went into a vertical dive, broke to pieces at 16,000 feet over Hermies, and crashed within our lines (G.95). Sgts J Bainbridge & J Johnston, 22 Squadron, attacked and destroyed an EA two-seater. 2nd Lt S Oades & 2/AM J Jones, 22 Squadron, shot down one EA which appeared to fall in flames. 2nd Lts J Macaulay & M St Clair-Fowles, 25 Squadron, were on a practice patrol and were attacked by three EA, one of which they shot down apparently out of control. An EA was shot down by anti-aircraft of the Third Army and fell in our lines, and another was shot down in flames by a French pilot and fell in the Second Army area.

Bombing – 41st Wing – Two raids were carried out into Germany in the afternoon, the first that have been possible for over a month, owing to incessant bad weather.

In one raid twelve 112lb bombs were dropped on railway sidings at Zweibrucken by 55 Squadron, 80 miles from their aerodrome, and in the second raid eight 112lb and eight 25lb bombs were dropped by 55 Squadron on the Burbach works at Saarbrucken. Anti-aircraft fire was heavy and accurate but the machines were not troubled by EA, and all our machines returned safely.

HONOURS AND AWARDS
The Military Cross – Lt E T Owles; 2nd Lt R R Bentley; 2nd Lt
P T Carden; 2nd Lt C F Nathan; Lt S L Quine.

DECEMBER 6
With aeroplane observation, 38 hostile batteries were successfully engaged for destruction. 829 photographs were taken during the day, and 5502 rounds fired at ground targets.

Enemy Aircraft – Sopwith Camels of 8 Squadron RNAS had several different engagements. Flight Cdr R Compston, assisted by other pilots, drove one EA down out of control, and in another fight he and other pilots shot down a two-seater which fell hopelessly out of control into the mist, while Flight Cdr G W Price and Flight Sub-Lt H Day shot down another out of control. 2nd Lt B Bate & Lt C Ffolliott, 18 Squadron, were taking photographs and were approaching Valenciennes when they were attacked by a large EA formation. After a short combat with the leading machine at close range the tail of the EA snapped as though shot through the longerons and crashed to earth. While on Offensive Patrol Lt J Kirkpatrick & 2nd Lt W Harmer, 20 Squadron, met an EA which flew directly at them out of the sun. The Observer, Lt Harmer, fired a drum into the EA at close range and it turned over, fell out of control, then crashed. Lts A Pitman & C Pearson, 57 Squadron, while on photography, attacked two EA scouts and shot one down from which a wing fell off. Several EA were driven down by pilots of 19 Squadron and 2nd Lt F S Meek, 29 Squadron, shot one down which was seen by other pilots to be burning on the ground afterwards. Capt J T B McCudden, 56 Squadron, saw a Rumpler two-seater apparently engaged on photography over Vendelles, so manoeuvred for position and opened fire. After a short burst from both guns a lot of material resembling maps and such like fell from the EA which fell out of control with the Observer hanging over the side of the fuselage. When about 8000 feet from the ground the right-hand wings fell off and the wreckage fell in our lines. Lt F G Huxley, 68 Squadron AFC, was flying at 2000 feet when he saw two two-seaters below him, so dived and shot one down in flames. A patrol of 84 Squadron shot down one EA completely out of control, while another was driven down out of control by Capt Thomas,41 Squadron. 2nd Lt S Oades & 2/AM J Jones, 22 Squadron, destroyed an EA, while 2nd Lts W Pudney & G Hayward of the same squadron drove one down out of control.

BOMBING
Bomb raids were carried out against targets at Moncheaux aerodrome, Billy Montigny, Maquion, Valenciennes Railway Station. On the night of 5th/6th, Nos 101 and 102 Squadrons bombed Gontrode aerodrome and railway stations at Douai and Dechy.

41st Wing – Eleven DH4s of 55 Squadron dropped bombs on the Burbach Works, Saarbrucken, from 13,000 feet. Anti-aircraft fire was heavy and accurate but all our machines returned safely.

DECEMBER 7

Low clouds prevented much flying during the day.

Artillery Co-operation – With aeroplane observation, 26 hostile batteries were successfully engaged for destruction, while with balloon observation of the 2nd Brigade four hostile batteries were successfully dealt with and 31 other targets. 5140 rounds were fired at ground targets by aeroplanes at low altitudes.

Enemy Aircraft – One EA scout landed in our lines near Vermelles under control. It was little damaged but appeared to have been hit by both anti-aircraft and machine gun fire. (G.97). Capt W Anderson & Lt J Bell, 69 Squadron AFC, were engaged in artillery observation when they met an EA two-seater and drove it down out of control, and it was seen to crash by ground observers.

HONOURS AND AWARDS

The Military Cross – Lt H Hammond, Dorset Regiment & RFC;
2nd Lt H Howard, Northumberland Fusiliers & RFC.

DECEMBER 8

Little flying was possible owing to unfavourable weather until the afternoon. With aeroplane observation 21 hostile batteries were successfully engaged for destruction. 315 photographs were taken during the day, and 6178 rounds fired at ground targets.

Enemy Aircraft – Capt O C Bryson and Lt A Fairclough, 19 Squadron, engaged a two-seater EA which they shot down out of control.

DECEMBER 9

On the 9th instant practically no work in the air was done owing to the weather.

HONOURS AND AWARDS

The Military Cross – Lt J B Williams, GR & RFC; 2nd Lt P J Moloney, RFC (SR).

DECEMBER 10

Artillery Co-operation – With aeroplane observation 24 hostile batteries were successfully engaged for destruction. 556 photographs were taken during the day, and 4277 rounds fired.

Enemy Aircraft – EA were active, especially on the Third Army front, where they endeavoured to stop our artillery machines from working. Four Bristol Fighters of 20 Squadron attacked seven EA, and Sgt F Johnson, who had as Observer Capt J H Hedley, shot down one which crashed. Lts A Pitman & C Pearson, 57 Squadron were taking photographs when they saw a two-seater EA climbing upwards. They continued with their photography until the EA had reached their height, then engaged and shot it down out of control. Lt J MacDonald, 24 Squadron, saw an EA formation attacking an aeroplane of his patrol below him, so dived and fired at close range into one EA which fell out of control. Another DH5 of this squadron, Lt A Brown, also hit one EA and it went down in a vertical dive. Lt L Franklin, 56 Squadron, shot down an EA scout out of control, and Lt G Thompson, 46 Squadron, also shot one down apparently out of control.

Lt M Mealing, 56 Squadron, with other SE5s, drove away a formation of five EA, and when diving after them saw an enemy balloon which he shot down in flames.

DECEMBER 11

Enemy aircraft were inactive and no combats took place. With aeroplane observation five hostile batteries were successfully engaged, while with balloon observation two were engaged and 21 other targets dealt with. A total of 1052 rounds were fired at ground targets.

41st Wing – Seven DH4s of 55 Squadron left the ground in fine weather to bomb the boot factory at Pirmasens but found the target obscured by clouds, so flew to a gap farther north from which point they saw a large railway junction north-east of Pirmasens and dropped twelve 112lb and ten 25lb bombs from 13,000 feet. All our machines returned safely.

COMMUNIQUÉ No.118

12 – 17 December 1917

On December 12, No.45 Squadron (Sopwith Camels) started a five-days journey to Italy, there to join Nos.28 and 66 Squadrons (Camels) and Nos.34 and 42 Squadrons (RE8s) to form the 51st Wing, VII Brigade, in support of Italian forces. The combat on December 17 between six Albatros scouts and an RE8 of 69 Squadron AFC, crewed by Lt J L M Sandy and Sgt H F Hughes, led to a near unique result. Both men had been killed by a single armour-piercing bullet, yet the RE8 with its dead crew continued to fly steadily in wide left-hand circles until its petrol was exhausted before descending and crashing near St Pol. Neither man received further injury in the crash. The Albatros they shot down in our lines was from Marine Jagdstaffel 2 and coded G.101.

During the period under review (12th to 17th December inclusive) we have claimed officially seven EA brought down by aeroplanes and seven driven down out of control. Approximately nine tons of bombs have been dropped, and 37,000 rounds fired at German troops and other targets.

DECEMBER 12
Captain E T Owles & Lt Black, 12 Squadron, made five flights during the day. In the first they reconnoitred the whole Corps front from a height of 300 feet, then did four contact patrols during which they fired 2200 rounds and dropped ten bombs. In one instance they saw enemy troops penetrating into one of our trenches, so dived and drove them back with machine gun fire and by dropping bombs on them from a height of 40 feet.
Artillery Co-operation – With aeroplane observation five hostile batteries were engaged for destruction.
Enemy Aircraft – Capt W W Rogers, 1 Squadron, flying a Nieuport, saw two formations of eight or nine Gothas flying west, so climbed up with his patrol. Observing one Gotha turning back, he attacked it and after firing three-quarters of a drum at from 20 to 30 yards range the EA burst into flames, fell to pieces, and crashed just north of Frelinghien. Another EA was brought down in our lines by Lt V Wigg, 65 Squadron, who, with the assistance of Lt C Matthews, drove one down out of control and then attacked a second which was finally shot down in flames in our lines (G.98). The following pilots each drove down an EA out of control; Lt K Seth Smith and 2nd Lt F Quigley, 70 Squadron; Capts A McKay and W M Fry, 23 Squadron; and Capt E Hughes, 3 Squadron. Anti- Aircraft of the Second Army shot down an EA which fell in our lines. None of our machines were brought down or missing.

DECEMBER 13
Low clouds and ground mist made work in the air practically impossible. Enemy aircraft were inactive and no combats took place. 8702 rounds were fired at ground targets and 70 25lb bombs were dropped. One EA was shot down by infantry of the Third Army.

DECEMBER 14
Practically no work was possible owing to low clouds, mist and rain.

HONOURS AND AWARDS
Distinguished Service Order – Capt A E McKeever, MC;
Capt J T B McCudden, MC.
Bar to the Military Cross – Capt L J McLean, MC.
The Military Cross – Capt V A H Robeson; Capt C E Barrington; Capt A S G Lee;
Capt H T F Russell; Capt J A Slater; Lt R S S Brown;
2nd Lt P W S Bulman; 2nd Lt J H Cooper; 2nd Lt R L M Ferrie;
2nd Lt A M Kinnear; Capt J M Child; Capt J C L Barnett;
Capt G C Wilson; Capt R C Phillips; Lt F G Huxley;
Lt R W Howard; Lt L H Holden; Lt H Taylor; Lt R F S Mauduit.

DECEMBER 15
With aeroplane observation 29 hostile batteries were successfully engaged and 30 neutralised. 4627 rounds were fired at ground targets, and 1287 plates exposed, while nearly three tons of bombs were dropped during the day.
Enemy Aircraft – A patrol of 30 Sopwith Camels of 43 Squadron fought five EA scouts and shot one down out of control. SE5s of 40 Squadron attacked four EA scouts near Douai and Capt J H Tudhope hit one which appeared to fall out of control, while in another patrol 2nd Lt R C Wade attacked a two-seater which fell apparently out of control. Nieuport Scouts of 29 Squadron met five EA scouts and a two-seater, and 2nd Lt P de Fontenay shot one down which fell vertically, after which 2nd Lt F S Meek dived and fired at it and it was seen to fall out of control. Major A D Carter, 19 Squadron, attacked a two-seater from behind at about 25 yards range and shot it down in flames, while Lts E Blyth and M Jennings of the same squadron shot down a two-seater which was seen by ground observers to crash. The following account is given by Captain J T B McCudden, 56 Squadron, of his encounters with two different two-seater EA; "While looking for EA I thought would probably be about over our lines, I saw one two-seater going at 18,500 feet over Gouzeaucourt at 10.30. I stayed in the sun at 19,800 feet and dived at the EA over Metz. Owing to a miscalculation of the EA's speed I was only able to fire a few shots at it as I was closing in too fast. EA continued to glide down with me following him but he got off too far east as the wind was very strong and we were going at 160 mph. I returned west, climbing, and at 11am saw an EA two-seater going north-west over Villers at 16,000 feet. I pursued the EA who turned east and secured a firing position at 200 yards range, just north of Gonnelieu at 11.5, and after firing about 30 shots from both guns the EA spun to the right and then went into a spiral dive for about 5000 feet, then went down in an almost vertical dive and hit the ground half a mile east of Bois de Vancelles and nothing was left of it."Lt A Blenkiron, 56 Squadron, shot down an EA scout out of control during a fight between eight EA and SE5s. In these combats none of our machines were shot down.

DECEMBER 16
The weather was fine in the morning but in the afternoon snow fell and completely stopped work. With aeroplane observation 19 hostile batteries were successfully engaged for destruction. A total of 7499 rounds were fired at ground targets, and 120 photographs taken.

Enemy Aircraft – An Offensive Patrol of 29 Squadron attacked 13 EA scouts over Roulers and four were shot down, probably out of control; one by each of the pilots Lts J Coombe and A Wingate-Grey, Capt R Rusby and 2nd Lt E S Meek. All our machines returned safely.

HONOURS AND AWARDS
The Military Cross – Capt W H N Shakespeare.

DECEMBER 17
Snow fell heavily on the whole front except on the Second Army.
Enemy Aircraft – Six Albatros scouts attacked Lt J L M Sandy & Sgt H F Hughes, 69 Squadron AFC, flying an RE8. The pilot and Observer refused to dive away from the EA but fought and shot one down within our lines. Lts E J Jones & K C Hodgson of the same squadron went to their assistance and fired away all their ammunition so returned for more, but did not find the enemy. Lt Sandy and Sgt Hughes were shot down and killed. An Offensive Patrol of 1 Squadron engaged EA scouts and two-seaters near Gheluvelt, and Capt W W Rogers and 2nd Lt G Moore shot down one EA each out of control, while 2nd Lt P Kelsey of the same squadron engaged an EA scout over Passchendaele which went down in flames, broke to pieces, and crashed in our lines north of Ypres. (G.100).

COMMUNIQUÉ No.119

18 – 24 December 1917

In part replacement for the withdrawal of the three Sopwith Camel units (Nos.28, 45 and 66 Squadrons) from the RFC front-line strength in France, No.71 Squadron, also equipped with Camels, arrived at St Omer on December 18, yet another Australian unit. For Captain James McCudden, 56 Squadron, already officially credited with 27 combat victories, the coming weeks were to see him dramatically increase his tally, particularly two-seater EA.

During the period under review (18th to 24th inclusive) we have claimed officially 19 EA brought down by aeroplanes and five driven down out of control. During this period we have lost only five machines missing and three shot down. Approximately 25,300 rounds were fired at ground targets and 13½ tons of bombs dropped.

DECEMBER 18
Photography – 1057 plates were exposed.
Enemy Aircraft – Pilots of 19 Squadron took part in a number of different fights with considerable success. A two-seater EA was attacked by Capt O C Bryson and Lt A Fairclough and was shot down out of control. Later in the day Lt Fairclough saw six EA and with his formation attacked them from above. He got good bursts into two EA, both of which he saw go down steeply. In the same combat Capt G Taylor sent another EA down apparently out of control. An anti-aircraft battery witnessed the fight and saw two EA crash. Capt P Huskinson of the same squadron drove down another EA which was obviously hit, and Major A D Carter drove down two EA out of control. 2nd Lt F Gorringe, 70 Squadron, saw an EA approaching the lines, so got into the sun, then dived and shot it down and it was seen to crash and burn on the ground. Capt A McKay, 23 Squadron, was patrolling in the vicinity of Becelaere when he saw two two-seater EA, so led his patrol to attack. He got on the tail of one which did not see him, opened fire at close range, and the EA spun straight to the ground and was completely wrecked. Shortly after, he attacked another and after firing 100 rounds from close range the EA two-seater went down completely out of control. 2nd Lt G Bremridge, 65 Squadron, was flying with other pilots of his squadron when an EA scout dived on his tail, but this was driven off by Lt G Knocker. 2nd Lt Bremridge then followed the EA and shot it down out of control. Capt J Gilmour, also 65 Squadron, took part in a large fight between Camels and a large EA formation, and dived at a single-seater which he shot down in flames. He then attacked a two-seater and shot it down out of control. Major J Cunningham in the same fight got to within 20 yards of an EA scout which was on another Camel's tail and shot it to pieces. He then attacked another scout with which he nearly collided, and last saw this EA falling completely out of control. Five Nieuports of 1 Squadron attacked seven EA scouts and Capt W W Rogers shot one down out of control, while 2nd Lt W Patrick fired 50 rounds into one from about 10 yards range just when it was firing at a Nieuport, and the EA fell down vertically with its engine full on and was seen by anti-aircraft to crash. In all this fighting only three of our aeroplanes were missing or brought down. These were three of 65

Squadron and the only ones missing during the day. One EA was brought down near Gavrelle by machine gun fire from the ground (First Army), and another shot down by anti-aircraft fire of the Second Army and fell in our lines near St Julien (G.103).

Bombing – 9th Wing – On the night of the 17th/18th December, No. 101 Squadron bombed Roulers and Ledeghem Stations and Rumbeke aerodrome. One machine was hit by AA fire on the outward journey carrying away portions of the lower plane and breaking the main spar and aileron. The pilot, however, proceeded and dropped his bombs on Rumbeke aerodrome.

HONOURS AND AWARDS
The Distinguished Service Cross – Flight Sub-Lt W L Jordan RNAS.
Second Bar to the Military Cross – Capt A C Youdale, MC.
The Military Cross – 2nd Lt B D Bate; 2nd Lt L E Shaw-Lawrence.
(Editor's note: Capt Youdale was killed in action, 23rd December).

DECEMBER 19
Dense haze greatly interfered with work. In all, 683 photographs were taken during the day, and 6520 rounds fired at ground targets, and three tons of bombs dropped.
Enemy Aircraft – A patrol of 40 Squadron met four EA scouts, and Capt G H Lewis and Capt J H Tudhope each shot down one out of control. Pilots of 19 Squadron again had a considerable amount of fighting with successful results. Capt O C Bryson and Lt A Fairclough attacked a two-seater which they destroyed. In another patrol Lt Fairclough shot a two-seater down out of control, then attacked another which went down vertically. Major A D Carter drove down one which appeared to be hit, and 2nd Lt H Galer drove one down which he followed near the ground and appeared to be completely out of control. 2nd Lt F Hobson, 70 Squadron, was leading a patrol of Camels when he saw three two-seater EA below. He dived and destroyed one, then attacked a second but was himself attacked from behind, so lost sight of this EA, but another pilot saw it fall in flames. 2nd Lt F Gorringe and 2nd Lt F Quigley attacked a scout which was manoeuvred extraordinarily well by a man who appeared to be a very experienced pilot. The EA, however, was eventually driven down and was last seen falling near the ground into mist. There is little doubt that it was destroyed. 2nd Lt F Lewis & Cpl G Holmes, 53 Squadron, were taking photographs when they were attacked by an EA formation, and hit one EA which fell out of control. An SE5 formation of 56 Squadron saw eight EA scouts south of Masnieres, so dived at them. Capt R A Maybery failed to return from this combat and was last seen behind an EA which he had shot down in flames. This pilot has accounted for 20 EA and his is the only machine missing during the day.
(Editor's note: Captain Richard Aveline Maybery, MC, was killed by Vizefeldwebel Artur Weber, Jagdstaffel 5).

DECEMBER 20
Very little work was possible owing to thick fog and mist.

HONOURS AND AWARDS
The Military Cross – Capt O C Bryson.
The Distinguished Conduct Medal – No.2015 Sgt F Hopper.

DECEMBER 21

A thick ground mist and fog made aerial work practically impossible.

DECEMBER 22

A total of 582 photographs were taken during the day, and 5595 rounds fired at ground targets. With aeroplane observation 55 hostile batteries were successfully engaged for destruction.

Enemy Aircraft – Capt J D Payne was leading an Offensive Patrol of 29 Squadron which attacked four EA and got on the tail of one which he shot down out of control. Capt O C Bryson and Lt E Olivier, 19 Squadron, fought eight EA and one was seen to fall completely out of control. 2nd Lt F Hobson was leading a patrol of 70 Squadron which engaged six EA scouts, and shot one down out of control. 2nd Lt G Elliott of the same squadron attacked a two-seater EA which he shot down out of control and it was seen to burn after crashing. A patrol of 20 Squadron engaged seven EA over Moorslede; Sgt F Johnson & Capt J H Hedley shot one down out of control, then engaged two others, and Capt Hedley fired 80 rounds at close range into one which burst into flames and crashed. One EA scout secured a favourable position under his machine so 2nd Lt R M Makepeace & Lt Brooke dived and attacked this EA which went down in a vertical dive and was followed until it was seen to crash. 2nd Lt Bacon & 1/AM Connor, 10 Squadron, were attacked by five EA scouts but returned safely after having shot one down out of control. Capt J T B McCudden, 56 Squadron, when looking for EA saw two EA flying west, so attacked one and shot the gunner and hit the engine, and the EA glided west partially under control, so he left this EA and attacked the other, but saw the pilot of the first EA had turned and was gliding east. He therefore turned, fired a burst at 50 yards range, and the EA went into a spiral spin and crashed in our lines south- west of St Quentin.(G.104).

HONOURS AND AWARDS

The Military Cross – Capt W W Rogers.
The Military Medal – No.87595 1/AM H Else.

DECEMBER 23

A total of 631 photographs were taken during the day, and 5861 rounds fired at ground targets.

Enemy Aircraft – Seven EA were brought down; five within our lines. Three of these were by Capt J T B McCudden, 56 Squadron, who shot down a fourth on the enemy's side, and two were by anti-aircraft fire. This is the first occasion on which one pilot has shot down four EA in a day, and Capt McCudden's accounts are as follows; " Left ground at 10.50 to look for EA west of our lines, and at 11.15am saw three EA two-seaters together over Vendelles, north-west of St Quentin at 13,000 feet. As they were above I could not engage them decisively but drove them all east of the lines. At about 11.10am an LVG came west just north of St Quentin at 17,000. Chased him and caught him up over Etreillers. He then turned south. I secured a firing position and fired a burst from both guns, when EA's engine stopped and water came pouring out from the radiator in the centre-section. EA turned south and I tried to turn him west because the Observer was waving his right arm, apparently in token of surrender, but the EA was still going south-east very fast. However, I fired another burst at close range, whereupon he went down in a steep dive and crashed completely between the canal and the road at Anguilcourt, which is north-east of La Fere, at 11.25am. I returned north climbing and at 11.50 saw a Rumpler at 17,500 just south of Peronne. I climbed for 20 minutes and attacked EA over Beauvois at 18,200 feet at 12.15. Going south-east, EA fought extraordinarily well and we got down to 8000 feet over Roupy, when after a burst from both guns at close range EA's right-hand wings fell off and the wreckage fell in our lines near Contescourt at 12.20. Returned north climbing and at 12.50 attacked two LVGs over Gouzeaucourt at 16,000. However, both machines co-operated very well, using their front guns as well as the rear, and I fought them east of the lines and then left them as I had no more petrol. Leading my formation east over Ypres towards the lines at 14,000 feet, at 2.30 I saw a Rumpler coming west over Metz at 14,000. EA saw my formation and turned east, nose down. I caught up to the EA at 13,000 feet over Bois de Gouzeaucourt and engaged him down to 6000 feet, when EA went into a spiral dive and crashed in our lines, north-west of Gouzeaucourt at 2.40pm. Reformed my patrol and crossed lines at 13,000 over Masnieres. At about 3.5pm engaged six Albatros scouts over Fontaine at 18,000. My patrol fought these EA down to 8000 feet over Bourlon Wood and then left EA who dived east. The fight was indecisive except that Lt E D G Galley, in fighting one EA end on, got hit in the oil tank and had to land at an Advanced Landing Ground, and apparently hit the EA's engine and it went off down east as if to land. The EA scouts (red-nosed Albatros) kept rolling and spinning down. After the fight, whilst reforming the patrol over Flesquieres, I saw an LVG coming west over Trescault at 12,000 feet. I got into position at close range, fired about 20 shots, when EA went down absolutely out of control, alternately stalling, turning upside down, then spinning a short distance before stalling again etc. EA took five minutes to reach the ground and in a vertical dive landed on a train in our lines, a few hundred yards west of Metz at 3.30pm. Returned at 3.50pm." 2nd Lt F Gorringe, 70 Squadron, observed a large amount of anti-aircraft fire over Ypres so flew in that direction and found an EA which he shot down. Lt J Ralston, 84 Squadron, drove down one EA out of control, while another fell out of control after being engaged by Capt E R Pennell and 2nd Lt W Brown. None of our machines were missing during the day, but one was shot down in "No Man's Land".

DECEMBER 24
Very little flying was done owing to dense fog.
Bombing – 41st Wing – Ten DH4s of 55 Squadron dropped sixteen 112lb and two 230lb bombs on the factory at Ludwigshaven, west of Mannheim, on the Rhine. Direct hits were obtained in the sidings at Badische and Heinrichlanz Works and in the Gas Works, and a fire started in the town. Anti-aircraft fire was very heavy over Mannheim and one DH4 was evidently hit as it went down under control near Speyer. Eleven EA attempted to attack the bombers but were kept at a distance of 300 yards. All our machines returned safely except the one mentioned. A photographic reconnaissance was also carried out by 2nd Lt Thaskrah & Lt D Fluke, 55 Squadron, who photographed Puzieux and Mars-le-Tour. The DH4 was attacked by two EA who followed it from Chambley on the outward journey until it recrossed the lines.

HONOURS AND AWARDS
The Military Cross – Capt R L Chidlaw-Roberts ; Capt I A J Duff ; 2nd Lt W E Davie.

COMMUNIQUÉ No.120

25 – 31 December 1917

During the month of December 1917 we have officially claimed 57 EA brought down by aeroplanes (of which 17 fell in our lines) and 28 driven down out of control (nine others were brought down in our lines by anti-aircraft, infantry, and machine gun fire). Sixty-six tons of bombs were dropped, and 122,836 rounds fired at ground targets. We had 30 machines missing.

DECEMBER 25
Very little work was possible owing to snow and mist. 116 plates were exposed, and 2300 rounds fired at ground targets.

DECEMBER 26
Snow-storms interfered with aerial work. 459 photographs were taken, seventy 25lb bombs dropped, and 5443 rounds fired at ground targets.

Enemy Aircraft – 2nd Lt F Quigley, 70 Squadron, attacked a two-seater which dived vertically after a burst of fire, but was followed and more shots fired into it. When it had gone down to 1500 feet, 2nd Lt Quigley circled round and watched the EA pilot attempting to flatten out, but it then crashed and burst into flames.

DECEMBER 27
Very little flying was possible owing to snow-storms and high wind. 5270 rounds were fired at ground targets, 63 photographs taken, and 136 bombs dropped.

Enemy Aircraft – Flight Cdr G W Price and Flight Sub-Lt H Day, 8 Squadron RNAS, shot down one EA which appeared to fall out of control. 2nd Lts Hanna & Burnand, 35 Squadron, observed a Pfalz scout on our side of the line in the vicinity of Vermand, so attacked and forced it to land in our lines north of Vermand. (G.110).

Miscellaneous – With reference to the raid on Mannheim by the 41st Wing on the 24th instant, the DAILY EXPRESS, Geneva, states; "The Kaiser and his Staff had a narrow escape during the British raid on Mannheim, the Kaiser's train passing through the station only one hour before the structure was partially wrecked by bombs. The line was destroyed some distance beyond the station. Bombs fell on the palace of the Palatinate and on the suspension bridge which crosses the Neckar. Both were badly damaged. Amunition factory was blown up and a number of persons killed or injured. Heavy damage was done."

DECEMBER 28
Artillery Co-operation – With aeroplane observation, 29 hostile batteries were successfully engaged for destruction. 1245 photographs were taken, 5200 rounds fired at ground targets, and approximately five tons of bombs dropped.

Enemy Aircraft – Thirteen EA were brought down during the day, seven of which fell in our lines. Three of the latter were by anti-aircraft which shot one down on the other side also, and five were driven down out of control. We had only three machines missing. Lt G E H McElroy, 40 Squadron, destroyed a two-seater approaching our lines. A patrol of 8 Squadron RNAS attacked an EA scout and

Flight Sub-Lt W L Jordan shot it down out of control. Two more were shot down out of control; Flight Cdr G W Price and Flight Sub- Lt H Day accounting for one, and Flight Sub-Lt W Crundall the other. Pilots of 70 Squadron destroyed three EA. 2nd Lt F Gorringe destroyed one of these, a second was destroyed by 2nd Lt G R Howsam, and the third by 2nd Lt F Hobson who dived at one which Lt K Seth Smith had driven down. This EA, a two-seater, landed on its nose, when 2nd Lt Hobson fired another burst, after which it burst into flames and was seen to burn up. Major A D Carter, 19 Squadron, followed an EA down, firing, until it fell out of control and crashed. Lt J Green & W McMillan, 13 Squadron, saw an EA apparently doing photography, so attacked it, and the EA, a Rumpler, eventually landed in our lines west of Monchy-le-Preux, and on examination was found to have been hit by an anti-aircraft shell. (G.117). 2nd Lts Robinson and G A Lambourn, 46 Squadron, shot down a two-seater in flames which broke to pieces before reaching the ground near Gouzeaucourt in our lines.

Capt J T B McCudden, 56 Squadron, during one flight, engaged four EA and shot three of them down in our lines. The following is his report: "Left aerodrome at 10.15 to look for EA west of the lines. At 11.10 I saw a Rumpler coming west over Boursies. I got into position at 75 yards, fired a short burst from both guns, and EA at once went into a right-hand spiral dive and its right-hand wings fell off at about 17,000, and the wreckage fell in our lines north of Velu Wood at 11.15. At 11.30 saw a Rumpler going north over Haplincourt at 17,000. I secured a firing position and fired a good burst from both guns, when flames at once came from the EA's fuselage and he went down in a right-hand flat spin and crashed in our lines near Flers (as near as I could judge), as I remained at 17,000 feet so as not to lose time by going down and having to climb up again. EA crashed about 11.35am. I now saw an LVG being shelled by our AA over Havrincourt at 16,000. AA fire did not stop until I was within range of EA. I obtained a good position at fairly long range, fired a burst with the object of making him dive, which he did. EA dived very steeply (about 200 mph) starting at about 16,000 feet, and at about 9000 feet I fired another burst into the EA at 100 yards range, when flames issued from EA's fuselage, then he broke up over Havrincourt Wood, the wreckage falling in our lines. The EA had been diving so fast that the Observer could not fire even if I gave him the chance. I climbed again at 12.15 and at 18,000 saw an LVG being shelled by our AA over Lagnicourt. EA dived down east and I caught up to him just east of the lines and fired a good burst from Lewis at 100 yards, when a small burst of flame came from EA but at once went out again. EA dived steeply, kicking his rudder from side to side, and I last saw him gliding north-east over Marquion at 12.20 at 9000 feet under control. Returned at 12.25 as I had no more petrol".

Anti-aircraft of the First Army shot down an EA which crashed near Auchy, and AA of the Third Army shot one down at Saillisel, one at Transloy, and one at Monchy which a machine of 13 Squadron also attacked.

DECEMBER 29

Low clouds and mist prevented much work being done. 801 photographs were taken during the day, 188 bombs dropped, and 4960 rounds fired at ground targets.

Enemy Aircraft – 2nd Lt F Westfield & Lt Fenelon, 10 Squadron, were attacked by three EA scouts, but the RE8 returned safely after shooting one down completely out of control. Pilots of 19 Squadron had considerable successful fighting but had one machine missing. Major A D Carter shot one EA down out of control, while Lt T G Candy shot another down out of control. Lt A Fairclough destroyed one EA and shot another down out of control, while Lt J D de Pencier hit one which fell out of control, and Capt P Huskinson shot two down out of control. Captain J T B McCudden, 56 Squadron, brought down two EA in our lines. The following are his reports; "Left aerodrome at 9am. Crossed the lines east of Gouzeaucourt at 9.45 at 14,000. Saw three EA two-seaters coming west. I dived on these followed by my patrol and drove an LVG down from 13,500 to the ground, when EA made a pretence of landing in our lines, but put his engine on again and made north-east at about ten feet. I headed him west again, but he again turned east, so I fired another burst into him and he got into a flat spin and crashed near Havrincourt at 9.55am. Climbed and only found two members of my patrol. I then approached four Albatros scouts over Bois de Vancelles, who went down east. Several EA two-seaters patrolling east of the Canal at Vendhuille at about 3000, too low to engage. Returned 10.50." Second Report – "Left ground at 11.25am to look for EA west of the lines. At 11.55 attacked an LVG over Lagnicourt at 16,000. I fired a short burst into EA at 100 yards when water and steam came from the EA's centre-section. EA dived very steeply and by the time I caught up to EA again he was too far east of the line to re-engage. Last saw him gliding down north over Haucourt at 4000 at 12am under control. At 1.50pm I dived on an LVG over Gouzeaucourt at 15,000. EA saw me and started a left-hand circle, the EA gunner firing at long range. After half a dozen turns EA pushed his nose down as we were drifting west. I now fired a drum of Lewis and 100 rounds of Vickers into him at 100 yards range and then his right-hand wings fell off and the wreckage fell in our lines north-east of Epehy at 1.55pm. Returned at 2.5 as I had no more petrol."

HONOURS AND AWARDS
The Distinguished Service Order – Major A D Carter.
Bar to the Military Cross – Capt C T Lally, MC.
The Distinguished Conduct Medal – No.7756 1/AM A Leyland.

DECEMBER 30
No service flying possible on account of unfavourable weather.

DECEMBER 31
Low clouds and mist interfered with work.

COMMUNIQUÉ No.121

1 – 7 January 1918

During January No.1 Squadron RFC was re-equipped, receiving SE5As in place of its Nieuport Scouts, while 64 Squadron exchanged its De Havilland 5s for SE5As. 2nd Lt A Beauchamp Proctor, 84 Squadron, mentioned on January 3, ended his war as Captain, VC, DSO, MC, DFC, credited with 54 combat victories.

During the period under review (1st to 7th January) we have claimed officially 24 EA brought down and eight driven down out of control. Approximately 23 tons of bombs have been dropped and 42,154 rounds fired at ground targets. Eleven of our machines are missing.

JANUARY 1
With aeroplane observation 14 hostile batteries were engaged successfully for destruction. A total of 1585 photographs were taken during the day; 4750 rounds fired at ground targets, and approximately four tons of bombs dropped.
Enemy Aircraft – Flight Cdr R Compston and Flight Sub-Lt A J Dixon, 8 Squadron RNAS, drove down an EA scout apparently out of control, and in another patrol Flight Cdr Compston fought and drove down another. This EA was then attacked by Capt E Mannock, 40 Squadron, and crashed in our lines at Fampoux. 2nd Lt F Gorringe, 70 Squadron, and Lt C Smith of the same squadron each attacked an EA which went down apparently on fire. 2nd Lt J S Chick & Lt H R Kincaid, 11 Squadron, were taking photographs when they attacked an EA scout and shot it down out of control. Capt A M Swyny & 2nd Lt A Lyons, 8 Squadron, attacked an EA which they shot down out of control. DH4s of 25 Squadron, when bombing, were attacked by seven EA scouts. Three EA were sent down possibly out of control. Anti-aircraft of the Fifth Army shot down an EA which fell in our lines. (G.120). Only one of our aeroplanes failed to return during the day.

JANUARY 2
Thick mist and low clouds prevented much flying being done. 125 photographs were taken during the day, 2500 rounds fired, and 44 25lb bombs dropped.
Enemy Aircraft – Flight Cdr G W Price, 8 Squadron RNAS, picked out one of seven Albatros scouts which his patrol met, and after a good burst from about 50 yards range from behind its tail, the EA immediately burst into flames and crashed.

JANUARY 3
1860 photographs were taken during the day, 5087 rounds fired at ground targets, and approximately three tons of bombs dropped. With aeroplane observation,45 hostile batteries were successfully engaged for destruction.
Enemy Aircraft – A patrol of 8 Squadron RNAS, consisting of Flight Cdr R Compston, Flight Lt R L Jordan, and Flight Sub-Lt P M Dennett, attacked a two-seater EA which was driven down and crashed. Flight Cdr Compston attacked another two-seater which he shot down out of control. Capt R Chidlaw-Roberts and Lt C F Cunningham, 60 Squadron, attacked a two-seater which was seen by anti-

aircraft to fall in flames. 2nd Lt F Gorringe, 70 Squadron, drove an EA down until it crashed, and 2nd Lt F Quigley of the same squadron shot down a two-seater out of control. A formation of Nieuport Scouts of 29 Squadron attacked an EA scout which Capt E W Molesworth shot down out of control, and a second was driven down out of control by 2nd Lts L Tims and F Williams. Capt H Rusby attacked an enemy balloon which was pulled down smoking.

While on photographic work, 2nd Lts W Beaver & H E Easton, 20 Squadron, attacked and shot down an EA scout which crashed and burst into flames. Lt H M Beck, 3 Squadron, shot down a two-seater out of control. Capt H Maddocks, 54 Squadron, shot down a two-seater in flames, and 2nd Lt A W Beauchamp Proctor, 84 Squadron, shot down a two-seater out of control, while a third was shot down in flames by Lt J Larson, 84 Squadron. Bombing DH4s of 27 Squadron had hard fighting and drove down two EA; one was hit by 2nd Lt W Henney & Lt P Driver; the other by 2nd Lt C Gannaway & Lt J Proger; while a third was shot down out of control by Lt E Green & Cpl R Allan, 25 Squadron, who were returning home alone when four EA scouts attacked them. Capt K R Park & Lt J Robertson, 48 Squadron, were taking photographs when six EA attacked them. They shot one scout down out of control and evaded the rest although the Bristol Fighter's engine was hit.

JANUARY 4

With aeroplane observation, 31 hostile batteries were successfully engaged for destruction, while five and 28 other targets were dealt with by balloon observation. A total of 1594 photographs were taken during the day, 547 bombs dropped, and 9500 rounds fired.

Bombing – 9th Wing – On the night 3rd/4th, 101 and 102 Squadrons bombed Gontrode, Ramegnies Chin, Ingelmunster, Eschem railway, Blandain railway, Maria Aalter, Scheldewendeke, and Ennetieres.

41st Wing – On the night 3rd/4th, ten machines of 100 Squadron left the ground at 5.30pm to attack factories and railways in the neighbourhood of Mazieres. The temperature on the ground was Minus 27 degrees Centigrade, and considerable trouble was experienced with engines. Eventually five of the machines crossed the lines but only two reached the chief objective – a factory – which was brilliantly lit up. Two 230lb and eight 25lb bombs were dropped, and a very large explosion took place close to the blast furnaces. One 230lb and six 25lb bombs were dropped on a railway station just north of Metz, probably Woippy, and one 230lb and six 25lb bombs on a railway junction south of Metz, probably Saint Privat. All machines returned.

Enemy Aircraft – Four machines of 8 Squadron RNAS had several combats, and in one Flight Sub-Lts W L Jordan, E G Johnstone and P M Dennett shot down a two-seater out of control. A second patrol shot down another two-seater out of control, while a third patrol shot down an EA scout out of control. 2nd Lt F Gorringe, 70 Squadron, fought a German pilot who manoeuvred skillfully but was beaten and fell in flames. In another patrol 2nd Lt Gorringe and Lt H Soulby attacked two two-seater EA and drove one down which crashed. A patrol of 65 Squadron engaged four two-seater EA and several scouts in a fight lasting half an hour. Capt J Gilmour shot down a two-seater in flames. In another patrol he destroyed an EA scout. 2nd Lt G Knocker and Lt E Eaton of the same squadron each shot down a scout out of control. A formation of Spads of 23 Squadron dived to help RE8s which were being attacked, and Capt W Fry shot down a scout which crashed, while 2nd Lt C Fowler shot one down which fell in flames and broke to pieces before reaching the ground.

2nd Lt G Moore, 1 Squadron, destroyed an EA scout. No.20 Squadron had a number of combats. In one 2nd Lts G Jooste & S H P Masding shot down an EA scout which crashed; while, on a photographic reconnaissance, 2nd Lt R M Makepeace & Capt J H Hedley were attacked by five scouts and shot one down completely out of control. Two other EA were driven down out of control; one by 2nd Lts R Pohlmann & O Hinson, 25 Squadron, and the other by 2nd Lts G Walker & W Jones, 35 Squadron, who were also attacked when on photographic reconnaissance.

HONOURS AND AWARDS
Bar to the Distinguished Service Order – Capt J T B McCudden, DSO, MC.
The Military Cross – 2nd Lt F G Quigley.

JANUARY 5
Very little work was possible owing to low clouds and mist.
41st Wing – On the night 4th/5th, nine machines of 100 Squadron again left to bomb factories at Maizieres, but owing to low clouds and heavy mist some machines failed to find the target and instead bombed Marly railway station, Maizieres, Courcelles railway station, Wurtemberg Junction, and a rail junction between Woippy and Devant-les-Ponts. All machines returned.
Enemy Aircraft – One EA scout was shot down out of control by 2nd Lt M Gonne, 54 Squadron.

JANUARY 6
With aeroplane observation, 39 hostile batteries were successfully engaged for destruction. 926 photographs were taken during the day, 12,594 rounds fired at ground targets from low altitudes, and 318 bombs dropped.
Enemy Aircraft – While engaged on photography over Valenciennes, 2nd Lt Stewart & Lt Mackay, 18 Squadron, were attacked by five EA scouts. One scout was shot down out of control, but the camera and plates of the DH4 were completely destroyed by bullets. Another DH4 of 18 Squadron, 2nd Lts Fenn & Priestman, was attacked by seven scouts and the fight lasted 20 minutes before the EA were evaded and one shot down out of control. Pilots of 8 Squadron RNAS fought ten EA scouts and Flight Cdr R Compston shot one down out of control. While on another patrol, Flight Cdr G W Price destroyed a two-seater, and later in the day Flight Sub-Lt H Day shot down a two-seater which crashed. 2nd Lts Green & Wilson, 57 Squadron, shot down an EA scout apparently out of control, and Sgt Clayton & 2nd Lt Sloot of the same squadron who were attacked by eight scouts. 2nd Lts W Beaver & H E Easton, 20 Squadron, shot down one EA out of control, while a second was shot down out of control by Capt P Huskinson, 19 Squadron. Capt J D Payne, 29 Squadron, Capt W M Fry, 23 Squadron, and 2nd Lt F Quigley, 70 Squadron, each destroyed an EA, and the EA shot down by Capt Fry fell in our lines (G.123). In one of the fights 2nd Lt F Gorringe, 70 Squadron, assisted in the destruction of one EA. Lts F R McCall & F C Farrington, 13 Squadron, were engaged on artillery work when attacked by an Albatros scout. The Observer opened fire at close range and the EA crashed into the wire on the enemy's side near Noyelles.

JANUARY 7
Very little flying was done owing to bad weather. Twenty-eight plates were exposed

during the day, and 3140 rounds fired at ground targets.

Enemy Aircraft – A two-seater was shot down out of control by Lt F Hobson, 70 Squadron. 2nd Lts R Nixon & E Church, 11 Squadron, were attacked by seven EA scouts and shot one down completely out of control.

HONOURS AND AWARDS

Bar to the Military Cross – Capt C A Stevens, MC.

COMMUNIQUÉ No.122

8 - 14 January 1918

Despite the continuing wintry weather conditions, a good deal of active flying was accomplished during the week. 2nd Lt A A McLeod, 2 Squadron, mentioned on January 14, was to gain a Victoria Cross on March 27th,1918 in a lone epic fight against superior odds.

During the period under review (8th to 14th January) we have claimed officially 13 EA brought down and six driven down out of control. Approximately 13 tons of bombs have been dropped, and 33,098 rounds fired at ground targets. Nine of our machines are missing.

JANUARY 8
Very little work was possible owing to snow-storms. There were no combats.

JANUARY 9
Weather was fine in the morning but in the afternoon snow stopped flying. With aeroplane observation, 39 hostile batteries were successfully engaged for destruction. 868 photographs were taken during the day, 3050 rounds fired at ground targets, and 136 bombs dropped.

Enemy Aircraft – Only a few combats took place. Lt E Peverell, 70 Squadron, attacked a two-seater which dived at once and in attempting to land turned over on its nose and crashed. 2nd Lts Kingsbury & Dorey, 21 Squadron, while on photography, were attacked by EA scouts and shot one down apparently out of control. Another machine of this squadron engaged in the same work was attacked by seven EA, and Capt G Zimmer enabled his Observer, 2nd Lt H Somerville to fire at close range into one scout which immediately fell out of control and in flames. Capt W Patrick, 1 Squadron, shot down a two-seater out of control, and Capt J D Payne, 29 Squadron, drove down a two-seater apparently out of control.

Capt J T B McCudden, 56 Squadron, attacked two EA and the following is his account; "Crossed lines at 10.40am over Flesquieres at 14,000 feet. At about 11.5 attacked two two-seaters over Bourlon Wood at 12,000 feet. I engaged a new type EA at 50 yards range but could not see EA through my Aldis Sight owing to water freezing on the lens, so had to sight by tracer. EA then went down in a spiral with petrol or water issuing from him, and I last saw him gliding down under control north of Raillencourt at about 500 feet at 11.10am.

"At 11.20 drove an Albatros scout away from over Ribecourt. At 11.30 attacked an LVG over Graincourt at 9,000 feet and after a short burst from both guns EA's engine stopped and he started coming west, after which he did a flat spiral glide. I got under his tail again and fired at close range, but the Vickers got a No.4 (*stoppage*) and Lewis finished drum, but EA continued to go down steeply and finally hit the ground in a fast glide down wind."

A patrol of 41 Squadron met five EA scouts and a two-seater which they attacked, but the scouts immediately dived away east. The pilot, however, succeeded in catching up the two-seater and shot it down completely out of control. Lt R

Dodds & 2nd Lt W Hart, 48 Squadron, were taking photographs when three EA attacked. One EA two-seater was shot down out of control. Shortly afterwards, they engaged three scouts and shot one down out of control.

JANUARY 10

With aeroplane observation, 29 hostile batteries were engaged successfully for destruction. 323 photographs were taken, 6416 rounds fired at ground targets, and 166 bombs dropped.

Enemy Aircraft – Capt Stevenson & Lt Rosborough, 16 Squadron, were on artillery work when attacked by five EA scouts, but returned safely after shooting one scout down out of control. Lt H Symons, 65 Squadron, was testing his engine when he saw two EA diving at an RE8, so dived and shot one down completely out of control and drove the other away.

JANUARY 11

Very little flying was done owing to low clouds and the high wind. On the night of the 9th/10th, Capt E Wilcox and 2/AM Rennie, 101 Squadron, left the ground at 5.20pm to test the weather. Having reached 1000 feet, the pilot decided to cross the lines, although the weather was getting worse and the wind stronger. He flew to Menin on which he dropped eight 25lb bombs, then turned in order to re-cross the lines.

He had a dead head-wind against which it was practically impossible to make any way, the wind having a velocity of about 50 mph. The hostile anti-aircraft soon realised the difficulties with which the machine had to contend and were not slow to take advantage of it. Owing to the very high wind the machine drifted by Lille in spite of efforts to prevent it, and immediately a heavy barrage of machine guns and anti-aircraft guns, firing tracer and burning shells ("flaming onions") was opened up at the FE2b. This lasted for some considerable time as the FE was unable to get away. The machine having been fitted with wireless, the aerodrome from time to time received messages from it and these proved to be of the greatest assistance. By this means intimation was received that bombs had been dropped and the whereabouts and condition of the machine. The FE still continued to drift south and Capt Wilcox was unable to do anything to prevent it. For a short time he was lost and a message was received asking for rockets. These were fired and the assistance of the searchlight section (anti-aircraft) was asked for. They put on their lights which proved to be very useful to the pilot. By this time another message was received stating that the FE was near Bethune and being shelled heavily by our own AA guns in spite of having fired the colour of the night. Eventually No.23 Lighthouse was reached and the pilot shortly after saw the aerodrome. The Squadron commander, Major W B Hargrave, says; "This flight is in my opinion the finest that any night-flying pilot has yet put up. It was impossible for Capt Wilcox to go higher than 2000 feet as the wind above that was 90 mph (viz. 30 mph faster than the speed of the machine). Capt Wilcox's machine was very badly hit both while on this and the other side of the lines".

(Editor's note: It was later ascertained that the report of Capt Wilcox re-being shelled by Allied AA was incorrect. No guns of the First Army fired at all that night. and the FE was over German lines)

HONOURS AND AWARDS
The Military Cross – 2nd Lt (T/Capt) H A Smith.

JANUARY 12
Low clouds and wind greatly interfered with work. With aeroplane observation,19 hostile batteries were successfully engaged for destruction. 59 photographs were taken during the day, 8014 rounds fired at ground targets, and 165 bombs dropped.
Enemy Aircraft – EA were not active and his scouts kept well east of the lines.

HONOURS AND AWARDS
Distinguished Service Cross – Flight Cdr G W Price, RNAS.
Military Cross – 2nd Lt A C B Harrison; Capt L G S Payne;
                Lt (T/Capt) G Talbot-Willcox.

JANUARY 13
Weather was mainly fine and a large amount of flying was done by all Brigades. With aeroplane observation, 39 hostile batteries were successfully engaged for destruction. 1667 plates were exposed, 421 bombs dropped, and 10,889 rounds fired.
Enemy Aircraft – EA were extremely active. Lt G E H McElroy, 40 Squadron, shot down an EA two-seater out of control near Pont-a-Vendin, Capt J H Tudhope of the same squadron shot down a DFW out of control. Capt Robinson & 2nd Lt Venmore, 57 Squadron, while on photography, were attacked by ten Albatros scouts. The Observer fired at one under its tail and it went down rolling and spinning, then fired at another EA which burst into flames and fell to pieces. The Observer then took 12 more photographs but the pilot was forced to return as his machine was becoming unmanageable, two flying wires, rudder control, and petrol pipe having been shot away. 2nd Lts T Colville-Jones and H G Crowe, 20 Squadron, while on O.P., dived at an EA two-seater, fired 150 rounds, and EA went down emitting smoke and crashed. Capt J T B McCudden, 56 Squadron, reports as follows; "Left aerodrome at 8.40am to pursue EA. At 9.35 I saw an LVG going north over Belinglise at 8.000. I glided from in the sun and secured a firing position at 50 yards without being seen, fired a short burst from both guns, when EA went into a right-hand spiral glide which got steeper. He then crashed just north of Lehancourt at 62B,H31b at 9.40am. Went north and saw two DFWs being shelled at about 5000 feet north-east of Ronnsoy at 9.50. Engaged one at close range and fired a long burst from both guns. EA went down steeply emitting smoke and water and hit the ground in a vertical dive just east of Vendhuille at 57B.S27, a, as far as I could judge, as I could not pay too much attention to it, as I was being engaged by the other DFW. This EA continued to circle round and got well east of the line like this, so I left him. Went north and saw two LVGs going west over Epehy at 10 am. I engaged one at 200 yards range at 9,000 feet and fired 200 rounds of Vickers into him. EA stalled, went down in a vertical dive, left-hand wings fell off and EA burst into flames and crashed in our lines just east of Lampire at 62B .F16b at 10.15am. Returned 11.5." 2nd Lts Rough & Dreschfield, 49 Squadron, attacked a two-seater and fired 20 rounds and the EA turned away climbing. A Triplane then fired on them and 2nd Lt Dreschfield shot it down in a spin completely out of control. An Offensive Patrol of 84 Squadron met several two-seater EA, two of which were destroyed and two

more driven down out of control. 2nd Lt J V Sorsoleil attacked one two-seater over Graincourt, opening fire from 200 yards. He closed under its tail and fired a second burst and the EA went down vertically and was seen to crash south-west of Graincourt. Lt J Ralston dived on a two -seater near Forenville, got on its tail, and shot it down to crash in the vicinity of the enemy's reserve trenches. 2nd Lt H A Payne attacked an Albatros two-seater, getting on its tail and firing a good burst with both guns, and the EA turned over steeply and fell out of control. Capt E R Pennell attacked a large two-seater near Bantouzelle, diving on it and firing with both guns from close range. The EA stalled, then fell vertically out of control. No.41 Section's balloon was destroyed by an EA Triplane; the Observers both made safe parachute descents, but the Triplane was brought down in our lines by anti-aircraft fire. *(Editor's note: This was Fokker Dr1, 144/17 of Jagdstaffel 11, piloted by Leutnant Stapenhorst, coded G.125).*

JANUARY 14
232 photographs were taken during the day, 131 bombs dropped, and 3387 rounds fired.
Bombing – 41st Wing – At noon on the 14th, 12 DH4s of 55 Squadron carried out a successful raid on the munitions factories and railway centre at Karlsruhe in Germany. One and a quarter tons of bombs were dropped. Anti-aircraft fire was very heavy and accurate over the objective, and the formation was attacked by seven EA, but only three were able to attain the height of our machines and these were kept at a distance by the Observers. All our machines returned safely.
Enemy Aircraft – Very few combats took place. Capt G M Cox, 65 Squadron, shot down a two-seater in flames at Westroosebeke which crashed.
Miscellaneous – 2nd Lt A A McLeod & Lt Thomson, 2 Squadron, attacked an enemy balloon over Bauvin which folded up and fell quickly.

HONOURS AND AWARDS
The Distinguished Service Order – Capt B E Baker, MC.
Distinguished Service Cross – Flight Sub-Lt H Day.

COMMUNIQUÉ No.123

15 – 21 January 1918

On January 18, Major General Hugh Trenchard relinquished his command of the RFC in France, and was appointed the first Chief of Air Staff for the newly forming Royal Air Force; being succeeded as GOC RFC in the Field by Major-General John Salmond. On January 19,the three all-Australian squadrons in France (Nos.68, 69 & 71) were officially retitled as Nos.2, 3 and 4 Squadrons, Australian Flying Corps.

During the period under review,15th to 21st January, we have claimed officially nine EA brought down and four driven down out of control. Six of our machines are missing. Approximately 11 tons of bombs have been dropped, and 34,112 rounds fired at ground targets. The weather generally throughout the week was adverse to flying.

JANUARY 15
Heavy rain during the day prevented any flying.
41st Wing – On the night of the 14th/15th, eleven machines of 100 Squadron bombed the steel works at Diedhofen (Thionville) in Germany, a rail junction two miles south-east of Metz, and Ebingen rail junction. All our machines returned.

JANUARY 16
High wind and rain all day made flying practically impossible. 2nd Lt A A McLeod & Lt A W Hammond, 2 Squadron, attempted an artillery patrol, and fired 225 rounds at an anti-aircraft gun and a group of men near La Bassee, and dropped two bombs on La Bassee.

JANUARY 17
Low clouds, rain and mist made operations impossible.

JANUARY 18
Forty-two hostile batteries were successfully engaged for destruction, 69 photographs were taken, 115 bombs dropped, and 7791 rounds fired at ground targets.
Enemy Aircraft – 2nd Lt A E Wylie, 65 Squadron, shot down one EA near Westroosbeke. Major R S Maxwell, 54 Squadron, fired a burst at 70 yards at an EA scout which turned over, the right bottom wing came partly away, and the EA went down in a steep spiral. 2nd Lt G Clapham of the same squadron attacked an Albatros scout and fired at point-blank range, and the EA went down in flames. One EA was brought down near Lens by infantry.

JANUARY 19
Weather was fine all day, sky covered in high clouds, and good visibility. 90 hostile batteries were successfully engaged for destruction, 870 photographs taken, 317 bombs dropped, and 14 ,458 rounds fired at ground targets.
Enemy Aircraft – Capt J L Trollope, 43 Squadron, while on Offensive Patrol over

Vitry, shot down a DFW which was seen to crash. Lt G H McElroy, 40 Squadron, shot an Albatros scout down out of control, and 2nd Lt W Harrison, also 40 Squadron, shot down a DFW out of control. Flight Cdr G W Price, 8 Squadron RNAS, attacked three Albatros scouts near Vitry, fired 300 rounds into one which fell over sideways and fell vertically. In a general engagement between 8 Squadron RNAS and 14 Albatros scouts, Flight Sub-Lt E G Johnstone attacked one EA and followed it down to 8000 feet, firing all the while. The EA was seen to fall completely out of control. Flight Sub-Lt P M Dennett shot another EA down out of control. Flight Lt W L Jordan fired 50 rounds into one EA which turned on its side and spun, and Flight Sub-Lts Dennett and Johnstone followed it down, each firing 250 rounds, and the EA fell out of control. 2nd Lt F Hobson, 70 Squadron, dived at a two-seater EA which fell out of control, then burst into flames. 2nd Lt G R Howsam of the same squadron also attacked a two-seater EA and sent it down out of control. 2nd Lt T C Jones & Lt L H Phelps, 20 Squadron, brought down an Albatros scout out of control. Capt R V Harrison & Lt T C Noel, 20 Squadron, saw four EA and dived on one and fired 20 rounds. The EA went down out of control. Sgt E Clayton & 2nd Lt L Sloot, 57 Squadron, when returning from a bomb raid, were attacked over Roulers by six Albatros scouts. The Observer fired 200 rounds and one EA went down in a vertical dive for 8000 feet. Capt R Hilton & Lt A Clayton, 9 Squadron, were attacked by six EA, two of which dived on the RE8. The Observer opened fire at 100 yards and the leading EA was seen to lose a wing and crash.

A patrol of four machines of 54 Squadron engaged seven Albatros scouts, and Capt K Shelton dived on two of them and followed them down to 500 feet, one of them falling out of control and seen later crashed on the ground.

JANUARY 20

Seventy-two hostile batteries were successfully engaged for destruction; 323 photographs were taken; 222 bombs dropped; and 10,572 rounds fired at ground targets.
Enemy Aircraft - Capt J T B McCudden, 56 Squadron, brought down one EA.

JANUARY 21

Low clouds and rain prevented much flying being done. 22 hostile batteries were successfully engaged for destruction; 140 bombs dropped, and 9086 rounds fired at ground targets.
41st Wing – On the night of the 21st/22nd, 17 machines of 100 Squadron started out to bomb the steel works at Thionville and the Bernsdorf railway sidings. Only 12 machines crossed the lines and dropped bombs. One machine of 16 Squadron RNAS dropped twelve 112lb bombs on the rail junction at Arnaville, south of Metz.

COMMUNIQUÉ No.124

22 – 28 January 1918

During the period under review (January 22nd to 28th inclusive) we have claimed officially 26 EA crashed and 19 driven down out of control. Approximately 37 tons of bombs were dropped, and 77,911 rounds fired at ground targets.

JANUARY 22
Seventy-nine hostile batteries were successfully engaged for destruction. A total of 1258 photographs were taken, 576 bombs dropped, and 18,670 rounds fired at ground targets. On the night of the 21st/22nd, 101 Squadron bombed aerodromes at, Heule, Rumbeke, Moorslede, and Harlebeke.

Enemy Aircraft – A patrol of 8 Squadron RNAS attacked seven Albatros scouts in the vicinity of Vitry. Flight Cdr G W Price and Flight Sub-Lt H Day each shot an EA down out of control. A patrol of 70 Squadron were attacked by seven EA scouts. In the fighting Lt K A Seth Smith dived on one 500 feet below him and it half-rolled over and went down completely out of control. 2nd Lt G R Howsam of the same squadron destroyed one EA. Capt F Quigley attacked one EA from the side and Lt Howsam attacked it from beneath its tail, and the EA started to spin, then burst into flames. An Albatros scout attacked Capt Quigley from above; he turned and fired at it nose-on. The EA dived and Lt J Todd followed it down, firing at it, and it crashed north-east of Houthulst Forest. Capt Quigley and Lt Howsam engaged another Albatros scout and followed it down until it became enveloped in a cloud of black smoke. Lt Howsam, while on a bomb raid, attacked a two-seater EA over Houthulst Forest, and after firing 400 rounds into it the EA burst into flames and crashed north-east of the Forest. Capt W Molesworth, 29 Squadron, engaged an EA at 100 yards range and it fell out of control emitting a long string of smoke. A patrol of eleven Bristol Fighters of 20 Squadron were attacked by about 20 Albatros scouts. 2nd Lts D G Cooke & H G Crowe shot down one completely out of control, and dived on another which was seen to fall issuing smoke and crash in flames south of Moorslede. Capt R K Kirkman & 2/AM J McMechan shot down one Albatros scout out of control. Sgt H O Smith & 2nd Lt C J Agelasto shot one down which crashed. Lt J McCone, 41 Squadron, dived on an EA firing two bursts and observed tracers entering the cockpit. The EA turned to the right and Lt McCone got off another burst of 40 rounds, and the EA immediately went down completely out of control, side-slipping and spinning, and was followed down to within 2000 feet of the ground.

Miscellaneous – Flight Cdr R Munday, 8 Squadron RNAS, made a night attack on a balloon. He crossed the lines at 3000 feet, dived to 1000 feet making for a point where he judged the balloon to be. He twice dived to within 100 feet, firing two bursts of 100 rounds each. When passing the balloon the second time at about 30 feet it burst into flames.

JANUARY 23
Enemy aircraft activity was very slight; no combats took place. 69 photographs were taken, 59 bombs dropped, and 5015 rounds fired at ground targets.

JANUARY 24

A total of 1309 photographs were taken, 446 bombs dropped, and 14,812 rounds fired at ground targets.

Enemy Aircraft – Capt A H O'Hara Wood, 4th Squadron AFC, shot down a DFW which fell straight into the ground north of La Bassee. Lt G McElroy, 40 Squadron, shot a DFW down completely out of control. No.8 Squadron RNAS, while on Offensive Patrol, met a formation of Albatros scouts. Flight Cdr R Munday fired 250 rounds at one EA at close range and it fell on its back and went down in a nose-dive. Flight Sub-Lt J B White attacked one EA firing 150 rounds at point- blank range and tracers were seen going into the pilot's cockpit. The EA turned over sideways and fell out of control. Another patrol of this squadron met several Albatros scouts, and Flight Sub-Lts W L Jordan and E G Johnstone both fired bursts at one EA which went down apparently out of control. Later, Flight Sub-Lts Johnstone and R Johns attacked a single Albatros scout close to the lines. They fired between them 200 rounds and the EA was last seen at 1500 feet still descending quite out of control. When on wireless patrol, Flight Cdr G W Price of the same squadron dived on an Albatros scout over La Bassee. He fired 300 rounds into the EA which fell vertically and was confirmed as crashed by AA observers. Flight Sub-Lt W H Sneath got in a good burst at one EA scout which he met east of Lens, and the EA dived for a short distance, then fell completely out of control, slipping from side to side, and was confirmed as crashed by AA observers.

While on an Offensive Patrol, Capt F Quigley, 70 Squadron, attacked a two-seater EA which eventually crashed in a hedge. 2nd Lt G R Howsam fired 400 rounds into an Albatros two-seater which crashed in a field. 2nd Lt A Koch attacked a two-seater into which he fired 150 rounds at close range and the EA fell in a spin completely out of control, and was seen still spinning down at 1000 feet.

Whilst on photography, 2nd Lts W Green & H Gros, 57 Squadron, were attacked by ten EA – five from below and five from above. 2nd Lt Gros, the Observer, fired a burst at a Triplane below him and it burst into flames. Another drum was fired at an Albatros scout which fell in a side-slip and was last seen falling out of control. Capt R F S Drewitt, 23 Squadron, while on Offensive Patrol, attacked one of six Albatros scouts which fell over, got into a spin, and was lost sight of as it entered the clouds. Capt W Molesworth, 29 Squadron, while leading a patrol, attacked a two-seater EA from behind and fired a drum at 150 yards range. The EA fell completely out of control. He then attacked another EA at about 100 yards range. A burst of smoke appeared and the EA dived east out of control and crashed. 2nd Lt J Coombe of the same patrol fired 80 rounds at 150 yards range at an EA which went down out of control. Whilst on Offensive Patrol, 2nd Lt F Clark, 60 Squadron, was attacked by an Albatros scout. Lt A W Morey of the same squadron did a left-hand bank towards the EA and collided with it. Both machines crashed. 2nd Lt P de Fontenay, 29 Squadron, sent an EA down in a spin which was confirmed as crashed by another pilot. Lt E Comber-Taylor & Sgt J Morris, 7 Squadron, whilst on photography, were attacked by about 12 EA. Sgt Morris fired 170 rounds as each EA attacked. One EA went down out of control, and another appeared to have a piece of the machine shot off.

Capt J T B McCudden, 56 Squadron, attacked a DFW when at 30 yards range and apparently hit the pilot as the gunner was seen to be leaning into the pilot's cockpit as if taking control, so Capt McCudden fired another burst and the EA went down alternatively diving and stalling and eventually got into a spin. It was last seen at 2000 feet still spinning.

COMMUNIQUÉ No. 124

Miscellaneous – At Aix-la-Chapelle a telegram was put up by the Germans on the 29th December 1917, saying that Mannheim had been bombarded. It is reported that the Central railway station, the electric power station, the chemical factory and a locomotive repair works were seriously damaged. The Mannheim fire brigade did not succeed in extinguishing the flames and the brigades of Ludwigshaven, Schwetsingen and Karlsruhe were called in to help. Several hundred thousand marks' damage was done. Five children, one woman and two men were killed. (Agent).

JANUARY 25

Sixty-five hostile batteries were successfully engaged for destruction; 1791 photographs were taken; 261 25lb and fourteen 112lb bombs were dropped, and 9672 rounds fired at ground targets. On the night of the 24th/25th, 101 Squadron bombed Oostacker, Rumbeke, Abeele, Bisseghem and Heule aerodromes, and Lendelede Station, Beveren and Roulers, while 102 Squadron bombed Roulers. Other targets were bombed by machines of 100 Squadron and 16 Squadron RNAS.
Enemy Aircraft – A patrol of 8 Squadron RNAS on a special mission observed five Albatros scouts near Beaumont. Flight Lt W L Jordan dived on two of these and fired 100 rounds into one at about 50 yards range. The EA fell on its side and went down slipping from side to side. Flight Lt Jordan and Flight Sub-Lt E G Johnstone followed the EA down and fired between them another 250 rounds and the EA was seen to crash. An Offensive Patrol of 40 Squadron observed a two-seater EA below and 2nd Lt J Hambley dived at it and opened fire. Tracers were seen to enter the fuselage and engine of the EA which stalled and fell over sideways, and then got into a vertical nose-dive. It was last seen at about 3000 feet still falling out of control. 2nd Lt D Richardson, 18 Squadron, while on photography, saw five EA and attacked, firing a burst at about 30 yards at one EA which went down in a spin completely out of control emitting a cloud of smoke. Capt R Boby & Lt W Wells, 22 Squadron, whilst on Offensive Patrol, observed 14 Albatros scouts in three groups below them. They dived and attacked one EA which spiralled, turned upside down, and fell completely out of control.

Capt H Hamersley, 60 Squadron, attacked an Albatros scout which fell out of control. 2nd Lt G Bremridge, 65 Squadron, attacked one of two EA two-seaters doing artillery work, and it burst into flames and crashed. 2nd Lt G R Howsam, 70 Squadron, dived on an Albatros scout which was attacking an RE8, and followed it down to 1000 feet firing all the way. The EA eventually fell over on its back and went down completely out of control. 2nd Lts J Allen & F Wakeford, 57 Squadron, whilst on photography, were attacked by an Albatros scout which fell out of control.

Sgt Gay & 2nd Lt A Flavell of the same squadron were attacked by nine Albatros scouts, and after a burst of 120 rounds from the Observer's gun, one EA fell out of control. An Offensive Patrol of 20 Squadron engaged 12 Albatros scouts. In the combat that ensued, Capt R Kirkman & 2nd Lt A Keith drove down one EA which was seen by No.60 Squadron to be falling with its wings folded back. 2nd Lts D McGoun & J Agelasto fired at one EA which went down out of control and was confirmed as crashed on the ground by another pilot. They then engaged another EA which was shot down out of control. Lt D Leigh-Pemberton & Capt N Taylor attacked an EA and shot it down out of control. Sgt F Johnson & 2nd Lt D Prosser attacked an EA which eventually broke up, the wings folding back. This EA was seen crashed on the ground. 2nd Lts D Weston & W Noble fired at one EA whose wing fell off. They then shot down another out of control.

205

2nd Lts C Matheson & C Brown, 3rd Squadron AFC, were attacked by two EA two-seaters, one of which they shot down in flames. A patrol of 56 Squadron, led by Capt J T B McCudden, attacked a DFW. Several pilots fired at it and after Lt T Durrant had fired a final burst the EA went down out of control. Capt McCudden attacked an EA completely out of control which has since been confirmed by infantry in the trenches to have crashed. Capt G H Bowman attacked one two-seater from under its tail and the enemy Observer disappeared into the cockpit leaving his gun pointing up. Lt A V Blenkiron then dived on it and drove it down completely out of control. Capt Bowman then got behind another EA which went into a steep dive and eventually crashed. Lt M E Mealing attacked a two-seater at close range. A large piece of this EA fell off and it fell out of control. At the same time 2nd Lt D Woodman dived on another EA which also went down out of control.

Lt Taylor, 41 Squadron, dived on one of eight Albatros scouts, fired 50 rounds at 40 yards range, and it fell over and nose-dived, and AA observers confirm that the EA crashed. 2nd Lt D Lawson, Lt W Kellog, and Capt M Gonne, 54 Squadron, all attacked an EA which was last seen diving vertically in flames. Capt Gonne then got directly behind another EA which was evidently unaware of his presence. After a short burst at point-blank range, the EA went down completely out of control and was watched down for 10,000 feet when it was lost in the haze. 2nd Lt E Krohn, 84 Squadron, shot down a two-seater EA which was last seen diving in flames. 2nd Lts H Elliott & R S Herring, 48 Squadron, whilst on photography, were attacked by an Albatros scout. 2nd Lt Herring fired two bursts and the EA turned over on its back and dropped in a spin, but owing to the haze was not seen to crash.

HONOURS AND AWARDS
Military Cross – Capt P D Robinson.
Military Medal – 1st/AM H Doran.

JANUARY 26
During the day 272 photographs were taken, 731 bombs dropped, and 6400 rounds fired at ground targets. Enemy aircraft activity was practically nil all day – no combats took place. One EA was brought down by anti-aircraft guns of the Fourth Army.

HONOURS AND AWARDS
Distinguished Conduct Medal – No.11559 Cpl C J French.

JANUARY 27
Very little flying was done owing to thick mist. No combats took place all day.

JANUARY 28
During the day a record number of photographs were taken, 2404 plates being exposed in all. Seventy hostile batteries were successfully engaged for destruction. A total of 381 25lb, two 230lb, and nineteen 112lb bombs were dropped, and 13,007 rounds fired at ground targets.
Enemy Aircraft – Enemy aircraft were very active and a considerable amount of fighting took place in which two EA were brought down, and 13 driven down out of control. Flight Cdr G W Price, 8 Squadron RNAS, fired 200 rounds into an EA two-seater at 20 to 50 yards range and it nose-dived, burst into flames at 4000 feet,

then crashed near La Bassee. 2nd Lt G Clapham, 54 Squadron, dived on one of three EA scouts and it went down out of control and was seen to crash. In other combats EA were claimed as driven down out of control by the following pilots; Flight Lt W L Jordan, 8 Squadron RNAS; 2nd Lt H M Hutton and 2nd Lt H S Wolff, 40 Squadron; Capt Meek, Lt A G Wingate-Grey, Lt P de Fontenay and Lt J G Coombe, all 29 Squadron; Sgt Noel & 2nd Lt Stennett, 57 Squadron; 2nd Lt H G Hegarty, 60 Squadron; 2nd Lt T Colville-Jones & Lt L H Phelps, 20 Squadron; 2nd Lt J Todd, 70 Squadron; 2nd Lt J S Chick & Capt R M Makepeace, 11 Squadron; 2nd Lts F Ransley & R Herring, 48 Squadron.

COMMUNIQUÉ No.125

29 January – 4 February 1918

During the period under review (January 29 to February 4) we have claimed officially 27 EA brought down (three of which fell in our lines) and 25 EA driven down out of control. Two hostile balloons were destroyed. Five of our machines are missing. Approximately 33 tons of bombs have been dropped, and 64,816 rounds fired at ground targets.

JANUARY 29

Seventy hostile batteries were successfully engaged for destruction with aeroplane observation, and 40 zone calls sent down.

Bombing – Night – Bomb raids were made on the night 28th/29th on Meurchin, Annoeullin, Carvin, Haubourdin, Brebieres, Izel, Vitry, Quiery-la-Motte, Annay, Pont-a-Vendin, Billy Montigny, Drocourt and Henin Lietard.

Bombing – Day – Bomb raids were carried out on Bohain, Hoogte, Seclin, Gulleghem ammunition dump, and aerodromes at Marquain, Gontrode and Cruyshautem.

Enemy Aircraft – Eight EA were brought down and four driven down out of control. 2nd Lt A T W Lindsay, 54 Squadron, brought down an enemy balloon in flames. Flight Sub-Lt H Day, 8 Squadron RNAS, attacked one of five Albatros scouts at close range and drove it down out of control. Flight Cdr R Munday attacked one EA at close range, firing 150 rounds, and tracers were seen to enter the EA's fuselage, which turned practically over and fell in a vertical dive completely out of control. Flight Sub-Lt R Johns shot one EA down completely out of control, and two others were driven down. A patrol of 70 Squadron attacked some EA scouts. Capt F Quigley followed an Albatros down to 6000 feet firing all the way & the EA went down in flames. Lt E Peverell dived on another EA which was sent down in a spin obviously out of control. Lt K Seth Smith attacked an Albatros scout nose-on at about 30 yards range and it fell out of control. 2nd Lt A Koch attacked two EA, one of which was driven down out of control. Capt F Hobson attacked an Albatros scout and drove it down out of control. Two patrols of 29 Squadron attacked fifteen Albatros scouts. Capt W Molesworth drove down one which turned east, then burst into flames. Capt F S Meek dived on one EA after firing 50 rounds into it from 60 yards range. It zoomed up sharply, one wing crumpled, and then burst into flames. 2nd Lt L Tims got on the tail of one EA and drove it down out of control. 2nd Lt G R Howsam, 32 Squadron, drove an EA scout down out of control, and it was seen to crash. 2nd Lt T M Williams, 65 Squadron, attacked an EA scout at point-blank range and it fell out of control with smoke coming out of the fuselage. Lt C Matthews attacked an EA which fell completely out of control and was seen by another pilot to break up in the air. Capt J Gilmour shot down a large two-seater which was observed to crash. Lt H Symons drove down an EA scout and a two-seater, both out of control. Lt R Fagan & 2nd Lt A Matt, 82 Squadron, whilst on photography, were attacked by six Albatros scouts, one of which was shot down and crashed in the French lines. The Armstrong Whitworth was badly shot about. 2nd Lt E Clear was forced to leave his patrol owing to engine trouble, but on his way home he saw two two-seater EA and attacked one. After firing a burst, the German

Observer was seen to fall forward over his gun. A second burst was fired and the EA went down in flames. 2nd Lt Clear was then attacked by five Albatros scouts but in spite of a failing engine managed to regain his aerodrome. 2nd Lts W Henney & A Wright, 27 Squadron, while on photography, were attacked by three EA and shot one down out of control.

JANUARY 30
During the night of the 29th/30th, 306 bombs were dropped and 525 rounds fired, and during the day 303 bombs were dropped, 10,652 rounds fired, and 1384 photographs taken. Fifty-two hostile batteries were successfully engaged for destruction.
Enemy Aircraft – 2nd Lts S Oades & S Bunting, 22 Squadron, shot a two-seater EA down in flames which was seen to crash. 2nd Lt W Casson, 43 Squadron, shot down a two-seater EA out of control. Lt J Coombe, 29 Squadron, attacked one of nine Albatros scouts and sent one down in a spin. Lt J Hewett, 23 Squadron, shot down an Albatros scout out of control, falling side to side. 2nd Lts D McGoun & C J Agelasto, 20 Squadron, shot down an Albatros scout at 30 yards range, which fell out of control and crashed. Lt R Bennett & 2/AM B Matthews of the same squadron shot down an Albatros scout completely out of control. Lt K Junor, 56 Squadron, dived on two EA scouts and opened fire from 100 yards. One scout went down in a series of sharp dives and at 8000 feet burst into flames, then crashed. Capt J T B McCudden attacked four EA scouts, into one of which he fired a short burst from both guns at 50 yards range when pieces of what appeared to be three-ply fell off the EA. Turning to the left, the EA went down in a vertical dive, absolutely out of control. Capt McCudden then flew behind a Pfalz and fired a short burst from both guns. The EA went down in a spiral, finally stalling and side-slipping, and was last seen at 6000 feet still out of control. Capt G H Bowman led a patrol against seven Albatros scouts and shot one down which crashed. A patrol of 84 Squadron, led by Capt F Leask, attacked six EA scouts and a two-seater, which were eventually reinforced by six more EA. In the fighting two EA were driven down completely out of control; one by Capt Leask, and the other by 2nd Lt J A McCudden.
(Editor's note: Lt John Anthony McCudden, MC, credited with eight combat victories, was a younger brother of Major J T B McCudden, VC and was killed in action on 18 March 1918 by Leutnant Hans Joachim Wolff of Jagdstaffel 11).

JANUARY 31
Weather was fine but a thick mist prevailed all day. No fighting took place.

FEBRUARY 1
Thick mist all day on all Brigade fronts prevented any service flying being carried out.

FEBRUARY 2
1224 photographs were taken, 285 25lb and twelve 112lb bombs were dropped, and 13,285 rounds fired at ground targets.
Enemy Aircraft – Lt G McElroy, 40 Squadron, shot down one EA out of control. Flight Cdr R Compston, 8 Squadron RNAS, shot down an Albatros scout and a two-seater, both completely out of control, and the two-seater was seen to crash. While on a roving commission, Sgt Gay & 2nd Lt Flavell, 57 Squadron, were attacked by

five Albatros scouts and a two-seater. The Observer fired 200 rounds at 250 yards range and one scout fell enveloped in a large cloud of smoke. Capt F Gorringe, 70 Squadron, attacked one of two two-seaters, firing 100 rounds, which was seen to crash by anti-aircraft gunners. Capt J T B McCudden, 56 Squadron, attacked an LVG at 100 yards range. He fired a long burst from both guns after which the EA went down vertically, fell onto its back, and the EA gunner fell out. The EA finally crashed in our lines.(G.130). Capt R Chappell, 41 Squadron, shot down an Albatros scout which crashed, but was then attacked by six EA scouts. He put his machine into a spin and on coming out saw one EA in front of him and five still above. He attacked the single EA which did a long side-slip and was last seen about 2000 feet from the ground still spinning and completely out of control. 2nd Lt Jones, 41 Squadron, shot down one EA which was last seen still spinning about 4000 feet below. Lt G C Cuthbertson, 54 Squadron, attacked an Albatros scout which was attacking a Sopwith Camel. The EA fell, then broke up in the air. Capt K Shelton, 54 Squadron, descended to an altitude of 50 feet and fired on a balloon which was then on the ground. It was seen to burst into flames. Two machines of 35 Squadron, while on photography, were attacked by five Fokker Triplanes. A patrol of 54 Squadron and several more EA scouts joined in. Two Triplanes were driven down and forced to land. Capt J M Child,84 Squadron, attacked a large two-seater DFW and apparently hit its Observer who disappeared into his cockpit. Owing to gun trouble Capt Child was unable to carry on the combat.

FEBRUARY 3

1173 photographs were taken, 451 25lb and 20 112lb bombs were dropped, and 14,418 rounds fired at ground targets.
Enemy Aircraft – Five EA were destroyed and nine driven down out of control. 2nd Lts W Beaver & H Easton, 20 Squadron, dived on an Albatros scout which fell out of control and burst into flames when near the ground. Several pilots of 8 Squadron RNAS fired at one EA which fell and was seen to crash. Capt H Maddocks, while leading a patrol of 54 Squadron, met five EA scouts. He dived at the nearest one which went down 2000 feet, then burst into flames. He then attacked a second EA which burst into flames and fell. Lt G Cuthbertson attacked and shot down one EA which was seen to crash by another pilot. In other combats, EA were claimed as driven down out of control by Capt A H O'Hara-Wood, 4th Squadron AFC; Capt O Horsley, 40 Squadron; Flight Cdr R J O Compston, 8 Squadron RNAS; Flight Cdr R Munday, 8 Squadron RNAS; 2nd Lts Green & Gros, 57 Squadron; 2nd Lt H Lewis, 23 Squadron; Capt J Gilmour and 2nd Lt G Knocker, 65 Squadron; 2nd Lt G Lipsett, 41 Squadron.

FEBRUARY 4

300 photographs were taken, 275 bombs dropped, and 11,521 rounds fired at ground targets. 21 hostile batteries were successfully engaged for destruction from aeroplane observation.
Enemy Aircraft – Five EA were brought down, one of which fell in our lines, and eight driven down out of control.

2nd Lt A Atkey & Lt C Ffolliott, 18 Squadron, when returning from a photographic and bombing expedition, were attacked by about ten EA scouts. Lt F folliott fired a burst at the leader which went down out of control, a portion of its tail plane detaching itself. A burst was then fired at another EA which went down out of control. The remainder of the EA then broke off combat. 2nd Lt Atkey's machine was badly shot about, the magazine gun and the Observer's drum being shot through and one elevator wire shot away. 2nd Lt H Hegarty and Lt H Crompton, 60 Squadron, both attacked an EA scout which spun down and crashed in our lines.(G.131). Lt Duncan and 2nd Lt J Priestley of the same squadron both attacked one of a formation of Albatros scouts. One of the planes fell off the EA which burst into flames.

An Offensive Patrol of 20 Squadron engaged 20 Albatros scouts. Lt D Leigh-Pemberton & Capt N W Taylor fired at one which burst into flames. 2nd Lts D J Weston & W Noble attacked a second EA which went down in a slow spin. Lt R Bennett & 1/AM Mather fired 200 rounds at a third EA which fell out of control. They were then attacked by three scouts and 1/AM Mather fired a drum into one of these and it burst into flames and fell to pieces in the air. 2nd Lts D E Cooke & C J Agelasto attacked a fifth EA which they shot down out of control. 2nd Lts E Lindup & Dougall attacked a sixth EA with the back gun and it fell completely out of control. 2nd Lt T Colville-Jones & Capt J H Hedley shot an EA down which crashed. 2nd Lt L Roberts & Lt M Farquharson-Roberts shot down an EA out of control. Lt T Colville-Jones and Capt J H Hedley dived on an enemy balloon which was seen to crumple on the ground.

HONOURS AND AWARDS
The Military Cross – Capt M E Gonne; 2nd Lt G R Howsam; Capt R K Kirkman; Capt R T O Windsor; Lt R S Larkin; Capt T Grant.

COMMUNIQUÉ No.126

5 – 11 February 1918

February 1918 saw No.35 Squadron exchange its Armstrong Whitworth FK8s ("Big Acks") for Bristol F2b Fighters to continue its main roles of army co-operation.

During the period under review, February 5th to 11th inclusive, we have claimed officially seven EA brought down and five driven down out of control, and one hostile balloon brought down. Nine of our machines are missing. Approximately 13 tons of bombs were dropped, 49,966 rounds were fired at ground targets, and 1261 photographs taken. Seventy-seven hostile batteries were successfully engaged for destruction from aeroplane observation on February 5th.

FEBRUARY 5
Enemy Aircraft – Lt G McElroy, 40 Squadron, singled out a DFW and when within 100 yards range fired 100 rounds. Pieces were seen to fall from the EA's tail and fuselage and it went down in a slow spin and crashed. He then observed a DFW which was pointed out to him by anti-aircraft fire; he dived, fired about 200 rounds, and the EA burst into flames. A patrol of 8 Squadron RNAS attacked two Albatros scouts. Flight Lt R McDonald and Flight Sub-Lts H Day and H H Fowler all engaged one EA which went down completely out of control and crashed. Major J Cunningham, 65 Squadron, attacked an Albatros scout which was diving on another member of his patrol and fired a burst from both guns at 50 yards range. The EA fell completely out of control, its tail plane folding up, and was seen to crash. Other EA claimed as driven down out of control were by 2nd Lts D G Cooke & C J Agelasto and 2nd Lts W Beaver & H Easton, 20 Squadron; Capt W Molesworth, 29 Squadron; 2nd Lt F Williams, 29 Squadron; 2nd Lt E Peacock, 65 Squadron; 2nd Lt A A Leitch, 65 Squadron; Lt J Aldred and Lt E Peverell, 70 Squadron; Capt F Soden, 60 Squadron; Lt G Shaw & Sgt F Hopper, 25 Squadron.
Miscellaneous – Capt J Gilmour, 65 Squadron, attacked a hostile balloon. The occupants descended by parachute and the balloon went down issuing black smoke.

FEBRUARY 6
105 photographs were taken, 262 bombs dropped, and 9405 rounds fired at ground targets.
Enemy Aircraft – A patrol of 3 Squadron attacked six Albatros scouts, and Lt G Alderson and 2nd Lt C J Kent each shot down one EA which are reported by AA to have crashed. In this fight Capt Sutton collided with one EA and had his fin taken off and had to retire from the combat.

FEBRUARY 7
Mist, rain and strong wind interfered with operations.

HONOURS AND AWARDS
Bar to the Distinguished Service Cross – Flight Cdr G W Price; Flight Lt W L Jordan.

212

The Distinguished Service Cross – Flight Sub-Lt E G Johnstone.
Bar to the Military Cross – Capt W E Moleswort.
Military Cross – Capt J H Tudhope; Lt G E H McElroy; Capt K M St C G Leask.

FEBRUARY 8
Low clouds, high wind and rain made flying practically impossible. No combats took place.

FEBRUARY 9
52 photographs were taken, 138 bombs dropped, and 8057 rounds fired at ground targets.
Enemy Aircraft – EA activity was very slight and only one decisive combat took place. 2nd Lt H H Hartley & Lt R S Herring, 48 Squadron, shot down one EA completely out of control, and it was last seen at a height of 2000 feet still out of control.

FEBRUARY 10
Weather very overcast with a high wind and little flying was done. 35 photographs were taken, 50 bombs dropped, and 4327 rounds fired at ground targets.

HONOURS AND AWARDS
2nd Bar to the Distinguished Service Cross – Flight Cdr R J O Compston, DSC.
The Military Cross – 2nd Lt A B Whiteside.

FEBRUARY 11
144 photographs taken, 102 bombs dropped, and 4376 rounds fired at ground targets. EA activity very slight. No combats took place.

COMMUNIQUÉ No. 127

12 – 18 February 1918

During the period under review, February 12th to 18th inclusive, we have claimed officially 39 EA brought down and 19 driven down out of control. Eleven of our machines are missing. Approximately 26 tons of bombs have been dropped, 43,000 rounds fired at ground targets, and 6657 photographs taken.

FEBRUARY 12
Little flying was possible owing to continuing bad weather. EA activity was slight, and no combats took place.
Bombing – Twelve DH4s of 55 Squadron carried out a raid on the barracks and railway station at Offenburg in Germany. All our machines returned.

HONOURS AND AWARDS
The Military Cross – 2nd Lt A J Wright: 2nd Lt R W Hobbs.

FEBRUARY 13
Practically no flying was done owing to rain and mist.

FEBRUARY 14
Weather was again very misty and the sky completely overcast.

HONOURS AND AWARDS
The Distinguished Service Order – Capt G H Bowman.
The Military Cross – Capt R N Welton; 2nd Lt R A George.

FEBRUARY 15
The mist still continued but showed signs of clearing in the afternoon. A total of 2350 rounds were fired into enemy trenches and at various targets behind the enemy's lines. A Friedrichshafen crashed in the Third Army area (G.133).

FEBRUARY 16
Weather was very fine and visibility good. 83 hostile batteries were successfully engaged for destruction; a total of 2547 photographs were taken, this being a record. Over seven tons of bombs were dropped, and 10,410 rounds fired.
Enemy Aircraft – Capt H H Balfour, 43 Squadron, while leading a patrol, observed two EA formations. He attacked one EA at point- blank range and drove it down out of control, then got on the tail of another EA which went down in a spin and crashed. 2nd Lt G Bailey, 43 Squadron, saw an Albatros scout attacking an RE8,so dived on its tail, fired, and the EA went down in flames and crashed. Major C Miles, 43 Squadron, drove an EA down completely out of control. 2nd Lt C King, 43 Squadron, shot an EA scout down out of control. Capt J Trollope, 43 Squadron, fought an EA down to 5000 feet which eventually crashed. Lt G McElroy, 40 Squadron, shot one EA down obviously out of control. Capt G H Lewis and Lt A Usher, 40 Squadron, both attacked an EA which fell out of control. 2nd Lt P J

Clayson, 1 Squadron, attacked an EA scout flying low over our lines, so dived and fired at close range and the EA went down and turned over in a ploughed field in our lines (G.134). 2nd Lts W Beaver & H Easton, 20 Squadron, shot down an EA two-seater out of control.

The following is an account of combats by Captain J T B McCudden, 56 Squadron, who brought down four EA, one of which fell in our lines;

"Left aerodrome at 9.40am and crossed the lines over Bantouzelle at 16,000 feet at 10.25. Many EA scouts about, mostly above us, who withdrew north and east. At 10.35 saw a Rumpler getting height over Caudry at 16,500. I secured a good position and fired a long burst with both guns, after which EA went down in a vertical dive and then all four wings fell off and the wreckage fell south-west of Caudry. At about 10.45 saw a DFW south of Bois de Vaucelles at about 15,000 feet. I secured a firing position at 100 yards range and after firing a long burst from both guns EA went down in flames, after which it fell to pieces, the wreckage falling just north-east of Le Catelet. I now engaged an LVG which went down damaged with water coming from radiator after being fired at by Lt K Junor and self. At 11.5 I fired a green light as one of my elevators was out of action and my Aldis and windscreen were covered in ice, due to a radiator leak. On re-crossing the lines I engaged a Rumpler at 15,500 feet over Hargicourt at 11.10 am. After firing a long burst from both guns EA went down fairly steeply south-east emitting smoke and was seen by Capt W Fielding-Johnson to go into a right-hand spiral dive, apparently out of control. (This machine was afterwards confirmed as having burst into flames near the ground.) Left aerodrome at 11.45 am and at 12.30 engaged a Rumpler at 15,500 feet as it was recrossing the lines over Lagnicourt. I secured a good position but EA immediately turned. However, I got into position again and fired a short burst from both guns after which the EA went down vertically and fell to pieces, and the wreckage fell in our lines in the vicinity of Lagnicourt. (G.137). Returned at 1.20pm."

2nd Lt J A McCudden, 84 Squadron, attacked a two-seater Rumpler and fired a good burst from both guns. EA dived and 2nd Lt McCudden followed it down to 1000 feet, firing from time to time, and EA was seen to crash. 2nd Lt J Sorsoleil, 84 Squadron, was attacked by five Albatros scouts who were escorting the Rumpler shot down by 2nd Lt McCudden and he attacked one EA which burst into flames. Lt J Larson, 84 Squadron, attacked an EA scout. The pilot appeared to be hit and EA stalled and fell over on its back, and was last seen falling out of control. Capt F Brown, 84 Squadron, attacked one of four EA scouts which he shot down completely out of control. He then attacked a second scout and tracers were seen to enter the EA which fell out of control. Capt Brown's engine then started to give trouble and he made for our lines. On the way he met a two-seater LVG and fired 150 rounds into it at 30 yards range, after which it fell and was seen to crash. Lt G Johnson, 84 Squadron, attacked an Albatros scout with both guns and it fell out of control and crashed. Capt J Ralston, 24 Squadron, attacked an Albatros scout which fell out of control. He had not time to change his drum before he was attacked by a second Albatros scout, and though wounded, regained his aerodrome. Major G H Bowman, 41 Squadron, shot down one EA out of control. Capt G Thomson, 46 Squadron, dived at an EA two-seater and fired 70 rounds. EA went down vertically giving out smoke and was confirmed by AA as being out of control.

A Friedrichshafen was brought down by AA fire in the First Army area. (G.136). An EA LVG landed at Catigny in our lines. (G.135).

FEBRUARY 17

Eighty-seven hostile batteries were successfully engaged for destruction from aeroplane observation. 2256 photographs were taken, 122 tons of bombs dropped, and 17,034 rounds fired at ground targets.

Enemy Aircraft – 2nd Lt W Casson, 43 Squadron, whilst leading a patrol, fired a long burst at the nearest of four EA two-seaters. The left-hand bottom plane of the EA crumpled up and the machine fell and crashed. 2nd Lts S A Oades & S W Bunting, 22 Squadron, brought down an EA scout after firing 100 rounds into it at close range.

Lt G McElroy, 40 Squadron, whilst on escort duty, opened fire from close range at an EA scout which fell and crashed on the outskirts of Lille. Later in his flight he saw an EA approaching our lines near Lens, which he attacked and drove down, and finally saw it crash and catch fire. 2nd Lt R Wade, 40 Squadron, fired several bursts into an EA scout which fell in flames and was seen to crash. 2nd Lt E Lindup & Cpl M Mather, 20 Squadron, in formation with 11 Bristol Fighters, fired 100 rounds into one of 16 EA encountered. The EA went down completely out of control and crashed west of Moorslede. Sgt F Johnson & Capt J H Hedley, 20 Squadron, also destroyed an EA which was seen to crash. Lt K Junor, 56 Squadron, when at 14,000 feet, was attacked by a single Albatros scout which fired a short burst, then dived away east. He dived after it and fired both guns at 100 yards range and EA burst into flames and crashed in a field. Lt M Mealing, 56 Squadron, attacked one of five EA scouts and it crashed to the ground.

Hostile EA were driven down out of control by the following: Capt D Flockart, 4th Squadron AFC; Lt F Woolhouse, 4th Squadron AFC; Capt J Trollope. 2nd Lts H Daniel, H Highton, A Dobie and Capt H H Balfour, all of 43 Squadron; 2nd Lt R Wade, 40 Squadron; 2nd Lts D McGoun & Masding, 20 Squadron; Sgt F Johnson & Capt J H Hedley, 20 Squadron; Lt R Bennett & Cpl F Archer, 20 Squadron; Capt J Hamilton, 29 Squadron; Capt W Fielding-Johnson, 56 Squadron; Capt J T B McCudden, 56 Squadron; 2nd Lt D Judson, 3 Squadron; 2nd Lt A W B Proctor, 84 Squadron; 2nd Lt G Travers, 84 Squadron.

FEBRUARY 18

58 hostile batteries were successfully engaged for destruction from aeroplane observation. A total of 1797 photographs were taken, six tons of bombs dropped, and 10,779 rounds fired at ground targets.

Bombing – On the night of 17th/18th, bomb raids were made on Henin Lietard, Auby, Blanc Maison, Douai, Vitry, Beaumont, Bois Grenier, Esquerchin, Quiery, Bohain, Fournes, Dechy, and Faumont aerodrome. By day on the 18th, five DH4s of 55 Squadron bombed the barracks and railway station at Treves, while four other DH4s bombed the station and steel works at Thionville. AA fire was considerable and accurate, two machines being hit, but all machines returned.

Enemy Aircraft – Capt J Allport & Lt A W Hammond, 2 Squadron, while on photography, were attacked by six EA scouts. Lt Hammond shot two down; one burst into flames and crashed, and the other fell to pieces. A patrol of three Bristol Fighters of 22 Squadron met four EA scouts and 2nd Lt S H Wallage brought one down. Capt F Gorringe, 70 Squadron, was attacked by several Albatros scouts and shot down one which burst into flames and crashed. Capt H Hamersley, 2nd Lts R B Clark, C O Evans and W M Kent, 60 Squadron, engaged four EA Triplanes. One was brought down by Capt Hamersley and seen to crash from 12,000 feet; another was driven down to about 300 feet by Lts Evans and Clark and finally crashed into a tree. Lt Kent drove down a third and saw it crash. Capt J T B McCudden, 56 Squadron, when leading a formation, dived on four EA scouts. He fired a short burst into the leader whose machine burst into flames, the pilot falling out. He then fired a long burst into another scout from 100 yards range and it went into a steep dive and crashed.

Hostile EA were also driven down out of control by Lt R Howard, 2nd Squadron AFC; Capt F Huxley, 2nd Squadron AFC; Capt G McElroy, 40 Squadron; Flight Lt W L Jordan, 8 Squadron RNAS; Flight Sub-Lts E G Johnstone, C R Walworth, and Flight Cdr R Compston, all of 8 Squadron RNAS; Capt H Balfour, 2nd Lts C King, Orcutt and Grandy, all of 43 Squadron; 2nd Lts S A Oades & S W Bunting, 22 Squadron; 2nd Lts L P Roberts & W Noble, 20 Squadron ; 2nd Lt J Todd, 70 Squadron; Capt R Rusby, 29 Squadron; 2nd Lts A K Cowper, R T Mark, and H B Richardson, all 24 Squadron; 2nd Lt Saunders, 84 Squadron; K Wensley & 2nd Lt Creek, 25 Squadron.

COMMUNIQUÉ No. 128

19 – 25 February 1918

In a week of varying weather conditions, combat losses increased on both sides of the lines. Lt G Jones, 4th Squadron AFC, mentioned on February 21st, eventually rose to become Air Marshal Sir George Jones, KBE,CB,DFC, Chief of Air Staff of the Royal Australian Air Force.

During the period under review, February 19th to 25th inclusive, we have officially claimed 58 EA brought down and 22 driven down out of control. Twenty-two of our machines are missing. Approximately 58¼ tons of bombs have been dropped and 9290 photographs taken.

FEBRUARY 19

Twenty-one hostile batteries were successfully engaged for destruction from aeroplane observation, a total of 1190 photographs taken, and 4 tons of bombs dropped. On the night of 18th/19th, eight machines of 100 Squadron bombed the railway station and barracks at Treves. One machine failed to return. Two other machines of 100 Squadron bombed the railway and gas works at Thionville. Both machines returned. By day, eleven DH4s of 55 Squadron bombed Treves. One DH4 is missing.

Enemy Aircraft – Lt R Mackenzie and Lt L Benjamin, 2nd Squadron AFC, attacked an EA scout which fell out of control and was seen by ground observers to crash near Vendin-le-Vieil. 2nd Lt R Owen, 43 Squadron, was attacked by five Albatros scouts. He fired a burst of 20 rounds at the nearest EA which went down out of control and was seen by anti-aircraft to fall in flames near the Bois du Biez. 2nd Lt W Kent, 60 Squadron, fired both his guns at an EA scout from a range of 400 yards. The Albatros burst into flames and crashed in our lines near Hollebeke.(G.138).

2nd Lts A Cowper, R Mark, R Hamersley, and P McDougall, 24 Squadron, each fired about 100 rounds into a two-seater EA which burst into flames and fell into Servais village. Capt R Grosvenor, 84 Squadron, dived on a large formation of EA scouts escorting a two-seater which dived away east. Capt Grosvenor followed the two-seater which stalled right in front of him and enabled him to get in a good burst. The EA went down and crashed into a wood south of St Quentin. 2nd Lt J Sorsoleil, 84 Squadron, attacked one of ten EA scouts. This scout started to spin and finally crashed near St Gobain woods. He was then attacked by one of the other scouts but managed to get on its tail and fired both guns. The EA dived vertically and crashed in the same wood as the previous EA. 2nd Lt J A McCudden,84 Squadron, was attacked by several EA scouts and sent one down out of control which crashed in the Forest of St Gobain. 2nd Lt A W B Proctor, 84 Squadron, engaged one of several EA scouts at about 15,000 feet and it crashed. Lt J Hewett, 23 Squadron, attacked one of two two-seater EA. He dived at this machine and zoomed up under it three times firing bursts from both guns at each dive. The EA went down in a slow glide and was seen by Lt Faulkner to crash into a house in Crecy. 2nd Lt A Lindsay, 54 Squadron, met five EA scouts escorting a two-seater. Getting on one EA's tail, he fired a short burst and the EA fell vertically and crashed near Monceau. Lt N Clark, 54 Squadron, attacked an EA scout and followed it down 8000 feet, firing short bursts, when part of the EA machine broke off and the remainder crashed into the ground near Monceau. EA were driven down out of control by the following; Capt L W Jarvis, 56 Squadron; 2nd Lts A Cowper, P McDougall, R Hamersley and R Mark, 24 Squadron; Capt R Grosvenor, 84 Squadron (two); 2nd Lt J A McCudden and Lt J Larson, 84 Squadron.

FEBRUARY 20
During the morning the sky was overcast with mist which turned to rain in the afternoon. No combats took place all day. By day, eight DH4s of 55 Squadron bombed factories and stations at Pirmasens in Germany from a height of 15,000 feet, and also bombed the Gas Works. All machines returned.

FEBRUARY 21
Weather fine all day with excellent visibility. Seventy hostile batteries were successfully engaged for destruction from aeroplane observation, and a total of 1216 photographs taken, and 44 tons of bombs dropped.

Enemy Aircraft – Enemy aircraft were fairly active all day, the activity being most marked in the afternoon. 2nd Lt W Adams, 4th Squadron, AFC, was attacked by two EA scouts and shot one down which crashed. Lt G Jones, 4th Squadron AFC, attacked one of five EA scouts and followed it from 15,000 to 10,000 feet, firing about 100 rounds at point-blank range. One wing of the EA broke off and it crashed. Lt A Clark, 2nd Squadron AFC, when leading his patrol, fired about 50 rounds from a range of 40 yards into an EA which was diving at him, and it fell over on its left wing, dropped vertically, and was seen to crash. Capt W Molesworth, 29 Squadron, chased a two-seater EA which he saw being "archied" over Ypres. He got on its tail, fired 20 rounds, and it burst into flames and fell in our lines between Hooge and Gheluvelt.(G.140). Lt R Bennett & Cpl Veale, 20 Squadron, whilst on patrol with eight Bristol Fighters, dived at a two-seater EA and fired a burst of about 50 rounds from the front gun at about 200 yards range. The EA side-slipped and was seen to crash. Capt J T B McCudden, 56 Squadron, attacked a two-seater EA at a height of 9000 feet over Acheville. After only four shots had been fired from each gun the EA burst into flames and crashed on the railway line just south of Mericourt. Capt G Hughes & Capt H Claye, 62 Squadron, whilst leading a formation at 13,000 feet, saw a large two-seater EA flying south over Armentieres at a height of 7000 feet. The pilot dived to within 200 feet of the EA, then zoomed up to within 50 yards under its tail, the pilot firing 50 rounds from his front gun. The EA turned east, then broke to pieces in the air. Hostile machines were driven down out of control by the following; Lt L Benjamin, 2nd Squadron AFC; Flight Cdr R Munday, 8 Squadron RNAS; Capt H Symons, 65 Squadron; 2nd Lt F Martin & 2nd Lt W Venmore, 57 Squadron; Capt G McElroy, 24 Squadron.

HONOURS AND AWARDS
The following is an extract from Fifth Supplement to *LONDON GAZETTE*, dated 8th February 1918:-

" The undermentioned officers have been brought to the notice of the Secretary of State for War, by the Army Council, for very valuable services rendered in connection with the war up to 31st December 1917. Pitcher, Maj and Bt-Lt-Col (Temp Brig.Gen) D Le G, Ind Army. "

FEBRUARY 22

The sky was covered with low clouds and there was occasional rain. A total of 89 photographs were taken and 73 tons of bombs dropped. There were no combats all day.

FEBRUARY 23

Weather was bad most of the day with very short intervals. No combats took place. On 19th inst. Capt W Fielding-Johnson, MC, 56 Squadron, drove down an EA scout out of control which has since been confirmed by AA observers as having crashed.

FEBRUARY 24

Sky was covered in low clouds with a few short intervals. 29 hostile batteries were successfully engaged for destruction from aeroplane observation. 203 bombs were dropped. Enemy aircraft activity was very slight, only a few indecisive combats taking place.

FEBRUARY 25

Low clouds most of the day. A total of four tons of bombs were dropped. Enemy aircraft activity was very slight; only one indecisive combat taking place.

HONOURS AND AWARDS

Bar to the Military Cross – Lt G E H McElroy, MC.
Military Cross – 2nd Lt J A McCudden; Lt F E Brown; 2nd Lt G McPherson; 2nd Lt D F Hurr.

COMMUNIQUÉ No.129

26 February – 4 March 1918

During the period under review, February 26th to March 4th inclusive, we have claimed officially 15 EA brought down and three driven down out of control. In addition, three EA were brought down by AA fire. Ten of our machines are missing. Approximately 29 ¼ tons of bombs were dropped, and 4333 photographs taken.

FEBRUARY 26
Weather fine with a very strong west wind in the morning; squalls and rain in the afternoon. 82 hostile batteries were successfully engaged for destruction from aeroplane observation.

Enemy Aircraft – EA were active on the whole front. 2nd Lt A Dobie, 43 Squadron, attacked a two-seater EA which nose-dived into the ground and was seen to crash. 2nd Lt C King, 43 Squadron, drove down a two-seater EA from 12,000 to 6000 feet, firing about 160 rounds at close range. He then drove three EA scouts down to the ground, and while contour chasing saw two Albatros scouts above him. He attacked one and drove it down completely out of control, and it was seen to crash. Sgt E Elton & Sgt C Hagan, 22 Squadron, were attacked by ten Albatros scouts. Sgt Hagan got a long burst into one EA which was diving on his tail, and the EA pilot was seen to collapse over the fuselage and the EA crashed. They then dived on another EA below and after firing a burst from short range the EA collapsed in the air and fell to pieces. 2nd Lts S Oades & S Bunting, 22 Squadron, attacked one of five Albatros scouts met near Douai. The EA burst into flames and fell to pieces. Capt W Molesworth, 29 Squadron, whilst leading a patrol, fired two drums at a two-seater EA which was diving east; it went into a vertical dive and was seen to crash southeast of Becelaere by No.10 Squadron. Sgt E Clayton & 2nd Lt L Sloot, 57 Squadron, fired two drums into the leading EA of three scouts which attacked them. Its wings fell off and it burst into flames. Capt J T B McCudden, 56 Squadron, attacked a two-seater EA at 17,000 feet as he was recrossing the lines after two indecisive combats. He opened fire at 200 yards and kept firing until the EA burst into flames and fell to pieces. He then went south and attacked an EA scout doing escort duty, at which he opened fire at a range of 200 yards, continuing until the EA fell to pieces, the wreckage falling near Cherisy.

2nd Lt A Cowper, 24 Squadron, was dived on by an EA scout which overshot him on our side of the lines, allowing him to get on its tail and fire a long burst. The EA dived down to 500 feet and 2nd Lt Cowper kept east, heading it off whenever it tried to recross the lines. The EA flew west at a height of 200 feet and 2nd Lt Cowper finally forced it to land intact at No.52 Squadron's aerodrome. (Pfalz D.III, G.141). Another EA, on being attacked by 2nd Lt Cowper, broke up in the air and fell in pieces. Whilst on patrol, Capt G E H McElroy, 24 Squadron, attacked a Triplane which burst into flames and crashed about four miles from Laon. 2nd Lt P McDougall, 24 Squadron, on patrol with Capt McElroy, attacked another Triplane from above. After an engagement of ten minutes the EA spun and was seen to crash. 2nd Lt J McDonald, 24 Squadron, drove an EA Triplane down to 4000 feet, firing short bursts from close range. The EA went down completely out of control and was seen to crash. He then saw a Triplane being attacked by other pilots of his patrol; he joined in and after a long fight at a height of about 200 feet drove the EA into the wood east of Samoussy into which it crashed. Hostile machines were driven down out of control by the following : 2nd Lt M Peiler, 23 Squadron; 2nd Lt S Oades & 2nd Lt S Bunting, 22 Squadron; Sgt C Noel & Cpl T Hodgson, 57 Squadron; Major G H Bowman, 41 Squadron; Lt K Junor, 56 Squadron; 2nd Lt R Hamersley and 2nd Lt H Richardson, 24 Squadron.

Bombing – A total of 2507 photographs were taken, and 15½ tons of bombs dropped.

FEBRUARY 27
The sky was overcast all day with rain in the afternoon.

Enemy Aircraft – EA activity was very slight, only a few combats taking place. 2nd Lt G R Howsam, 70 Squadron, attacked an EA two-seater near Warneton at 500 feet and it crashed into a hedge south-east of Comines.

Bombing – A total of 83 photographs were taken, and 138 bombs dropped.

HONOURS AND AWARDS
The Military Cross – 2nd Lt W M Blackie.

FEBRUARY 28
Weather was bad with occasional bright intervals. Twenty hostile batteries were successfully engaged for destruction from aeroplane observation. EA activity was very slight all day. A total of 194 photographs were taken, and 246 bombs dropped.

MARCH 1
Low clouds throughout the day. Seventeen hostile batteries were successfully engaged for destruction from aeroplane observation.

Enemy Aircraft – EA activity was very slight. Hostile machines were driven down out of control by Capt W D Patrick, 2nd Lts F McGoun, P Clayson, 1 Squadron; Capt N Millman & 2nd Lt H Cooper, 48 Squadron (two); Capt J Morris, 23 Squadron; Capt G E H McElroy, 24 Squadron; Lt G Cuthbertson, 54 Squadron; 2nd Lt A W B Proctor, 84 Squadron. An EA (DFW) was brought down in our lines by EA of the Third Army, (G.143).

Bombing – A total of 527 photographs were taken, and 62 tons of bombs dropped.

HONOURS AND AWARDS
The Distinguished Service Cross - Flight Cdr R Munday, RNAS.
The Military Cross – Capt G H B Streatfield; Capt J M Allport; Lt A W Hammond;
2nd Lt J V Sorsoleil.

MARCH 2
Clouds were low all day with a very strong wind and snow at times. EA activity was nil.

MARCH 3
Low clouds and mist throughout the day prevented all flying.

MARCH 4
Low clouds, mist and rain on the whole front made flying practically impossible.

COMMUNIQUÉ No.130

5 – 12 March 1918

In the month of March, No.12 Squadron, though retaining its (mainly) RE8 aircraft, was issued with a Flight of Bristol F2b Fighters. Enemy aircraft activity was steadily increasing, building towards the planned German land offensive of March 21.

During the period under review, 5th to 12th March, we have claimed officially 50 EA brought down (three of which fell in our lines) and 45 driven down out of control. Approximately 46 tons of bombs were dropped, and 11,694 photographs taken. Thirteen of our machines are missing.

MARCH 5
790 photographs were taken and 77 bombs dropped.
Enemy Aircraft – Capt J L Trollope, 43 Squadron, shot down one EA out of control. 2nd Lt C W Usher, 40 Squadron, attacked an EA scout and after a short combat the EA dived steeply and was confirmed by AA observers to have burst into flames 2000 feet from the ground. 2nd Lts S A Oades & S W Bunting, 22 Squadron, attacked a two-seater EA and on firing a burst into it, its right wing folded back and it went down in a spinning dive. They then attacked an EA scout which turned over and spun down completely out of control.

MARCH 6
Sixty hostile batteries were successfully engaged for destruction from aeroplane observation; 2562 photographs were taken; and over eight tons of bombs dropped.
Enemy Aircraft – Sgt E J Elton & 2nd Lt G S L Hayward, 22 Squadron, shot down an EA scout which crashed near Dechy. 2nd Lt R J Owen, 43 Squadron, was attacked by eight EA scouts, one of which he shot down and was confirmed by "B" Battery, AA to have crashed near the Bois du Biez. Lt F J Scott, 4th Squadron AFC, shot down a Rumpler two-seater, which was confirmed by an Observer of No.5 Squadron to have crashed near Lens. 2nd Lt F Belway & 1/AM F Rose, 13 Squadron, shot down an EA scout which landed intact in our lines south of Feuchy. (Albatros DV. G.144). 2nd Lt H P Richardson, 24 Squadron, dived on one of five EA scouts and after firing about 60 rounds both left planes broke off the EA which fell between Fontaine and Croin.

Lts R H Little & L N Jones, 48 Squadron, attacked a formation of EA scouts but were themselves attacked by another EA formation from above. One EA was shot down out of control and seen to crash. Capt G E H McElroy, 24 Squadron, shot down one EA scout which was seen to hit the ground north-east of Bellecourt. He then attacked an Albatros scout and fired 200 rounds from close range. The EA went down smoking and before reaching the ground burst into flames. Capt K G Leask, 84 Squadron, was attacked by a large number of EA scouts, one of which he shot down out of control and was seen to crash near Renansart. 2nd Lt D M Clements, 24 Squadron, succeeded in shooting down an EA which collided with him in the air, and both machines crashed on our side of the lines. (Albatros DVa. G.145). Capt R J Tipton, 40 Squadron, observed seven EA scouts and singled out one and opened fire with both guns. EA went down vertically and crashed on this side of the lines. (Pfalz D.III. G.146). 2nd Lt J W Wallwork, 2nd Lt W L Harrison, and Capt I P R Napier, all of 40 Squadron, each attacked an EA and in each case shot it down out of control. All three EA were reported by ground observers to have crashed – one west of Lens, one north of Lens, and one just north of Mericourt. EA were shot down out of control by the following: 2nd Lt D A Stewart & Lt H W M Mackay, 18 Squadron (three); Sgt E J Elton & 2nd Lt G S L Hayward, 22 Squadron; 2nd Lts H F Davison & J L Morgan, 22 Squadron; 2nd Lts G W Bulmer & S J Hunter, 22 Squadron ; Capt J H Tudhope, 40 Squadron; 2nd Lt W L Harrison, 40 Squadron; Capt A G Waller & Sgt M Kilroy, 18 Squadron ; Sgts W McCleery & W Dyke, 18 Squadron; 2nd Lt B E Sharwood-Smith & Sgt J C Lowe, 57 Squadron; Capt R W Chappell, 41 Squadron; Capt G E Thomson, 46 Squadron; 2nd Lt D R MacLaren, 46 Squadron; Lt G D Jenkins, 46 Squadron; Lt F R McCall & 2nd Lt F C Farrington, 13 Squadron; Capt A J Brown, 24 Squadron; 2nd Lt A K Cowper, 24 Squadron; 2nd Lt E Pybus & Lt T W Cave, 35 Squadron; Capt A H G Fellowes, 54 Squadron ; 2nd Lt P A MacDougall, 24 Squadron; 2nd Lt G J Dawe, 24 Squadron.

MARCH 7

278 photographs were taken, and 32 tons of bombs dropped.
Enemy Aircraft – EA activity was very slight. Capt J F Morris, 23 Squadron, shot down a Rumpler two-seater in flames.

MARCH 8

54 hostile batteries were successfully engaged for destruction from aeroplane observation; 2534 photographs were taken, and 9 ½ tons of bombs dropped.
Enemy Aircraft – One EA was brought down by AA fire in the Third Army area. Capt D Flockart, 4th Squadron AFC, attacked the rear of two Albatros scouts and it burst into flames, turned on its back, started spinning, then its wings fell off about 1000 feet lower down. Flight Lt A B Ellwood with Flight Sub-Lts K D MacLeod and C S Devereux, 3 Squadron RNAS, attacked a two-seater which immediately dived east. They followed, firing at about 100 yards range, and the EA continued to dive, and a large trail of yellow smoke was seen coming from it. It was last seen on the ground on fire near Tortequesne. Capt H W Woollett, 43 Squadron, shot down an Albatros scout in flames.

2nd Lts H F Davison & J L Morgan, 22 Squadron, shot down an EA scout and the EA's wing was seen to break off in the air. Sgts E J Elton & S Belding, 22 Squadron, shot down an Albatros scout which crashed south-west of Lille. Capt O C Bryson, 19 Squadron, shot down an EA scout; its wings folded back and it went down in a spin. Capt E R Tempest, 64 Squadron, shot down an EA scout which was confirmed by AA as crashed. Lt A K Cowper, 24 Squadron, attacked the leader of three EA and fired 100 rounds at close range. The EA dived side-slipping right to the ground and was seen to crash. 2nd Lt H H Hartley & Lt J H Robertson, 48 Squadron, attacked an EA which fell slowly spinning to the ground and was seen to crash. Capt G E H McElroy, 24 Squadron, got on the tail of an EA Triplane and fired both guns at very close range. Pieces were seen to fall from the EA which was seen to crash in a field. Lt H D Barton, 24 Squadron, saw a Triplane attacking an SE5. He opened fire at 20 yards and the EA did a half-stall and went down vertically with black smoke issuing. EA were driven down out of control by the following: Lt G Noland, 4th Squadron AFC; Capt O Horsley, 40 Squadron; 2nd Lts H F Davison & J L Morgan, 22 Squadron (two – the pilot of one was seen to fall out of his cockpit onto the centre-section); 2nd Lt L J Sweeney & Lt H G Burgess, 4 Squadron; 2nd Lt A L Paxton, 2nd Squadron AFC; Lt L H Holden, 2nd Squadron AFC; Capt P Huskinson, 19 Squadron; Capt F G Quigley, 70 Squadron; 2nd Lt G R Howsam, 70 Squadron; Capt J A Slater, 64 Squadron; 2nd Lt R H Topliss, 64 Squadron; 2nd Lt T Rose, 64 Squadron; Capt G E Thomson, 46 Squadron; Lt M E Mealing, 56 Squadron; 2nd Lt L A Payne & Lt G H H Scutt, 48 Squadron; 2nd Lts E S Smetham Jones & G Dixon, 48 Squadron; Lt W A McMichael & E G Humphrey, 48 Squadron; 2nd Lt H H Hartley & Lt J H Robertson, 48 Squadron; Lt J E Drummond & 2nd Lt N Sillars, 48 Squadron; Capt G E H McElroy, 24 Squadron; Capt N C Millman & 2nd Lt H A Cooper, 48 Squadron; 2nd Lt J Gray & Lt J A McGinnis, 27 Squadron.

MARCH 9

Forty-one hostile batteries were successfully engaged for destruction from aeroplane observation. 2097 photographs were taken, and nine tons of bombs dropped.

Bombing – 9th Wing – An attack on three hostile aerodromes was made by 61 machines of the 22nd Wing, 88 bombs being dropped. Squadrons were led by their Squadron Commanders and the whole watched from above by the Wing Commander. No.23 Squadron, covered by 24 Squadron, dropped 14 bombs from low altitude on Bertry aerodrome. Four direct hits were obtained on hangars and five fell amongst machines which were out on the aerodrome. They flew back to the lines at a height of 100 feet, attacking horse transport on the roads and in an orchard, a company of infantry, and a group of officers on horses, and a balloon which was hauled down emitting smoke. Busigny and Escaufort aerodromes were attacked by machines of Nos.48 and 54 Squadrons, covered by 84 Squadron. No.54 Squadron dropped 22 bombs from 500 feet and obtained five direct hits on hangars. Machines returned at a low height, firing at horse transport, troops at drill, cavalry, and trains. Pilots of 48 Squadron dropped thirty-two 25lb bombs from 400 feet, obtaining direct hits on hangars, two of which were set on fire. They returned at low altitude engaging ground targets en route.

Enemy Aircraft – Capt J H Tudhope. 40 Squadron, shot down an Albatros scout which was seen to crash and burst into flames. Flight Lt J A Glen and Flight Sub-Lt O P Adam, 3 Squadron RNAS, shot down an EA two-seater in flames. 2nd Lt G R Howsam, 70 Squadron, attacked one of five Albatros scouts which he shot down, the EA being seen to go to the ground. Capt F Quigley, 70 Squadron, attacked an Albatros scout which went down in a steep spiral and on fire, then engaged an Albatros two-seater which he shot down and it crashed in a field. Capt G M Cox, 65 Squadron, attacked a Fokker Triplane which stalled, then went into a spin with one of its planes folded up. Capt P Huskinson, 19 Squadron, shot down a Pfalz scout which crashed and burst into flames south-east of Wervicq. Capt H A Hamersley, 60 Squadron, shot down an EA scout out of control. When at about 2000 feet from the ground the EA's wings fell off and it crashed near Dadizeele. Capt J F Morris, Lt J F N Macrae, and 2nd Lt G W R Poisley, 23 Squadron, all fired bursts at an EA which they drove down to crash in a field near Walincourt. Lt H V Puckridge, 19 Squadron, attacked an EA which spun down for several thousand feet and was eventually seen to burst into flames by another pilot of the same squadron. EA were shot down out of control by the following: 2nd Lt W L Harrison, 40 Squadron; 2nd Lt H S Wolff, 40 Squadron; 2nd Lt W E Warden, 40 Squadron; 2nd Lt J W Wallwork, 40 Squadron (two); Capt R J Tipton, 40 Squadron; Lt R E Bion, 40 Squadron; 2nd

Lt G A Lingham, 43 Squadron; 2nd Lt H Daniel, 43 Squadron; Lt A G Clark, 2nd Squadron AFC; Capt R W Howard, 2nd Squadron AFC; 2nd Lt L H T Capel & Cpl M B Mather, 20 Squadron (two); 2nd Lt G R Howsam, 70 Squadron; 2nd Lt H L Whiteside, 70 Squadron; 2nd Lts D G Cooke & J J Scaramanga, 20 Squadron; Lt J A Duncan, 60 Squadron; Capt H D Crompton, 60 Squadron; 2nd Lt E J Blyth, 19 Squadron; 2nd Lt J S Griffith, 60 Squadron; Capt F G Quigley, 70 Squadron (two); 2nd Lt G Bremridge, 65 Squadron; Lt H W Soulby, 70 Squadron; 2nd Lt D C M Brooks & Lt H R Kincaid, 11 Squadron; Sgts D W Beard & H W Scammell, 11 Squadron; 2nd Lts W F Mayoss & W Haddow, 15 Squadron; Flight Sub-Lt C E Siedle and A/G L Middleton, 5 Squadron RNAS; Capt G E H McElroy, 24 Squadron; Lt H V L Tubbs, 24 Squadron; 2nd Lts J Baird & F Keith, 48 Squadron; 2nd Lt H H Hartley & Lt J H Robertson, 48 Squadron; Capt N C Millman & 2nd Lt H A Cooper, 48 Squadron. Capt H J Hamilton, 1 Squadron, destroyed a hostile balloon.

MARCH 10
Thirty-two hostile batteries were successfully engaged from aeroplane observation. 1533 photographs were taken, and 5½ tons of bombs dropped.

Bombing – Eleven DH4s of 55 Squadron attacked, in broad daylight, the Daimler Works at Stuttgart in Germany, 150 miles from their aerodrome, from a height of 12,500 feet. All our machines returned except one which evidently had engine trouble on the return flight just before crossing the lines, as the pilot fired a green light and went down under control.

Enemy Aircraft – 2nd Lt D A Stewart & Sgt C Beardmore, 18 Squadron, whilst on a bomb raid, were attacked by several formations of EA scouts. They shot one down out of control which was reported by AA to have crashed. Flight Lt A T Whealy, 3 Squadron RNAS, shot down an EA scout which was seen by other pilots to crash. 2nd Lt D R MacLaren, 46 Squadron, shot down an EA scout, the tail of which was seen to fall to pieces. 2nd Lt E A Clear, 84 Squadron, shot down a two-seater EA which crashed in a field near Estrees. Capt M Le Blanc-Smith, 73 Squadron, shot down a Fokker Triplane which was reported to crash. Capts G F Hughes & H Claye, 62 Squadron, shot down an Albatros scout in flames. EA were shot down out of control by the following: Capt A G Waller & Sgt M V Kilroy, 18 Squadron; 2nd Lt G Darvill & Sgt A Pollard, 18 Squadron; Capt R W Howard, 2nd Squadron AFC; Flight Lt A B Ellwood, 3 Squadron RNAS; Flight Sub-Lt F J S Britnell, 3 Squadron RNAS; Flight Lt W H Chisam, 3 Squadron RNAS; Capt R S C McClintock, 64 Squadron; 2nd Lt W H Brown, 84 Squadron; 2nd Lt D Gardiner, 80 Squadron; Capt St C C Taylor, 80 Squadron (two); Lts C W Robinson & C D Wells, 62 Squadron (two); Capts G F Hughes & H Claye, 62 Squadron; 2nd Lt C Allen & Lt J M Hay, 62 Squadron; 2nd Lt M H Cleary & Lt N T Watson, 62 Squadron.

Miscellaneous – 2nd Lt F P Magoun, 1 Squadron, attacked a hostile balloon which went down in deflated condition. Capt G B Moore, Lt H A Rigby, and 2nd Lt A E Sweeting, 1 Squadron, all attacked a hostile balloon which crumpled up and went down deflated, the observer jumping out. 2nd Lt J C Bateman, 1 Squadron, attacked a hostile balloon which disappeared below the clouds in deflated condition. One low-flying EA was brought down by infantry.

MARCH 11
Seventeen hostile batteries were successfully engaged from aeroplane observation. 1800 plates were exposed, and eight tons of bombs dropped.

Enemy Aircraft – Sgt E J Elton & 2nd Lt G S L Hayward, 22 Squadron, shot down an EA scout which crashed at Faches. Flight Cdr F C Armstrong, 3 Squadron RNAS, shot down an Albatros scout, the tail of the EA falling off in the air. 2nd Lt W L Harrison, 40 Squadron, shot down a two-seater EA which crashed near the Canal, west of La Bassee. Capt J A Slater, 64 Squadron, shot down an Albatros scout in flames. 2nd Lts F H Davies & E M Cleland, 13 Squadron, while on artillery patrol, were attacked by five Albatros scouts, one of which they shot down and it crashed near Sailly. Capt F E Brown and Lt G O Johnson, both of 84 Squadron, attacked an EA scout which finally crashed near Lavergies. 2nd Lt E R Varley, 23 Squadron, attacked one of two EA, and it rolled over on its back and was seen to crash by AA observers. 2nd Lt S W Symons & Sgt W N Holmes, 62 Squadron, brought down a Fokker Triplane which burst into flames near the ground. 2nd Lt G S Hodson, 73 Squadron, attacked a Fokker Triplane which he shot down, the EA's wings finally breaking off in the air. Capt T S Sharpe, 73 Squadron, attacked a Fokker Triplane at very close range and it crashed near Hancourt. EA were shot down out of control by the following: Lt L H Holden, 2nd Squadron AFC; Capt H H Balfour, 43 Squadron, Capt H W Woollett, 43 Squadron; Capt J L Trollope, 43 Squadron; 2nd Lt R J Owen, 43 Squadron; Sgt E J Elton & 2nd Lt G S L Hayward, 22 Squadron; 2nd Lt S H Wallage & Sgt J H Jones, 22 Squadron (two); Capt J A Slater, 64 Squadron; Capt D J Bell, 3 Squadron; Capt D H Oliver & 2nd Lt W H Eastoe, 59 Squadron; Capt A J Brown, 2nd Lts P Nolan, R T Mark, H T Richardson and 2nd Lt E W Lindeberg drove down one EA; 2nd Lt E J Smetham-Jones & Lt A C Cooper, 48 Squadron; 2nd Lt H H Hartley & Lt J H Robertson, 48 Squadron; Capt R F S Drewitt, 23 Squadron; Capts G F Hughes & H Claye, 62 Squadron; 2nd Lt R G Lawson,73 Squadron; 2nd Lt W a' B Probart, 73 Squadron.

Miscellaneous – Capt F G Quigley, 70 Squadron, attacked an enemy balloon and smoke was seen coming out of its side. 2nd Lt A Koch, Lt K A Seth-Smith, and 2nd Lt W M Carlaw of the same squadron then attacked it and the balloon went down in flames. Two men were seen in the basket when the balloon was set on fire.

COMMUNIQUÉ No.131

12 – 18 March 1918

During the period under review we have claimed officially 98 EA brought down, and 46 EA driven down out of control. Approximately 95 ½ tons of bombs have been dropped, 10,441 photographs taken, and 163,567 rounds fired at ground targets. Thirty-six of our machines are missing.

MARCH 12

Eighty-six hostile batteries were successfully engaged from aeroplane observation. 2134 photographs were taken, and 15½ tons of bombs dropped.

Bombing – Raids were made on Brancourt-le-Grand, Haubourdin, Sallaumines, Moisnil, Tourcoing, Ledeghem, Wervicq, Dury, Mons, Bavai. No.55 Squadron carried out a long distance bomb raid, the third within the last four days, when nine DH4s bombed Coblenz railway station and nearby barracks and factories. All machines returned.

Enemy Aircraft – Lt L H Holden, 2nd Squadron AFC, shot an EA down out of control which was reported by "A" Battery, AA, to have gone down in flames near Wingles. Lt R W Mackenzie, 2nd Squadron AFC, on the same patrol, dived on a two-seater EA which fell out of control and was reported by "A" Battery, AA, to have gone down in flames. Capt H H Balfour, 43 Squadron, attacked a two-seater EA and its Observer was seen to collapse in the cockpit. After Capt Balfour fired several more bursts the EA suddenly dived vertically, then spun slowly with clouds of black smoke coming out of the fuselage, finally catching fire.

Lt J W Aldred, 70 Squadron, shot down an EA scout which was seen to crash. Capt F G Quigley, 70 Squadron, shot down one of four EA scouts which was seen shortly afterwards smoking on the ground near Dadizeele. Capt Quigley shot down a second EA scout which burst into flames at about 4000 feet. 2nd Lt H L Whiteside, 70 Squadron, attacked an Albatros scout and followed it down to a height of 5000 feet, and it finally crashed. Lts H W Sellars & C C Robson, 11 Squadron, attacked an Albatros two-seater which fell in flames in our lines near Doignies. 2nd Lts J P Seabrook & C Wrigglesworth, 11 Squadron, engaged a large number of EA scouts and shot one down which crashed in a field south-east of Cambrai. Capt A P Maclean & Lt F H Cantlon, 11 Squadron, engaged one EA with their rear gun at 100 yards range and it burst into flames. Lt M E Mealing, 56 Squadron, attacked a two-seater EA over Ribecourt which dived steeply, then crashed in our lines.

Capt J F Morris, 43 Squadron, was attacked by five EA. He dived on the nearest and fired 150 rounds at close range; the EA dived away and was seen to crash by A/177 Battery RFA. Capt R F S Drewitt, 23 Squadron, shot down an EA scout which was attacking an SE5. The EA eventually crashed near the canal just east of Bellenglise. 2nd Lt N Roberts & Cpl W Lauder, 48 Squadron, shot down a Fokker Triplane which was seen to crash in a wood at St Claude, NNE of St Quentin. 2nd Lts P A MacDougall & W Selwyn, both of 24 Squadron, each attacked a two-seater EA which dived away east. It was followed by 2nd Lt MacDougall who shot it down. Capt A J Brown, 24 Squadron, shot down an EA which crashed near the enemy's front lines. Capt T W Withington and Major J A Cunningham, both of 65

Squadron, each shot down an EA scout completely out of control, which were both reported crashed east of Ypres by other pilots. EA were shot down out of control by the following : 2nd Lt A McN Denovan, 1 Squadron; Flight Cdr L H Rochford, 3 Squadron RNAS; 2nd Lt A K Lomax, 43 Squadron; Capt W B Tunbridge, 4th Squadron AFC; Capt H J Hamilton, 1 Squadron; 2nd Lt P J Clayson, 1 Squadron; Capt F G Quigley, 70 Squadron; Lt K A Seth-Smith, 70 Squadron; 2nd Lt J Todd, 70 Squadron; 2nd Lt W M Carlaw, 70 Squadron; 2nd Lt J S Chick & Lt P Douglas, 11 Squadron; Capt A P Maclean & Lt F H Cantlon, 11 Squadron; Capt C C Haynes & Lt J L Smith, 11 Squadron; Capt G E Thomson, 46 Squadron; Capt A J Brown, 24 Squadron (two); 2nd Lt H T Richardson,24 Squadron, Capt L D Baker, 23 Squadron; 2nd Lt C A Hore & Cpl J Cruickshank, 48 Squadron (two); Flight Cdr A M Shook, 4 Squadron RNAS; Lt G E Gibbons & Lt S A W Knights, 62 Squadron; 2nd Lt P R Hampton & 2nd Lt L Lane, 62 Squadron.

During the night of the 11th/12th inst.,a "Friedrichshafen" landed in our lines in the Third Army area; the four occupants being taken prisoner.(G.147).

MARCH 13
59 hostile batteries were successfully engaged from aeroplane observation; 1547 photographs taken, and 17 tons of bombs dropped.

Bombing – Raids were carried out on targets at Marquillies, Haubourdin, Pont-a-Vendin, Wavrin, Fournes, Courtrai, Ledeghem, Staden, Wervicq, Cantin, Etreux aerodrome, St Quentin, Denain. On the afternoon of the 13th, nine DH4s of 55 Squadron left to bomb the railway station and barracks at Freiburg in Germany. Eight DHs reached the objective and dropped bombs from 14,000 feet. After bombing they were attacked by 16 EA. Three DH4s are missing.

Enemy Aircraft – EA activity was great all day on all Army fronts, large formations being encountered east of Cambrai and east of La Bassee.

Capt F E Brown, 84 Squadron, shot down an EA scout which crashed in Hamblieres village. 2nd Lt P K Hobson, 84 Squadron, shot down an EA scout which broke to pieces in the air, the top and bottom left-hand planes breaking away. Capt D J Bell, 3 Squadron, attacked a two-seater Albatros at very close range. The left plane of the EA came off and the wreckage crashed near Villers. A patrol of 1 Squadron attacked an EA scout which they shot down completely out of control, and was confirmed as crashed by Signals, 49th Division. The following pilots of 1 Squadron took part in the combat; Capt W D Patrick, Capt G B Moore, Capt H J Hamilton, 2nd Lt A Hollis, Lt H Rigby.

2nd Lt M F Peiler, 43 Squadron, dived on one of 12 EA which were attacking three Armstrong Whitworths. The EA went down and crashed. 2nd Lt C F King, 43 Squadron, attacked one of two EA scouts which went down in a slow spin and finally crashed. 2nd Lt A K Lomax, 43 Squadron, attacked a third EA which he shot down south-east of Bois du Biez. 2nd Lt G A Lingham, 43 Squadron, also attacked an EA scout which fell and crashed near La Bassee. Capt H W Woollett, 43 Squadron, whilst leading this patrol, attacked two of the EA scouts, one of which he shot to pieces, the machine collapsing in the air and falling to bits. Lt R W McKenzie, 2 Squadron AFC, dived on an Albatros scout which crashed between Wingles and Meurchin. 2nd Lt G S Hodson, 73 Squadron, shot down an EA scout which crashed near Wambaix, south-east of Cambrai. Capt A H Orlebar, 73 Squadron, attacked a Fokker Triplane and it immediately dived, its top plane coming off. Capt C C Taylor, 80 Squadron, shot down an EA scout which broke up before reaching the ground. Capt F L Luxmoore, 54 Squadron, engaged a two-seater EA which was also attacked by 2nd Lt J R Moore, 54 Squadron. The EA eventually crashed. 2nd Lt H F Davison & 2nd Lt J L Morgan, 22 Squadron, shot down an EA in flames which crashed near Annoeullin. Lt F G C Weare & 2nd Lt S J Hunter, 22 Squadron, shot down an EA scout which spun down and crashed between Seclin and Houplin. Lt W L Wells & 2nd Lt P S Williams, 22 Squadron, also shot down an EA scout which crashed just west of Emmerin. Sgt E J Elton & 2nd Lt G S L Hayward, 22 Squadron, shot one EA down out of control and followed it down, and after firing another burst, the EA broke to pieces, the wings falling off. They then attacked another EA which crashed near Herrin. Capt G F Hughes & Capt H Claye, 62 Squadron, in a general engagement between his patrol and a very large formation of EA scouts, shot down one Fokker Triplane which was confirmed by other patrol members to have crashed. He then attacked one of three Triplanes diving on his tail, and this EA went down vertically, its top plane seen falling away in pieces. Capt Hughes was then attacked by at least six other Albatros scouts and Fokker Triplanes. His Observer's gun was out of action but he finally out-distanced all the EA, and recrossed the lines at 3000 feet.

(Editor's note: The first Fokker Triplane shot down was piloted by Leutnant Lothar von Richthofen, younger brother of the "Red Baron", Manfred von Richthofen. Injuries from his crash put Lothar in hospital for several weeks.)

EA were driven down out of control by the following: Capt A J Brown, 24 Squadron; Lt R T Mark, 24 Squadron; 2nd Lt A K Cowper, 24 Squadron; 2nd Lt H W Sellars & C C Robson, 11 Squadron; 2nd Lt C L Stubbs, 84 Squadron; 2nd Lt J S Chick & Lt P Douglas, 11 Squadron; Capt C C Haynes & Lt D S Allison, 11 Squadron; Capt A Roulstone & Lt D F V Page, 57 Squadron; 2nd Lts D Latimer & J J Scaramanga, 20 Squadron; 2nd Lt E Lindup & Cpl F Archer, 20 Squadron; Capt G M Cox, 65 Squadron; Lt A C Dean, 43 Squadron; 2nd Lt H S Montgomerie & Lt W H Wardrope, 2 Squadron; 2nd Lt M F Peiler, 43 Squadron; Capt H W Woollett, 43 Squadron; Capt A H Orlebar, 73 Squadron; Lt B Balfour, 65 Squadron; 2nd Lt G L Ormerod & Sgt A Burton, 22 Squadron; Lt A R James & Lt J M Hay, 62 Squadron; 2nd Lt W E Staton & 2nd Lt H E Merritt, 62 Squadron (two); Capt S W Symons & Sgt W N Holmes, 62 Squadron.

Miscellaneous – The work done by No.102 Squadron on the night of the 12th/13th constitutes a record as regards the number of bombs dropped by one squadron in one night. All pilots except three, made three trips, four pilots made four trips, and two made five trips.

MARCH 14

Low clouds and mist and rain in the morning prevented flying, though weather improved a little in the afternoon. 36 hostile batteries were successfully engaged from aeroplane observation, 436 photographs were taken, and 4½ tons of bombs dropped. EA activity was very slight and no combats took place. An attack on Mont d'Origny aerodrome was carried out by 19 machines of Nos.24, 48 and 84 Squadrons. 42 bombs were dropped on and 4760 rounds fired at hangars and other favourable targets. 24 Squadron dropped 12 bombs from 100 to 2000 feet. One hangar was set on fire and two others damaged. 48 Squadron dropped 16 bombs from 1000 to 2000 feet on various targets and fired over 8600 rounds at troops on the road, billets and lorries. 84 Squadron missed the objective and got four bombs on barges at Bernot from 500 feet; one barge was hit.

MARCH 15

34 hostile batteries were successfully engaged from aeroplane observation. 1648 photographs were taken, and 12 tons of bombs dropped.

Enemy Aircraft – EA were very active up to noon, after which the activity decreased. Capt W Fielding-Johnson, 56 Squadron, shot down an EA scout which was reported to have burst into flames. Lt M Mealing, 56 Squadron, attacked an EA scout which went down at a terrific speed in a spin and was seen to crash. Later, an EA two-seater was met south-east of Inchy. Lt Mealing engaged it first, firing a good burst from both guns. He left the EA as he saw some water and a small stream of flame come out of the EA's engine cowling. Capt Fielding-Johnson then attacked it, firing at very close range, and the EA fell and crashed. 2nd Lt J S Chick & Lt P Douglas, 11 Squadron, shot down one EA in flames. Sgt D W Beard & Sgt H W Scarnell, 11 Squadron, attacked one EA and the EA pilot fell forward in his seat; the EA immediately nose-dived and shortly after broke up in the air. Capt R F S Drewitt, 23 Squadron, dived on a two-seater EA which went down in a steep glide, followed by Capt Drewitt and Lt G G MacPhee, and crashed. 2nd Lt A W B Proctor, 84 Squadron, attacked an EA from underneath and it spun down to crash in our lines south of Villeret.

2nd Lt E A Clear, 84 Squadron, shot down an Albatros scout which crashed near Mesnil St Laurent. 2nd Lt C T Travers, 84 Squadron, attacked one of three EA scouts and after firing 150 rounds into it the EA started to dive with smoke and flames coming out of the fuselage. 2nd Lt A K Cowper, 24 Squadron, dived on one of two Rumpler two-seaters firing about 100 rounds from 50 to 10 yards range. The EA started to go down steeply and 2nd Lt R T Mark got on its tail and fired 100 rounds at 60 yards range. The EA continued to dive and was finally attacked by 2nd Lt H B Richardson and was seen to crash into the wood north of Premonte. 2nd Lt F P McGoun, 1 Squadron, and 2nd Lt L W Mawbey, attacked an EA which stalled, went into a vertical dive, then crashed south of Ledeghem. Capt W D Patrick, 1 Squadron, got on the tail of an Albatros scout and fired a long burst from both guns. The EA was seen to crash. Major A D Carter, 19 Squadron, shot down an EA scout whose right wings folded back as it spun down. 2nd Lt D A Stewart & Sgt A O Pollard, 18 Squadron, were attacked by five Pfalz scouts from underneath. They fired at one which then spun down and crashed. EA were driven down out of control by the following; Lt M Mealing, 56 Squadron; 2nd Lt H J Walkerdine, 56 Squadron, Capt L R Wren & 2nd Lt E Gilroy, 11 Squadron; Lt H W Sellars & Lt C C Robson, 11 Squadron; 2nd Lt J S Chick & Lt P Douglas, 11 Squadron; Sgt D W Beard & Sgt H W Scarnell, 11 Squadron (two); Capt J A Slater, 64 Squadron; 2nd Lt J F T Barrett, 64 Squadron; 2nd Lt H B Redler, 24 Squadron; Capt F M Kitto, 54 Squadron; Lt J F Larson, 84 Squadron; Major A D Carter, 19 Squadron; Capt P Huskinson, 19 Squadron; 2nd Lt N W Hustings, 19 Squadron; Capt J Leacroft, 19 Squadron (two); Lt A W Adams, 4th Squadron AFC; Lt J C Courtney, 4th Squadron AFC; Capt A G Waller & Lt J Brisbane, 18 Squadron; Lts A R James & J M Hay, 62 Squadron.

(Editor's Note: 2nd Lt H B Redler's "Out of Control" EA was in fact a Fokker Triplane flown by Hauptmann Adolf von Tutschek, the 27-victory commander of Jagdgeschwader 2, who was killed).

HONOURS AND AWARDS

Bar to the Military Cross – Capt H H Balfour, KRRC and RFC.
The Military Cross – 2nd Lt C F King, General List RFC; Lt G C Cuthbertson,
                       General List RFC.

MARCH 16

27 hostile batteries were successfully engaged from aeroplane observation. 1560 photographs were taken, and 21¾ tons of bombs dropped.

Enemy Aircraft – Capt D J Bell, 3 Squadron, fired just ten rounds at an EA at about 15 yards range and it spun down, then broke up in the air. He then saw an EA some 2000 feet below him, so dived, got below its tail, and fired a short burst at very close range. The EA's left wing broke off. Capt G E Thomson, 46 Squadron, attacked a two-seater EA which stalled, then fell in flames. Capt R W Chappell, 41 Squadron, attacked one of three EA two-seaters, firing both guns at about 125 yards range. A large cloud of smoke and a sheet of flame came from the EA's cockpit and it fell in a spin. Lt W L Wells & 2nd Lt G S L Hayward, 22 Squadron, attacked one of three Albatros scouts. The EA immediately turned upside down and fell several thousand feet completely out of control, then crashed near Beaumont. 2nd Lt H L Christie & Sgt S Belding, 22 Squadron, shot an EA down in flames which crashed in a wood at Carvin. Sgt E J Elton & 2nd Lt R Critchley, 22 Squadron, also shot down an EA in flames. Lt F G C Weare & 2nd Lt S J Hunter, 22 Squadron, attacked one of three Pfalz scouts which fell completely out of control and crashed south-west of Esquerchin. Flight Lt W H Chisham, 3 Squadron RNAS, attacked an EA two-seater which dived vertically and was seen to crash from "C" Battery observation post. Flight Cdr L H Rochford, Flight Lts J A Glen and A B Ellwood, 3 Squadron RNAS, all attacked an EA two-seater which finally fell in flames. 2nd Lt E R Varley, 23 Squadron, attacked a two-seater EA flying north over Lehaucourt and it fell emitting smoke and crashed. Capt R F S Drewitt, 23 Squadron, shot down another two-seater in flames (confirmed by AA observers). Lt N Clark, 54 Squadron, followed an EA two-seater down to 200 feet and it spun into the ground and burst into flames. Lt G O Johnson, 84 Squadron, attacked a two-seater EA down to 1000 feet and it finally crashed between Villers Outreaux and Sarain. Flight Lt E Dickson & Sub-Lt Scott, 5 Squadron RNAS, when returning from a bomb raid, went to the assistance of one of their machines which was being attacked by four EA, and shot one EA down which was seen to crash. They then went to the assistance of another of their machines being attacked by no less than 12 EA of various types. A front gun of their machine ran out of ammunition, the back gun jammed several times, and they finally ran out of ammunition altogether. Their machine was very badly shot about, bullets entering the petrol tanks, the fuselage in a number of places, planes and tail. Flight Lt T Watkins & Squadron Cdr S J Goble, 5 Squadron RNAS, shot down one of five EA scouts which was seen to crash. 2nd Lt H B Richardson, 24 Squadron, shot down an EA scout which crashed into a wood.

EA were also driven down out of control by the following: Sgt C W Noel & 2nd Lt L L T Sloot, 57 Squadron (two); Flight Lt H T Mellings, 10 Squadron RNAS; 2nd Lt C E Mayer, 3 Squadron; Capt L W Jarvis, 56 Squadron; 2nd Lt H J Walkerdine, 56 Squadron; Capt G E Thomson, 46 Squadron; Capt S P Smith, 46 Squadron; Lt W L Wells & 2nd Lt G S L Hayward, 22 Squadron (two); 2nd Lt W F J Harvey & Sgt A Burton, 22 Squadron; Sgt E J Elton & 2nd Lt R Critchley, 22 Squadron; 2nd Lt G W Bulmer & 2nd Lt P S Williams, 22 Squadron (two); Lt G F Malley, 4th Squadron AFC; 2nd Lt A W Adams, 4th Squadron AFC; Capt J F Gordon & 2nd Lt J C O'Reilly King, 25 Squadron; Lt P Burrows & 2nd Lt R S Herring, 48 Squadron (two); Flight Lt T Watkins & Squadron Cdr S J Goble, 5 Squadron RNAS; Lt H V L Tubbs and 2nd Lt J J Dawe, 24 Squadron; Lt F H Taylor, 41 Squadron.

MARCH 17

106 hostile batteries were successfully engaged from aeroplane observation. 134 photographs were taken. 13¼ tons of bombs were dropped.

Enemy Aircraft – EA were very active and a considerable amount of fighting took place. Capt J L Trollope, 43 Squadron, attacked one of four EA at close range and it dived vertically, burst into flames, then broke up in the air. Lt M R N Jennings, 19 Squadron, shot down an EA seen to crash. Lt A B Fairclough, 19 Squadron and 2nd Lt E Olivier both attacked one EA scout which went down in flames. Capt J Leacroft, 19 Squadron, shot down one EA in flames which was seen to crash, while Lt N W Hustings of the same squadron shot down an EA out of control which was confirmed to have crashed. Capt P Huskinson, 19 Squadron, dived on an EA scout and followed it down to 3500 feet, and saw it crash near Roulers. Major J A Cunningham, 65 Squadron, attacked an EA scout which turned east and dived. Major Cunningham followed, firing both guns at close range, and the EA crashed at Zuidhoek. Lt J K V Peden, 3 Squadron, whilst on low bombing, engaged one of two EA and sent it down to crash. 2nd Lt A A M Arnot, 3 Squadron, whilst on Offensive Patrol, got on the tail of an EA scout and fired a long burst at about 10 yards range. The EA immediately caught fire and fell. Capt E R Tempest, 64 Squadron, dived on one of five EA scouts and shot it down in flames. Capt W H Park & 2nd Lt H J Greenwood, 11 Squadron, engaged the leader of four EA scouts and shot it down to crash and burn on the ground. 2nd Lt A W B Proctor, 84 Squadron, got on the tail of one EA scout and fired 100 rounds. The EA did a steep dive, followed by a zoom and a quick left-hand turn, whereupon the bottom left-hand plane gave way and the whole left wing crumpled up against the fuselage. 2nd Lt C L Stubbs, 84 Squadron, attacked an EA scout which he followed down to 5000 feet continually firing, and the EA crashed in a village. 2nd Lt J V Sorsoleil, 84 Squadron, shot down an EA which crashed one mile east of Moretz. Lt N Clark, 54 Squadron, attacked an EA two-seater which caught fire in the pilot's seat whilst in the air, and burst into flames on hitting the ground. Lt J R Rodger, 80 Squadron, dived on the rear machine of four EA scouts and shot it down out of control, and AA report that this EA burst into flames.

Capt H A Whistler, 80 Squadron, engaged an EA scout but was immediately attacked from the rear by three other EA. He zoomed up and came down behind the last EA, firing about 100 rounds at close range, and the EA fell, turning over and over, finally crashing in a wood. Lt R A Preeston, 80 Squadron, whilst flying in formation, dived on one EA of a large number which were attacking his formation, and he was immediately attacked by three more EA which he managed to shake off. Finding himself alone, he turned west and climbed to 12,000 feet where he was attacked by 12 EA. He fired a short burst into one EA which overshot him in a dive, then, being outnumbered, he spun and dived to about 2000 feet. He succeeded in reaching our side of the lines after a running fight the whole of the way. (With reference to this combat, the 66th Division report that at 11.10am one British scout put up a wonderful fight with eight EA, and No.35 Squadron report one EA still falling out of control 300 feet from the ground at the same place and time. The EA was one of a large EA formation which were fighting a lone Camel).

2nd Lt A K Cowper, 24 Squadron, attacked an EA which dived and he followed it for 1000 feet still firing. The EA went into a slow spin and finally crashed in a field south-west of Ramicourt. 2nd Lt E A Clear dived on a Fokker Triplane which was attacking one of his formation. The EA made a sharp turn to the left, and at the same time an EA "V-Strutter" also turned round a bank of clouds and crashed into the Triplane practically end-on. The planes of both EA folded back and they both dropped like a stone.

EA were brought down out of control by the following: Capt J L Trollope, 43 Squadron; Flight Lt A T Whealy, 3 Squadron RNAS; Major A D Carter, 19 Squadron; Capt A Roulstone, 57 Squadron; 2nd Lt A E Venmore, 57 Squadron; 2nd Lt H E Stewart, 3 Squadron; 2nd Lt W C Dennett, 3 Squadron; Capt G E Thomson, 46 Squadron; Capt E R Tempest, 64 Squadron; 2nd Lt A W B Proctor, 84 Squadron (two); 2nd Lt J Loupinsky & Sgt A Remington, 25 Squadron; Lt G E Gibbons & 2nd Lt S A W Knights, 62 Squadron; Capt H A Whistler, 80 Squadron; 2nd Lt R T Mark, 24 Squadron; 2nd Lt H B Richardson, 24 Squadron; 2nd Lt W H Brown, 84 Squadron (two); Capt F E Brown, 84 Squadron (two).

MARCH 18
Ninety-six hostile batteries were successfully engaged from aeroplane observation. 1682 photographs were taken, and 14 tons of bombs dropped.

Bombing – Raids were made on Mouchin aerodrome, Don, Seclin, Haubourdin, Premont ammunition dump, Emerchicourt aerodrome, Fournes, La Carnoy, Zarren, Iwuy Dump, Oisy-le-Verger, Busigny aerodrome, and Etreux aerodrome. Ten DH4s of 55 Squadron set out to bomb military objectives at Mannheim on the Rhine. Nine reached the target and dropped eighteen 112 lb and ten 25 lb bombs from 13,500 feet. The DH4s were attacked by two formations of EA scouts, 14 in total, and two EA were sent down out of control though were not seen to actually crash. All our machines returned.

Enemy Aircraft – EA activity was great, and fighting throughout the day was intense. Sgt E J Elton & 2nd Lt R Critchley, 22 Squadron, attacked an EA which went into a vertical dive. Its top wing came off and it was seen to crash. 2nd Lt W F J Harvey & 2nd Lt J L Morgan, 22 Squadron, shot down an EA in flames. Flight Sub-Lt S Smith, 3 Squadron RNAS, attacked one of five EA scouts, fired 300 rounds into it, and it fell out of control and crashed, witnessed by the rest of his patrol. Flight Lt E T Hayne, 3 Squadron RNAS, dived on an EA two-seater and fired 100 rounds at point-blank range. The EA dived below him and was then attacked by Flight Sub-Lt R C Berlyn at close range. The EA's Observer was seen to fall on his gun, and the EA crashed alongside houses about a mile east of Henin Lietard. Capt H W Woollett, 43 Squadron, attacked a two-seater and followed it due east until he got to close quarters, then fired about 90 rounds into it. The EA spun down and was seen to crash and immediately went up like an explosion, clouds of black smoke appearing from it.

2nd Lt W L Harrison, 40 Squadron, shot a two-seater down in flames. Capt R W Howard, 2nd Squadron AFC, fired 60 rounds into an EA two-seater; smoke immediately issued from its fuselage and it dived steeply out of control and in flames. Capt W E Molesworth when leading a patrol of 29 Squadron met an EA patrol. He engaged the leader, firing 20 rounds at 100 yards range. The EA fell out of control and crashed south-east of Rumbeke. In the same patrol 2nd Lt F J Williams, 29 Squadron, fired a drum into another EA at about 50 yards range. The left wing of the EA was completely shot away and was seen to fall off. Capt H A Hamersley, 60 Squadron, attacked one of several EA scouts over Roulers and its right-hand bottom plane came off. The EA went into a spin and its top plane collapsed, and it crashed just east of Rumbeke aerodrome. 2nd Lt W H Brown, 84

Squadron, was attacked by a Fokker Triplane which fired at him from a stalled position.

2nd Lt Brown dived on the Triplane firing both guns and it immediately dived away. He continued to dive after the EA, firing a long burst from short range, and the Triplane started spinning, then went into a vertical dive which continued until it hit the ground. 2nd Lts E R Varley and H A F Goodison, 23 Squadron, saw AA bursts east of Urvillers and dived to attack an EA, finally forcing it to land in our lines near Essigny-le-Grand. Flight Sub-Lt G B McBain & Aerial Gunlayer W Jones, 5 Squadron RNAS, engaged one of five EA scouts which went into a dive, seemed to lose control, and its tail plane dropped off. 2nd Lt E A Richardson, 54 Squadron, during an engagement between Camels, SE5s and a large EA formation, attacked a Fokker Triplane which nose-dived, burst into flames, then broke up in the air. A patrol of 84 Squadron saw several EA north of Busigny. 2nd Lt E A Clear singled out one red Fokker Triplane and fired a burst from his Lewis gun. The EA went into a spin, then flattened out. 2nd Lt Clear expected this and followed the EA down, firing another burst at 30 yards range. The EA stalled, then fell completely out of control and was followed down to 9000 feet by 2nd Lt Clear who was then compelled to leave the EA owing to gun stoppages. This EA is confirmed as crashed by 54 Squadron.

Major C M Crowe (attached to 56 Squadron) saw an EA two-seater over Inchy and attacked with both guns at close range. It fell out of control and was seen to crash. Capt W S Fielding-Johnson, 56 Squadron, saw about ten EA attacking a patrol of Camels. He attacked one EA scout which fell and crashed. He then attacked another which did a left-hand spin and crashed into the ground on its back. 2nd Lt H J Walkerdine, 56 Squadron, in the same combat, shot down one EA scout which was seen to crash, then attacked another which also crashed, confirmed by Capt Fielding-Johnson. Lt F H Taylor, 41 Squadron, whilst on a test flight, saw five EA two-seaters over Lecluse. He dived on one EA firing about 100 rounds and it dived through the clouds and was lost to sight, but was confirmed as crashed by two AA batteries.

EA were also driven down out of control by the following: Capt F C G Weare & 2nd Lt G S L Hayward, 22 Squadron; 2nd Lt H L Christie & Sgt R Pritchard, 22 Squadron; Flight Lt E T Hayne, 3 Squadron RNAS; Lt A G Wingate-Grey, 29 Squadron; Capt J G Coombe, 29 Squadron; 2nd Lt F J Davies, 29 Squadron; 2nd Lt C F Cunningham, 60 Squadron; 2nd Lt J S Griffiths, 60 Squadron; Lt J F Larson, 84 Squadron; Capt F E Brown, 84 Squadron; 2nd Lt W H Brown, 84 Squadron; Flight Lt E Dickson & Sub-Lt W H Scott, 5 Squadron RNAS; Flight Cdr C P O Bartlett & Aerial Gunlayer Naylor, 5 Squadron RNAS; 2nd Lt N M Drysdale, 54 Squadron; Capt B P G Beanlands, 2nd Lt H B Redler, 24 Squadron; Lt A K Cowper, 24 Squadron; Capt K G Leask, 84 Squadron; Lt G O Johnson, 84 Squadron; Capt E R Tempest , 64 Squadron; Lt H W Sellars & Lt C C Robson, 11 Squadron; Major C M Crowe, attached 56 Squadron; 2nd Lt C A Bridgland & 2nd Lt E R Stewart, 55 Squadron; Capt S B Collett & Lt G Breyer-Ash, 55 Squadron.

Miscellaneous – No.5 Squadron RNAS bombed Busigny aerodrome with a view to drawing up EA which were to be attacked by Nos.54 and 84 Squadrons. The plan was successful, a fierce fight taking place in which four EA were brought down and eight driven down out of control.

COMMUNIQUÉ No.132

19 – 25 March 1918

On March 21st a German offensive, known as the Great Battle of France, commenced; its object being to mount a decisive break in the Allied lines before American resources became available in significant strength to bolster the Allied armies in France. While aerial combats increased in intensity, the prime activity for RFC and RNAS squadrons on the main battle front was low-level harassment of German troops and emplacements. Of particular note is Captain John Trollope's claims for six EA brought down in a single day on March 24th – a new RFC record. Four days later, however, he was shot down, badly wounded, in German territory by Leutnant Paul Billik, Jagdstaffel 52.

During the period under review we have claimed officially 132 EA brought down, four of which fell in our lines, and 88 driven down out of control. In addition, six were brought down by AA or machine gun fire from the ground. Forty of our machines are missing. Approximately 138 tons of bombs were dropped, and 3795 photographs taken.

MARCH 19
Rain almost entirely prevented flying during the day. Thirty-five hostile batteries were successfully engaged from aeroplane observation.
Enemy Aircraft – EA were not active and no combats took place.

HONOURS AND AWARDS
The Distinguished Service Order – Capt W B Farrington.
Bar to the Military Cross – Capt P Huskinson, MC.
The Military Cross – 2nd Lt D A Stewart; Capt D G B Jardine; Capt G E Thomson.
The Distinguished Conduct Medal – No.20624 Cpl M B Mather.

MARCH 20
Enemy Aircraft – EA were inactive. No combats took place.

MARCH 21
Weather very misty but a great deal of low flying took place. Thirteen hostile batteries were successfully engaged from aeroplane observation. 711 photographs were taken, and 152 tons of bombs dropped.
Enemy Aircraft – EA were active, much fighting taking place during the day. In addition to EA brought down in combat, one EA was brought down in our lines by infantry.
2nd Lt D R MacLaren, 46 Squadron, while returning from low bombing saw an LVG below him flying east. He dived on the EA's tail, fired about 100 rounds, and EA went into a spin and crashed at the western corner of Douai. He then attacked an enemy balloon and its Observer jumped out with parachute; the balloon burst into flames. On getting over the lines the same pilot saw a two-seater below him over Graincourt. He dived on it from the front, firing about 50 rounds. The EA immediately turned east and went down under control. 2nd Lt MacLaren gave

chase, firing in all another 50 rounds and the EA finally crashed completely just east of Marquion.

Lt H W Sellars & Lt C C Robson, 11 Squadron, attacked an Albatros two-seater doing artillery observation. The EA dived vertically and then spun out of control after three bursts had been fired at it from the Bristol Fighter. Lt Robson observed smoke coming from its engine and it crashed this side of the line north of the Bapaume – Cambrai road. Shortly afterwards Lts Sellars & Robson were attacked by three Albatros scouts. Two bursts were fired at the nearest which burst into flames and crashed north of Morchies.

An Offensive Patrol of 3 Squadron RNAS attacked an EA two-seater and shot it down out of control, and the wreckage fell near Vaulx. Lt C R Keary, 23 Squadron, was attacked by two EA scouts simultaneously. He managed to get on the tail of one, fired both guns, and the EA went down and was seen to crash. Capt W L Wells & Cpl W Beales, 48 Squadron, shot down an EA scout which was seen to crash. Capt J F Morris, 23 Squadron, observed tracers coming up past his right wing as he was attacked from below by an EA scout. He dived on the EA, fired 200 rounds at close range, and the EA dived straight into the ground and crashed. Lt R St J Dix & Lt R M Montgomery, 82 Squadron, dived on an EA two-seater which was doing contact patrol work at about 1500 feet. The EA crashed just north of La Folie. Lt Richardson, 62 Squadron, shot down an EA scout which crashed near Magny-la-Fosse. 2nd Lt W E Staton & Lt J R Gordon, 62 Squadron, in a general engagement between a patrol of Bristol Fighters and a formation of EA Triplanes and scouts, engaged a Triplane at very close range. Tracers were seen to hit the EA pilot and the Triplane went into a vertical nose-dive, then fell in flames. Capt T L Purdom & 2nd Lt P V G Chambers, 62 Squadron, in the same engagement, shot down an Albatros scout and its top plane came off. Capt J A Slater, 64 Squadron, shot down an Albatros scout which was seen to crash. Lt A G Vlasto, 46 Squadron, attacked an EA doing contact patrol work, getting on its tail and opening fire at 400 yards and continuing to fire till within 50 yards. The EA went down vertically into the ground.

EA were driven down out of control by the following; Capt P W S Bulman, 3 Squadron; Lt F L Hird, 3 Squadron; 2nd Lt J L Butler, 3 Squadron; 2nd Lt A D Shannon & Sgt B J Maisey, 11 Squadron; Lt E E Stock & Cpl J H Bowler, 48 Squadron; 2nd Lt H B Richardson, 24 Squadron (two); 2nd Lt A K Cowper, 24 Squadron (two); 2nd Lt H M Arthur & 2nd Lt J Bruce-Norton, 62 Squadron ; Capt J A Slater, 64 Squadron; 2nd Lt V W Thompson, 64 Squadron; Lt H N C Robinson, 46 Squadron; Lt M E Mealing, 56 Squadron; Lt T Durrant, 56 Squadron: Lt E D G Galley, 56 Squadron; Lt H J Burden, 56 Squadron; Flight Cdr L H Rochford, Flight Lt J A Glen, 3 Squadron RNAS (one); Flight Cdr F C Armstrong, 3 Squadron RNAS; Lt A E Robertson, 4th Squadron AFC; Lt A H Cobby, 4th Squadron AFC (two); Lt E F Pflaum, 4th Squadron AFC.

HONOURS AND AWARDS
Bar to the Military Cross – Lt S S Jones, MC.
The Military Cross – Capt G D Moore; Capt G F Hughes; Capt C H Brewer; 2nd Lt W L Harrison; Capt R Dodds.

MARCH 22
Thick mist prevented flying till late in the morning. Seventeen hostile batteries were

successfully engaged from aeroplane observation, 807 photographs taken, and 21 tons of bombs dropped.

Enemy Aircraft – EA were very active on the battle front. Low-flying EA engaged our infantry with machine gun fire. Two EA were brought down by AA fire in our lines, and one by infantry. Flight Lt A T Whealy, 3 Squadron RNAS, shot down an Albatros scout which finally fell in our lines in the enemy's barrage.

Flight Lt E Pierce, 3 Squadron RNAS, attacked an EA which spun down followed by a thin trail of white steam and finally crashed just across the lines. Flight Cdr F C Armstrong, 3 Squadron RNAS, attacked one of nine EA at close range which crashed in the trenches in the enemy's barrage. Flight Cdr L Rochford, 3 Squadron RNAS, shot down an EA scout which crashed near Bousies. Capt F Hobson, 70 Squadron, got under the tail of an EA two-seater and fired a short burst. The EA turned over and went down. Capt Hobson continued to fire at this EA down to 7000 feet when it burst into flames and fell approximately at Sailly, north-west of Cambrai. Capt F G Quigley, 70 Squadron, dived on an Albatros scout and saw his tracers going into the EA's fuselage and tail. The EA suddenly dropped one wing and dived almost vertically towards our line, hitting the ground between Inchy and Bourlon. 2nd Lt D R MacLaren, 46 Squadron, fired 50 rounds at an EA two-seater which crashed on its back. 2nd Lt A W Franklyn, 3 Squadron, shot down an EA scout which was seen to crash. 2nd Lt A A M Arnot, 3 Squadron, attacked one of many EA scouts which was confirmed as crashed. Capt D J Bell, 3 Squadron, attacked the leader of a large formation of EA scouts, and it fell in flames. Lt K W Junor, 56 Squadron, fired both guns at an EA scout which crashed on the edge of Havrincourt Wood. 2nd Lt W S Stephenson, 73 Squadron, attacked an EA scout. Tracers were seen to enter the EA's cockpit and it stalled, rolled backwards, then fell completely out of control with engine full on and nose-dived into the ground. 2nd Lt W a'B Probart, 73 Squadron, attacked one of five EA scouts and shot it down in flames. Capt A H Orlebar, 73 Squadron, opened fire on one of a large formation of EA scouts and it burst into flames and fell. Capt H G Forrest, 2nd Squadron AFC, fired 40 rounds at close range into an EA two-seater and the EA's Observer ceased firing and the EA went down out of control, rolling over and over in flames. Capt W B Tunbridge, 4th Squadron AFC, dived on one of three EA two-seaters, and Lt Wright also attacked it. It nose-dived and was seen to crash. 2nd Lt R T Mark, 24 Squadron, shot down an EA in flames. 2nd Lt H B Richardson, 24 Squadron, attacked the rear machine of several EA scouts. This EA dived vertically from 7000 feet and crashed between Peronne and the canal. 2nd Lt P G Nolan, 24 Squadron, was one of several pilots who shot down an EA two-seater in flames over Matigny. Capt T Colville-Jones & 2nd Lt J A Galbraith, 48 Squadron, shot down an Albatros scout which crashed in a field about one mile south-east of Monchy Lagache.

2nd Lt A C G Brown & 2nd Lt G G Bartlett, 48 Squadron, attacked one of five EA which were circling round a Bristol Fighter. 2nd Lt Brown dived on the nearest EA firing short bursts. The EA attempted to zoom up to the right of 2nd Lt Brown, then put its nose down and flew into the ground. 2nd Lt E E Stock, 54 Squadron, dived on an EA two-seater over Caulaincourt. The EA Observer ceased to fire, and the EA was then attacked by 2nd Lt R C Crowden, 54 Squadron, and it crashed near Attilly. Flight Cdr A R Brown, 9 Squadron RNAS, attacked one of seven EA two-seaters and it fell in a vertical dive and was seen to crash. 2nd Lt A Koch, 70 Squadron, attacked an EA two-seater and it crashed in the trenches about 2000 yards east of Lagnicourt.

EA were brought down out of control by the following: Flight Lt A B Ellwood, 3 Squadron RNAS; Flight Lt L D Bawlf, 3 Squadron RNAS; Lt H G W Debenham, 46 Squadron; 2nd Lt A Koch, 70 Squadron; Capt F Hobson, 70 Squadron; 2nd Lt J Todd, 70 Squadron; Capt F G Quigley, 70 Squadron; Capt C J Marchant and 2nd Lt D R MacLaren, 46 Squadron (one); 2nd Lt G R Riley, 3 Squadron; Capt F Billinge, 56 Squadron; 2nd Lt W Porter, 56 Squadron; 2nd Lt G S Hodson, 73 Squadron; Capt H G Forrest, 2nd Squadron AFC; Lt R W Mackenzie, 2nd Squadron AFC; Lt A R Rackett, 2nd Squadron AFC; 2nd Lt A C G Brown & 2nd Lt G G Bartlett, 48 Squadron; Capt F E Brown, 84 Squadron; Flight Cdr C R Lupton & Aerial Gunlayer Wood, 5 Squadron RNAS; Flight Cdr C P O Bartlett & Aerial Gunlayer Naylor, 5 Squadron RNAS; Capt R C Phillips, 2nd Squadron AFC; 2nd Lt G Pilditch, 73 Squadron; Capt A H Orlebar, 73 Squadron; Lt L H Holden, 2nd Squadron AFC.

MARCH 23

Thirty-nine hostile batteries were successfully engaged from aeroplane observation, 825 photographs taken, and 33 tons of bombs dropped.

Enemy Aircraft – EA were very active, especially on the battle front, fighting taking place at a height not over 10,000 feet. Flight Lt A B Ellwood, together with Flight Sub-Lt McLeod, 3 Squadron RNAS, shot down an EA scout which crashed in the vicinity of Noreuil. Flight Cdr R C Armstrong, 3 Squadron RNAS, shot down an EA scout which crashed near Vaulx. Lt G F Malley, 4th Squadron AFC, shot down an Albatros scout which was seen to crash. He then attacked another EA scout together with Lt P K Schafer, which also crashed.

Capt H G Forrest, 2nd Squadron AFC, together with Lt L Benjamin, shot down an EA scout in flames. Capt J H Tudhope, 40 Squadron, shot down a two-seater which crashed in the vicinity of Fontaine-les-Croisilles. 2nd Lts G W Bulmer & P S Williams, 22 Squadron, shot down an EA scout which crashed. Lt R W Mackenzie, 2nd Squadron AFC, engaged an EA two-seater and it burst into a cloud of smoke and fell in flames. Capt J L Trollope, 43 Squadron, attacked one of two EA two-seaters which fell in flames in our lines near Mercatel. Lt H B Fairclough, 19 Squadron, attacked an EA two-seater which was also attacked by Capt J Leacroft. The EA eventually burst into flames and broke to pieces in the air; the wreckage falling in Lille. Capt R H Rusby, 29 Squadron, shot an EA two-seater down in flames. 2nd Lts W Beaver & H E Easton, 20 Squadron, attacked one of six EA scouts which crashed south of Roncq. Capt T S Sharpe, 73 Squadron, shot down an Albatros scout which crashed near Douchy. He then attacked a formation of five LVGs, diving and opening fire at the centre EA which fell and crashed near Roisel. He next attacked the rear LVG which also fell and crashed. Capt E R Tempest, 64 Squadron, dived into the middle of a formation of Pfalz scouts, firing at close range into one which fell in a vertical nose-dive and was seen to crash. 2nd Lt H N C Robinson, 46 Squadron, shot down an EA two-seater which crashed in a shell hole. Capt G E Thomson, 46 Squadron, dived on the rear machine of a formation of EA scouts. The EA turned on its back, went down in a spin, finally crashing. Later, in a general engagement with EA Triplanes and scouts, Capt Thomson shot down one EA seen to crash. 2nd Lt J P Seabrook & Lt A Reeve, 11 Squadron, shot down an EA scout in flames, and Sgt D W Beard & 2nd Lt H H Stewart, also 11 Squadron, shot down a second scout in flames. Capt H R Child & 2nd Lt J P Y Dickie, 11 Squadron, attacked an EA two-seater which turned on its back and spun to the ground, seen to crash. 2nd Lt J H Smith, 46 Squadron, attacked an EA scout which broke to pieces in the air. 2nd Lt D R MacLaren, 46 Squadron, fired 100 rounds into a two-seater which spun down and crashed. Capt C J Marchant, 46 Squadron, shot down a two-seater which broke to pieces in the air, and saw it crash and burst into flames. Lt H G W Debenham, 46 Squadron, attacked an Albatros scout which spun down and was seen to crash. 2nd Lt H N C Robinson, 46 Squadron, shot down a two-seater which crashed north of Vaulx.

2nd Lt C Marsden, 46 Squadron, shot down a two-seater which crashed. Capt J A Slater, 64 Squadron, shot down an EA scout which was seen to crash. Lt M E Mealing, 56 Squadron, attacked a balloon which crumpled up and fell to the ground, the Observer jumping out. He then dived on an EA two-seater over Noreuil which did a right-hand turn and crashed nose-first into a fence. 2nd Lt P S Burge, 64 Squadron, fired both guns at a Fokker Triplane which dived at him. As the EA went past him he got on its tail and fired 50 rounds at close range, whereupon the EA turned onto its back and crashed into trees in Bourlon Wood. Lt I M Harris, 64 Squadron, attacked an Albatros scout which fell in a spin and crashed. Capt R S C McClintock, 64 Squadron, shot down an EA scout which was seen to crash. Lt C A Bisonette, 64 Squadron, shot a two-seater down which crashed into Havrincourt Wood. Capt F Hobson, 70 Squadron, shot down an EA scout which crashed near Morchies. Capt F G Quigley, 70 Squadron, shot down an EA scout which crashed between Morchies and the Bapaume-Cambrai road. Capt W L Wells & Cpl W Beales, 48 Squadron, in conjuction with 2nd Lt A K Cowper, 24 Squadron, shot down a two-seater which crashed north of Dury. Capt L D Baker, 23 Squadron, together with Lt H Goodison, saw a two-seater escorted by four EA scouts. Three of the escort immediately made off east on seeing Capt Baker and Lt Goodison attacking the two-seater. This EA glided straight down and on each attempt to turn east these pilots succeeded in cutting it off, and it eventually landed in a ploughed field in our lines just west of Champion aerodrome. Lt E H Peverell, 70 Squadron, attacked a two-seater which turned on its back, started to spin, and continued to do so right to the ground.

EA were driven down out of control by the following: Flight Lt A T Whealy, 3 Squadron RNAS; Lt F J Scott, 4th Squadron AFC; Capt R C Phillips, 2nd Squadron AFC; 2nd Lt H V Highton, 43 Squadron; Capt D M McGoun & 2nd Lt F N Harrison, 22 Squadron; Capts R K Kirkman & J H Hedley, 20 Squadron (two); Capt T L Purdom & 2nd Lt P V G Chambers, 62 Squadron; Lt W J Shorter and 2nd Lt H N C Robinson, 46 Squadron (one); Capt G E Thomson, 46 Squadron; Capt R W Chappell, 41 Squadron; 2nd Lt E F H Davis, 41 Squadron; Capt D J Bell, 3 Squadron; Lt F H Taylor, 41 Squadron; Capt C J Marchant, 46 Squadron; 2nd Lt D R MacLaren, 2nd Lt R K McConnell, 46 Squadron; 2nd Lt H N C Robinson and 2nd Lt G Hudson, 46 Squadron (one); Lt A G Vlasto, 46 Squadron; Capt D W Forshaw, 46 Squadron; 2nd Lt M M Freehill, 46 Squadron; Capt J A Slater, 64 Squadron; Lt A A Duffus, 64 Squadron; Capt R S C McClintock, 64 Squadron; Lt J P McCone, 41 Squadron; 2nd Lt A Koch, 70 Squadron; Capt D J Bell, 3 Squadron.

MARCH 24

Weather fine and a great deal of work carried out, especially on the battle front where our machines harassed the enemy's troops with bombs and machine gun fire from very low altitudes. Twenty hostile batteries were successfully engaged from aeroplane observation, 1197 photographs taken, and 36¾ tons of bombs dropped. *Bombing* – During the night of the 23rd/24th, one Handley Page of 16 Squadron

RNAS dropped ten 112 lb bombs on the railway station, works, and bridge over the river at Konz, just south of Treves. Eleven machines of 100 Squadron attacked Frescaty, south-west of Metz. During the day, 12 DH4s of 55 Squadron attacked military objectives at Mannheim. On the return journey 32 EA attacked the DH4 formation and a fierce fight ensued. One EA was shot down in flames and two others brought down, one of which crashed in the centre of Mannheim. In addition, five EA were driven down out of control. All our machines returned except two, one of which is believed to have gone down under control.

Enemy Aircraft – EA activity was very great, especially on the battle front. In addition to machines from the 3rd and 5th Brigades, machines from the 1st Brigade and the 9th Wing did a great deal of low flying, attacking enemy troops on the ground all along the battle front. In addition to EA brought down in aerial combats, two EA were brought down by AA fire, one of which fell in our lines. 2nd Lt W L Harrison, 40 Squadron, shot down an EA two-seater which crashed near St Leger. Capt R C Phillips, 2nd Squadron AFC, dived on one of three two-seaters escorted by scouts. After he had fired 150 rounds at 50 yards range, the right wing of the EA fell off and the EA fell out of control and crashed. In a general engagement between a patrol of 19 Squadron and ten EA scouts, Capt J Leacroft shot down one out of control and saw a piece of the EA break off. This EA was seen to crash.

The following are the reports of combats by Capt J L Trollope, 43 Squadron, who accounted for six EA in one day, thus creating a record:

"Whilst leading my patrol east of Mercatel, I saw three DFWs some way away trying to cross the line. I worked round east and attacked one but was forced by gun jams to break off. I corrected my guns and then attacked another DFW. I fired about 100 rounds at point-blank range. EA went down in a spin and broke up about 1000 feet below me. This was seen by Lt Owen. I then attacked another DFW with Lt R J Owen and after firing 75 rounds the machine burst into flames and fluttered down on fire. This was confirmed by Lt Owen who also attacked it. I then saw an Albatros scout coming down onto one of our formation. I dived on him and fired about 100 rounds. EA fell completely out of control. This was seen to crash by Capt H W Woollett.

"When I was leading my patrol over Sailly Saillisel at about 6000 feet, I saw four EA two-seaters trying to interfere with RE8s. I dived down with my formation and attacked one EA. I fired a short burst at close range and the EA fell to bits in the air. I saw two of my patrol engaging the other three two-seaters at close range and I saw two EA go down completely out of control and crash. I gathered all my patrol and flew about looking for the other EA. I saw two pink two-seaters below me, very close to the ground. I attacked each in turn from about 20 feet and they nose-dived into the ground, and I saw both crash. I climbed up and saw the rest of my patrol engaged by a large formation of EA scouts. I got into the scrap and was forced to return through lack of ammunition."

2nd Lt C J S Dearlove & Lt E C Batchelor, 12 Squadron, were attacked by two EA scouts, one of which they shot down and saw crash. Lt M E Mealing, 56 Squadron, got on the tail of a Pfalz scout and fired bursts into it; the EA went down and crashed just west of Tincourt. 2nd Lt H N C Robinson, 46 Squadron, shot down an EA two-seater which crashed. Capt S P Smith, 46 Squadron, also shot down a two-seater, seen to crash. Capt H W Woollett, 43 Squadron, dived on a two-seater which was attempting to cross our lines. He fired 100 rounds at 75 yards range and the EA burst into flames and went down on fire, crashing south-east of Arras. Capt

Woollett then dived on another two-seater which fell spinning and crashed about two miles south of the Scarpe. 2nd Lt R J Owen and 2nd Lt C F King, 43 Squadron, each attacked an EA two-seater which broke up in the air. 2nd Lt Owen, in conjunction with Capt Trollope attacked a two-seater which fell out of control. 2nd Lt H Daniel, 43 Squadron, shot down an EA scout which was seen to crash. 2nd Lt A S Hemming, 41 Squadron, attacked a Fokker Triplane which turned over with smoke issuing from the cockpit and eventually burst into flames. Lt F H Taylor, 41 Squadron, attacked a Fokker Triplane which fell and was seen to crash. Lt Taylor then attacked an enemy balloon. Capt H T F Russell, 41 Squadron, shot down a Fokker Triplane which was seen to crash. Capt F G C Weare & 2nd Lt G S L Hayward, 22 Squadron, shot down an EA scout which crashed near Cherisy. Later, they fired a short burst into another EA scout which crashed at Vis. 2nd Lt W F J Harvey & Lt H F Moore, 22 Squadron, shot down an EA scout which was seen to crash. Capt J F Morris, 23 Squadron, whilst on low flying, attacked an EA two-seater and fought it down to 100 feet, finally driving it to the ground, the EA crashing badly near Canizy. He was then attacked by seven Pfalz scouts and in the fight succeeded in getting good bursts into five of them. One Pfalz was shot down in flames and crashed on our side of the lines. Capt Morris's machine was badly shot about and he had to make a forced landing. Capt T Colville-Jones & Lt D Wishart-Orr, 48 Squadron, shot down a two-seater which crashed just east of Ham. Capt F M Kitto, 54 Squadron, attacked an EA in the neighbourhood of Attilly. The EA tried to get away east but Capt Kitto forced it to fight over Holnon Wood, eventually forcing it down to the ground just west of St Quentin, where it crashed. Capt Kitto later attacked an EA near Mons and it dived vertically into the ground. 2nd Lt E W Lindeburg, 24 Squadron, saw EA taking off from Mons and attacked one at 2000 feet which went straight into the ground. 2nd Lt H B Redler, 24 Squadron, shot down a two-seater which crashed near Pithon. 2nd Lt A K Cowper, 24 Squadron, with 2nd Lts Nolan and Farrell of the same squadron attacked a two-seater which was seen to crash. Capt K G Leask, 84 Squadron, shot down an EA scout which crashed. Lt J D Hewett, 23 Squadron, shot down an EA two-seater which fell out of control and then burst into flames before crashing near the Ham-Nesle road. The pilot and Observer in the EA jumped out at 2000 feet.

2nd Lt H B Redler, 24 Squadron, attacked one of five EA two-seaters which he forced to land in a field to the south of Berlancourt; the EA turned over and crashed on landing. Capt W L Wells & Cpl W Beales, 48 Squadron, shot down a two-seater in a spin which crashed, then shot down an EA scout in flames, seen to crash. 2nd Lts P H O'Lieff & S R Wells, 55 Squadron, when returning from the raid on Mannheim, were attacked by several EA scouts and shot one down which was seen to crash. 2nd Lts E J Whyte & W G Robins, 55 Squadron, when returning from bombing Mannheim, were also attacked by several EA scouts and shot one down which fell in a spinning nose-dive and crashed in the centre of the town.

EA were driven down out of control by the following: Lt A G Clark, 2nd Squadron AFC; Capt O Horsley, 40 Squadron; Lt E J Blyth, 19 Squadron; Major A D Carter, 19 Squadron and Lt G B Irving, 19 Squadron (one); Capt J Leacroft, 19 Squadron; Lt E F Pflaum, 4th Squadron AFC; Flight Cdr L H Rochford and six other pilots of 3 Squadron RNAS (one); 2nd Lt J Hanman & Lt C R Cuthbert, 12 Squadron; 2nd Lt H L Whiteside & 70 Squadron; Capt R W Chappell, 41 Squadron (two); 2nd Lt H D Arkell, 41 Squadron; Lt R H Stacey, 41 Squadron; 2nd Lt W F J Harvey & H F Moore, 22 Squadron; Capt P W S Bulman, 3 Squadron; 2nd Lt E E Stock, 54 Squadron; 2nd

Lt R J Hamersley, 24 Squadron; 2nd Lt W Legge & Sgt A S Allan, 55 Squadron; 2nd Lts P H O'Lieff & S R Wells, 55 Squadron (two); 2nd Lt R C Sansom & Sgt J Ryan, 55 Squadron.

HONOURS AND AWARDS
Bar to the Military Cross – Capt F G Quigley.
The Military Cross – 2nd Lt F N S Creek; Lt J F N Macrae; 2nd Lt E Pybus; Lt T W Cave; 2nd Lt P A MacDougall; Lt K W Junor; Lt M E Mealing; 2nd Lt H N C Robinson; 2nd Lt J S Chick; Capt E R Tempest.

MARCH 25
Twenty-two hostile batteries were successfully engaged from aeroplane observation, 483 photographs taken, and 33 tons of bombs dropped.
Bombing – 8th Brigade – During the night of the 24th/25th, one Handley Page of 16 Squadron RNAS carried out the first raid on Cologne; the railway station being the objective. The machine was in the air for eight hours and 35 minutes. During the same night, machines of 100 Squadron dropped almost three tons of bombs on railway stations at Metz and Thionville. All our machines returned.
Enemy Aircraft – Machines of the 1st, 3rd and 5th Brigades flew at low altitudes and attacked enemy troops, concentrating in the neighbourhood of Vaulx and Ervillers, and fired over 90,000 rounds at massed enemy troops, convoys and other targets. Capt R W Chappell, 41 Squadron, whilst leading a patrol over Sailly, saw 20 EA (Albatros scouts and Fokker Triplanes). He dived on one Albatros which was seen to crash. 2nd Lt W F J Harvey & Lt H F Moore, 22 Squadron, fired a long burst into an EA scout, the left wing of which folded back and was seen to crash. Capt D M McGoun & 2nd Lt F N Harrison, 22 Squadron, shot down an EA seen to crash on the east side of St Leger. Capt H W Woollett, 43 Squadron, attacked one of two EA scouts and it was seen to crash. 2nd Lt H N C Robinson, 46 Squadron, shot down an EA two-seater which crashed.

Capt H S C McClintock, 64 Squadron, whilst flying at a height of only 100 feet in a heavy ground mist almost collided with an EA two-seater. He fired two short bursts and the EA crashed to the ground. 2nd Lts H C Adams & F Catterall, 18 Squadron, were attacked by two formations of EA scouts, who followed them down from 10,500 feet to 1500 feet, then broke off the combat. In the meantime one EA was seen to burst into flames and break in half. 2nd Lt G L Hobbs & Lt H E A Chippendale, 15 Squadron, were attacked by seven EA scouts, one of which they shot down in flames. Capt R A Grosvenor, 84 Squadron, and 2nd Lt W H Brown, also 84 Squadron, both dived at an EA two-seater which crashed into Flers where it burst into flames.

EA were driven down out of control by Lt S A Puffer, 41 Squadron; Lt W J Gillespie, 41 Squadron; 2nd Lts H F Davison & J L Morgan, 22 Squadron.

COMMUNIQUÉ No.133

26 – 31 March 1918

The German Army High Command's "Great Battle of France", launched on March 21st, failed in its prime objective of dividing the Allied armies, and by March 29th had ground to a virtual halt. Aircraft of the RFC and RNAS played a significant part in stemming the German offensive, flying throughout each day at low level, strafing and harassing German troops wherever they could be found, and offering fierce opposition to any German aircraft encountered.

During the period under review, 26th to 31st March, we have claimed officially 76 EA brought down, two of which fell in our lines, and 18 driven down out of control. In addition, seven were brought down by AA or machine gun fire from the ground. 59 of our machines are missing. Approximately 167 tons of bombs were dropped, and 612 photographs taken.

MARCH 26

Enemy Aircraft – During the day nearly all our aeroplanes were employed dropping bombs and firing from low altitude on enemy troops in the neighbourhood of Peronne and Bapaume. EA were also active and a certain amount of fighting took place. Capt N Deakin & Lt C T Anderson, 2 Squadron, were attacked by five EA scouts, one of which they shot down in flames and saw crash. 2nd Lt A C Atkey & Lt J Brisbane, 18 Squadron, were attacked by four EA scouts. They engaged the leader which they shot down, and it was seen to crash in flames. 2nd Lt R B Smith & Sgt A Pollard, 18 Squadron, were chased by eleven EA scouts and a Fokker Triplane; the latter dived at them and they shot it down in a spin and watched it crash. 2nd Lt D A Stewart & Capt L Y Collins, 18 Squadron, shot down an EA two-seater which was seen to crash into a wood south of Bapaume. 2nd Lt A E Robertson, 4th Squadron AFC, fired 30 rounds at 50 yards range at a Fokker Triplane which went down in an almost vertical side-slip which turned into a nose-dive, then was seen to crash. Lt F J Scott, 4th Squadron AFC, whilst attacking ground objects, saw an EA two-seater below him. He attacked, firing 150 rounds into the cockpit. The EA turned over on its back and nose-dived into the ground with the engine full on and crashed. Capt F G C Weare & 2nd Lt G S L Hayward, 22 Squadron, dived on a formation of five Pfalz scouts, one of which they shot down completely out of control, and it was seen to crash. 2nd Lts H F Davison & J L Morgan, 22 Squadron, in the same engagement, shot down one EA scout and followed it down to 4000 feet, observed it to be on fire, then saw it hit the ground still burning. Sgt E J Elton & 2nd Lt R Critchley, 22 Squadron, in the same fight, also shot down an EA scout which was seen to crash east of Albert. Capt F E Hobson, 70 Squadron, saw several EA scouts attacking some of our RE8s and low-flying scouts. He engaged one of these EA and it spun into the ground north of the Bapaume-Cambrai road. 2nd Lt D R MacLaren 46 Squadron, attacked an EA two-seater which was working at about 2000 feet. After a burst of 75 rounds had been fired into it the EA went down in a spin and was seen to crash. 2nd Lt W E Warden, 40 Squadron, fired 200 rounds from both guns into one EA scout and it fell out of control and crashed near Grevillers. 2nd Lt H R Gould & Lt J M Brisbane, 18 Squadron, were followed by ten EA scouts on which they turned and engaged, shooting one down which was seen to crash. Capt M R N Jennings, 19 Squadron, saw seven EA scouts and a Fokker Triplane about 1000 feet below him. He fired at one Albatros scout at close range and it fell out of control and crashed. Lt A H Rigby, 1 Squadron, fired about a drum of Lewis and about 50 rounds from his Vickers into one of nine EA scouts which dived on him. The EA immediately went down and burst into flames. 2nd Lt J E A R Daley, 24 Squadron, shot one EA scout down in a spin which crashed in flames. 2nd Lt H B Redler, 24 Squadron, attacked a two-seater EA, firing 100 rounds from underneath. The EA dived east emitting masses of smoke and crashed into Barleux. 2nd Lt H B Richardson, 24 Squadron, attacked one of two EA two-seaters and both dived east, but the one attacked by 2nd Lt Richardson crashed in a field at Dreslincourt.

EA were driven down out of control by the following: Lt L Benjamin, 2nd Squadron AFC; 2nd Lt A C Atkey & Lt J Brisbane, 18 Squadron; 2nd Lt A E Robertson, 4th Squadron AFC (two); Capt F G C Weare & 2nd Lt G S L Hayward, 22 Squadron; Capt J Gilmour, 65 Squadron ; 2nd Lt W L Harrison, 40 Squadron; 2nd Lt P D Learoyd, 40 Squadron.

MARCH 27
Thirty hostile batteries were successfully engaged from aeroplane observation, 177 photographs taken, and over 50 tons of bombs dropped.

Enemy Aircraft – Our machines were again concentrated on low bombing and machine-gunning enemy infantry in the neighbourhood of Cambrai, Bapaume, Peronne and Chaulnes. In spite of this, an appreciable amount of fighting in the air took place. 2nd Lt P J Clayson, 1 Squadron, while flying over Achiet-le-Grand, engaged the rear machine of five EA scouts. The EA immediately fell over on its right wing, went down vertically with engine full on, then crashed near Ablainzeville. Capt R C Phillips, 2nd Squadron AFC, engaged an EA which was firing at our troops. He dived on it, firing about 100 rounds, and it crashed on our side of the lines near Meaulte. Capt Phillips also engaged one of several Triplanes which attacked his formation, fired 50 rounds, and the EA burst into flames and fell slowly to earth. 2nd Lt D A Stewart & Capt L Y Collins, 18 Squadron, were engaged by three EA south-west of Albert, one of which they shot down and it was seen to crash. 2nd Lt T Hoskins, 2nd Squadron AFC, fired about 200 rounds at a Fokker Triplane which he met near Albert. The EA rolled over and burst into a cloud of smoke and flames and fell completely out of control, then crashed in flames.

2nd Lt H F Davison & 2nd Lt J L Morgan, 22 Squadron, shot down one of four Fokker Triplanes, which was seen to crash on the railway siding south-east of Albert. 2nd Lt A R Knowles & Lt E A Matthews, 11 Squadron, were attacked by six EA scouts. They engaged the leader which went down out of control and crashed on the outskirts of Meaulte. Shortly after they met two EA scouts and shot one down in flames which was seen burning on the ground in the vicinity of Morlancourt. Capt L W Jarvis, 56 Squadron, engaged one of several EA scouts in conjunction with 2nd Lt Walkerdine. The EA stalled, turned over, then crashed in a ploughed field.

Lt E G Leake & 2nd Lt T H Upfill, 59 Squadron, were attacked by an EA scout which dived out of the clouds onto their tail, firing all the time. About 100 rounds were fired into the EA, apparently putting its engine out of action. The EA failed to cross the crater zone and crashed just south of Serre. Lt F R McCall & Lt B S Andrew, 13 Squadron, attacked two EA two-seaters which were trying to cross our lines. 200 rounds were fired into one which crashed in its own lines; confirmed by "K" Battery, AA.

2nd Lt R T Mark, 24 Squadron, fired 50 rounds at close range into an EA two-seater over Goyencourt. The EA did a slow spiral and crashed near Fresnoy-les-Roye. Flight Cdr C P O Bartlett & Aerial Gunlayer Naylor, 5 Squadron RNAS, fired a long burst with rear guns into an EA scout which was seen to crash. 2nd Lt C G D Napier & J M J Moore, 48 Squadron, shot down an EA two-seater which crashed near the River Avre, south-west of Roye. 2nd Lts F C Ransley & J M J Moore, 48 Squadron, attacked an EA two-seater which crashed in the Bois de Tailles. Flight Lt E Dickson & Flight Sub-Lt Stewart, 5 Squadron RNAS, shot down an EA scout. Its left wing folded back and it was seen to crash.

EA were driven down out of control by the following : 2nd Lts H F Davison & J L Morgan, 22 Squadron; 2nd Lt D R MacLaren, 46 Squadron; 2nd Lts C G D Napier & J M J Moore, 48 Squadron; Capt G E H McElroy, 24 Squadron.

MARCH 28

A high wind prevailed all day and a certain amount of rain in the afternoon, in spite of which a great deal of work was done, mostly consisting of bombing and machine-gunning the enemy's troops etc from a low altitude.

Enemy Aircraft – In addition to the EA brought down in aerial combat during the day, two EA were brought down by AA fire, one of which fell in our lines. 2nd Lt H I Pole & Lt L C Spence, 2 Squadron, were attacked by six Fokker Triplanes and an EA scout, and they shot down one Triplane out of control which burst into flames before reaching the ground and was seen burning on the ground west of Estrees. 2nd Lts R S Durno & R H Boyd, 5 Squadron, attacked an EA which was apparently doing contact patrol work. The EA turned east, nose-dived, and crashed. Sgt W McCleery & 2nd Lt H Gould, 18 Squadron, shot down one of six EA scouts in flames which crashed. 2nd Lt R V Irwin & Sgt C Beardmore, 18 Squadron, followed down an EA scout which had dived on them, and after a long burst from the front gun the EA dived perpendicularly when not more than 100 feet from the ground and crashed. Lt F J Scott, 4th Squadron AFC shot down an EA which turned over on its back, then spun into the ground. Lt E R Jeffree, 4th Squadron AFC, whilst firing on enemy troops in the vicinity of Albert, saw four Fokker Triplanes below him, so dived on to one, firing about 20 rounds. The EA rolled over on its back, then spun into the ground. He then attacked another Triplane which also spun down and was seen to crash. Capt G B Moore, 1 Squadron, attacked an EA two-seater from 70 yards range and it glided down and crashed near Bazentin, north-east of Albert. Flight Cdr C P O Bartlett & Aerial Gunlayer Naylor, 5 Squadron RNAS, whilst on a bomb raid, were attacked by five EA scouts and three Fokker Triplanes. Two of these EA manoeuvring to get on the tail of Flight Cdr Bartlett's machine collided and went down locked together and caught fire on reaching the ground. 2nd Lt C F King, 43 Squadron, in a general engagement between eight EA scouts and a patrol of his squadron, shot down one EA scout which was seen crashed.

EA were driven down out of control by the following: 2nd Lts E Lindup & H G Crowe, 20 Squadron; Lts R G Bennett & J D Boyd, 20 Squadron; Flight Lt E Dickson & Sub-Lt Stewart, 5 Squadron RNAS; Flight Cdr C P O Bartlett & Aerial Gunlayer Naylor, 5 Squadron RNAS; 2nd Lt H H Browning, 4th Squadron AFC.

MARCH 29

Little flying was possible in the morning owing to bad weather, which improved in the afternoon.

Enemy Aircraft – Machines were again engaged in bombing from a low altitude and firing at enemy troops, and were chiefly employed between the Somme and Hangest. EA were very active just south of the Somme.

2nd Lt C H E Allen & Sgt J B Wright, 25 Squadron, were attacked by one EA scout which they shot down in flames. 2nd Lt C Marsden, 48 Squadron, was attacked by seven EA scouts when flying at 1500 feet. He fired 50 rounds into the EA leader which fell vertically and crashed. The remaining EA forced 2nd Lt Marsden down to 30 feet, his elevator controls being shot away, and he crashed within a few yards of our front line. His machine was completely wrecked and, as it was so near the front line, he burst the petrol tank with his revolver and burned the machine. 2nd Lt H F Proctor, 32 Squadron, dived on an EA scout which was flying east at about 1000 feet. He followed it down to 500 feet, firing 200 rounds at point-blank range, and the EA crashed just south of Proyart.

2nd Lt A E Hulme & Sgt A Remington, 25 Squadron, shot down one of ten EA scouts which attacked their formation; it went down in a spin and crashed between Raincourt and Herleville. 2nd Lts S Jones & H Pullan, 25 Squadron, shot down an EA scout seen to crash near Proyart. 2nd Lts E J Smetham-Jones and J C Fitton, 48 Squadron, when flying at a height of 900 feet, shot down an EA scout just east of Bayonvillers. Capt A K Cowper, 24 Squadron, attacked an EA two-seater, firing both guns, and the EA dived east very steeply and crashed. Lts J K Watson & Benton, 52 Squadron, were attacked by five EA scouts, one of which they shot down to crash in a field between Caix and Rosieres. Capt G E H McElroy, 24 Squadron, saw five EA scouts behind their lines west of Foucaucourt. He climbed above the clouds and approached the EA through a gap, apparently unobserved, then dived on one Albatros scout, firing 100 rounds into it at a range of from 100 to 20 yards. Pieces were seen to fall off the EA's fuselage and it went down completely out of control, crashing between Foucaucourt and the River Somme. Capt Mc Elroy also shot down one EA out of control.

HONOURS AND AWARDS

Bar to the Military Cross – Capt D J Bell, MC.
The Military Cross – Lt R W Mackenzie; Lt A B Fairclough; 2nd Lt G S L Hayward.

MARCH 30

Weather fine in the morning but turned to rain in the afternoon. In spite of this machines of the 3rd and 5th Brigades continued their attacks with bombs and machine guns on enemy infantry. 21½ tons of bombs were dropped and 179 photographs taken.

Enemy Aircraft – South of the Somme EA were very active during the morning, being chiefly employed in firing from low altitude at our infantry. AA guns of the First and Second Armies both brought down an EA in our lines. Flight Lt J Gamon & Sub-Lt Stringer, 5 Squadron RNAS, when returning from a bomb raid, were attacked by three Fokker Triplanes one of which they shot down to crash. 2nd Lt E A Clear, 84 Squadron, dived on one of four EA two-seaters firing both guns, and the EA crashed near Cerisy. Lt A H Cobby, 4th Squadron AFC, attacked an EA scout which was sitting on the tail of a Camel. The EA started to spin and one wing broke off, and it was seen to crash. 2nd Lt L Balderson & Capt F Kempster, 18 Squadron, shot an EA scout down in flames. Sgt E J Elton & 2nd Lt R Critchley, 22 Squadron, in a general engagement between a patrol of Bristol Fighters and EA of various descriptions, shot down one EA two-seater which crashed near Rosieres, then attacked another EA which crashed near Lihons. They also shot down an EA which crashed between Vauvillers and Soyecourt. 2nd Lts H F Davison & J L Morgan, 22 Squadron, shot down an EA two-seater which crashed into a wood east of Barvillers.

Capt H A Hamersley, 60 Squadron, attacked one of several EA scouts which crashed on the roof of a house in Hem and burst into flames. He also shot down one EA completely out of control which was confirmed as having crashed. Capt W H Copeland, 60 Squadron, shot down an EA scout which crashed in the centre of the village of Boire. 2nd Lt H G Hegarty, 60 Squadron, dived on one EA scout flying at 1200 feet and drove it down to 500 feet. The EA went over in a vertical bank, then crashed in the village of Theux. Lt W J A Duncan, 60 Squadron, fired 150 rounds into an EA two-seater, which was also attacked by 2nd Lt J S Griffith of the same squadron, and the EA crashed in the village of Becourt. 2nd Lt W F J Harvey & Lt H F Moore, 22 Squadron, fired 150 rounds into an enemy balloon. Almost immediately a cloud of smoke obscured the balloon from view, and when this cleared away nothing was seen of the balloon.

EA were driven down out of control by the following; 2nd Lt J G Kennedy, 65 Squadron; Capt H G Forrest, 2nd Squadron AFC; Lt R St J Dix, and 2nd Lt F G Dyson, 82 Squadron; Capt F G C Weare & 2nd Lt G S L Hayward, 22 Squadron; 2nd Lts H F Davison & Lt J L Morgan, 22 Squadron; 2nd Lt J N Bartlett, 60 Squadron; Capt J A Slater and 2nd Lt P S Burge, 64 Squadron (one).

HONOURS AND AWARDS
Victoria Cross – Capt J T B McCudden, DSO, MC, MM.
Bar to the Military Cross – Capt W S Fielding-Johnson, MC.
The Military Cross – Capt J L Trollope; Lt W L Wells; 2nd Lt H J Walkerdyne;
                2nd Lt F H Davies.
The Distinguished Conduct Medal – No.1429 Sgt E J Elton, MM.

MARCH 31
Weather was very overcast with occasional rain showers.
Enemy Aircraft – Very few EA were encountered with the exception of south of the Somme, but a good many two-seaters appeared to be doing contact patrol work. 2nd Lt R C Crowden, 54 Squadron, shot down an EA scout to crash near Warfusee. 2nd Lt G S Hodson, 73 Squadron, shot down an EA scout out of control. 2nd Lts W E Green & H S Gros, 57 Squadron, shot down one EA scout out of control.

Editor's note: One surprising omission from this Communiqué was mention of the epic lone combat between 2nd Lt A A McLeod and his Observer Lt A W Hammond, flying an Armstrong Whitworth FK8 of No.2 Squadron, and nine Fokker Triplanes, some of these being from Jagdstaffel 10 of the "Richthofen Circus", in the afternoon of March 27th. Both men sustained multiple wounds in the fight, then had the FK8 set on fire, but McLeod climbed out of his burning cockpit onto the lower left wing root and guided the flaming aircraft down to a crash-landing in "No Man's Land", then extracted his Observer from the burning wreckage and dragged him to the nearest Allied trench. McLeod's selfless courage brought him the award of a Victoria Cross – the last RFC man to receive the little bronze cross. Tragically, Alan Arnett McLeod fell victim to virulent influenza later, and died on November 6th, 1918 in Canada.

PERSONNEL INDEX

INDEX